KU-051-751

WITHDRAWN

PENGUIN BOOKS

ORIENTALISM

Edward W. Said is University Professor at Columbia University, where he has taught English and Comparative Literature since 1963. He was born in Jerusalem in 1935 and educated at Victoria College, Cairo, Mount Hermon School, Massachusetts, and at Princeton and Harvard universities. In 1974 he was Visiting Professor of Comparative Literature at Harvard, in 1975–6 Fellow of the Center for Advanced Study in Behavioral Science at Stanford, and in 1979 Visiting Professor of Humanities at Johns Hopkins University. He was editor of the *Arab Studies Quarterly*, and a member of the Council of Foreign Relations, New York, the American Academy of Arts and Letters, the American Philosophical Society and the Royal Society of Literature. He has received Harvard University's Bowdoin Prize and the Lionel Trilling Award at Columbia in 1976 and in 1994. In 1998, Said received the Sultan Owais Prize for general cultural achievement; he became an Honorary Fellow of the Middle Eastern Studies Association in 1999; and in 2002, he received the Prince of Asturias Prize. His books include *Joseph Conrad and the Fiction of Autobiography*; *Beginnings: Intention and Method*; *The Question of Palestine*; *Literature and Society*; *The World, The Text and the Critic*; *Covering Islam*; *After the Last Sky*; *Blaming the Victims*; *Culture and Imperialism*; *Representations of the Intellectual*; *Out of Place: A Memoir*; *The End of the Peace Process: Oslo and After*; *Peace and Its Discontents: Gaza to Jericho 1993–1995*; *Parallels and Paradoxes: Explorations of Music and Society*; and *Freud and the Non-European*.

Edward W. Said is married and has one son and one daughter.

ORIENTALISM

PENGUIN BOOKS

PENGUIN BOOKS

Published by the Penguin Group
Penguin Books Ltd, 80 Strand, London WC2R 0RL, England
Penguin Putnam Inc., 375 Hudson Street, New York, New York 10014, USA
Penguin Books Australia Ltd, 250 Camberwell Road, Camberwell, Victoria 3124, Australia
Penguin Books Canada Ltd, 10 Alcorn Avenue, Toronto, Ontario, Canada M4V 3B2
Penguin Books India (P) Ltd, 11 Community Centre, Panchsheel Park, New Delhi – 110 017, India
Penguin Books (NZ) Ltd, Cnr Rosedale and Airborne Roads, Albany, Auckland, New Zealand
Penguin Books (South Africa) (Pty) Ltd, 24 Sturdee Avenue, Rosebank 2196, South Africa

Penguin Books Ltd, Registered Offices: 80 Strand, London WC2R 0RL, England

www.penguin.com

First published by Routledge & Kegan Paul Ltd 1978
Published in Peregrine Books 1985
Reprinted in Penguin Books 1991
Reprinted with a new Afterword 1995
Reprinted with a new Preface 2003
6

Copyright © Edward W. Said, 1978, 1995, 2003
Published by arrangement with Pantheon Books, a Division of Random House Inc.
All rights reserved

Printed in England by Clays Ltd, St Ives plc
Typeset in Times Roman

Grateful acknowledgment is made to the following for permission to reprint previously published material:

George Allen & Unwin, Ltd.: Excerpts from *Subjects of the Day: Being a Selection of Speeches and Writings* by George Nathaniel Curzon.

George Allen & Unwin, Ltd.: Excerpts from *Revolution in the Middle East and Other Case Studies, proceedings of a seminar*, edited by P. J. Vatikiotis.

American Jewish Committee: Excerpts from "The Return of Islam" by Bernard Lewis, in *Commentary*, vol. 61, no. 1 (January 1976). Reprinted from *Commentary* by permission. Copyright © 1976 by the American Jewish Committee.

Basic Books, Inc.: Excerpts from "Renan's Philological Laboratory" by Edward W. Said, in *Art, Politics, and Will: Essays in Honor of Lionel Trilling*, edited by Quentin Anderson et al. Copyright © 1977 by Basic Books, Inc.

The Bodley Head and McIntosh & Otis, Inc.: Excerpts from *Flaubert in Egypt*, translated and edited by Francis Steegmuller. Reprinted by permission of Francis Steegmuller and The Bodley Head.

Jonathan Cape, Ltd., and The Letters of T. E. Lawrence Trust: Excerpt from *The Letters of T. E. Lawrence*, edited by David Garnett.

Jonathan Cape, Ltd., The Seven Pillars Trust, and Doubleday & Co., Inc.: Excerpt from *The Seven Pillars of Wisdom: A Triumph* by T. E. Lawrence. Copyright 1926, 1935 by Doubleday & Co., Inc.

Doubleday & Co., Inc., and A. P. Watt & Sons, Ltd.: Excerpt from *Verse* by Rudyard Kipling.

The Georgia Review: Excerpts from "Orientalism," which originally appeared in *The Georgia Review* (Spring 1977). Copyright © 1977 by the University of Georgia.

Harper & Row, Publishers, Inc.: Excerpt from a poem by Bornier (1862), quoted in *De Lesseps of Suez* by Charles Beatty.

Macmillan & Co., London and Basingstoke: Excerpts from *Modern Egypt*, vol. 2, by Evelyn Baring, Lord Cromer.

Macmillan Publishing Co., Inc.: Excerpt from "Propaganda" by Harold Lasswell, in *The Encyclopedia of the Social Sciences*, edited by Edwin R. A. Seligman, vol. 12 (1934).

Macmillan Publishing Co., Inc., and A. P. Watt & Sons, Ltd.: Excerpt from "Byzantium" by William Butler Yeats, in *The Collected Poems*. Copyright 1933 by Macmillan Publishing Co., Inc., renewed 1961 by Bertha Georgie Yeats.

The New York Times Company: Excerpts from "Arabs, Islam, and the Dogmas of the West" by Edward W. Said, in *The New York Times Book Review*, October 31, 1976. Copyright © 1976 by The New York Times Company. Reprinted by permission.

Northwestern University Press: Excerpt from "The Arab Portrayed" by Edward W. Said, in *The Arab-Israeli Confrontation of June 1967: An Arab Perspective*, edited by Ibrahim Abu-Lughod. Copyright © 1970 by Northwestern University Press.

Prentice-Hall, Inc.: Excerpt from *The Persians* by Aeschylus, translated by Anthony J. Podleck. Copyright © 1970 by Prentice-Hall, Inc.

FOR JANET AND IBRAHIM

Contents

Preface (2003)

Nine years ago, in the spring of 1994, I wrote an afterword for *Orientalism* in which, in trying to clarify what I believed I had and had not said, I stressed not only the many discussions that had opened up since my book appeared in 1978, but also the ways in which a work about representations of "the Orient" lends itself to increasing misrepresentation and misinterpretation. That I find the very same thing today more ironic than irritating is a sign of how much my age has crept up on me, along with the necessary diminutions in expectations and pedagogic zeal which usually frame the road to seniority. The recent death of my two main intellectual, political and personal mentors, Eqbal Ahmad and Ibrahim Abu-Lughod (who is one of the work's dedicatees) has brought sadness and loss, as well as resignation and a certain stubborn will to go on. It isn't at all a matter of being optimistic, but rather of continuing to have faith in the ongoing and literally unending process of emancipation and enlightenment that, in my opinion, frames and gives direction to the intellectual vocation.

Nevertheless it is still a source of amazement to me that *Orientalism* continues to be discussed and translated all over the world, in thirty-six languages. Thanks to the efforts of my dear friend and colleague Professor Gaby Peterberg, now of UCLA, formerly of Ben Gurion University in Israel, there is a Hebrew version of the book available, which has stimulated considerable discussion and debate among Israeli readers and students. In addition, a Vietnamese translation has appeared under Australian auspices; I hope it's not immodest to say that an Indochinese intellectual space seems to have opened up for the propositions of this book. In any case, it gives me great pleasure to note as an author who had never dreamed of any such happy fate for his work that interest in what I tried to do in my book hasn't completely died down, particularly in the many different lands of the "Orient" itself.

In part, of course, that is because the Middle East, the Arabs and Islam have continued to fuel enormous change, struggle, controversy and, as I write these lines, war. As I said many years ago, *Orientalism* is the product of circumstances that are fundamentally, indeed radically, fractious. In my memoir *Out of Place* (1999) I described the strange and contradictory worlds in which I grew up, providing for myself and my readers a detailed account of the settings that I think formed me in Palestine, Egypt and Lebanon. But that was only a very personal account that stopped short of all the years of my own political engagement that started after the 1967 Arab–Israeli war, a war in whose continuing aftermath (Israel is still in military occupation of the Palestinian territories and the Golan Heights) the terms of struggle and the ideas at stake that were crucial for my generation of Arabs and Americans seem to go on. Nevertheless I do want to affirm yet again that this book and, for that matter, my intellectual work generally have really been enabled by my life as a university academic. For all its often noted defects and problems, the American university—and mine, Columbia, in particular—is still one of the few remaining places in the United States where reflection and study can take place in an almost utopian fashion. I have never taught *anything* about the Middle East, being by training and practice a teacher of the mainly European and American humanities, a specialist in modern comparative literature. The university and my pedagogic work with two generations of first-class students and excellent colleagues have made possible the kind of deliberately meditated and analyzed study that this book contains, which for all its urgent worldly references is still a book about culture, ideas, history and power, rather than Middle Eastern politics *tout court*. That was my notion from the beginning, and it is very evident and a good deal clearer to me today.

Yet *Orientalism* is very much a book tied to the tumultuous dynamics of contemporary history. I emphasize in it accordingly that neither the term Orient nor the concept of the West has any ontological stability; each is made up of human effort, partly affirmation, partly identification of the Other. That these supreme fictions lend themselves easily to manipulation and the organization of collective passion has never been more evident than in our time, when the mobilizations of fear, hatred, disgust and resurgent self-pride and arrogance—much of it having to do with Islam and the Arabs on one side, "we" Westerners on the other—are very large-scale enterprises. *Orientalism*'s first page opens with a 1975 description of the Lebanese Civil War that ended in 1990, but the violence and the ugly shedding of human blood continues up to this minute. We have had the failure of the Oslo peace process, the outbreak of the second intifada, and the awful suffering of the Palestinians on the reinvaded West Bank and Gaza, with Israeli F-16's and Apache helicopters used routinely on the defenseless civilians as part of their collective punishment. The suicide bombing phenomenon has appeared with all its hideous damage, none more lurid and apocalyptic of course than the events of September 11 and their aftermath in the wars against Afghanistan and Iraq. As I write these lines, the illegal and unsanctioned imperial invasion and occupation of Iraq by Britain and the United States proceeds, with a prospect of physical ravagement, political unrest and more invasions that is truly awful to contemplate. This is all part of what is supposed to be a clash of civilizations, unending, implacable, irremediable. Nevertheless, I think not.

I wish I could say, however, that general understanding of the Middle East, the Arabs and Islam in the United States has improved somewhat, but alas, it really hasn't. For all kinds of reasons, the situation in Europe seems to be considerably better. In the US, the hardening of attitudes, the tightening of the grip of demeaning generalization and triumphalist cliché, the dominance of crude power allied with simplistic contempt of dissenters and "others," has found a fitting correlative in the looting, pillaging and destruction of Iraq's libraries and museums. What our leaders and their intellectual lackeys seem incapable of understanding is that history cannot be swept clean like a blackboard, clean so that "we" might inscribe our own future there and impose our own forms of life for these lesser people to follow. It is quite common to hear high officials in Washington and elsewhere speak of changing the map of the Middle East, as if ancient societies and myriad peoples can be shaken up like so many peanuts in a jar. But this has often happened with the "Orient," that semi-mythical construct which since Napoleon's invasion of Egypt in the late eighteenth century has been made and re-made countless times by power acting through an expedient form of knowledge to assert that this is the Orient's nature, and we must deal with it accordingly. In the process the uncountable sediments of history, which include innumerable histories and a dizzying variety of peoples, languages, experiences and cultures, all these are swept aside or ignored, relegated to the sand heap along with the treasures ground into meaningless fragments that were taken out of Baghdad's libraries and museums. My argument is that history is made by men and women, just as it can also be unmade and re-written, always with various silences and elisions, always with shapes imposed and disfigurements tolerated, so that "our" East, "our" Orient becomes "ours" to possess and direct.

I should say again that I have no "real" Orient to argue for. I do, however, have a very high regard for the powers and gifts of the peoples of that region to struggle on for their vision of what they are and want to be. There has been so massive and calculatedly aggressive an attack on the contemporary societies of the Arab and Muslim for their backwardness, lack of democracy, and abrogation of women's rights that we simply forget that such notions as modernity, enlightenment and democracy are by no means simple and agreed-upon concepts that one either does or does not find, like Easter eggs in the living-room. The breathtaking insouciance of jejune publicists who speak in the name of foreign policy and who have no live notion (or any knowledge at all) of the language of what real people actually speak has fabricated an arid landscape ready for American power to construct there an *ersatz* model of free market "democracy," without even a trace of doubt that such projects don't exist outside of Swift's Academy of Lagado.

What I do argue also is that there is a difference between knowledge of other peoples and other times that is the result of understanding, compassion, careful study and analysis for their own sakes, and on the other hand knowledge—if that is what it is—that is part of an overall campaign of self-affirmation, belligerency and outright war. There is, after all, a profound difference between the will to understand for purposes of co-existence and humanistic enlargement of horizons, and the will to dominate for the purposes of control and external dominion. It is surely one of the intellectual catastrophes of history that an imperialist war confected by a small group of unelected US officials (they've been called chickenhawks, since none of them ever served in the military) was waged against a devastated Third World dictatorship on thoroughly ideological grounds having to do with world dominance, security control, and scarce resources, but disguised for its true intent, hastened and reasoned for by Orientalists who betrayed their calling as scholars. The major influences on George W. Bush's Pentagon and National Security Council were men such as Bernard Lewis and Fouad Ajami, experts on the Arab and Islamic world who helped the American hawks to think about such preposterous phenomena as the Arab mind and centuries-old Islamic decline that only American power could reverse. Today, bookstores in the US are filled with shabby screeds bearing screaming headlines about Islam and terror, Islam exposed, the Arab threat and the Muslim menace, all of them written by political polemicists pretending to knowledge imparted to them and others by experts who have supposedly penetrated to the heart of these strange Oriental peoples over there who have been such a terrible thorn in "our" flesh. Accompanying such warmongering expertise have been the omnipresent CNNs and Foxs of this world, plus myriad numbers of evangelical and right-wing radio hosts, plus innumerable tabloids and even middle-brow journalists, all of them re-cycling the same unverifiable fictions and vast generalizations so as to stir up "America" against the foreign devil.

Even with all its terrible failings and its appalling dictator (who was partly created by US policy two decades ago), were Iraq to have been the world's largest exporter of bananas or oranges, surely there would have been no war, no hysteria over mysteriously vanished weapons of mass destruction, no transporting of an enormous army, navy and air force 7000 miles away to destroy a country scarcely known even to the educated American, all in the name of "freedom." Without a well-organized sense that these people over there were not like "us" and didn't appreciate "our" values—the very core of traditional Orientalist dogma as I describe its creation and circulation in this book—there would have been no war.

So from the very same directorate of paid professional scholars enlisted by the Dutch conquerors of Malaysia and Indonesia, the British armies of India, Mesopotamia, Egypt, West Africa, the French armies of Indochina and North Africa, came the American advisers to the Pentagon and the White House, using the same clichés, the same demeaning stereotypes, the same justifications of power and violence (after all, runs the chorus, power is the only language they understand) in this case as in the earlier ones. These people have now been joined in Iraq by a whole army of private contractors and eager entrepreneurs to whom shall be confided everything from the writing of textbooks and the constitution to the

refashioning and privatisation of Iraqi political life and its oil industry. Every single empire in its official discourse has said that it is not
like all the others, that its circumstances are special, that it has a
mission to enlighten, civilize, bring order and democracy, and that
it uses force only as a last resort. And, sadder still, there always is a
chorus of willing intellectuals to say calming words about benign or
altruistic empires, as if one shouldn't trust the evidence of one's
eyes watching the destruction and the misery and death brought by
the latest *mission civilizatrice*.

One specifically American contribution to the discourse of empire
is the specialized jargon of policy expertise. You don't need Arabic
or Persian or even French to pontificate about how the democracy
domino effect is just what the Arab world needs. Combative and
woefully ignorant policy experts whose world experience is limited
to the Beltway grind out books on "terrorism" and liberalism, or
about Islamic fundamentalism and American foreign policy, or about
the end of history, all of it vying for attention and influence quite
without regard for truthfulness or reflection or real knowledge. What
matters is how efficient and resourceful it sounds, and who might go
for it, as it were. The worst aspect of this essentializing stuff is that
human suffering in all its density and pain is spirited away. Memory
and with it the historical past are effaced as in the common, dismiss-
ively contemptuous American phrase, "you're history."

Twenty-five years after its publication, *Orientalism* once again
raises the question of whether modern imperialism ever ended, or
whether it has continued in the Orient since Napoleon's entry into
Egypt two centuries ago. Arabs and Muslims have been told that
victimology and dwelling on the depredations of empire are only
ways of evading responsibility in the present. You have failed, you
have gone wrong, says the modern Orientalist. This, of course, is
also V. S. Naipaul's contribution to literature, that the victims of
empire wail on while their country goes to the dogs. But what a
shallow calculation of the imperial intrusion that is, how summarily
it scants the immense distortion introduced by the empire into the
lives of "lesser" peoples and "subject races" generation after generation, how little it wishes to face the long succession of years
through which empire continues to work its way in the lives of, say,
Palestinians or Congolese or Algerians or Iraqis. We allow justly
that the Holocaust has permanently altered the consciousness of our
time: why do we not accord the same epistemological mutation in

what imperialism has done, and what Orientalism continues to do? Think of the line that starts with Napoleon, continues with the rise of Oriental studies and the takeover of North Africa, and goes on in similar undertakings in Vietnam, in Egypt, in Palestine and, during the entire twentieth century, in the struggle over oil and strategic control in the Gulf, in Iraq, Syria, Palestine and Afghanistan. Then think contrapuntally of the rise of anti-colonial nationalism, through the short period of liberal independence, the era of military coups, of insurgency, civil war, religious fanaticism, irrational struggle and uncompromising brutality against the latest bunch of "natives." Each of these phases and eras produces its own distorted knowledge of the other, each its own reductive images, its own disputatious polemics.

My idea in *Orientalism* is to use humanistic critique to open up the fields of struggle, to introduce a longer sequence of thought and analysis to replace the short bursts of polemical, thought-stopping fury that so imprison us in labels and antagonistic debate whose goal is a belligerent collective identity rather than understanding and intellectual exchange. I have called what I try to do "humanism," a word I continue to use stubbornly despite the scornful dismissal of the term by sophisticated post-modern critics. By humanism I mean first of all attempting to dissolve Blake's mind-forg'd manacles so as to be able to use one's mind historically and rationally for the purposes of reflective understanding and genuine disclosure. More-over, humanism is sustained by a sense of community with other interpreters and other societies and periods: strictly speaking, there-fore, there is no such thing as an isolated humanist.

This is to say that every domain is linked to every other one, and that nothing that goes on in our world has ever been isolated and pure of any outside influence. The disheartening part is that the more the critical study of culture shows us that this is the case, the less influence such a view seems to have, and the more territorially reductive polarizations like "Islam *v*. the West" seem to conquer.

For those of us who by force of circumstance actually live the pluri-cultural life as it entails Islam and the West, I have long felt that a special intellectual and moral responsibility attaches to what we do as scholars and intellectuals. Certainly I think it is incumbent upon us to complicate and/or dismantle the reductive formulae and the abstract but potent kind of thought that leads the mind away from concrete human history and experience and into the realms of ideological fiction, metaphysical confrontation and collective passion. This is not to say that we cannot speak about issues of injustice and suffering, but that we need to do so always within a context that is amply situated in history, culture and socio-economic reality. Our role is to widen the field of discussion, not to set limits in accord with the prevailing authority. I have spent a great deal of my life during the past thirty-five years advocating the rights of the Palestinian people to national self-determination, but I have always tried to do that with full attention paid to the reality of the Jewish people and what they suffered by way of persecution and genocide. The paramount thing is that the struggle for equality in Palestine/Israel should be directed toward a humane goal, that is, co-existence, and not further suppression and denial. Not accidentally, I indicate that Orientalism and modern anti-Semitism have common roots. Therefore it would seem to be a vital necessity for independent intellectuals always to provide alternative models to the reductively simplifying and confining ones, based on mutual hostility, that have prevailed in the Middle East and elsewhere for so long.

Let me now speak about a different alternative model that has been extremely important to me in my work. As a humanist whose field is literature, I am old enough to have been trained forty years ago in the field of comparative literature, whose leading ideas go back to Germany in the late eighteenth and early nineteenth centuries. Before that I must mention the supremely creative contribution of Giambattista Vico, the Neopolitan philosopher and philologist whose ideas anticipate and later infiltrate the line of German thinkers I am about to cite. They belong to the era of Herder and Wolf, later to be followed by Goethe, Humboldt, Dilthey, Nietzsche, Gadamer, and finally the great Twentieth Century Romance philologists Erich Auerbach, Leo Spitzer and Ernst Robert Curtius. To young people of the current generation the very idea of philology suggests something impossibly antiquarian and musty, but philology in fact is the most basic and creative of the interpretive arts. It is exemplified for me most admirably in Goethe's interest in Islam generally, and Hafiz in particular, a consuming passion which led to the composition of the *West-Östlicher Diwan*, and it inflected Goethe's later ideas about *Weltliteratur*, the study of all the literatures of the world as a symphonic whole which could be apprehended theoretically as having preserved the individuality of each work without losing sight of the whole.

There is a considerable irony to the realization, then, that, as today's globalized world draws together in some of the lamentable ways I have been talking about here, we may be approaching the kind of standardization and homogeneity that Goethe's ideas were specifically formulated to prevent. In an essay published in 1951 entitled "Philologie der Weltliteratur", Erich Auerbach made exactly that point at the outset of the postwar period, which was also the beginning of the Cold War. His great book *Mimesis*, published in Berne in 1946 but written while Auerbach was a wartime exile teaching Romance languages in Istanbul, was meant to be a testament to the diversity and concreteness of the reality represented in Western literature from Homer to Virginia Woolf; but reading the 1951 essay one senses that for Auerbach the great book he wrote was an elegy for a period when people could interpret texts philologically, concretely, sensitively and intuitively, using erudition and an excellent command of several languages to support the kind of understanding that Goethe advocated for his understanding of Islamic literature.

Positive knowledge of languages and history was necessary, but it was never enough, any more than the mechanical gathering of facts would constitute an adequate method of grasping what an author like Dante, for example, was all about. The main requirement for the kind of philological understanding Auerbach and his predecessors were talking about and tried to practice was one that sympathetically and subjectively entered into the life of a written text as seen from the perspective of its time and its author (*eingefühling*). Rather than alienation and hostility to another time and different culture, philology as applied to *Weltliteratur* involved a profound humanistic spirit deployed with generosity and, if I may use the word, hospitality. Thus the interpreter's mind actively makes a place in it for a foreign Other. And this creative making of a place for works that are otherwise alien and distant is the most important facet of the interpreter's philological mission.

All this was obviously undermined and destroyed in Germany by National Socialism. After the war, Auerbach notes mournfully, the standardization of ideas, and greater and greater specialization of knowledge, gradually narrowed the opportunities for the kind of investigative and everlastingly inquiring kind of philological work that he had represented, and, alas, it's an even more depressing fact that since Auerbach's death in 1957 both the idea and practice of humanistic research have shrunk in scope as well as in centrality. The book culture based on archival research as well as general principles of mind that once sustained humanism as a historical discipline have almost disappeared. Instead of reading in the real sense of the word, our students today are often distracted by the fragmented knowledge available on the internet and in the mass media.

Worse yet, education is threatened by nationalist and religious orthodoxies often disseminated by the mass media as they focus ahistorically and sensationally on the distant electronic wars that give viewers the sense of surgical precision but that in fact obscure the terrible suffering and destruction produced by modern "clean" warfare. In the demonization of an unknown enemy, for whom the label "terrorist" serves the general purpose of keeping people stirred up and angry, media images command too much attention and can be exploited at times of crisis and insecurity of the kind that the post-9/11 period has produced. Speaking both as an American and as an Arab I must ask my reader not to underestimate the kind of simplified view of the world that a relative handful of Pentagon civilian elites have formulated for US policy in the entire Arab and Islamic worlds, a view in which terror, pre-emptive war, and unilateral regime change—backed up by the most bloated military budget in history—are the main ideas debated endlessly and impoverishingly by a media that assigns itself the role of producing so-called "experts" who validate the government's general line.

Reflection, debate, rational argument, moral principle based on a secular notion that human beings must create their own history, have been replaced by abstract ideas that celebrate American or Western exceptionalism, denigrate the relevance of context, and regard other cultures with derisive contempt. Perhaps you will say that I am making too many abrupt transitions between humanistic interpretation on the one hand and foreign policy on the other, and that a modern technological society which along with unprecedented power possesses the internet and F-16 fighter-jets must in the end be commanded by formidable technical-policy experts like Donald Rumsfeld and Richard Perle. But what has really been lost is a sense of the density and interdependence of human life, which can neither be reduced to a formula nor be brushed aside as irrelevant. Even the language of the war is dehumanizing in the extreme: "We'll go in there, take out Saddam, destroy his army with clean surgical strikes, and everyone will think it's great," said a congresswoman on national television. It seems to me entirely symptomatic of the precarious moment we are living through that when Vice President Cheney made his hard-line speech on August 26, 2002, about the imperative to attack Iraq, he quoted as his single Middle east "expert" in support of military intervention against Iraq an Arab academic who as a paid consultant to the mass media on a nightly basis keeps repeating his hatred of his own people and the renunciation of his background. Such a *trahison des clercs* is a sign of how genuine humanism can degenerate into jingoism and false patriotism.

That is one side of the global debate. In the Arab and Muslim countries the situation is scarcely better. As Roula Khalaf in an excellent *Financial Times* essay (September 4, 2002) argues, the region has slipped into an easy anti-Americanism that shows little understanding of what the US is really like as a society. Because the governments are relatively powerless to affect US policy toward them, they turn their energies to repressing and keeping down their own populations, which results in resentment, anger and helpless imprecations that do nothing to open up societies where secular ideas about human history and development have been overtaken by failure and frustration, as well as by an Islamism built out of rote learning, the obliteration of what are perceived to be other, competitive forms of secular knowledge, and an inability to analyze and exchange ideas within the generally discordant world of modern discourse. The gradual disappearance of the extraordinary tradition of Islamic *ijtihad* has been one of the major cultural disasters of our time, with the result that critical thinking and individual wrestling with the problems of the modern world have simply dropped out of sight. Orthodoxy and dogma rule instead.

This is not to say that the cultural world has simply regressed on one side to a belligerent neo-Orientalism and on the other to blanket rejectionism. The recent United Nations World Summit in Johannesburg, for all its limitations, did in fact reveal a vast area of common global concern whose detailed workings on matters having to do with the environment, famine, the gap between advanced and developing countries, health and human rights, suggest the welcome emergence of a new collective constituency that gives the often facile notion of "one world" a new urgency. In all this, however, we must admit that no one can possibly know the extraordinarily complex unity of our globalized world, despite the reality that, as I said at the outset, the world does have a real interdependence of parts that leaves no genuine opportunity for isolation.

The point I want to conclude with now is to insist that the terrible reductive conflicts that herd people under falsely unifying rubrics like "America," "The West" or "Islam" and invent collective identities for large numbers of individuals who are actually quite diverse, cannot remain as potent as they are, and must be opposed, their murderous effectiveness vastly reduced in influence and mobilizing power. We still have at our disposal the rational interpretive skills that are the legacy of humanistic education, not as a sentimental piety enjoining us to return to traditional values or the classics but as the active practice of worldly secular rational discourse. The secular world is the world of history as made by human beings. Human agency is subject to investigation and analysis, which it is the mission of understanding to apprehend, criticize, influence and judge. Above all, critical thought does not submit to state power or to commands to join in the ranks marching against one or another approved enemy. Rather than the manufactured clash of civilizations, we need to concentrate on the slow working together of cultures that overlap, borrow from each other, and live together in far more interesting ways than any abridged or inauthentic mode of understanding can allow. But for that kind of wider perception we need time and patient and skeptical inquiry, supported by faith in communities of interpretation that are difficult to sustain in a world demanding instant action and reaction.

Humanism is centered upon the agency of human individuality and subjective intuition, rather than on received ideas and approved authority. Texts have to be read as texts that were produced and live on in the historical realm in all sorts of what I have called worldly ways. But this by no means excludes power, since on the contrary what I have tried to show in my book have been the insinuations, the imbrications of power into even the most recondite of studies.

And lastly, most important, humanism is the only, and, I would go as far as saying, the final, resistance we have against the inhuman practices and injustices that disfigure human history. We are today abetted by the enormously encouraging democratic field of cyberspace, open to all users in ways undreamed of by earlier generations either of tyrants or of orthodoxies. The world-wide protests before the war began in Iraq would not have been possible were it not for the existence of alternative communities across the globe, informed by alternative news sources and keenly aware of the environmental, human rights, and libertarian impulses that bind us together in this tiny planet. The human, and humanistic, desire for enlightenment and emancipation is not easily deferred, despite the incredible strength of the opposition to it that comes from the Rumsfelds, Bin Ladens, Sharons and Bushes of this world. I would like to believe that *Orientalism* has had a place in the long and often interrupted road to human freedom.

E.W.S.

New York
May 2003

Acknowledgments

I have been reading about Orientalism for a number of years, but most of this book was written during 1975–1976, which I spent as a Fellow at the Center for Advanced Study in the Behavioral Sciences, Stanford, California. In this unique and generous institution, it was my good fortune not only to have benefitted agreeably from several colleagues, but also from the help of Joan Warmbrunn, Chris Hoth, Jane Kielsmeier, Preston Cutler, and the center's director, Gardner Lindzey. The list of friends, colleagues, and students who read, or listened to, parts or the whole of this manuscript is so long as to embarrass me, and now that it has finally appeared as a book, perhaps even them. Nevertheless I should mention with gratitude the always helpful encouragement of Janet and Ibrahim Abu-Lughod, Noam Chomsky, and Roger Owen, who followed this project from its beginning to its conclusion. Likewise I must gratefully acknowledge the helpful and critical interest of the colleagues, friends, and students in various places whose questions and discussion sharpened the text considerably. André Schiffrin and Jeanne Morton of Pantheon Books were ideal publisher and copy editor, respectively, and made the ordeal (for the author, at least) of preparing the manuscript an instructive and genuinely intelligent process. Mariam Said helped me a great deal with her research on the early modern history of Orientalist institutions. Apart from that, though, her loving support really made much of the work on this book not only enjoyable but possible.

E. W. S.

New York
September–October 1977

They cannot represent themselves; they must be represented.

> —Karl Marx, *The Eighteenth Brumaire of Louis Bonaparte*

The East is a career.

> —Benjamin Disraeli, *Tancred*

Orient – from exotic fantasy
to nothing

Complete
reverse in
modern
times

Construction of Orient

Our colonies
+ own culture
comes from
our construction
of theirs

Introduction

I

On a visit to Beirut during the terrible civil war of 1975–1976 a French journalist wrote regretfully of the gutted downtown area that "it had once seemed to belong to . . . the Orient of Chateaubriand and Nerval."[1] He was right about the place, of course, especially so far as a European was concerned. The Orient was almost a European invention, and had been since antiquity a place of romance, exotic beings, haunting memories and landscapes, remarkable experiences. Now it was disappearing; in a sense it had happened, its time was over. Perhaps it seemed irrelevant that Orientals themselves had something at stake in the process, that even in the time of Chateaubriand and Nerval Orientals had lived there, and that now it was they who were suffering; the main thing for the European visitor was a European representation of the Orient and its contemporary fate, both of which had a privileged communal significance for the journalist and his French readers.

Americans will not feel quite the same about the Orient, which for them is much more likely to be associated very differently with the Far East (China and Japan, mainly). Unlike the Americans, the French and the British—less so the Germans, Russians, Spanish, Portuguese, Italians, and Swiss—have had a long tradition of what I shall be calling *Orientalism*, a way of coming to terms with the Orient that is based on the Orient's special place in European Western experience. The Orient is not only adjacent to Europe; it is also the place of Europe's greatest and richest and oldest colonies, the source of its civilizations and languages, its cultural contestant, and one of its deepest and most recurring images of the Other. In addition, the Orient has helped to define Europe (or the West) as its contrasting image, idea, personality, experience. Yet none of this Orient is merely imaginative. The Orient is an integral part of European *material* civilization and culture. Orientalism expresses and represents that part culturally and even ideologically as a mode of discourse with supporting institutions, vocabulary, scholarship, imagery, doctrines, even colonial bureaucracies and colonial styles. In contrast, the American understanding of the Orient will seem considerably less dense, although our recent Japanese, Korean, and Indochinese adventures ought now to be creating a more sober, more realistic "Oriental" awareness. Moreover, the vastly expanded American political and economic role in the Near East (the Middle East) makes great claims on our understanding of that Orient.

It will be clear to the reader (and will become clearer still throughout the many pages that follow) that by Orientalism I mean several things, all of them, in my opinion, interdependent. The most readily accepted designation for Orientalism is an academic one, and indeed the label still serves in a number of academic institutions. Anyone who teaches, writes about, or researches the Orient—and this applies whether the person is an anthropologist, sociologist, historian, or philologist—either in its specific or its general aspects, is an Orientalist, and what he or she does is Orientalism. Compared with *Oriental studies* or *area studies*, it is true that the term *Orientalism* is less preferred by specialists today, both because it is too vague and general and because it connotes the high-handed executive attitude of nineteenth-century and early-twentieth-century European colonialism. Nevertheless books are written and congresses held with "the Orient" as their main focus, with the Orientalist in his new or old guise as their main authority. The point is that even if it does not survive as it once did, Orientalism lives on academically through its doctrines and theses about the Orient and the Oriental.

Related to this academic tradition, whose fortunes, transmigrations, specializations, and transmissions are in part the subject of this study, is a more general meaning for Orientalism. Orientalism is a style of thought based upon an ontological and epistemological distinction made between "the Orient" and (most of the time) "the Occident." Thus a very large mass of writers, among whom are poets, novelists, philosophers, political theorists, economists, and imperial administrators, have accepted the basic distinction between East and West as the starting point for elaborate theories, epics, novels, social descriptions, and political accounts concerning the

Orient, its people, customs, "mind," destiny, and so on. *This* Orientalism can accommodate Aeschylus, say, and Victor Hugo, Dante and Karl Marx. A little later in this introduction I shall deal with the methodological problems one encounters in so broadly construed a "field" as this.

The interchange between the academic and the more or less imaginative meanings of Orientalism is a constant one, and since the late eighteenth century there has been a considerable, quite disciplined—perhaps even regulated—traffic between the two. Here I come to the third meaning of Orientalism, which is something more historically and materially defined than either of the other two. Taking the late eighteenth century as a very roughly defined starting point Orientalism can be discussed and analyzed as the corporate institution for dealing with the Orient—dealing with it by making statements about it, authorizing views of it, describing it, by teaching it, settling it, ruling over it: in short, Orientalism as a Western style for dominating, restructuring, and having authority over the Orient. I have found it useful here to employ Michel Foucault's notion of a discourse, as described by him in *The Archaeology of Knowledge* and in *Discipline and Punish*, to identify Orientalism. My contention is that without examining Orientalism as a discourse one cannot possibly understand the enormously systematic discipline by which European culture was able to manage—and even produce—the Orient politically, sociologically, militarily, ideologically, scientifically, and imaginatively during the post-Enlightenment period. Moreover, so authoritative a position did Orientalism have that I believe no one writing, thinking, or acting on the Orient could do so without taking account of the limitations on thought and action imposed by Orientalism. In brief, because of Orientalism the Orient was not (and is not) a free subject of thought or action. This is not to say that Orientalism unilaterally determines what can be said about the Orient, but that it is the whole network of interests inevitably brought to bear on (and therefore always involved in) any occasion when that peculiar entity "the Orient" is in question. How this happens is what this book tries to demonstrate. It also tries to show that European culture gained in strength and identity by setting itself off against the Orient as a sort of surrogate and even underground self.

Historically and culturally there is a quantitative as well as a qualitative difference between the Franco-British involvement in the Orient and—until the period of American ascendancy after

World War II—the involvement of every other European and Atlantic power. To speak of Orientalism therefore is to speak mainly, although not exclusively, of a British and French cultural enterprise, a project whose dimensions take in such disparate realms as the imagination itself, the whole of India and the Levant, the Biblical texts and the Biblical lands, the spice trade, colonial armies and a long tradition of colonial administrators, a formidable scholarly corpus, innumerable Oriental "experts" and "hands," an Oriental professorate, a complex array of "Oriental" ideas (Oriental despotism, Oriental splendor, cruelty, sensuality), many Eastern sects, philosophies, and wisdoms domesticated for local European use—the list can be extended more or less indefinitely. My point is that Orientalism derives from a particular closeness experienced between Britain and France and the Orient, which until the early nineteenth century had really meant only India and the Bible lands. From the beginning of the nineteenth century until the end of World War II France and Britain dominated the Orient and Orientalism; since World War II America has dominated the Orient, and approaches it as France and Britain once did. Out of that closeness, whose dynamic is enormously productive even if it always demonstrates the comparatively greater strength of the Occident (British, French, or American), comes the large body of texts I call Orientalist.

It should be said at once that even with the generous number of books and authors that I examine, there is a much larger number that I simply have had to leave out. My argument, however, depends neither upon an exhaustive catalogue of texts dealing with the Orient nor upon a clearly delimited set of texts, authors, and ideas that together make up the Orientalist canon. I have depended instead upon a different methodological alternative—whose backbone in a sense is the set of historical generalizations I have so far been making in this Introduction—and it is these I want now to discuss in more analytical detail.

II

I have begun with the assumption that the Orient is not an inert fact of nature. It is not merely *there*, just as the Occident itself is not just *there* either. We must take seriously Vico's great obser-

vation that men make their own history, that what they can know
is what they have made, and extend it to geography: as both geographical and cultural entities—to say nothing of historical entities
—such locales, regions, geographical sectors as "Orient" and "Occident" are man-made. Therefore as much as the West itself, the
Orient is an idea that has a history and a tradition of thought,
imagery, and vocabulary that have given it reality and presence in
and for the West. The two geographical entities thus support and to
an extent reflect each other.

Having said that, one must go on to state a number of reasonable
qualifications. In the first place, it would be wrong to conclude that
the Orient was *essentially* an idea, or a creation with no corresponding reality. When Disraeli said in his novel *Tancred* that
the East was a career, he meant that to be interested in the East
was something bright young Westerners would find to be an all-
consuming passion; he should not be interpreted as saying that the
East was *only* a career for Westerners. There were—and are—
cultures and nations whose location is in the East, and their lives,
histories, and customs have a brute reality obviously greater than
anything that could be said about them in the West. About that
fact this study of Orientalism has very little to contribute, except
to acknowledge it tacitly. But the phenomenon of Orientalism as
I study it here deals principally, not with a correspondence between
Orientalism and Orient, but with the internal consistency of Orientalism and its ideas about the Orient (the East as career) despite
or beyond any correspondence, or lack thereof, with a "real"
Orient. My point is that Disraeli's statement about the East refers
mainly to that created consistency, that regular constellation of
ideas as the pre-eminent thing about the Orient, and not to its
mere being, as Wallace Stevens's phrase has it.

A second qualification is that ideas, cultures, and histories cannot
seriously be understood or studied without their force, or more
precisely their configurations of power, also being studied. To believe that the Orient was created—or, as I call it, "Orientalized"
—and to believe that such things happen simply as a necessity of
the imagination, is to be disingenuous. The relationship between
Occident and Orient is a relationship of power, of domination, of
varying degrees of a complex hegemony, and is quite accurately
indicated in the title of K. M. Panikkar's classic *Asia and Western
Dominance*.[2] The Orient was Orientalized not only because it was
discovered to be "Oriental" in all those ways considered common-

place by an average nineteenth-century European, but also because it *could be*—that is, submitted to being—*made* Oriental. There is very little consent to be found, for example, in the fact that Flaubert's encounter with an Egyptian courtesan produced a widely influential model of the Oriental woman; she never spoke of herself, she never represented her emotions, presence, or history. *He* spoke for and represented her. He was foreign, comparatively wealthy, male, and these were historical facts of domination that allowed him not only to possess Kuchuk Hanem physically but to speak for her and tell his readers in what way she was "typically Oriental." My argument is that Flaubert's situation of strength in relation to Kuchuk Hanem was not an isolated instance. It fairly stands for the pattern of relative strength between East and West, and the discourse about the Orient that it enabled.

This brings us to a third qualification. One ought never to assume that the structure of Orientalism is nothing more than a structure of lies or of myths which, were the truth about them to be told, would simply blow away. I myself believe that Orientalism is more particularly valuable as a sign of European-Atlantic power over the Orient than it is as a veridic discourse about the Orient (which is what, in its academic or scholarly form, it claims to be). Nevertheless, what we must respect and try to grasp is the sheer knitted-together strength of Orientalist discourse, its very close ties to the enabling socio-economic and political institutions, and its redoubtable durability. After all, any system of ideas that can remain unchanged as teachable wisdom (in academies, books, congresses, universities, foreign-service institutes) from the period of Ernest Renan in the late 1840s until the present in the United States must be something more formidable than a mere collection of lies. Orientalism, therefore, is not an airy European fantasy about the Orient, but a created body of theory and practice in which, for many generations, there has been a considerable material investment. Continued investment made Orientalism, as a system of knowledge about the Orient, an accepted grid for filtering through the Orient into Western consciousness, just as that same investment multiplied—indeed, made truly productive—the statements proliferating out from Orientalism into the general culture.

Gramsci has made the useful analytic distinction between civil and political society in which the former is made up of voluntary (or at least rational and noncoercive) affiliations like schools, families, and unions, the latter of state institutions (the army, the police, the central bureaucracy) whose role in the polity is direct domination. Culture, of course, is to be found operating within civil society, where the influence of ideas, of institutions, and of other persons works not through domination but by what Gramsci calls consent. In any society not totalitarian, then, certain cultural forms predominate over others, just as certain ideas are more influential than others; the form of this cultural leadership is what Gramsci has identified as *hegemony*, an indispensable concept for any understanding of cultural life in the industrial West. It is hegemony, or rather the result of cultural hegemony at work, that gives Orientalism the durability and the strength I have been speaking about so far. Orientalism is never far from what Denys Hay has called the idea of Europe,[3] a collective notion identifying "us" Europeans as against all "those" non-Europeans, and indeed it can be argued that the major component in European culture is precisely what made that culture hegemonic both in and outside Europe: the idea of European identity as a superior one in comparison with all the non-European peoples and cultures. There is in addition the hegemony of European ideas about the Orient, themselves reiterating European superiority over Oriental backwardness, usually overriding the possibility that a more independent, or more skeptical, thinker might have had different views on the matter.

In a quite constant way, Orientalism depends for its strategy on this flexible *positional* superiority, which puts the Westerner in a whole series of possible relationships with the Orient without ever losing him the relative upper hand. And why should it have been otherwise, especially during the period of extraordinary European ascendancy from the late Renaissance to the present? The scientist, the scholar, the missionary, the trader, or the soldier was in, or thought about, the Orient because he *could be there*, or could think about it, with very little resistance on the Orient's part. Under the general heading of knowledge of the Orient, and within the umbrella of Western hegemony over the Orient during the period from the end of the eighteenth century, there emerged a complex Orient suitable for study in the academy, for display in the museum, for reconstruction in the colonial office, for theoretical illustration in anthropological, biological, linguistic, racial, and historical theses about mankind and the universe, for instances of economic and sociological theories of development, revolution, cultural personality, national or religious character. Additionally, the imaginative examination of things Oriental was based more or less exclusively upon a sovereign Western consciousness out of whose unchallenged centrality an Oriental world emerged, first according to general ideas about who or what was an Oriental, then according to a detailed logic governed not simply by empirical reality but by a battery of desires, repressions, investments, and projections. If we can point to great Orientalist works of genuine scholarship like Silvestre de Sacy's *Chrestomathie arabe* or Edward William Lane's *Account of the Manners and Customs of the Modern Egyptians*, we need also to note that Renan's and Gobineau's racial ideas came out of the same impulse, as did a great many Victorian pornographic novels (see the analysis by Steven Marcus of "The Lustful Turk"[4]).

And yet, one must repeatedly ask oneself whether what matters in Orientalism is the general group of ideas overriding the mass of material—about which who could deny that they were shot through with doctrines of European superiority, various kinds of racism, imperialism, and the like, dogmatic views of "the Oriental" as a kind of ideal and unchanging abstraction?—or the much more varied work produced by almost uncountable individual writers, whom one would take up as individual instances of authors dealing with the Orient. In a sense the two alternatives, general and particular, are really two perspectives on the same material: in both instances one would have to deal with pioneers in the field like William Jones, with great artists like Nerval or Flaubert. And why would it not be possible to employ both perspectives together, or one after the other? Isn't there an obvious danger of distortion (of precisely the kind that academic Orientalism has always been prone to) if either too general or too specific a level of description is maintained systematically?

My two fears are distortion and inaccuracy, or rather the kind of inaccuracy produced by too dogmatic a generality and too positivistic a localized focus. In trying to deal with these problems I have tried to deal with three main aspects of my own contemporary reality that seem to me to point the way out of the methodological or perspectival difficulties I have been discussing, difficulties that might force one, in the first instance, into writing a coarse polemic on so unacceptably general a level of description as not to be worth the effort, or in the second instance, into writing so detailed and atomistic a series of analyses as to lose all track of the general lines of force informing the field, giving it its special cogency. How then to recognize individuality and to reconcile it with its intelligent, and by no means passive or merely dictatorial, general and hegemonic context?

III

I mentioned three aspects of my contemporary reality: I must explain and briefly discuss them now, so that it can be seen how I was led to a particular course of research and writing.

1. *The distinction between pure and political knowledge.* It is very easy to argue that knowledge about Shakespeare or Wordsworth is not political whereas knowledge about contemporary China or the Soviet Union is. My own formal and professional designation is that of "humanist," a title which indicates the humanities as my field and therefore the unlikely eventuality that there might be anything political about what I do in that field. Of course, all these labels and terms are quite unnuanced as I use them here, but the general truth of what I am pointing to is, I think, widely held. One reason for saying that a humanist who writes about Wordsworth, or an editor whose specialty is Keats, is not involved in anything political is that what he does seems to have no direct political effect upon reality in the everyday sense. A scholar whose field is Soviet economics works in a highly charged area where there is much government interest, and what he might produce in the way of studies or proposals will be taken up by policymakers, government officials, institutional economists, intelligence experts. The distinction between "humanists" and persons whose work has policy implications, or political significance, can be broadened further by saying that the former's ideological color is a matter of incidental importance to politics (although possibly of great moment to his colleagues in the field, who may object to his Stalinism or fascism or too easy liberalism), whereas the ideology of the latter is woven directly into his material—indeed, economics, politics, and sociology in the modern academy are ideological sciences—and therefore taken for granted as being "political."

Nevertheless the determining impingement on most knowledge

produced in the contemporary West (and here I speak mainly about
the United States) is that it be nonpolitical, that is, scholarly,
academic, impartial, above partisan or small-minded doctrinal
belief. One can have no quarrel with such an ambition in theory,
perhaps, but in practice the reality is much more problematic. No
one has ever devised a method for detaching the scholar from the
circumstances of life, from the fact of his involvement (conscious
or unconscious) with a class, a set of beliefs, a social position, or
from the mere activity of being a member of a society. These
continue to bear on what he does professionally, even though
naturally enough his research and its fruits do attempt to reach a
level of relative freedom from the inhibitions and the restrictions
of brute, everyday reality. For there is such a thing as knowledge
that is less, rather than more, partial than the individual (with his
entangling and distracting life circumstances) who produces it.
Yet this knowledge is not therefore automatically nonpolitical.

Whether discussions of literature or of classical philology are
fraught with—or have unmediated—political significance is a very
large question that I have tried to treat in some detail elsewhere.[5]
What I am interested in doing now is suggesting how the general
liberal consensus that "true" knowledge is fundamentally nonpolitical (and conversely, that overtly political knowledge is not
"true" knowledge) obscures the highly if obscurely organized
political circumstances obtaining when knowledge is produced.
No one is helped in understanding this today when the adjective
"political" is used as a label to discredit any work for daring to
violate the protocol of pretended suprapolitical objectivity. We may
say, first, that civil society recognizes a gradation of political importance in the various fields of knowledge. To some extent the
political importance given a field comes from the possibility of its
direct translation into economic terms; but to a greater extent
political importance comes from the closeness of a field to ascertain-
able sources of power in political society. Thus an economic study
of long-term Soviet energy potential and its effect on military
capability is likely to be commissioned by the Defense Department,
and thereafter to acquire a kind of political status impossible for a
study of Tolstoi's early fiction financed in part by a foundation.
Yet both works belong in what civil society acknowledges to be a
similar field, Russian studies, even though one work may be done
by a very conservative economist, the other by a radical literary

historian. My point here is that "Russia" as a general subject matter has political priority over nicer distinctions such as "economics" and "literary history," because political society in Gramsci's sense reaches into such realms of civil society as the academy and saturates them with significance of direct concern to it.

I do not want to press all this any further on general theoretical grounds: it seems to me that the value and credibility of my case can be demonstrated by being much more specific, in the way, for example, Noam Chomsky has studied the instrumental connection between the Vietnam War and the notion of objective scholarship as it was applied to cover state-sponsored military research.[6] Now because Britain, France, and recently the United States are imperial powers, their political societies impart to their civil societies a sense of urgency, a direct political infusion as it were, where and whenever matters pertaining to their imperial interests abroad are concerned. I doubt that it is controversial, for example, to say that an Englishman in India or Egypt in the later nineteenth century took an interest in those countries that was never far from their status in his mind as British colonies. To say this may seem quite different from saying that all academic knowledge about India and Egypt is somehow tinged and impressed with, violated by, the gross political fact—and yet *that is what I am saying* in this study of Orientalism. For if it is true that no production of knowledge in the human sciences can ever ignore or disclaim its author's involvement as a human subject in his own circumstances, then it must also be true that for a European or American studying the Orient there can be no disclaiming the main circumstances of *his* actuality: that he comes up against the Orient as a European or American first, as an individual second. And to be a European or an American in such a situation is by no means an inert fact. It meant and means being aware, however dimly, that one belongs to a power with definite interests in the Orient, and more important, that one belongs to a part of the earth with a definite history of involvement in the Orient almost since the time of Homer.

Put in this way, these political actualities are still too undefined and general to be really interesting. Anyone would agree to them without necessarily agreeing also that they mattered very much, for instance, to Flaubert as he wrote *Salammbô*, or to H. A. R. Gibb as he wrote *Modern Trends in Islam*. The trouble is that there is too great a distance between the big dominating fact, as I have described it, and the details of everyday life that govern the minute discipline of a novel or a scholarly text as each is being written. Yet if we eliminate from the start any notion that "big" facts like imperial domination can be applied mechanically and deterministically to such complex matters as culture and ideas, then we will begin to approach an interesting kind of study. My idea is that European and then American interest in the Orient was political according to some of the obvious historical accounts of it that I have given here, but that it was the culture that created that interest, that acted dynamically along with brute political, economic, and military rationales to make the Orient the varied and complicated place that it obviously was in the field I call Orientalism.

Therefore, Orientalism is not a mere political subject matter or field that is reflected passively by culture, scholarship, or institutions; nor is it a large and diffuse collection of texts about the Orient; nor is it representative and expressive of some nefarious "Western" imperialist plot to hold down the "Oriental" world. It is rather a *distribution* of geopolitical awareness into aesthetic, scholarly, economic, sociological, historical, and philological texts; it is an *elaboration* not only of a basic geographical distinction (the world is made up of two unequal halves, Orient and Occident) but also of a whole series of "interests" which, by such means as scholarly discovery, philological reconstruction, psychological analysis, landscape and sociological description, it not only creates but also maintains; it *is*, rather than expresses, a certain *will* or *intention* to understand, in some cases to control, manipulate, even to incorporate, what is a manifestly different (or alternative and novel) world; it is, above all, a discourse that is by no means in direct, corresponding relationship with political power in the raw, but rather is produced and exists in an uneven exchange with various kinds of power, shaped to a degree by the exchange with power political (as with a colonial or imperial establishment), power intellectual (as with reigning sciences like comparative linguistics or anatomy, or any of the modern policy sciences), power cultural (as with orthodoxies and canons of taste, texts, values), power moral (as with ideas about what "we" do and what "they" cannot do or understand as "we" do). Indeed, my real argument is that Orientalism is—and does not simply represent—a considerable dimension of modern political-intellectual culture, and as such has less to do with the Orient than it does with "our" world.

Because Orientalism is a cultural and a political fact, then, it does not exist in some archival vacuum; quite the contrary, I think it can be shown that what is thought, said, or even done about the Orient follows (perhaps occurs within) certain distinct and intellectually knowable lines. Here too a considerable degree of nuance and elaboration can be seen working as between the broad superstructural pressures and the details of composition, the facts of textuality. Most humanistic scholars are, I think, perfectly happy with the notion that texts exist in contexts, that there is such a thing as intertextuality, that the pressures of conventions, predecessors, and rhetorical styles limit what Walter Benjamin once called the "overtaxing of the productive person in the name of . . . the principle of 'creativity,' " in which the poet is believed on his own, and out of his pure mind, to have brought forth his work.[7] Yet there is a reluctance to allow that political, institutional, and ideological constraints act in the same manner on the individual author. A humanist will believe it to be an interesting fact to any interpreter of Balzac that he was influenced in the *Comédie humaine* by the conflict between Geoffroy Saint-Hilaire and Cuvier, but the same sort of pressure on Balzac of deeply reactionary monarchism is felt in some vague way to demean his literary "genius" and therefore to be less worth serious study. Similarly—as Harry Bracken has been tirelessly showing—philosophers will conduct their discussions of Locke, Hume, and empiricism without ever taking into account that there is an explicit connection in these classic writers between their "philosophic" doctrines and racial theory, justifications of slavery, or arguments for colonial exploitation.[8] These are common enough ways by which contemporary scholarship keeps itself pure.

Perhaps it is true that most attempts to rub culture's nose in the mud of politics have been crudely iconoclastic; perhaps also the social interpretation of literature in my own field has simply not kept up with the enormous technical advances in detailed textual analysis. But there is no getting away from the fact that literary studies in general, and American Marxist theorists in particular, have avoided the effort of seriously bridging the gap between the superstructural and the base levels in textual, historical scholarship; on another occasion I have gone so far as to say that the literary-cultural establishment as a whole has declared the serious study of imperialism and culture off limits.[9] For Orientalism brings one up directly against that question—that is, to realizing that political imperialism governs an entire field of study, imagination, and scholarly institutions—in such a way as to make its avoidance an intellectual and historical impossibility. Yet there will always remain the perennial escape mechanism of saying that a literary scholar and a philosopher, for example, are trained in literature and philosophy respectively, not in politics or ideological analysis. In other words, the specialist argument can work quite effectively to block the larger and, in my opinion, the more intellectually serious perspective.

Here it seems to me there is a simple two-part answer to be given, at least so far as the study of imperialism and culture (or Orientalism) is concerned. In the first place, nearly every nineteenth-century writer (and the same is true enough of writers in earlier periods) was extraordinarily well aware of the fact of empire: this is a subject not very well studied, but it will not take a modern Victorian specialist long to admit that liberal cultural heroes like John Stuart Mill, Arnold, Carlyle, Newman, Macaulay, Ruskin, George Eliot, and even Dickens had definite views on race and imperialism, which are quite easily to be found at work in their writing. So even a specialist must deal with the knowledge that Mill, for example, made it clear in *On Liberty* and *Representative Government* that his views there could not be applied to India (he was an India Office functionary for a good deal of his life, after all) because the Indians were civilizationally, if not racially, inferior. The same kind of paradox is to be found in Marx, as I try to show in this book. In the second place, to believe that politics in the form of imperialism bears upon the production of literature, scholarship, social theory, and history writing is by no means equivalent to saying that culture is therefore a demeaned or denigrated thing. Quite the contrary: my whole point is to say that we can better understand the persistence and the durability of saturating hegemonic systems like culture when we realize that their internal constraints upon writers and thinkers were *productive*, not unilaterally inhibiting. It is this idea that Gramsci, certainly, and Foucault and Raymond Williams in their very different ways have been trying to illustrate. Even one or two pages by Williams on "the uses of the Empire" in *The Long Revolution* tell us more about nineteenth-century cultural richness than many volumes of hermetic textual analyses.[10]

Therefore I study Orientalism as a dynamic exchange between

individual authors and the large political concerns shaped by the three great empires—British, French, American—in whose intellectual and imaginative territory the writing was produced. What interests me most as a scholar is not the gross political verity but the detail, as indeed what interests us in someone like Lane or Flaubert or Renan is not the (to him) indisputable truth that Occidentals are superior to Orientals, but the profoundly worked over and modulated evidence of his detailed work within the very wide space opened up by that truth. One need only remember that Lane's *Manners and Customs of the Modern Egyptians* is a classic of historical and anthropological observation because of its style, its enormously intelligent and brilliant details, not because of its simple reflection of racial superiority, to understand what I am saying here.

The kind of political questions raised by Orientalism, then, are as follows: What other sorts of intellectual, aesthetic, scholarly, and cultural energies went into the making of an imperialist tradition like the Orientalist one? How did philology, lexicography, history, biology, political and economic theory, novel-writing, and lyric poetry come to the service of Orientalism's broadly imperialist view of the world? What changes, modulations, refinements, even revolutions take place within Orientalism? What is the meaning of originality, of continuity, of individuality, in this context? How does Orientalism transmit or reproduce itself from one epoch to another? In fine, how can we treat the cultural, historical phenomenon of Orientalism as a kind of *willed human work*—not of mere unconditioned ratiocination—in all its historical complexity, detail, and worth without at the same time losing sight of the alliance between cultural work, political tendencies, the state, and the specific realities of domination? Governed by such concerns a humanistic study can responsibly address itself to politics *and* culture. But this is not to say that such a study establishes a hard-and-fast rule about the relationship between knowledge and politics. My argument is that each humanistic investigation must formulate the nature of that connection in the specific context of the study, the subject matter, and its historical circumstances.

2. *The methodological question.* In a previous book I gave a good deal of thought and analysis to the methodological importance for work in the human sciences of finding and formulating a first step, a point of departure, a beginning principle.[11] A major lesson

I learned and tried to present was that there is no such thing as a merely given, or simply available, starting point: beginnings have to be made for each project in such a way as to *enable* what follows from them. Nowhere in my experience has the difficulty of this lesson been more consciously lived (with what success—or failure —I cannot really say) than in this study of Orientalism. The idea of beginning, indeed the act of beginning, necessarily involves an act of delimitation by which something is cut out of a great mass of material, separated from the mass, and made to stand for, as well as be, a starting point, a beginning; for the student of texts one such notion of inaugural delimitation is Louis Althusser's idea of the *problematic*, a specific determinate unity of a text, or group of texts, which is something given rise to by analysis.[12] Yet in the case of Orientalism (as opposed to the case of Marx's texts, which is what Althusser studies) there is not simply the problem of finding a point of departure, or problematic, but also the question of designating which texts, authors, and periods are the ones best suited for study.

It has seemed to me foolish to attempt an encyclopedic narrative history of Orientalism, first of all because if my guiding principle was to be "the European idea of the Orient" there would be virtually no limit to the material I would have had to deal with; second, because the narrative model itself did not suit my descriptive and political interests; third, because in such books as Raymond Schwab's *La Renaissance orientale*, Johann Fück's *Die Arabischen Studien in Europa bis in den Anfang des 20. Jahrhunderts*, and more recently, Dorothee Metlitzki's *The Matter of Araby in Medieval England*[13] there already exist encyclopedic works on certain aspects of the European-Oriental encounter such as make the critic's job, in the general political and intellectual context I sketched above, a different one.

There still remained the problem of cutting down a very fat archive to manageable dimensions, and more important, outlining something in the nature of an intellectual order within that group of texts without at the same time following a mindlessly chronological order. My starting point therefore has been the British, French, and American experience of the Orient taken as a unit, what made that experience possible by way of historical and intellectual background, what the quality and character of the experience has been. For reasons I shall discuss presently I limited that already limited (but still inordinately large) set of questions to the Anglo-French-American experience of the Arabs and Islam, which for almost a thousand years together stood for the Orient. Immediately upon doing that, a large part of the Orient seemed to have been eliminated—India, Japan, China, and other sections of the Far East—not because these regions were not important (they obviously have been) but because one could discuss Europe's experience of the Near Orient, or of Islam, apart from its experience of the Far Orient. Yet at certain moments of that general European history of interest in the East, particular parts of the Orient like Egypt, Syria, and Arabia cannot be discussed without also studying Europe's involvement in the more distant parts, of which Persia and India are the most important; a notable case in point is the connection between Egypt and India so far as eighteenth- and nineteenth-century Britain was concerned. Similarly the French role in deciphering the Zend-Avesta, the pre-eminence of Paris as a center of Sanskrit studies during the first decade of the nineteenth century, the fact that Napoleon's interest in the Orient was contingent upon his sense of the British role in India: all these Far Eastern interests directly influenced French interest in the Near East, Islam, and the Arabs.

Britain and France dominated the Eastern Mediterranean from about the end of the seventeenth century on. Yet my discussion of that domination and systematic interest does not do justice to (a) the important contributions to Orientalism of Germany, Italy, Russia, Spain, and Portugal and (b) the fact that one of the important impulses toward the study of the Orient in the eighteenth century was the revolution in Biblical studies stimulated by such variously interesting pioneers as Bishop Lowth, Eichhorn, Herder, and Michaelis. In the first place, I had to focus rigorously upon the British-French and later the American material because it seemed inescapably true not only that Britain and France were the pioneer nations in the Orient and in Oriental studies, but that these vanguard positions were held by virtue of the two greatest colonial networks in pre-twentieth-century history; the American Oriental position since World War II has fit—I think, quite self-consciously —in the places excavated by the two earlier European powers. Then too, I believe that the sheer quality, consistency, and mass of British, French, and American writing on the Orient lifts it above the doubtless crucial work done in Germany, Italy, Russia, and elsewhere. But I think it is also true that the major steps in Oriental scholarship were first taken in either Britain and France, then elaborated upon by Germans. Silvestre de Sacy, for example, was not only the first modern and institutional European Orientalist, who worked on Islam, Arabic literature, the Druze religion, and Sassanid Persia; he was also the teacher of Champollion and of Franz Bopp, the founder of German comparative linguistics. A similar claim of priority and subsequent pre-eminence can be made for William Jones and Edward William Lane.

In the second place—and here the failings of my study of Orientalism are amply made up for—there has been some important recent work on the background in Biblical scholarship to the rise of what I have called modern Orientalism. The best and the most illuminatingly relevant is E. S. Shaffer's impressive *"Kubla Khan" and The Fall of Jerusalem*,[14] an indispensable study of the origins of Romanticism, and of the intellectual activity underpinning a great deal of what goes on in Coleridge, Browning, and George Eliot. To some degree Shaffer's work refines upon the outlines provided in Schwab, by articulating the material of relevance to be found in the German Biblical scholars and using that material to read, in an intelligent and always interesting way, the work of three major British writers. Yet what is missing in the book is some sense of the political as well as ideological edge given the Oriental material by the British and French writers I am principally concerned with; in addition, unlike Shaffer I attempt to elucidate subsequent developments in academic as well as literary Orientalism that bear on the connection between British and French Orientalism on the one hand and the rise of an explicitly colonial-minded imperialism on the other. Then too, I wish to show how all these earlier matters are reproduced more or less in American Orientalism after the Second World War.

Nevertheless there is a possibly misleading aspect to my study, where, aside from an occasional reference, I do not exhaustively discuss the German developments after the inaugural period dominated by Sacy. Any work that seeks to provide an understanding of academic Orientalism and pays little attention to scholars like Steinthal, Müller, Becker, Goldziher, Brockelmann, Nöldeke—to mention only a handful—needs to be reproached, and I freely reproach myself. I particularly regret not taking more account of the great scientific prestige that accrued to German scholarship by the middle of the nineteenth century, whose neglect was made into a denunciation of insular British scholars by George Eliot. I have in mind Eliot's unforgettable portrait of Mr. Casaubon in *Middle-*

march. One reason Casaubon cannot finish his Key to All Mythologies is, according to his young cousin Will Ladislaw, that he is unacquainted with German scholarship. For not only has Casaubon chosen a subject "as changing as chemistry: new discoveries are constantly making new points of view": he is undertaking a job similar to a refutation of Paracelsus because "he is not an Orientalist, you know."[15]

Eliot was not wrong in implying that by about 1830, which is when *Middlemarch* is set, German scholarship had fully attained its European pre-eminence. Yet at no time in German scholarship during the first two-thirds of the nineteenth century could a close partnership have developed between Orientalists and a protracted, sustained *national* interest in the Orient. There was nothing in Germany to correspond to the Anglo-French presence in India, the Levant, North Africa. Moreover, the German Orient was almost exclusively a scholarly, or at least a classical, Orient: it was made the subject of lyrics, fantasies, and even novels, but it was never actual, the way Egypt and Syria were actual for Chateaubriand, Lane, Lamartine, Burton, Disraeli, or Nerval. There is some significance in the fact that the two most renowned German works on the Orient, Goethe's *Westöstlicher Diwan* and Friedrich Schlegel's *Über die Sprache und Weisheit der Indier*, were based respectively on a Rhine journey and on hours spent in Paris libraries. What German Oriental scholarship did was to refine and elaborate techniques whose application was to texts, myths, ideas, and languages almost literally gathered from the Orient by imperial Britain and France.

Yet what German Orientalism had in common with Anglo-French and later American Orientalism was a kind of intellectual *authority* over the Orient within Western culture. This authority must in large part be the subject of any description of Orientalism, and it is so in this study. Even the name *Orientalism* suggests a serious, perhaps ponderous style of expertise; when I apply it to modern American social scientists (since they do not call themselves Orientalists, my use of the word is anomalous), it is to draw attention to the way Middle East experts can still draw on the vestiges of Orientalism's intellectual position in nineteenth-century Europe.

There is nothing mysterious or natural about authority. It is formed, irradiated, disseminated; it is instrumental, it is persuasive; it has status, it establishes canons of taste and value; it is virtually indistinguishable from certain ideas it dignifies as true, and from traditions, perceptions, and judgments it forms, transmits, reproduces. Above all, authority can, indeed must, be analyzed. All these attributes of authority apply to Orientalism, and much of what I do in this study is to describe both the historical authority in and the personal authorities of Orientalism.

My principal methodological devices for studying authority here are what can be called *strategic location*, which is a way of describing the author's position in a text with regard to the Oriental material he writes about, and *strategic formation*, which is a way of analyzing the relationship between texts and the way in which groups of texts, types of texts, even textual genres, acquire mass, density, and referential power among themselves and thereafter in the culture at large. I use the notion of strategy simply to identify the problem every writer on the Orient has faced: how to get hold of it, how to approach it, how not to be defeated or overwhelmed by its sublimity, its scope, its awful dimensions. Everyone who writes about the Orient must locate himself vis-à-vis the Orient; translated into his text, this location includes the kind of narrative voice he adopts, the type of structure he builds, the kinds of images, themes, motifs that circulate in his text—all of which add up to deliberate ways of addressing the reader, containing the Orient, and finally, representing it or speaking in its behalf. None of this takes place in the abstract, however. Every writer on the Orient (and this is true even of Homer) assumes some Oriental precedent, some previous knowledge of the Orient, to which he refers and on which he relies. Additionally, each work on the Orient *affiliates* itself with other works, with audiences, with institutions, with the Orient itself. The ensemble of relationships between works, audiences, and some particular aspects of the Orient therefore constitutes an analyzable formation—for example, that of philological studies, of anthologies of extracts from Oriental literature, of travel books, of Oriental fantasies—whose presence in time, in discourse, in institutions (schools, libraries, foreign services) gives it strength and authority.

It is clear, I hope, that my concern with authority does not entail analysis of what lies hidden in the Orientalist text, but analysis rather of the text's surface, its exteriority to what it describes. I do not think that this idea can be overemphasized. Orientalism is premised upon exteriority, that is, on the fact that the Orientalist, poet or scholar, makes the Orient speak, describes the Orient, renders its mysteries plain for and to the West. He is never concerned with the Orient except as the first cause of what he says. What he says and writes, by virtue of the fact that it is said or written, is meant to indicate that the Orientalist is outside the Orient, both as an existential and as a moral fact. The principal product of this exteriority is of course representation: as early as Aeschylus's play *The Persians* the Orient is transformed from a very far distant and often threatening Otherness into figures that are relatively familiar (in Aeschylus's case, grieving Asiatic women). The dramatic immediacy of representation in *The Persians* obscures the fact that the audience is watching a highly artificial enactment of what a non-Oriental has made into a symbol for the whole Orient. My analysis of the Orientalist text therefore places emphasis on the evidence, which is by no means invisible, for such representations *as representations*, not as "natural" depictions of the Orient. This evidence is found just as prominently in the so-called truthful text (histories, philological analyses, political treatises) as in the avowedly artistic (i.e., openly imaginative) text. The things to look at are style, figures of speech, setting, narrative devices, historical and social circumstances, *not* the correctness of the representation nor its fidelity to some great original. The exteriority of the representation is always governed by some version of the truism that if the Orient could represent itself, it would; since it cannot, the representation does the job, for the West, and *faute de mieux*, for the poor Orient. "Sie können sich nicht vertreten, sie müssen vertreten werden," as Marx wrote in *The Eighteenth Brumaire of Louis Bonaparte*.

Another reason for insisting upon exteriority is that I believe it needs to be made clear about cultural discourse and exchange within a culture that what is commonly circulated by it is not "truth" but representations. It hardly needs to be demonstrated again that language itself is a highly organized and encoded system, which employs many devices to express, indicate, exchange messages and information, represent, and so forth. In any instance of at least written language, there is no such thing as a delivered presence, but a *re-presence*, or a representation. The value, efficacy, strength, apparent veracity of a written statement about the Orient therefore relies very little, and cannot instrumentally depend, on the Orient as such. On the contrary, the written statement is a presence to the reader by virtue of its having excluded, displaced, made supererogatory any such *real thing* as "the Orient." Thus all of Orientalism stands forth and away from the Orient: that Orientalism makes sense at all depends more on the West than on the Orient, and this sense is directly indebted to various Western techniques of representation that make the Orient visible, clear, "there" in discourse about it. And these representations rely upon institutions, traditions, conventions, agreed-upon codes of understanding for their effects, not upon a distant and amorphous Orient.

The difference between representations of the Orient before the last third of the eighteenth century and those after it (that is, those belonging to what I call modern Orientalism) is that the range of representation expanded enormously in the later period. It is true that after William Jones and Anquetil-Duperron, and after Napoleon's Egyptian expedition, Europe came to know the Orient more scientifically, to live in it with greater authority and discipline than ever before. But what mattered to Europe was the expanded scope and the much greater refinement given its techniques for receiving the Orient. When around the turn of the eighteenth century the Orient definitively revealed the age of its languages— thus outdating Hebrew's divine pedigree—it was a group of Europeans who made the discovery, passed it on to other scholars, and preserved the discovery in the new science of Indo-European philology. A new powerful science for viewing the linguistic Orient was born, and with it, as Foucault has shown in *The Order of Things*, a whole web of related scientific interests. Similarly William Beckford, Byron, Goethe, and Hugo restructured the Orient by their art and made its colors, lights, and people visible through their images, rhythms, and motifs. At most, the "real" Orient provoked a writer to his vision; it very rarely guided it.

Orientalism responded more to the culture that produced it than to its putative object, which was also produced by the West. Thus the history of Orientalism has both an internal consistency and a highly articulated set of relationships to the dominant culture surrounding it. My analyses consequently try to show the field's shape and internal organization, its pioneers, patriarchal authorities, canonical texts, doxological ideas, exemplary figures, its followers, elaborators, and new authorities; I try also to explain how Orientalism borrowed and was frequently informed by "strong" ideas, doctrines, and trends ruling the culture. Thus there was (and is) a linguistic Orient, a Freudian Orient, a Spenglerian Orient, a Darwinian Orient, a racist Orient—and so on. Yet never has there been such a thing as a pure, or unconditional, Orient; similarly, never has there been a nonmaterial form of Orientalism, much less something so innocent as an "idea" of the Orient. In this underlying conviction and in its ensuing methodological consequences do I differ from scholars who study the history of ideas. For the emphases and the executive form, above all the material effectiveness, of statements made by Orientalist discourse are possible in ways that any hermetic history of ideas tends completely to scant. Without those emphases and that material effectiveness Orientalism would be just another idea, whereas it is and was much more than that. Therefore I set out to examine not only scholarly works but also works of literature, political tracts, journalistic texts, travel books, religious and philological studies. In other words, my hybrid perspective is broadly historical and "anthropological," given that I believe all texts to be worldly and circumstantial in (of course) ways that vary from genre to genre, and from historical period to historical period.

Yet unlike Michel Foucault, to whose work I am greatly indebted, I do believe in the determining imprint of individual writers upon the otherwise anonymous collective body of texts constituting a discursive formation like Orientalism. The unity of the large ensemble of texts I analyze is due in part to the fact that they frequently refer to each other: Orientalism is after all a system for citing works and authors. Edward William Lane's *Manners and Customs of the Modern Egyptians* was read and cited by such diverse figures as Nerval, Flaubert, and Richard Burton. He was an authority whose use was an imperative for anyone writing or thinking about the Orient, not just about Egypt: when Nerval borrows passages verbatim from *Modern Egyptians* it is to use Lane's authority to assist him in describing village scenes in Syria, not Egypt. Lane's authority and the opportunities provided for citing him discriminately as well as indiscriminately were there because Orientalism could give his text the kind of distributive currency that he acquired. There is no way, however, of understanding Lane's currency without also understanding the peculiar features of *his* text; this is equally true of Renan, Sacy, Lamartine, Schlegel, and a group of other influential writers. Foucault believes that in general the individual text or author counts for very little; empirically, in the case of Orientalism (and perhaps nowhere else) I find this not to be so. Accordingly my analyses employ close textual readings whose goal is to reveal the dialectic between individual text or writer and the complex collective formation to which his work is a contribution.

Yet even though it includes an ample selection of writers, this book is still far from a complete history or general account of Orientalism. Of this failing I am very conscious. The fabric of as thick a discourse as Orientalism has survived and functioned in Western society because of its richness: all I have done is to describe parts of that fabric at certain moments, and merely to suggest the existence of a larger whole, detailed, interesting, dotted with fascinating figures, texts, and events. I have consoled myself with believing that this book is one installment of several, and hope there are scholars and critics who might want to write others. There is still a general essay to be written on imperialism and culture; other studies would go more deeply into the connection between Orientalism and pedagogy, or into Italian, Dutch, German, and Swiss Orientalism, or into the dynamic between scholarship and imaginative writing, or into the relationship between administrative ideas and intellectual discipline. Perhaps the most important task of all would be to undertake studies in contemporary alternatives to Orientalism, to ask how one can study other cultures and peoples from a libertarian, or a nonrepressive and nonmanipulative, perspective. But then one would have to rethink the whole complex problem of knowledge and power. These are all tasks left embarrassingly incomplete in this study.

The last, perhaps self-flattering, observation on method that I want to make here is that I have written this study with several audiences in mind. For students of literature and criticism, Orientalism offers a marvelous instance of the interrelations between society, history, and textuality; moreover, the cultural role played by the Orient in the West connects Orientalism with ideology, politics, and the logic of power, matters of relevance, I think, to the literary community. For contemporary students of the Orient, from university scholars to policymakers, I have written with two ends in mind: one, to present their intellectual genealogy to them in a way that has not been done; two, to criticize—with the hope of stirring discussion—the often unquestioned assumptions on which their work for the most part depends. For the general reader, this study deals with matters that always compel attention, all of them connected not only with Western conceptions and treatments of the Other but also with the singularly important role played by Western culture in what Vico called the world of nations. Lastly, for readers in the so-called Third World, this study proposes itself as a step towards an understanding not so much of Western politics and of the non-Western world in those politics as of the *strength* of Western cultural discourse, a strength too often mistaken as merely decorative or "superstructural." My hope is to illustrate the formidable structure of cultural domination and, specifically for formerly colonized peoples, the dangers and temptations of employing this structure upon themselves or upon others.

The three long chapters and twelve shorter units into which this book is divided are intended to facilitate exposition as much as possible. Chapter One, "The Scope of Orientalism," draws a large circle around all the dimensions of the subject, both in terms of historical time and experiences and in terms of philosophical and political themes. Chapter Two, "Orientalist Structures and Re-structures," attempts to trace the development of modern Orientalism by a broadly chronological description, and also by the description of a set of devices common to the work of important poets, artists, and scholars. Chapter Three, "Orientalism Now," begins where its predecessor left off, at around 1870. This is the period of great colonial expansion into the Orient, and it culminates in World War II. The very last section of Chapter Three characterizes the shift from British and French to American hegemony; I attempt there finally to sketch the present intellectual and social realities of Orientalism in the United States.

3. *The personal dimension.* In the *Prison Notebooks* Gramsci says: "The starting-point of critical elaboration is the consciousness of what one really is, and is 'knowing thyself' as a product of the historical process to date, which has deposited in you an infinity of traces, without leaving an inventory." The only available English translation inexplicably leaves Gramsci's comment at that, whereas in fact Gramsci's Italian text concludes by adding, "therefore it is imperative at the outset to compile such an inventory."[16]

Much of the personal investment in this study derives from my awareness of being an "Oriental" as a child growing up in two British colonies. All of my education, in those colonies (Palestine and Egypt) and in the United States, has been Western, and yet that deep early awareness has persisted. In many ways my study of Orientalism has been an attempt to inventory the traces upon me, the Oriental subject, of the culture whose domination has been so powerful a factor in the life of all Orientals. This is why for me the

Islamic Orient has had to be the center of attention. Whether what I have achieved is the inventory prescribed by Gramsci is not for me to judge, although I have felt it important to be conscious of trying to produce one. Along the way, as severely and as rationally as I have been able, I have tried to maintain a critical consciousness, as well as employing those instruments of historical, humanistic, and cultural research of which my education has made me the fortunate beneficiary. In none of that, however, have I ever lost hold of the cultural reality of, the personal involvement in having been constituted as, "an Oriental."

The historical circumstances making such a study possible are fairly complex, and I can only list them schematically here. Anyone resident in the West since the 1950s, particularly in the United States, will have lived through an era of extraordinary turbulence in the relations of East and West. No one will have failed to note how "East" has always signified danger and threat during this period, even as it has meant the traditional Orient as well as Russia. In the universities a growing establishment of area-studies programs and institutes has made the scholarly study of the Orient a branch of national policy. Public affairs in this country include a healthy interest in the Orient, as much for its strategic and economic importance as for its traditional exoticism. If the world has become immediately accessible to a Western citizen living in the electronic age, the Orient too has drawn nearer to him, and is now less a myth perhaps than a place crisscrossed by Western, especially American, interests.

One aspect of the electronic, postmodern world is that there has been a reinforcement of the stereotypes by which the Orient is viewed. Television, the films, and all the media's resources have forced information into more and more standardized molds. So far as the Orient is concerned, standardization and cultural stereotyping have intensified the hold of the nineteenth-century academic and imaginative demonology of "the mysterious Orient." This is nowhere more true than in the ways by which the Near East is grasped. Three things have contributed to making even the simplest perception of the Arabs and Islam into a highly politicized, almost raucous matter: one, the history of popular anti-Arab and anti-Islamic prejudice in the West, which is immediately reflected in the history of Orientalism; two, the struggle between the Arabs and Israeli Zionism, and its effects upon American Jews as well as upon both the liberal culture and the population at large; three, the almost total absence of any cultural position making it possible either to identify with or dispassionately to discuss the Arabs or Islam. Furthermore, it hardly needs saying that because the Middle East is now so identified with Great Power politics, oil economics, and the simple-minded dichotomy of freedom-loving, democratic Israel and evil, totalitarian, and terroristic Arabs, the chances of anything like a clear view of what one talks about in talking about the Near East are depressingly small.

My own experiences of these matters are in part what made me write this book. The life of an Arab Palestinian in the West, particularly in America, is disheartening. There exists here an almost unanimous consensus that politically he does not exist, and when it is allowed that he does, it is either as a nuisance or as an Oriental. The web of racism, cultural stereotypes, political imperialism, dehumanizing ideology holding in the Arab or the Muslim is very strong indeed, and it is this web which every Palestinian has come to feel as his uniquely punishing destiny. It has made matters worse for him to remark that no person academically involved with the Near East—no Orientalist, that is—has ever in the United States culturally and politically identified himself wholeheartedly with the Arabs; certainly there have been identifications on some level, but they have never taken an "acceptable" form as has liberal American identification with Zionism, and all too frequently they have been radically flawed by their association either with discredited political and economic interests (oil-company and State Department Arabists, for example) or with religion.

The nexus of knowledge and power creating "the Oriental" and in a sense obliterating him as a human being is therefore not for me an exclusively academic matter. Yet it is an *intellectual* matter of some very obvious importance. I have been able to put to use my humanistic and political concerns for the analysis and description of a very worldly matter, the rise, development, and consolidation of Orientalism. Too often literature and culture are presumed to be politically, even historically innocent; it has regularly seemed otherwise to me, and certainly my study of Orientalism has convinced me (and I hope will convince my literary colleagues) that society and literary culture can only be understood and studied together. In addition, and by an almost inescapable logic, I have found myself writing the history of a strange, secret sharer of Western anti-Semitism. That anti-Semitism and, as I have discussed it in its Islamic branch, Orientalism resemble each other very closely is a historical, cultural, and political truth that needs only to be mentioned to an Arab Palestinian for its irony to be perfectly understood. But what I should like also to have contributed here is a better understanding of the way cultural domination has operated. If this stimulates a new kind of dealing with the Orient, indeed if it eliminates the "Orient" and "Occident" altogether, then we shall have advanced a little in the process of what Raymond Williams has called the "unlearning" of "the inherent dominative mode."[17]

1

The Scope of Orientalism

. . . le génie inquiet et ambitieux de Européens . . . impatient d'employer les nouveaux instruments de leur puissance . . .

—Jean-Baptiste-Joseph Fourier, *Préface historique* (1809), *Description de l'Égypte*

I
Knowing the Oriental

On June 13, 1910, Arthur James Balfour lectured the House of Commons on "the problems with which we have to deal in Egypt." These, he said, "belong to a wholly different category" than those "affecting the Isle of Wight or the West Riding of Yorkshire." He spoke with the authority of a long-time member of Parliament, former private secretary to Lord Salisbury, former chief secretary for Ireland, former secretary for Scotland, former prime minister, veteran of numerous overseas crises, achievements, and changes. During his involvement in imperial affairs Balfour served a monarch who in 1876 had been declared Empress of India; he had been especially well placed in positions of uncommon influence to follow the Afghan and Zulu wars, the British occupation of Egypt in 1882, the death of General Gordon in the Sudan, the Fashoda Incident, the battle of Omdurman, the Boer War, the Russo-Japanese War. In addition his remarkable social eminence, the breadth of his learning and wit—he could write on such varied subjects as Bergson, Handel, theism, and golf—his education at Eton and Trinity College, Cambridge, and his apparent command over imperial affairs all gave considerable authority to what he told the Commons in June 1910. But there was still more to Balfour's speech, or at least to his need for giving it so didactically and moralistically. Some members were questioning the necessity for "England in Egypt," the subject of Alfred Milner's enthusiastic book of 1892, but here designating a once-profitable occupation that had become a source of trouble now that Egyptian nationalism was on the rise and the continuing British presence in Egypt no longer so easy to defend. Balfour, then, to inform and explain.

Recalling the challenge of J. M. Robertson, the member of Tyneside, Balfour himself put Robertson's question again: "What right have you to take up these airs of superiority with regard to people whom you choose to call Oriental?" The choice of "Oriental" was canonical; it had been employed by Chaucer and Mandeville, by Shakespeare, Dryden, Pope, and Byron. It designated Asia or the East, geographically, morally, culturally. One could speak in Europe of an Oriental personality, an Oriental atmosphere, an Oriental tale, Oriental despotism, or an Oriental mode of production, and be understood. Marx had used the word, and now Balfour was using it; his choice was understandable and called for no comment whatever.

> I take up no attitude of superiority. But I ask [Robertson and anyone else] . . . who has even the most superficial knowledge of history, if they will look in the face the facts with which a British statesman has to deal when he is put in a position of supremacy over great races like the inhabitants of Egypt and countries in the East. We know the civilization of Egypt better than we know the civilization of any other country. We know it further back; we know it more intimately; we know more about it. It goes far beyond the petty span of the history of our race, which is lost in the prehistoric period at a time when the Egyptian civilisation had already passed its prime. Look at all the Oriental countries. Do not talk about superiority or inferiority.

Two great themes dominate his remarks here and in what will follow: knowledge and power, the Baconian themes. As Balfour justifies the necessity for British occupation of Egypt, supremacy in his mind is associated with "our" knowledge of Egypt and not principally with military or economic power. Knowledge to Balfour means surveying a civilization from its origins to its prime to its decline—and of course, it means *being able to do that*. Knowledge means rising above immediacy, beyond self, into the foreign and distant. The object of such knowledge is inherently vulnerable to scrutiny; this object is a "fact" which, if it develops, changes, or otherwise transforms itself in the way that civilizations frequently do, nevertheless is fundamentally, even ontologically stable. To have such knowledge of such a thing is to dominate it, to have authority over it. And authority here means for "us" to deny autonomy to "it"—the Oriental country—since we know it and it exists, in a sense, *as* we know it. British knowledge of Egypt *is* Egypt for Balfour, and the burdens of knowledge make such questions as inferiority and superiority seem petty ones. Balfour nowhere denies British superiority and Egyptian inferiority; he takes them for granted as he describes the consequences of knowledge.

> First of all, look at the facts of the case. Western nations as soon as they emerge into history show the beginnings of those capacities for self-government . . . having merits of their own. . . . You may look through the whole history of the Orientals in what is called, broadly speaking, the East, and you never find traces of self-

government. All their great centuries—and they have been very great—have been passed under despotisms, under absolute government. All their great contributions to civilisation—and they have been great—have been made under that form of government. Conqueror has succeeded conqueror; one domination has followed another; but never in all the revolutions of fate and fortune have you seen one of those nations of its own motion establish what we, from a Western point of view, call self-government. That is the fact. It is not a question of superiority and inferiority. I suppose a true Eastern sage would say that the working government which we have taken upon ourselves in Egypt and elsewhere is not a work worthy of a philosopher—that it is the dirty work, the inferior work, of carrying on the necessary labour.

Since these facts are facts, Balfour must then go on to the next part of his argument.

Is it a good thing for these great nations—I admit their greatness —that this absolute government should be exercised by us? I think it is a good thing. I think that experience shows that they have got under it far better government than in the whole history of the world they ever had before, and which not only is a benefit to them, but is undoubtedly a benefit to the whole of the civilised West. . . . We are in Egypt not merely for the sake of the Egyptians, though we are there for their sake; we are there also for the sake of Europe at large.

Balfour produces no evidence that Egyptians and "the races with whom we deal" appreciate or even understand the good that is being done them by colonial occupation. It does not occur to Balfour, however, to let the Egyptian speak for himself, since presumably any Egyptian who would speak out is more likely to be "the agitator [who] wishes to raise difficulties" than the good native who overlooks the "difficulties" of foreign domination. And so, having settled the ethical problems, Balfour turns at last to the practical ones. "If it is our business to govern, with or without gratitude, with or without the real and genuine memory of all the loss of which we have relieved the population [Balfour by no means implies, as part of that loss, the loss or at least the indefinite post-ponement of Egyptian independence] and no vivid imagination of all the benefits which we have given to them; if that is our duty, how is it to be performed?" England exports "our very best to these countries." These selfless administrators do their work "amidst tens of thousands of persons belonging to a different creed, a different race, a different discipline, different conditions of life." What makes their work of governing possible is their sense of being supported at home by a government that endorses what they do. Yet

> directly the native populations have that instinctive feeling that those with whom they have got to deal have not behind them the might, the authority, the sympathy, the full and ungrudging support of the country which sent them there, those populations lose all that sense of order which is the very basis of their civilisation, just as our officers lose all that sense of power and authority, which is the very basis of everything they can do for the benefit of those among whom they have been sent.

Balfour's logic here is interesting, not least for being completely consistent with the premises of his entire speech. England knows Egypt; Egypt is what England knows; England knows that Egypt cannot have self-government; England confirms that by occupying Egypt; for the Egyptians, Egypt is what England has occupied and now governs; foreign occupation therefore becomes "the very basis" of contemporary Egyptian civilization; Egypt requires, indeed insists upon, British occupation. But if the special intimacy between governor and governed in Egypt is disturbed by Parliament's doubts at home, then "the authority of what . . . is the dominant race— and as I think ought to remain the dominant race—has been undermined." Not only does English prestige suffer; "it is vain for a handful of British officials—endow them how you like, give them all the qualities of character and genius you can imagine—it is impossible for them to carry out the great task which in Egypt, not we only, but the civilised world have imposed upon them."[1]

As a rhetorical performance Balfour's speech is significant for the way in which he plays the part of, and represents, a variety of characters. There are of course "the English," for whom the pronoun "we" is used with the full weight of a distinguished, powerful man who feels himself to be representative of all that is best in his nation's history. Balfour can also speak for the civilized world, the West, and the relatively small corps of colonial officials in Egypt. If he does not speak directly for the Orientals, it is because they after all speak another language; yet he knows how they feel since he knows their history, their reliance upon such as he, and their expectations. Still, he does speak for them in the sense that what they might have to say, were they to be asked and might they be able to answer, would somewhat uselessly confirm what is already evident: that they are a subject race, dominated by a race that knows them and what is good for them better than they could possibly know themselves. Their great moments were in the past; they are useful in the modern world only because the powerful and up-to-date empires have effectively brought them out of the wretchedness of their decline and turned them into rehabilitated residents of productive colonies.

Egypt in particular was an excellent case in point, and Balfour was perfectly aware of how much right he had to speak as a member of his country's parliament on behalf of England, the West, Western civilization, about modern Egypt. For Egypt was not just another colony: it was the vindication of Western imperialism; it was, until its annexation by England, an almost academic example of Oriental backwardness; it was to become the triumph of English knowledge and power. Between 1882, the year in which England occupied Egypt and put an end to the nationalist rebellion of Colonel Arabi, and 1907, England's representative in Egypt, Egypt's master, was Evelyn Baring (also known as "Over-baring"), Lord Cromer. On July 30, 1907, it was Balfour in the Commons who had supported the project to give Cromer a retirement prize of fifty thousand pounds as a reward for what he had done in Egypt. Cromer *made* Egypt, said Balfour:

> Everything he has touched he has succeeded in. . . . Lord Cromer's services during the past quarter of a century have raised Egypt from the lowest pitch of social and economic degradation until it now stands among Oriental nations, I believe, absolutely alone in its prosperity, financial and moral.[2]

How Egypt's moral prosperity was measured, Balfour did not venture to say. British exports to Egypt equaled those to the whole of Africa; that certainly indicated a sort of financial prosperity, for Egypt and England (somewhat unevenly) together. But what really mattered was the unbroken, all-embracing Western tutelage of an Oriental country, from the scholars, missionaries, businessmen, soldiers, and teachers who prepared and then implemented the occupation to the high functionaries like Cromer and Balfour who saw themselves as providing for, directing, and sometimes even forcing Egypt's rise from Oriental neglect to its present lonely eminence.

If British success in Egypt was as exceptional as Balfour said, it was by no means an inexplicable or irrational success. Egyptian affairs had been controlled according to a general theory expressed both by Balfour in his notions about Oriental civilization and by Cromer in his management of everyday business in Egypt. The most important thing about the theory during the first decade of the twentieth century was that it worked, and worked staggeringly well. The argument, when reduced to its simplest form, was clear, it was precise, it was easy to grasp. There are Westerners, and there are Orientals. The former dominate; the latter must be dominated, which usually means having their land occupied, their internal affairs rigidly controlled, their blood and treasure put at the disposal of one or another Western power. That Balfour and Cromer, as we shall soon see, could strip humanity down to such ruthless cultural and racial essences was not at all an indication of their particular viciousness. Rather it was an indication of how streamlined a general doctrine had become by the time they put it to use— how streamlined and effective.

Unlike Balfour, whose theses on Orientals pretended to objective universality, Cromer spoke about Orientals specifically as what he had ruled or had to deal with, first in India, then for the twenty-five years in Egypt during which he emerged as the paramount consul-general in England's empire. Balfour's "Orientals" are Cromer's "subject races," which he made the topic of a long essay published in the *Edinburgh Review* in January 1908. Once again, knowledge of subject races or Orientals is what makes their management easy and profitable; knowledge gives power, more power requires more knowledge, and so on in an increasingly profitable dialectic of information and control. Cromer's notion is that England's empire will not dissolve if such things as militarism and commercial egotism at home and "free institutions" in the colony (as opposed to British government "according to the Code of Christian morality") are kept in check. For if, according to Cromer, logic is something "the existence of which the Oriental is disposed altogether to ignore," the proper method of ruling is not to impose ultrascientific measures upon him or to force him bodily to accept logic. It is rather to understand his limitations and "endeavor to find, in the contentment of the subject race, a more worthy and, it may be hoped, a stronger bond of union between the rulers and the ruled." Lurking everywhere behind the pacification of the subject race is imperial might, more effective for its refined understanding and infrequent use than for its soldiers, brutal tax gatherers, and incontinent force. In a word, the Empire must be wise; it must temper its cupidity with selflessness, and its impatience with flexible discipline.

To be more explicit, what is meant when it is said that the commercial spirit should be under some control is this—that in dealing with Indians or Egyptians, or Shilluks, or Zulus, the first question is to consider what these people, who are all, nationally speaking, more or less *in statu pupillari*, themselves think is best in their own interests, although this is a point which deserves serious consideration. But it is essential that each special issue should be decided mainly with reference to what, by the light of Western knowledge and experience tempered by local considerations, we conscientiously think is best for the subject race, without reference to any real or supposed advantage which may accrue to England as a nation, or—as is more frequently the case—to the special interests represented by some one or more influential classes of Englishmen. If the British nation as a whole persistently bears this principle in mind, and insists sternly on its application, though we can never create a patriotism akin to that based on affinity of race or community of language, we may perhaps foster some sort of cosmopolitan allegiance grounded on the respect always accorded to superior talents and unselfish conduct, and on the gratitude derived both from favours conferred and from those to come. There may then at all events be some hope that the Egyptian will hesitate before he throws in his lot with any future Arabi. . . . Even the Central African savage may eventually learn to chant a hymn in honour of Astraea Redux, as represented by the British official who denies him gin but gives him justice. More than this, commerce will gain.[3]

How much "serious consideration" the ruler ought to give proposals from the subject race was illustrated in Cromer's total opposition to Egyptian nationalism. Free native institutions, the absence of foreign occupation, a self-sustaining national sovereignty: these unsurprising demands were consistently rejected by Cromer, who asserted unambiguously that "the real future of Egypt . . . lies not in the direction of a narrow nationalism, which will only embrace native Egyptians . . . but rather in that of an enlarged cosmopolitanism."[4] Subject races did not have it in them to know what was good for them. Most of them were Orientals, of whose characteristics Cromer was very knowledgeable since he had had experience with them both in India and Egypt. One of the convenient things about Orientals for Cromer was that managing them, although circumstances might differ slightly here and there, was almost everywhere nearly the same.[5] This was, of course, because Orientals were almost everywhere nearly the same.

Now at last we approach the long-developing core of essential knowledge, knowledge both academic and practical, which Cromer and Balfour inherited from a century of modern Western Orientalism: knowledge about and knowledge of Orientals, their race, character, culture, history, traditions, society, and possibilities. This knowledge was effective: Cromer believed he had put it to use in governing Egypt. Moreover, it was tested and unchanging knowledge, since "Orientals" for all practical purposes were a Platonic essence, which any Orientalist (or ruler of Orientals) might examine, understand, and expose. Thus in the thirty-fourth chapter of his two-volume work *Modern Egypt*, the magisterial record of his experience and achievement, Cromer puts down a sort of personal canon of Orientalist wisdom:

> Sir Alfred Lyall once said to me: "Accuracy is abhorrent to the Oriental mind. Every Anglo-Indian should always remember that maxim." Want of accuracy, which easily degenerates into untruthfulness, is in fact the main characteristic of the Oriental mind.
>
> The European is a close reasoner; his statements of fact are devoid of any ambiguity; he is a natural logician, albeit he may not have studied logic; he is by nature sceptical and requires proof before he can accept the truth of any proposition; his trained intelligence works like a piece of mechanism. The mind of the Oriental, on the other hand, like his picturesque streets, is eminently wanting in symmetry. His reasoning is of the most slipshod description. Although the ancient Arabs acquired in a somewhat higher degree the science of dialectics, their descendants are singularly deficient in the logical faculty. They are often incapable of drawing the most obvious conclusions from any simple premises of which they may admit the truth. Endeavor to elicit a plain statement of facts from any ordinary Egyptian. His explanation will generally be lengthy, and wanting in lucidity. He will probably contradict himself half-a-dozen times before he has finished his story. He will often break down under the mildest process of cross-examination.

Orientals or Arabs are thereafter shown to be gullible, "devoid of energy and initiative," much given to "fulsome flattery," intrigue, cunning, and unkindness to animals; Orientals cannot walk on either a road or a pavement (their disordered minds fail to understand what the clever European grasps immediately, that roads and pavements are made for walking); Orientals are inveterate liars, they are "lethargic and suspicious," and in everything oppose the clarity, directness, and nobility of the Anglo-Saxon race.[6]

Cromer makes no effort to conceal that Orientals for him were always and only the human material he governed in British colonies. "As I am only a diplomatist and an administrator, whose proper study is also man, but from the point of view of governing him," Cromer says, ". . . I content myself with noting the fact that somehow or other the Oriental generally acts, speaks, and thinks in a manner exactly opposite to the European."[7] Cromer's descriptions are of course based partly on direct observation, yet here and there he refers to orthodox Orientalist authorities (in particular Ernest Renan and Constantin de Volney) to support his views. To these authorities he also defers when it comes to explaining why Orientals are the way they are. He has no doubt that *any* knowledge of the Oriental will confirm his views, which, to judge from his description of the Egyptian breaking under cross-examination, find the Oriental to be guilty. The crime was that the Oriental was an Oriental, and it is an accurate sign of how commonly acceptable such a tautology was that it could be written without even an appeal to European logic or symmetry of mind. Thus any deviation from what were considered the norms of Oriental behavior was believed to be unnatural; Cromer's last annual report from Egypt consequently proclaimed Egyptian nationalism to be an "entirely novel idea" and "a plant of exotic rather than of indigenous growth."[8]

We would be wrong, I think, to underestimate the reservoir of accredited knowledge, the codes of Orientalist orthodoxy, to which Cromer and Balfour refer everywhere in their writing and in their public policy. To say simply that Orientalism was a rationalization of colonial rule is to ignore the extent to which colonial rule was justified in advance by Orientalism, rather than after the fact. Men have always divided the world up into regions having either real or imagined distinction from each other. The absolute demarcation between East and West, which Balfour and Cromer accept with such complacency, had been years, even centuries, in the making. There were of course innumerable voyages of discovery; there were contacts through trade and war. But more than this, since the middle of the eighteenth century there had been two principal elements in the relation between East and West. One was a growing systematic knowledge in Europe about the Orient, knowledge reinforced by the colonial encounter as well as by the widespread interest in the alien and unusual, exploited by the developing sciences of ethnology, comparative anatomy, philology, and history; furthermore, to this systematic knowledge was added a sizable body of literature produced by novelists, poets, translators, and gifted travelers. The other feature of Oriental-European relations was that Europe was always in a position of strength, not to say domination. There is no way of putting this euphemistically. True, the relationship of strong to weak could be disguised or mitigated, as when Balfour acknowledged the "greatness" of Oriental civilizations. But the essential relationship, on political, cultural, and even religious grounds, was seen—in the West, which is what concerns us here— to be one between a strong and a weak partner.

Many terms were used to express the relation: Balfour and Cromer, typically, used several. The Oriental is irrational, depraved (fallen), childlike, "different"; thus the European is rational, virtuous, mature, "normal." But the way of enlivening the relationship was everywhere to stress the fact that the Oriental lived in a different but thoroughly organized world of his own, a world with its own national, cultural, and epistemological boundaries and principles of internal coherence. Yet what gave the Oriental's world its intelligibility and identity was not the result of his own efforts but rather the whole complex series of knowledgeable manipulations by which the Orient was identified by the West. Thus the two features of cultural relationship I have been discussing come together. Knowledge of the Orient, because generated out of strength, in a sense *creates* the Orient, the Oriental, and his world. In Cromer's and Balfour's language the Oriental is depicted as something one judges (as in a court of law), something one studies and depicts (as in a curriculum), something one disciplines (as in a school or prison), something one illustrates (as in a zoological manual). The point is that in each of these cases the Oriental is *contained* and *represented* by dominating frameworks. Where do these come from?

Cultural strength is not something we can discuss very easily— and one of the purposes of the present work is to illustrate, analyze, and reflect upon Orientalism as an exercise of cultural strength. In other words, it is better not to risk generalizations about so vague and yet so important a notion as cultural strength until a good deal of material has been analyzed first. But at the outset one can say that so far as the West was concerned during the nineteenth and twentieth centuries, an assumption had been made that the

Orient and everything in it was, if not patently inferior to, then in need of corrective study by the West. The Orient was viewed as if framed by the classroom, the criminal court, the prison, the illustrated manual. Orientalism, then, is knowledge of the Orient that places things Oriental in class, court, prison, or manual for scrutiny, study, judgment, discipline, or governing.

During the early years of the twentieth century, men like Balfour and Cromer could say what they said, in the way they did, because a still earlier tradition of Orientalism than the nineteenth-century one provided them with a vocabulary, imagery, rhetoric, and figures with which to say it. Yet Orientalism reinforced, and was reinforced by, the certain knowledge that Europe or the West literally commanded the vastly greater part of the earth's surface. The period of immense advance in the institutions and content of Orientalism coincides exactly with the period of unparalleled European expansion; from 1815 to 1914 European direct colonial dominion expanded from about 35 percent of the earth's surface to about 85 percent of it.[9] Every continent was affected, none more so than Africa and Asia. The two greatest empires were the British and the French; allies and partners in some things, in others they were hostile rivals. In the Orient, from the eastern shores of the Mediterranean to Indochina and Malaya, their colonial possessions and imperial spheres of influence were adjacent, frequently overlapped, often were fought over. But it was in the Near Orient, the lands of the Arab Near East, where Islam was supposed to define cultural and racial characteristics, that the British and the French encountered each other and "the Orient" with the greatest intensity, familiarity, and complexity. For much of the nineteenth century, as Lord Salisbury put it in 1881, their common view of the Orient was intricately problematic: "When you have got a . . . faithful ally who is bent on meddling in a country in which you are deeply interested —you have three courses open to you. You may renounce—or monopolize—or share. Renouncing would have been to place the French across our road to India. Monopolizing would have been very near the risk of war. So we resolved to share."[10]

And share they did, in ways that we shall investigate presently. What they shared, however, was not only land or profit or rule; it was the kind of intellectual power I have been calling Orientalism. In a sense Orientalism was a library or archive of information commonly and, in some of its aspects, unanimously held. What bound the archive together was a family of ideas[11] and a unifying set of values proven in various ways to be effective. These ideas explained the behavior of Orientals; they supplied Orientals with a mentality, a genealogy, an atmosphere; most important, they allowed Europeans to deal with and even to see Orientals as a phenomenon possessing regular characteristics. But like any set of durable ideas, Orientalist notions influenced the people who were called Orientals as well as those called Occidental, European, or Western; in short, Orientalism is better grasped as a set of constraints upon and limitations of thought than it is simply as a positive doctrine. If the essence of Orientalism is the ineradicable distinction between Western superiority and Oriental inferiority, then we must be prepared to note how in its development and subsequent history Orientalism deepened and even hardened the distinction. When it became common practice during the nineteenth century for Britain to retire its administrators from India and elsewhere once they had reached the age of fifty-five, then a further refinement in Orientalism had been achieved; no Oriental was ever allowed to see a Westerner as he aged and degenerated, just as no Westerner needed ever to see himself, mirrored in the eyes of the subject race, as anything but a vigorous, rational, ever-alert young Raj.[12]

Orientalist ideas took a number of different forms during the nineteenth and twentieth centuries. First of all, in Europe there was a vast literature about the Orient inherited from the European past. What is distinctive about the late eighteenth and early nineteenth centuries, which is where this study assumes modern Orientalism to have begun, is that an Oriental renaissance took place, as Edgar Quinet phrased it.[13] Suddenly it seemed to a wide variety of thinkers, politicians, and artists that a new awareness of the Orient, which extended from China to the Mediterranean, had arisen. This awareness was partly the result of newly discovered and translated Oriental texts in languages like Sanskrit, Zend, and Arabic; it was also the result of a newly perceived relationship between the Orient and the West. For my purposes here, the keynote of the relationship was set for the Near East and Europe by the Napoleonic invasion of Egypt in 1798, an invasion which was in many ways the very model of a truly scientific appropriation of one culture by another, apparently stronger one. For with Napoleon's occupation of Egypt processes were set in motion between East and West that still dominate our contemporary cultural and political perspectives. And the Napoleonic expedition, with its great collective monument of erudition, the *Description de l'Égypte*, provided a scene or setting for Orientalism, since Egypt and subsequently the other Islamic lands were viewed as the live province, the laboratory, the theater of effective Western knowledge about the Orient. I shall return to the Napoleonic adventure a little later.

With such experiences as Napoleon's the Orient as a body of knowledge in the West was modernized, and this is a second form in which nineteenth- and twentieth-century Orientalism existed. From the outset of the period I shall be examining there was everywhere amongst Orientalists the ambition to formulate their discoveries, experiences, and insights suitably in modern terms, to put ideas about the Orient in very close touch with modern realities. Renan's linguistic investigations of Semitic in 1848, for example, were couched in a style that drew heavily for its authority upon contemporary comparative grammar, comparative anatomy, and racial theory; these lent his Orientalism prestige and—the other side of the coin—made Orientalism vulnerable, as it has been ever since, to modish as well as seriously influential currents of thought in the West. Orientalism has been subjected to imperialism, positivism, utopianism, historicism, Darwinism, racism, Freudianism, Marxism, Spenglerism. But Orientalism, like many of the natural and social sciences, has had "paradigms" of research, its own learned societies, its own Establishment. During the nineteenth century the field increased enormously in prestige, as did also the reputation and influence of such institutions as the Société asiatique, the Royal Asiatic Society, the Deutsche Morgenländische Gesellschaft, and the American Oriental Society. With the growth of these societies went also an increase, all across Europe, in the number of professorships in Oriental studies; consequently there was an expansion in the available means for disseminating Orientalism. Orientalist periodicals, beginning with the *Fundgraben des Orients* (1809), multiplied the quantity of knowledge as well as the number of specialties.

Yet little of this activity and very few of these institutions existed and flourished freely, for in a third form in which it existed, Orientalism imposed limits upon thought about the Orient. Even the most imaginative writers of an age, men like Flaubert, Nerval, or Scott, were constrained in what they could either experience of or say about the Orient. For Orientalism was ultimately a political vision of reality whose structure promoted the difference between the familiar (Europe, the West, "us") and the strange (the Orient, the East, "them"). This vision in a sense created and then served the two worlds thus conceived. Orientals lived in their world, "we" lived in ours. The vision and material reality propped each other up, kept each other going. A certain freedom of intercourse was always the Westerner's privilege; because his was the stronger culture, he could penetrate, he could wrestle with, he could give shape and meaning to the great Asiatic mystery, as Disraeli once called it. Yet what has, I think, been previously overlooked is the constricted vocabulary of such a privilege, and the comparative limitations of such a vision. My argument takes it that the Orientalist reality is both antihuman and persistent. Its scope, as much as its institutions and all-pervasive influence, lasts up to the present.

But how did and does Orientalism work? How can one describe it all together as a historical phenomenon, a way of thought, a contemporary problem, and a material reality? Consider Cromer again, an accomplished technician of empire but also a beneficiary of Orientalism. He can furnish us with a rudimentary answer. In "The Government of Subject Races" he wrestles with the problem of how Britain, a nation of individuals, is to administer a wide-flung empire according to a number of central principles. He contrasts the "local agent," who has both a specialist's knowledge of the native and an Anglo-Saxon individuality, with the central authority at home in London. The former may "treat subjects of local interest in a manner calculated to damage, or even to jeopardize, Imperial interests. The central authority is in a position to obviate any danger arising from this cause." Why? Because this authority can "ensure the harmonious working of the different parts of the machine" and "should endeavour, so far as is possible, to realise the circumstances attendant on the government of the dependency."[14] The language is vague and unattractive, but the point is not hard to grasp. Cromer envisions a seat of power in the West, and radiating out from it towards the East a great embracing machine, sustaining the central authority yet commanded by it. What the machine's branches feed into it in the East—human material, material wealth, knowledge, what have you—is processed by the machine, then converted into more power. The specialist does the immediate translation of mere Oriental matter into useful substance: the Oriental becomes, for example, a subject race, an example of an "Oriental" mentality, all for the enhancement of the "authority" at home. "Local interests" are Orientalist special interests, the "central authority" is the general interest of the imperial society as a whole. What Cromer quite accurately sees is the management of knowledge by society, the fact that knowledge—no matter how special—is regulated first by the local concerns of a specialist, later by the general concerns of a social system of authority. The interplay between local and central interests is intricate, but by no means indiscriminate.

In Cromer's own case as an imperial administrator the "proper study is also man," he says. When Pope proclaimed the proper study of mankind to be man, he meant all men, including "the poor Indian"; whereas Cromer's "also" reminds us that certain men, such as Orientals, can be singled out as the subject for *proper* study. The proper study—in this sense—of Orientals is Orientalism, properly separate from other forms of knowledge, but finally useful (because finite) for the material and social reality enclosing all knowledge at any time, supporting knowledge, providing it with uses. An order of sovereignty is set up from East to West, a mock chain of being whose clearest form was given once by Kipling:

> Mule, horse, elephant, or bullock, he obeys his driver, and the driver his sergeant, and the sergeant his lieutenant, and the lieutenant his captain, and the captain his major, and the major his colonel, and the colonel his brigadier commanding three regiments, and the brigadier his general, who obeys the Viceroy, who is the servant of the Empress.[15]

As deeply forged as is this monstrous chain of command, as strongly managed as is Cromer's "harmonious working," Orientalism can also express the strength of the West and the Orient's weakness—as seen by the West. Such strength and such weakness are as intrinsic to Orientalism as they are to any view that divides the world into large general divisions, entities that coexist in a state of tension produced by what is believed to be radical difference.

For that is the main intellectual issue raised by Orientalism. Can one divide human reality, as indeed human reality seems to be genuinely divided, into clearly different cultures, histories, traditions, societies, even races, and survive the consequences humanly? By surviving the consequences humanly, I mean to ask whether there is any way of avoiding the hostility expressed by the division, say, of men into "us" (Westerners) and "they" (Orientals). For such divisions are generalities whose use historically and actually has been to press the importance of the distinction between some men and some other men, usually towards not especially admirable ends. When one uses categories like Oriental and Western as both the starting and the end points of analysis, research, public policy (as the categories were used by Balfour and Cromer), the result is usually to polarize the distinction—the Oriental becomes more Oriental, the Westerner more Western—and limit the human encounter between different cultures, traditions, and societies. In short, from its earliest modern history to the present, Orientalism as a form of thought for dealing with the foreign has typically shown the altogether regrettable tendency of any knowledge based on such hard-and-fast distinctions as "East" and "West": to channel thought into a West or an East compartment. Because this tendency is right at the center of Orientalist theory, practice, and values found in the West, the sense of Western power over the Orient is taken for granted as having the status of scientific truth.

A contemporary illustration or two should clarify this observation perfectly. It is natural for men in power to survey from time to time the world with which they must deal. Balfour did it frequently. Our contemporary Henry Kissinger does it also, rarely with more express frankness than in his essay "Domestic Structure and Foreign Policy." The drama he depicts is a real one, in which the United States must manage its behavior in the world under the pressures of domestic forces on the one hand and of foreign realities on the other. Kissinger's discourse must for that reason alone establish a polarity between the United States and the world; in addition, of course, he speaks consciously as an authoritative voice for the major Western power, whose recent history and present reality have placed it before a world that does not easily accept its power and dominance. Kissinger feels that the United States can deal less problematically with the industrial, developed West than it can with the developing world. Again, the contemporary actuality of relations between the United States and the so-called Third World (which includes China, Indochina, the Near East, Africa, and Latin America) is manifestly a thorny set of problems, which even Kissinger cannot hide.

Kissinger's method in the essay proceeds according to what linguists call binary opposition: that is, he shows that there are two styles in foreign policy (the prophetic and the political), two types of technique, two periods, and so forth. When at the end of the historical part of his argument he is brought face to face with the contemporary world, he divides it accordingly into two halves, the developed and the developing countries. The first half, which is the West, "is deeply committed to the notion that the real world is external to the observer, that knowledge consists of recording and classifying data—the more accurately the better." Kissinger's proof for this is the Newtonian revolution, which has not taken place in the developing world: "Cultures which escaped the early impact of Newtonian thinking have retained the essentially pre-Newtonian view that the real world is almost completely *internal* to the observer." Consequently, he adds, "empirical reality has a much different significance for many of the new countries than for the West because in a certain sense they never went through the process of discovering it."[16]

Unlike Cromer, Kissinger does not need to quote Sir Alfred Lyall on the Oriental's inability to be accurate; the point he makes is sufficiently unarguable to require no special validation. We had our Newtonian revolution; they didn't. As thinkers we are better off than they are. Good: the lines are drawn in much the same way, finally, as Balfour and Cromer drew them. Yet sixty or more years have intervened between Kissinger and the British imperialists. Numerous wars and revolutions have proved conclusively that the pre-Newtonian prophetic style, which Kissinger associates both with "inaccurate" developing countries and with Europe before the Congress of Vienna, is not entirely without its successes. Again unlike Balfour and Cromer, Kissinger therefore feels obliged to respect this pre-Newtonian perspective, since "it offers great flexibility with respect to the contemporary revolutionary turmoil." Thus the duty of men in the post-Newtonian (real) world is to "construct an international order *before* a crisis imposes it as a necessity": in other words, *we* must still find a way by which the developing world can be contained. Is this not similar to Cromer's vision of a harmoniously working machine designed ultimately to benefit some central authority, which opposes the developing world?

Kissinger may not have known on what fund of pedigreed knowledge he was drawing when he cut the world up into pre-Newtonian and post-Newtonian conceptions of reality. But his distinction is identical with the orthodox one made by Orientalists, who separate Orientals from Westerners. And like Orientalism's distinction Kissinger's is not value-free, despite the apparent neutrality of his tone. Thus such words as "prophetic," "accuracy," "internal," "empirical reality," and "order" are scattered throughout his description, and they characterize either attractive, familiar, desirable virtues or menacing, peculiar, disorderly defects. Both the traditional Orientalist, as we shall see, and Kissinger conceive of the difference between cultures, first, as creating a battlefront that separates them, and second, as inviting the West to control, contain, and otherwise govern (through superior knowledge and accommodating power) the Other. With what effect and at what considerable expense such militant divisions have been maintained, no one at present needs to be reminded.

Another illustration dovetails neatly—perhaps too neatly—with Kissinger's analysis. In its February 1972 issue, the *American Journal of Psychiatry* printed an essay by Harold W. Glidden, who is identified as a retired member of the Bureau of Intelligence and Research, United States Department of State; the essay's title ("The Arab World"), its tone, and its content argue a highly characteristic Orientalist bent of mind. Thus for his four-page, double-columned psychological portrait of over 100 million people, considered for a period of 1,300 years, Glidden cites exactly four sources for his views: a recent book on Tripoli, one issue of the Egyptian newspaper *Al-Ahram*, the periodical *Oriente Moderno*, and a book by Majid Khadduri, a well-known Orientalist. The article itself purports to uncover "the inner workings of Arab behavior," which from *our* point of view is "aberrant" but for Arabs is "normal." After this auspicious start, we are told that Arabs stress conformity; that Arabs inhabit a shame culture whose "prestige system" involves the ability to attract followers and clients (as an aside we are told that "Arab society is and always has been based on a system of client-patron relationships"); that Arabs can function only in conflict situations; that prestige is based solely on the ability to dominate others; that a shame culture—and therefore Islam itself—makes a virtue of revenge (here Glidden triumphantly cites the June 29, 1970 *Ahram* to show that "in 1969 [in Egypt] in 1070 cases of murder where the perpetrators were apprehended, it was found that 20 percent of the murders were based on a desire to wipe out shame, 30 percent on a desire to satisfy real or imaginary wrongs, and 31 percent on a desire for blood revenge"); that if from a Western point of view "the only rational thing for the Arabs to do is to make peace . . . for the Arabs the situation is not governed by this kind of logic, for objectivity is not a value in the Arab system."

Glidden continues, now more enthusiastically: "it is a notable fact that while the Arab value system demands absolute solidarity within the group, it at the same time encourages among its members a kind of rivalry that is destructive of that very solidarity"; in Arab society only "success counts" and "the end justifies the means";

Arabs live "naturally" in a world "characterized by anxiety expressed in generalized suspicion and distrust, which has been labelled free-floating hostility"; "the art of subterfuge is highly developed in Arab life, as well as in Islam itself"; the Arab need for vengeance overrides everything, otherwise the Arab would feel "ego-destroying" shame. Therefore, if "Westerners consider peace to be high on the scale of values" and if "we have a highly developed consciousness of the value of time," this is not true of Arabs. "In fact," we are told, "in Arab tribal society (where Arab values originated), strife, not peace, was the normal state of affairs because raiding was one of the two main supports of the economy." The purpose of this learned disquisition is merely to show how on the Western and Oriental scale of values "the relative position of the elements is quite different." QED.[17]

This is the apogee of Orientalist confidence. No merely asserted generality is denied the dignity of truth; no theoretical list of Oriental attributes is without application to the behavior of Orientals in the real world. On the one hand there are Westerners, and on the other there are Arab-Orientals; the former are (in no particular order) rational, peaceful, liberal, logical, capable of holding real values, without natural suspicion; the latter are none of these things. Out of what collective and yet particularized view of the Orient do these statements emerge? What specialized skills, what imaginative pressures, what institutions and traditions, what cultural forces produce such similarity in the descriptions of the Orient to be found in Cromer, Balfour, and our contemporary statesmen?

II

Imaginative Geography and Its Representations:
Orientalizing the Oriental

Strictly speaking, Orientalism is a field of learned study. In the Christian West, Orientalism is considered to have commenced its formal existence with the decision of the Church Council of

Vienne in 1312 to establish a series of chairs in "Arabic, Greek, Hebrew, and Syriac at Paris, Oxford, Bologna, Avignon, and Salamanca."[18] Yet any account of Orientalism would have to consider not only the professional Orientalist and his work but also the very notion of a field of study based on a geographical, cultural, linguistic, and ethnic unit called the Orient. Fields, of course, are made. They acquire coherence and integrity in time because scholars devote themselves in different ways to what seems to be a commonly agreed-upon subject matter. Yet it goes without saying that a field of study is rarely as simply defined as even its most committed partisans—usually scholars, professors, experts, and the like —claim it is. Besides, a field can change so entirely, in even the most traditional disciplines like philology, history, or theology, as to make an all-purpose definition of subject matter almost impossible. This is certainly true of Orientalism, for some interesting reasons.

To speak of scholarly specialization as a geographical "field" is, in the case of Orientalism, fairly revealing since no one is likely to imagine a field symmetrical to it called Occidentalism. Already the special, perhaps even eccentric attitude of Orientalism becomes apparent. For although many learned disciplines imply a position taken towards, say, *human* material (a historian deals with the human past from a special vantage point in the present), there is no real analogy for taking a fixed, more or less total geographical position towards a wide variety of social, linguistic, political, and historical realities. A classicist, a Romance specialist, even an Americanist focuses on a relatively modest portion of the world, not on a full half of it. But Orientalism is a field with considerable geographical ambition. And since Orientalists have traditionally occupied themselves with things Oriental (a specialist in Islamic law, no less than an expert in Chinese dialects or in Indian religions, is considered an Orientalist by people who call themselves Orientalists), we must learn to accept enormous, indiscriminate size plus an almost infinite capacity for subdivision as one of the chief characteristics of Orientalism—one that is evidenced in its confusing amalgam of imperial vagueness and precise detail.

All of this describes Orientalism as an academic discipline. The "ism" in Orientalism serves to insist on the distinction of this discipline from every other kind. The rule in its historical development as an academic discipline has been its increasing scope, not its greater selectiveness. Renaissance Orientalists like Erpenius and

Guillaume Postel were primarily specialists in the languages of the Biblical provinces, although Postel boasted that he could get across Asia as far as China without needing an interpreter. By and large, until the mid-eighteenth century Orientalists were Biblical scholars, students of the Semitic languages, Islamic specialists, or, because the Jesuits had opened up the new study of China, Sinologists. The whole middle expanse of Asia was not academically conquered for Orientalism until, during the later eighteenth century, Anquetil-Duperron and Sir William Jones were able intelligibly to reveal the extraordinary riches of Avestan and Sanskrit. By the middle of the nineteenth century Orientalism was as vast a treasure-house of learning as one could imagine. There are two excellent indices of this new, triumphant eclecticism. One is the encyclopedic description of Orientalism roughly from 1765 to 1850 given by Raymond Schwab in his *La Renaissance orientale*.[19] Quite aside from the scientific discoveries of things Oriental made by learned professionals during this period in Europe, there was the virtual epidemic of Orientalia affecting every major poet, essayist, and philosopher of the period. Schwab's notion is that "Oriental" identifies an amateur or professional enthusiasm for everything Asiatic, which was wonderfully synonymous with the exotic, the mysterious, the profound, the seminal; this is a later transposition eastwards of a similar enthusiasm in Europe for Greek and Latin antiquity during the High Renaissance. In 1829 Victor Hugo put this change in directions as follows: "Au siècle de Louis XIV on était helléniste, maintenant on est orientaliste."[20] A nineteenth-century Orientalist was therefore either a scholar (a Sinologist, an Islamicist, an Indo-Europeanist) or a gifted enthusiast (Hugo in *Les Orientales*, Goethe in the *Westöstlicher Diwan*), or both (Richard Burton, Edward Lane, Friedrich Schlegel).

The second index of how inclusive Orientalism had become since the Council of Vienne is to be found in nineteenth-century chronicles of the field itself. The most thorough of its kind is Jules Mohl's *Vingt-sept Ans d'histoire des études orientales*, a two-volume logbook of everything of note that took place in Orientalism between 1840 and 1867.[21] Mohl was the secretary of the Société asiatique in Paris, and for something more than the first half of the nineteenth century Paris was the capital of the Orientalist world (and, according to Walter Benjamin, of the nineteenth century). Mohl's position in the Société could not have been more central to the field of Orientalism. There is scarcely anything done by a

European scholar touching Asia during those twenty-seven years that Mohl does not enter under "études orientales." His entries of course concern publications, but the range of published material of interest to Orientalist scholars is awesome. Arabic, innumerable Indian dialects, Hebrew, Pehlevi, Assyrian, Babylonian, Mongolian, Chinese, Burmese, Mesopotamian, Javanese: the list of philological works considered Orientalist is almost uncountable. Moreover, Orientalist studies apparently cover everything from the editing and translation of texts to numismatic, anthropological, archaeological, sociological, economic, historical, literary, and cultural studies in every known Asiatic and North African civilization, ancient and modern. Gustave Dugat's *Histoire des orientalistes de l'Europe du XIIe au XIXe siècle* (1868–1870)[22] is a selective history of major figures, but the range represented is no less immense than Mohl's.

Such eclecticism as this had its blind spots, nevertheless. Academic Orientalists for the most part were interested in the classical period of whatever language or society it was that they studied. Not until quite late in the century, with the single major exception of Napoleon's Institut d'Égypte, was much attention given to the academic study of the modern, or actual, Orient. Moreover, the Orient studied was a textual universe by and large; the impact of the Orient was made through books and manuscripts, not, as in the impress of Greece on the Renaissance, through mimetic artifacts like sculpture and pottery. Even the rapport between an Orientalist and the Orient was textual, so much so that it is reported of some of the early-nineteenth-century German Orientalists that their first view of an eight-armed Indian statue cured them completely of their Orientalist taste.[23] When a learned Orientalist traveled in the country of his specialization, it was always with unshakable abstract maxims about the "civilization" he had studied; rarely were Orientalists interested in anything except proving the validity of these musty "truths" by applying them, without great success, to uncomprehending, hence degenerate, natives. Finally, the very power and scope of Orientalism produced not only a fair amount of exact positive knowledge about the Orient but also a kind of second-order knowledge—lurking in such places as the "Oriental" tale, the mythology of the mysterious East, notions of Asian inscrutability—with a life of its own, what V. G. Kiernan has aptly called "Europe's collective day-dream of the Orient."[24] One happy result of this is that an estimable number of important writers during the nineteenth century were Oriental enthusiasts: It is perfectly correct, I think, to speak of a genre of Orientalist writing as exemplified in the works of Hugo, Goethe, Nerval, Flaubert, Fitzgerald, and the like. What inevitably goes with such work, however, is a kind of free-floating mythology of the Orient, an Orient that derives not only from contemporary attitudes and popular prejudices but also from what Vico called the conceit of nations and of scholars. I have already alluded to the political uses of such material as it has turned up in the twentieth century.

Today an Orientalist is less likely to call himself an Orientalist than he was almost any time up to World War II. Yet the designation is still useful, as when universities maintain programs or departments in Oriental languages or Oriental civilizations. There is an Oriental "faculty" at Oxford, and a department of Oriental studies at Princeton. As recently as 1959, the British government empowered a commission "to review developments in the Universities in the fields of Oriental, Slavonic, East European and African studies . . . and to consider, and advise on, proposals for future development."[25] The Hayter Report, as it was called when it appeared in 1961, seemed untroubled by the broad designation of the word *Oriental*, which it found serviceably employed in American universities as well. For even the greatest name in modern Anglo-American Islamic studies, H. A. R. Gibb, preferred to call himself an Orientalist rather than an Arabist. Gibb himself, classicist that he was, could use the ugly neologism "area study" for Orientalism as a way of showing that area studies and Orientalism after all were interchangeable geographical titles.[26] But this, I think, ingenuously belies a much more interesting relationship between knowledge and geography. I should like to consider that relationship briefly.

Despite the distraction of a great many vague desires, impulses, and images, the mind seems persistently to formulate what Claude Lévi-Strauss has called a science of the concrete.[27] A primitive tribe, for example, assigns a definite place, function, and significance to every leafy species in its immediate environment. Many of these grasses and flowers have no practical use; but the point Lévi-Strauss makes is that mind requires order, and order is achieved by discriminating and taking note of everything, placing everything of which the mind is aware in a secure, refindable place, therefore giving things some role to play in the economy of objects and identities that make up an environment. This kind of rudimentary classification has a logic to it, but the rules of the logic by which a green fern in one society is a symbol of grace and in another is considered maleficent are neither predictably rational nor universal. There is always a measure of the purely arbitrary in the way the distinctions between things are seen. And with these distinctions go values whose history, if one could unearth it completely, would probably show the same measure of arbitrariness. This is evident enough in the case of fashion. Why do wigs, lace collars, and high buckled shoes appear, then disappear, over a period of decades? Some of the answer has to do with utility and some with the inherent beauty of the fashion. But if we agree that all things in history, like history itself, are made by men, then we will appreciate how possible it is for many objects or places or times to be assigned roles and given meanings that acquire objective validity only *after* the assignments are made. This is especially true of relatively uncommon things, like foreigners, mutants, or "abnormal" behavior.

It is perfectly possible to argue that some distinctive objects are made by the mind, and that these objects, while appearing to exist objectively, have only a fictional reality. A group of people living on a few acres of land will set up boundaries between their land and its immediate surroundings and the territory beyond, which they call "the land of the barbarians." In other words, this universal practice of designating in one's mind a familiar space which is "ours" and an unfamiliar space beyond "ours" which is "theirs" is a way of making geographical distinctions that *can be* entirely arbitrary. I use the word "arbitrary" here because imaginative geography of the "our land–barbarian land" variety does not require that the barbarians acknowledge the distinction. It is enough for "us" to set up these boundaries in our own minds; "they" become "they" accordingly, and both their territory and their mentality are designated as different from "ours." To a certain extent modern and primitive societies seem thus to derive a sense of their identities negatively. A fifth-century Athenian was very likely to feel himself to be nonbarbarian as much as he positively felt himself to be Athenian. The geographic boundaries accompany the social, ethnic, and cultural ones in expected ways. Yet often the sense in which someone feels himself to be not-foreign is based on a very unrigorous idea of what is "out there," beyond one's own territory. All kinds of suppositions, associations, and fictions appear to crowd the unfamiliar space outside one's own.

The French philosopher Gaston Bachelard once wrote an analysis of what he called the poetics of space.[28] The inside of a house, he said, acquires a sense of intimacy, secrecy, security, real or imag-

ined, because of the experiences that come to seem appropriate for
it. The objective space of a house—its corners, corridors, cellar,
rooms—is far less important than what poetically it is endowed
with, which is usually a quality with an imaginative or figurative
value we can name and feel: thus a house may be haunted, or
homelike, or prisonlike, or magical. So space acquires emotional
and even rational sense by a kind of poetic process, whereby the
vacant or anonymous reaches of distance are converted into
meaning for us here. The same process occurs when we deal with
time. Much of what we associate with or even know about such
periods as "long ago" or "the beginning" or "at the end of time"
is poetic—made up. For a historian of Middle Kingdom Egypt,
"long ago" will have a very clear sort of meaning, but even this
meaning does not totally dissipate the imaginative, quasi-fictional
quality one senses lurking in a time very different and distant from
our own. For there is no doubt that imaginative geography and
history help the mind to intensify its own sense of itself by dramatizing the distance and difference between what is close to it and what
is far away. This is no less true of the feelings we often have that
we would have been more "at home" in the sixteenth century or in
Tahiti.

Yet there is no use in pretending that all we know about time and
space, or rather history and geography, is more than anything else
imaginative. There are such things as positive history and positive
geography which in Europe and the United States have impressive
achievements to point to. Scholars now do know more about the
world, its past and present, than they did, for example, in Gibbon's
time. Yet this is not to say that they know all there is to know, nor,
more important, is it to say that what they know has effectively
dispelled the imaginative geographical and historical knowledge I
have been considering. We need not decide here whether this kind
of imaginative knowledge infuses history and geography, or whether
in some way it overrides them. Let us just say for the time being that
it is there as something *more* than what appears to be merely positive knowledge.

Almost from earliest times in Europe the Orient was something
more than what was empirically known about it. At least until the
early eighteenth century, as R. W. Southern has so elegantly shown,
European understanding of one kind of Oriental culture, the Islamic,
was ignorant but complex.[29] For certain associations with the East—
not quite ignorant, not quite informed—always seem to have

gathered around the notion of an Orient. Consider first the demarcation between Orient and West. It already seems bold by the time
of the *Iliad*. Two of the most profoundly influential qualities associated with the East appear in Aeschylus's *The Persians*, the earliest
Athenian play extant, and in *The Bacchae* of Euripides, the very
last one extant. Aeschylus portrays the sense of disaster overcoming
the Persians when they learn that their armies, led by King Xerxes,
have been destroyed by the Greeks. The chorus sings the following
ode:

> Now all Asia's land
> Moans in emptiness.
> Xerxes led forth, oh oh!
> Xerxes destroyed, woe woe!
> Xerxes' plans have all miscarried
> In ships of the sea.
> Why did Darius then
> Bring no harm to his men
> When he led them into battle,
> That beloved leader of men from Susa?[30]

What matters here is that Asia speaks through and by virtue of the
European imagination, which is depicted as victorious over Asia,
that hostile "other" world beyond the seas. To Asia are given the
feelings of emptiness, loss, and disaster that seem thereafter to
reward Oriental challenges to the West; and also, the lament that in
some glorious past Asia fared better, was itself victorious over
Europe.

In *The Bacchae*, perhaps the most Asiatic of all the Attic dramas,
Dionysus is explicitly connected with his Asian origins and with the
strangely threatening excesses of Oriental mysteries. Pentheus, king
of Thebes, is destroyed by his mother, Agave, and her fellow
bacchantes. Having defied Dionysus by not recognizing either his
power or his divinity, Pentheus is thus horribly punished, and the
play ends with a general recognition of the eccentric god's terrible
power. Modern commentators on *The Bacchae* have not failed to
note the play's extraordinary range of intellectual and aesthetic
effects; but there has been no escaping the additional historical detail
that Euripides "was surely affected by the new aspect that the
Dionysiac cults must have assumed in the light of the foreign
ecstatic religions of Bendis, Cybele, Sabazius, Adonis, and Isis,
which were introduced from Asia Minor and the Levant and swept

through Piraeus and Athens during the frustrating and increasingly irrational years of the Peloponnesian War."[31]

The two aspects of the Orient that set it off from the West in this pair of plays will remain essential motifs of European imaginative geography. A line is drawn between two continents. Europe is powerful and articulate; Asia is defeated and distant. Aeschylus *represents* Asia, makes her speak in the person of the aged Persian queen, Xerxes' mother. It is Europe that articulates the Orient; this articulation is the prerogative, not of a puppet master, but of a genuine creator, whose life-giving power represents, animates, constitutes the otherwise silent and dangerous space beyond familiar boundaries. There is an analogy between Aeschylus's orchestra, which contains the Asiatic world as the playwright conceives it, and the learned envelope of Orientalist scholarship, which also will hold in the vast, amorphous Asiatic sprawl for sometimes sympathetic but always dominating scrutiny. Secondly, there is the motif of the Orient as insinuating danger. Rationality is undermined by Eastern excesses, those mysteriously attractive opposites to what seem to be normal values. The difference separating East from West is symbolized by the sternness with which, at first, Pentheus rejects the hysterical bacchantes. When later he himself becomes a bacchant, he is destroyed not so much for having given in to Dionysus as for having incorrectly assessed Dionysus's menace in the first place. The lesson that Euripides intends is dramatized by the presence in the play of Cadmus and Tiresias, knowledgeable older men who realize that "sovereignty" alone does not rule men;[32] there is such a thing as judgment, they say, which means sizing up correctly the force of alien powers and expertly coming to terms with them. Hereafter Oriental mysteries will be taken seriously, not least because they challenge the rational Western mind to new exercises of its enduring ambition and power.

But one big division, as between West and Orient, leads to other smaller ones, especially as the normal enterprises of civilization provoke such outgoing activities as travel, conquest, new experiences. In classical Greece and Rome geographers, historians, public figures like Caesar, orators, and poets added to the fund of taxonomic lore separating races, regions, nations, and minds from each other; much of that was self-serving, and existed to prove that Romans and Greeks were superior to other kinds of people. But concern with the Orient had its own tradition of classification and hierarchy. From at least the second century B.C. on, it was lost on no traveler

or eastward-looking and ambitious Western potentate that Herodotus—historian, traveler, inexhaustibly curious chronicler—and
Alexander—king warrior, scientific conqueror—had been in the
Orient before. The Orient was therefore subdivided into realms
previously known, visited, conquered, by Herodotus and Alexander
as well as their epigones, and those realms not previously known,
visited, conquered. Christianity completed the setting up of main
intra-Oriental spheres: there was a Near Orient and a Far Orient, a
familiar Orient, which René Grousset calls "l'empire du Levant,"[33]
and a novel Orient. The Orient therefore alternated in the mind's
geography between being an Old World to which one returned, as to
Eden or Paradise, there to set up a new version of the old, and
being a wholly new place to which one came as Columbus came
to America, in order to set up a New World (although, ironically,
Columbus himself thought that he discovered a new part of the Old
World). Certainly neither of these Orients was purely one thing or
the other: it is their vacillations, their tempting suggestiveness, their
capacity for entertaining and confusing the mind, that are interesting.

Consider how the Orient, and in particular the Near Orient,
became known in the West as its great complementary opposite
since antiquity. There were the Bible and the rise of Christianity;
there were travelers like Marco Polo who charted the trade routes
and patterned a regulated system of commercial exchange, and
after him Lodovico di Varthema and Pietro della Valle; there were
fabulists like Mandeville; there were the redoubtable conquering
Eastern movements, principally Islam, of course; there were the
militant pilgrims, chiefly the Crusaders. Altogether an internally
structured archive is built up from the literature that belongs to
these experiences. Out of this comes a restricted number of typical
encapsulations: the journey, the history, the fable, the stereotype,
the polemical confrontation. These are the lenses through which the
Orient is experienced, and they shape the language, perception, and
form of the encounter between East and West. What gives the
immense number of encounters some unity, however, is the vacillation I was speaking about earlier. Something patently foreign and
distant acquires, for one reason or another, a status more rather
than less familiar. One tends to stop judging things either as
completely novel or as completely well known; a new median
category emerges, a category that allows one to see new things,
things seen for the first time, as versions of a previously known thing.

In essence such a category is not so much a way of receiving new information as it is a method of controlling what seems to be a threat to some established view of things. If the mind must suddenly deal with what it takes to be a radically new form of life—as Islam appeared to Europe in the early Middle Ages—the response on the whole is conservative and defensive. Islam is judged to be a fraudulent new version of some previous experience, in this case Christianity. The threat is muted, familiar values impose themselves, and in the end the mind reduces the pressure upon it by accommodating things to itself as either "original" or "repetitious." Islam thereafter is "handled": its novelty and its suggestiveness are brought under control so that relatively nuanced discriminations are now made that would have been impossible had the raw novelty of Islam been left unattended. The Orient at large, therefore, vacillates between the West's contempt for what is familiar and its shivers of delight in—or fear of—novelty.

Yet where Islam was concerned, European fear, if not always respect, was in order. After Mohammed's death in 632, the military and later the cultural and religious hegemony of Islam grew enormously. First Persia, Syria, and Egypt, then Turkey, then North Africa fell to the Muslim armies; in the eighth and ninth centuries Spain, Sicily, and parts of France were conquered. By the thirteenth and fourteenth centuries Islam ruled as far east as India, Indonesia, and China. And to this extraordinary assault Europe could respond with very little except fear and a kind of awe. Christian authors witnessing the Islamic conquests had scant interest in the learning, high culture, and frequent magnificence of the Muslims, who were, as Gibbon said, "coeval with the darkest and most slothful period of European annals." (But with some satisfaction he added, "since the sum of science has risen in the West, it should seem that the Oriental studies have languished and declined."[34]) What Christians typically felt about the Eastern armies was that they had "all the appearance of a swarm of bees, but with a heavy hand . . . they devastated everything": so wrote Erchembert, a cleric in Monte Cassino in the eleventh century.[35]

Not for nothing did Islam come to symbolize terror, devastation, the demonic, hordes of hated barbarians. For Europe, Islam was a lasting trauma. Until the end of the seventeenth century the "Ottoman peril" lurked alongside Europe to represent for the whole of Christian civilization a constant danger, and in time European civilization incorporated that peril and its lore, its great events, figures, virtues, and vices, as something woven into the fabric of life. In Renaissance England alone, as Samuel Chew recounts in his classic study *The Crescent and the Rose,* "a man of average education and intelligence" had at his fingertips, and could watch on the London stage, a relatively large number of detailed events in the history of Ottoman Islam and its encroachments upon Christian Europe.[36] The point is that what remained current about Islam was some necessarily diminished version of those great dangerous forces that it symbolized for Europe. Like Walter Scott's Saracens, the European representation of the Muslim, Ottoman, or Arab was always a way of controlling the redoubtable Orient, and to a certain extent the same is true of the methods of contemporary learned Orientalists, whose subject is not so much the East itself as the East made known, and therefore less fearsome, to the Western reading public.

There is nothing especially controversial or reprehensible about such domestications of the exotic; they take place between all cultures, certainly, and between all men. My point, however, is to emphasize the truth that the Orientalist, as much as anyone in the European West who thought about or experienced the Orient, performed this kind of mental operation. But what is more important still is the limited vocabulary and imagery that impose themselves as a consequence. The reception of Islam in the West is a perfect case in point, and has been admirably studied by Norman Daniel. One constraint acting upon Christian thinkers who tried to understand Islam was an analogical one; since Christ is the basis of Christian faith, it was assumed—quite incorrectly— that Mohammed was to Islam as Christ was to Christianity. Hence the polemic name "Mohammedanism" given to Islam, and the automatic epithet "imposter" applied to Mohammed.[37] Out of such and many other misconceptions "there formed a circle which was never broken by imaginative exteriorisation. . . . The Christian concept of Islam was integral and self-sufficient."[38] Islam became an image— the word is Daniel's but it seems to me to have remarkable implications for Orientalism in general—whose function was not so much to represent Islam in itself as to represent it for the medieval Christian.

> The invariable tendency to neglect what the Qur'an meant, or what Muslims thought it meant, or what Muslims thought or did in any given circumstances, necessarily implies that Qur'anic and other Islamic doctrine was presented in a form that would con-

vince Christians; and more and more extravagant forms would stand a chance of acceptance as the distance of the writers and public from the Islamic border increased. It was with very great reluctance that what Muslims said Muslims believed was accepted as what they did believe. There was a Christian picture in which the details (even under the pressure of facts) were abandoned as little as possible, and in which the general outline was never abandoned. There were shades of difference, but only with a common framework. All the corrections that were made in the interests of an increasing accuracy were only a defence of what had newly been realised to be vulnerable, a shoring up of a weakened structure. Christian opinion was an erection which could not be demolished, even to be rebuilt.[39]

This rigorous Christian picture of Islam was intensified in innumerable ways, including—during the Middle Ages and early Renaissance—a large variety of poetry, learned controversy, and popular superstition.[40] By this time the Near Orient had been all but incorporated in the common world-picture of Latin Christianity —as in the *Chanson de Roland* the worship of Saracens is portrayed as embracing Mahomet *and* Apollo. By the middle of the fifteenth century, as R. W. Southern has brilliantly shown, it became apparent to serious European thinkers "that something would have to be done about Islam," which had turned the situation around somewhat by itself arriving militarily in Eastern Europe. Southern recounts a dramatic episode between 1450 and 1460 when four learned men, John of Segovia, Nicholas of Cusa, Jean Germain, and Aeneas Silvius (Pius II), attempted to deal with Islam through *contraferentia*, or "conference." The idea was John of Segovia's: it was to have been a staged conference with Islam in which Christians attempted the wholesale conversion of Muslims. "He saw the conference as an instrument with a political as well as a strictly religious function, and in words which will strike a chord in modern breasts he exclaimed that even if it were to last ten years it would be less expensive and less damaging than war." There was no agreement between the four men, but the episode is crucial for having been a fairly sophisticated attempt—part of a general European attempt from Bede to Luther—to put a representative Orient in front of Europe, to *stage* the Orient and Europe together in some coherent way, the idea being for Christians to make it clear to Muslims that Islam was just a misguided version of Christianity. Southern's conclusion follows:

Most conspicuous to us is the inability of any of these systems of thought [European Christian] to provide a fully satisfying explanation of the phenomenon they had set out to explain [Islam] —still less to influence the course of practical events in a decisive way. At a practical level, events never turned out either so well or so ill as the most intelligent observers predicted; and it is perhaps worth noticing that they never turned out better than when the best judges confidently expected a happy ending. Was there any progress [in Christian knowledge of Islam]? I must express my conviction that there was. Even if the solution of the problem remained obstinately hidden from sight, the statement of the problem became more complex, more rational, and more related to experience. . . . The scholars who labored at the problem of Islam in the Middle Ages failed to find the solution they sought and desired; but they developed habits of mind and powers of comprehension which, in other men and in other fields, may yet deserve success.[41]

The best part of Southern's analysis, here and elsewhere in his brief history of Western views of Islam, is his demonstration that it is finally Western ignorance which becomes more refined and complex, not some body of positive Western knowledge which increases in size and accuracy. For fictions have their own logic and their own dialectic of growth or decline. Onto the character of Mohammed in the Middle Ages was heaped a bundle of attributes that corresponded to the "character of the [twelfth-century] prophets of the 'Free Spirit' who did actually arise in Europe, and claim credence and collect followers." Similarly, since Mohammed was viewed as the disseminator of a false Revelation, he became as well the epitome of lechery, debauchery, sodomy, and a whole battery of assorted treacheries, all of which derived "logically" from his doctrinal impostures.[42] Thus the Orient acquired representatives, so to speak, and representations, each one more concrete, more internally congruent with some Western exigency, than the ones that preceded it. It is as if, having once settled on the Orient as a locale suitable for incarnating the infinite in a finite shape, Europe could not stop the practice; the Orient and the Oriental, Arab, Islamic, Indian, Chinese, or whatever, become repetitious pseudo-incarnations of some great original (Christ, Europe, the West) they were supposed to have been imitating. Only the source of these rather narcissistic Western ideas about the Orient changed in time, not their character. Thus we will find it commonly believed in the twelfth and thirteenth centuries that Arabia was "on the fringe of the Christian world, a natural asylum for heretical outlaws,"[43] and that Mohammed was a cunning apostate, whereas in the twentieth century an Orientalist scholar, an erudite specialist, will be the one to point out how Islam is really no more than second-order Arian heresy.[44]

Our initial description of Orientalism as a learned field now acquires a new concreteness. A field is often an enclosed space. The idea of representation is a theatrical one: the Orient is the stage on which the whole East is confined. On this stage will appear figures whose role it is to represent the larger whole from which they emanate. The Orient then seems to be, not an unlimited extension beyond the familiar European world, but rather a closed field, a theatrical stage affixed to Europe. An Orientalist is but the particular specialist in knowledge for which Europe at large is responsible, in the way that an audience is historically and culturally responsible for (and responsive to) dramas technically put together by the dramatist. In the depths of this Oriental stage stands a prodigious cultural repertoire whose individual items evoke a fabulously rich world: the Sphinx, Cleopatra, Eden, Troy, Sodom and Gomorrah, Astarte, Isis and Osiris, Sheba, Babylon, the Genii, the Magi, Nineveh, Prester John, Mahomet, and dozens more; settings, in some cases names only, half-imagined, half-known; monsters, devils, heroes; terrors, pleasures, desires. The European imagination was nourished extensively from this repertoire: between the Middle Ages and the eighteenth century such major authors as Ariosto, Milton, Marlowe, Tasso, Shakespeare, Cervantes, and the authors of the *Chanson de Roland* and the *Poema del Cid* drew on the Orient's riches for their productions, in ways that sharpened the outlines of imagery, ideas, and figures populating it. In addition, a great deal of what was considered learned Orientalist scholarship in Europe pressed ideological myths into service, even as knowledge seemed genuinely to be advancing.

A celebrated instance of how dramatic form and learned imagery come together in the Orientalist theater is Barthélemy d'Herbelot's *Bibliothèque orientale*, published posthumously in 1697, with a preface by Antoine Galland. The introduction of the recent *Cambridge History of Islam* considers the *Bibliothèque*, along with George Sale's preliminary discourse to his translation of the Koran (1734) and Simon Ockley's *History of the Saracens* (1708, 1718), to be "highly important" in widening "the new understand-

ing of Islam" and conveying it "to a less academic readership."[45]
This inadequately describes d'Herbelot's work, which was not
restricted to Islam as Sale's and Ockley's were. With the exception
of Johann H. Hottinger's *Historia Orientalis,* which appeared in
1651, the *Bibliothèque* remained the standard reference work in
Europe until the early nineteenth century. Its scope was truly
epochal. Galland, who was the first European translator of *The
Thousand and One Nights* and an Arabist of note, contrasted
d'Herbelot's achievement with every prior one by noting the
prodigious range of his enterprise. D'Herbelot read a great number
of works, Galland said, in Arabic, Persian, and Turkish, with the
result that he was able to find out about matters hitherto concealed
from Europeans.[46] After first composing a dictionary of these three
Oriental languages, d'Herbelot went on to study Oriental history,
theology, geography, science, and art, in both their fabulous and
their truthful varieties. Thereafter he decided to compose two works,
one a *bibliothèque,* or "library," an alphabetically arranged dictionary, the second a *florilège,* or anthology. Only the first part was
completed.

Galland's account of the *Bibliothèque* stated that "orientale" was
planned to include principally the Levant, although—Galland says
admiringly—the time period covered did not begin only with the
creation of Adam and end with the "temps où nous sommes":
d'Herbelot went even further back, to a time described as "plus
haut" in fabulous histories—to the long period of the pre-Adamite
Solimans. As Galland's description proceeds, we learn that the
Bibliothèque was like "any other" history of the world, for what it
attempted was a complete compendium of the knowledge available
on such matters as the Creation, the Deluge, the destruction of
Babel, and so forth—with the difference that d'Herbelot's sources
were Oriental. He divided history into two types, sacred and profane
(the Jews and Christians in the first, the Muslims in the second),
and two periods, pre- and postdiluvian. Thus d'Herbelot was able
to discuss such widely divergent histories as the Mogul, the Tartar,
the Turkish, and the Slavonic; he took in as well all the provinces of
the Muslim Empire, from the Extreme Orient to the Pillars of
Hercules, with their customs, rituals, traditions, commentaries,
dynasties, palaces, rivers, and flora. Such a work, even though it
included some attention to "la doctrine perverse de Mahomet, qui
a causé si grands dommages au Christianisme," was more capa-
ciously thorough than any work before it. Galland concluded his

"Discours" by assuring the reader at length that d'Herbelot's *Bibliothèque* was uniquely "utile et agréable"; other Orientalists, like Postel, Scaliger, Golius, Pockoke, and Erpenius, produced Orientalist studies that were too narrowly grammatical, lexico-graphical, geographical, or the like. Only d'Herbelot was able to write a work capable of convincing European readers that the study of Oriental culture was more than just thankless and fruitless: only d'Herbelot, according to Galland, attempted to form in the minds of his readers a sufficiently ample idea of what it meant to know and study the Orient, an idea that would both fill the mind and satisfy one's great, previously conceived expectations.[47]

In such efforts as d'Herbelot's, Europe discovered its capacities for encompassing and Orientalizing the Orient. A certain sense of superiority appears here and there in what Galland had to say about about his and d'Herbelot's *materia orientalia*; as in the work of seventeenth-century geographers like Raphael du Mans, Europeans could perceive that the Orient was being outstripped and outdated by Western science.[48] But what becomes evident is not only the advantage of a Western perspective: there is also the triumphant technique for taking the immense fecundity of the Orient and mak-ing it systematically, even alphabetically, knowable by Western laymen. When Galland said of d'Herbelot that he satisfied one's expectations he meant, I think, that the *Bibliothèque* did not attempt to revise commonly received ideas about the Orient. For what the Orientalist does is to *confirm* the Orient in his readers' eyes; he neither tries nor wants to unsettle already firm convictions. All the *Bibliothèque orientale* did was represent the Orient more fully and more clearly; what may have been a loose collection of randomly acquired facts concerning vaguely Levantine history, Biblical imagery, Islamic culture, place names, and so on were transformed into a rational Oriental panorama, from A to Z. Under the entry for Mohammed, d'Herbelot first supplied all of the Prophet's given names, then proceeded to confirm Mohammed's ideological and doctrinal value as follows:

> C'est le fameux imposteur Mahomet, Auteur et Fondateur d'une hérésie, qui a pris le nom de religion, que nous appelons Ma-hometane. *Voyez* le titre d'Eslam.
> Les Interprètes de l'Alcoran et autres Docteurs de la Loy Musulmane ont appliqué à ce faux prophète tous les éloges, que les Ariens, Paulitiens ou Paulianistes & autres Héré-tiques ont attribué à Jésus-Christ, en lui ôtant sa Divinité. . . .[49]

(This is the famous imposter Mahomet, Author and Founder
of a heresy, which has taken on the name of religion, which we
call Mohammedan. See entry under *Islam*.

The interpreters of the Alcoran and other Doctors of Muslim
or Mohammedan Law have applied to this false prophet all the
praises which the Arians, Paulicians or Paulianists, and other
Heretics have attributed to Jesus Christ, while stripping him of
his Divinity. . . .)

"Mohammedan" is the relevant (and insulting) European
designation; "Islam," which happens to be the correct Muslim name,
is relegated to another entry. The "heresy . . . which we
call Mohammedan" is "caught" as the imitation of a Christian imitation
of true religion. Then, in the long historical account of Mohammed's
life, d'Herbelot can turn to more or less straight narrative. But it is
the *placing* of Mohammed that counts in the *Bibliothèque*. The
dangers of free-wheeling heresy are removed when it is transformed
into ideologically explicit matter for an alphabetical item. Mohammed no longer roams the Eastern world as a threatening, im-
moral debauchee; he sits quietly on his (admittedly prominent)
portion of the Orientalist stage.[50] He is given a genealogy, an
explanation, even a development, all of which are subsumed under
the simple statements that prevent him from straying elsewhere.

Such "images" of the Orient as this are images in that they
represent or stand for a very large entity, otherwise impossibly
diffuse, which they enable one to grasp or see. They are also
characters, related to such types as the braggarts, misers, or
gluttons produced by Theophrastus, La Bruyère, or Selden. Perhaps
it is not exactly correct to say that one *sees* such characters as the
miles gloriosus or Mahomet the imposter, since the discursive confinement of a character is supposed at best to let one apprehend a
generic type without difficulty or ambiguity. D'Herbelot's character
of Mahomet is an *image*, however, because the false prophet is part
of a general theatrical representation called *orientale* whose totality
is contained in the *Bibliothèque*.

The didactic quality of the Orientalist representation cannot be
detached from the rest of the performance. In a learned work like
the *Bibliothèque orientale*, which was the result of systematic study
and research, the author imposes a disciplinary order upon the
material he has worked on; in addition, he wants it made clear to
the reader that what the printed page delivers is an ordered, disciplined judgment of the material. What is thus conveyed by the

Bibliothèque is an idea of Orientalism's power and effectiveness, which everywhere remind the reader that henceforth in order to get at the Orient he must pass through the learned grids and codes provided by the Orientalist. Not only is the Orient accommodated to the moral exigencies of Western Christianity; it is also circumscribed by a series of attitudes and judgments that send the Western mind, not first to Oriental sources for correction and verification, but rather to other Orientalist works. The Orientalist stage, as I have been calling it, becomes a system of moral and epistemological rigor. As a discipline representing institutionalized Western knowledge of the Orient, Orientalism thus comes to exert a three-way force, on the Orient, on the Orientalist, and on the Western "consumer" of Orientalism. It would be wrong, I think, to underestimate the strength of the three-way relationship thus established. For the Orient ("out there" towards the East) is corrected, even penalized, for lying outside the boundaries of European society, "our" world; the Orient is thus *Orientalized*, a process that not only marks the Orient as the province of the Orientalist but also forces the uninitiated Western reader to accept Orientalist codifications (like d'Herbelot's alphabetized *Bibliothèque*) as the *true* Orient. Truth, in short, becomes a function of learned judgment, not of the material itself, which in time seems to owe even its existence to the Orientalist.

This whole didactic process is neither difficult to understand nor difficult to explain. One ought again to remember that all cultures impose corrections upon raw reality, changing it from free-floating objects into units of knowledge. The problem is not that conversion takes place. It is perfectly natural for the human mind to resist the assault on it of untreated strangeness; therefore cultures have always been inclined to impose complete transformations on other cultures, receiving these other cultures not as they are but as, for the benefit of the receiver, they ought to be. To the Westerner, however, the Oriental was always *like* some aspect of the West; to some of the German Romantics, for example, Indian religion was essentially an Oriental version of Germano-Christian pantheism. Yet the Orientalist makes it his work to be always converting the Orient from something into something else: he does this for himself, for the sake of his culture, in some cases for what he believes is the sake of the Oriental. This process of conversion is a disciplined one: it is taught, it has its own societies, periodicals, traditions, vocabulary, rhetoric, all in basic ways connected to and supplied by the prevailing cultural and political norms of the West. And, as I shall demonstrate, it tends to become more rather than less total in what it tries to do, so much so that as one surveys Orientalism in the nineteenth and twentieth centuries the overriding impression is of Orientalism's insensitive schematization of the entire Orient.

How early this schematization began is clear from the examples I have given of Western representations of the Orient in classical Greece. How strongly articulated were later representations building on the earlier ones, how inordinately careful their schematization, how dramatically effective their placing in Western imaginative geography, can be illustrated if we turn now to Dante's *Inferno*. Dante's achievement in *The Divine Comedy* was to have seamlessly combined the realistic portrayal of mundane reality with a universal and eternal system of Christian values. What Dante the pilgrim sees as he walks through the Inferno, Purgatorio, and Paradiso is a unique vision of judgment. Paolo and Francesca, for instance, are seen as eternally confined to hell for their sins, yet they are seen as enacting, indeed living, the very characters and actions that put them where they will be for eternity. Thus each of the figures in Dante's vision not only represents himself but is also a typical representation of his character and the fate meted out to him.

"Maometto"—Mohammed—turns up in canto 28 of the *Inferno*. He is located in the eighth of the nine circles of Hell, in the ninth of the ten Bolgias of Malebolge, a circle of gloomy ditches surrounding Satan's stronghold in Hell. Thus before Dante reaches Mohammed, he passes through circles containing people whose sins are of a lesser order: the lustful, the avaricious, the gluttonous, the heretics, the wrathful, the suicidal, the blasphemous. After Mohammed there are only the falsifiers and the treacherous (who include Judas, Brutus, and Cassius) before one arrives at the very bottom of Hell, which is where Satan himself is to be found. Mohammed thus belongs to a rigid hierarchy of evils, in the category of what Dante calls *seminator di scandalo e di scisma*. Mohammed's punishment, which is also his eternal fate, is a peculiarly disgusting one: he is endlessly being cleft in two from his chin to his anus like, Dante says, a cask whose staves are ripped apart. Dante's verse at this point spares the reader none of the eschatological detail that so vivid a punishment entails: Mohammed's entrails and his excrement are described with unflinching accuracy. Mohammed explains his punishment to Dante, pointing as well to Ali, who precedes him in the line of sinners whom the attendant devil is splitting in two; he also asks Dante to warn one Fra Dolcino, a renegade priest whose sect advocated community of women and goods and who was accused of having a mistress, of what will be in store for him. It will not have been lost on the reader that Dante saw a parallel between Dolcino's and Mohammed's revolting sensuality, and also between their pretensions to theological eminence.

But this is not all that Dante has to say about Islam. Earlier in the *Inferno*, a small group of Muslims turns up. Avicenna, Averroës, and Saladin are among those virtuous heathens who, along with Hector, Aeneas, Abraham, Socrates, Plato, and Aristotle, are confined to the first circle of the Inferno, there to suffer a minimal (and even honorable) punishment for not having had the benefit of Christian revelation. Dante, of course, admires their great virtues and accomplishments, but because they were not Christians he must condemn them, however lightly, to Hell. Eternity is a great leveler of distinctions, it is true, but the special anachronisms and anomalies of putting pre-Christian luminaries in the same category of "heathen" damnation with post-Christian Muslims does not trouble Dante. Even though the Koran specifies Jesus as a prophet, Dante chooses to consider the great Muslim philosophers and king as having been fundamentally ignorant of Christianity. That they can also inhabit the same distinguished level as the heroes and sages of classical antiquity is an ahistorical vision similar to Raphael's in his fresco *The School of Athens,* in which Averroës rubs elbows on the academy floor with Socrates and Plato (similar to Fénelon's *Dialogues des morts* [1700–1718], where a discussion takes place between Socrates and Confucius).

The discriminations and refinements of Dante's poetic grasp of Islam are an instance of the schematic, almost cosmological inevitability with which Islam and its designated representatives are creatures of Western geographical, historical, and above all, moral apprehension. Empirical data about the Orient or about any of its parts count for very little; what matters and is decisive is what I have been calling the Orientalist vision, a vision by no means confined to the professional scholar, but rather the common possession of all who have thought about the Orient in the West. Dante's powers as a poet intensify, make more rather than less representative, these perspectives on the Orient. Mohammed, Saladin,

Averroës, and Avicenna are fixed in a visionary cosmology—fixed, laid out, boxed in, imprisoned, without much regard for anything except their "function" and the patterns they realize on the stage on which they appear. Isaiah Berlin has described the effect of such attitudes in the following way:

> In [such a] . . . cosmology the world of men (and, in some versions, the entire universe) is a single, all-inclusive hierarchy; so that to explain why each object in it is as, and where, and when it is, and does what it does, is *eo ipso* to say what its goal is, how far it successfully fulfills it, and what are the relations of coordination and subordination between the goals of the various goal-pursuing entities in the harmonious pyramid which they collectively form. If this is a true picture of reality, then historical explanation, like every other form of explanation, must consist, above all, in the attribution of individuals, groups, nations, species, each to its own proper place in the universal pattern. To know the "cosmic" place of a thing or a person is to say what it is and what it does, and at the same time why it should be and do as it is and does. Hence to be and to have value, to exist and to have a function (and to fulfill it more or less successfully) are one and the same. The pattern, and it alone, brings into being and causes to pass away and confers purpose, that is to say, value and meaning, on all there is. To understand is to perceive patterns. . . . The more inevitable an event or an action or a character can be exhibited as being, the better it has been understood, the profounder the researcher's insight, the nearer we are to the one ultimate truth.

This attitude is profoundly anti-empirical.[51]

And so, indeed, is the Orientalist attitude in general. It shares with magic and with mythology the self-containing, self-reinforcing character of a closed system, in which objects are what they are *because* they are what they are, for once, for all time, for ontological reasons that no empirical material can either dislodge or alter. The European encounter with the Orient, and specifically with Islam, strengthened this system of representing the Orient and, as has been suggested by Henri Pirenne, turned Islam into the very epitome of an outsider against which the whole of European civilization from the Middle Ages on was founded. The decline of the Roman Empire as a result of the barbarian invasions had the paradoxical effect of incorporating barbarian ways into Roman and Mediterranean culture, Romania; whereas, Pirenne argues, the consequence of the

Islamic invasions beginning in the seventh century was to move the center of European culture away from the Mediterranean, which was then an Arab province, and towards the North. "Germanism began to play its part in history. Hitherto the Roman tradition had been uninterrupted. Now an original Romano–Germanic civilization was about to develop." Europe was shut in on itself: the Orient, when it was not merely a place in which one traded, was culturally, intellectually, spiritually *outside* Europe and European civilization, which, in Pirenne's words, became "one great Christian community, coterminous with the *ecclesia*. . . . The Occident was now living its own life."[52] In Dante's poem, in the work of Peter the Venerable and other Cluniac Orientalists, in the writings of the Christian polemicists against Islam from Guibert of Nogent and Bede to Roger Bacon, William of Tripoli, Burchard of Mount Syon, and Luther, in the *Poema del Cid,* in the *Chanson de Roland,* and in Shakespeare's *Othello* (that "abuser of the world"), the Orient and Islam are always represented as outsiders having a special role to play *inside* Europe.

Imaginative geography, from the vivid portraits to be found in the *Inferno* to the prosaic niches of d'Herbelot's *Bibliothèque orientale,* legitimates a vocabulary, a universe of representative discourse peculiar to the discussion and understanding of Islam and of the Orient. What this discourse considers to be a fact—that Mohammed is an imposter, for example—is a component of the discourse, a statement the discourse compels one to make whenever the name Mohammed occurs. Underlying all the different units of Orientalist discourse—by which I mean simply the vocabulary employed whenever the Orient is spoken or written about—is a set of representative figures, or tropes. These figures are to the actual Orient—or Islam, which is my main concern here—as stylized costumes are to characters in a play; they are like, for example, the cross that Everyman will carry, or the particolored costume worn by Harlequin in a *commedia dell'arte* play. In other words, we need not look for correspondence between the language used to depict the Orient and the Orient itself, not so much because the language is inaccurate but because it is not even trying to be accurate. What it is trying to do, as Dante tried to do in the *Inferno*, is at one and the same time to characterize the Orient as alien and to incorporate it schematically on a theatrical stage whose audience, manager, and actors are *for* Europe, and only for Europe. Hence the vacillation between the familiar and the alien; Mohammed is always the imposter (familiar, because he pretends to be like the Jesus we know) and always the Oriental (alien, because although he is in some ways "like" Jesus, he is after all not like him).

Rather than listing all the figures of speech associated with the Orient—its strangeness, its difference, its exotic sensuousness, and so forth—we can generalize about them as they were handed down through the Renaissance. They are all declarative and self-evident; the tense they employ is the timeless eternal; they convey an impression of repetition and strength; they are always symmetrical to, and yet diametrically inferior to, a European equivalent, which is sometimes specified, sometimes not. For all these functions it is frequently enough to use the simple copula *is*. Thus, Mohammed *is* an imposter, the very phrase canonized in d'Herbelot's *Bibliothèque* and dramatized in a sense by Dante. No background need be given; the evidence necessary to convict Mohammed is contained in the "is." One does not qualify the phrase, neither does it seem necessary to say that Mohammed *was* an imposter, nor need one consider for a moment that it may not be necessary to repeat the statement. It *is* repeated, he *is* an imposter, and each time one says it, he becomes more of an imposter and the author of the statement gains a little more authority in having declared it. Thus Humphrey Prideaux's famous seventeenth-century biography of Mohammed is subtitled *The True Nature of Imposture*. Finally, of course, such categories as imposter (or Oriental, for that matter) imply, indeed require, an opposite that is neither fraudulently something else nor endlessly in need of explicit identification. And that opposite is "Occidental," or in Mohammed's case, Jesus.

Philosophically, then, the kind of language, thought, and vision that I have been calling Orientalism very generally is a form of radical realism; anyone employing Orientalism, which is the habit for dealing with questions, objects, qualities, and regions deemed Oriental, will designate, name, point to, fix what he is talking or thinking about with a word or phrase, which then is considered either to have acquired, or more simply to be, reality. Rhetorically speaking, Orientalism is absolutely anatomical and enumerative: to use its vocabulary is to engage in the particularizing and dividing of things Oriental into manageable parts. Psychologically, Orientalism is a form of paranoia, knowledge of another kind, say, from ordinary historical knowledge. These are a few of the results, I think, of imaginative geography and of the dramatic boundaries it draws. There are some specifically modern transmutations of these Orientalized results, however, to which I must now turn.

III
Projects

It is necessary to examine the more flamboyant operational successes of Orientalism if only to judge how exactly wrong (and how totally opposite to the truth) was the grandly menacing idea expressed by Michelet, that "the Orient advances, invincible, fatal to the gods of light by the charm of its dreams, by the magic of its *chiaroscuro*."[53] Cultural, material, and intellectual relations between Europe and the Orient have gone through innumerable phases, even though the line between East and West has made a certain constant impression upon Europe. Yet in general it was the West that moved upon the East, not vice versa. *Orientalism* is the generic term that I have been employing to describe the Western approach to the Orient; Orientalism is the discipline by which the Orient was (and is) approached systematically, as a topic of learning, discovery, and practice. But in addition I have been using the word to designate that collection of dreams, images, and vocabularies available to anyone who has tried to talk about what lies east of the dividing line. These two aspects of Orientalism are not incongruent, since by use of them both Europe could advance securely and unmetaphorically upon the Orient. Here I should like principally to consider material evidence of this advance.

Islam excepted, the Orient for Europe was until the nineteenth century a domain with a continuous history of unchallenged Western dominance. This is patently true of the British experience in India, the Portuguese experience in the East Indies, China, and Japan, and the French and Italian experiences in various regions of the Orient. There were occasional instances of native intransigence to disturb the idyll, as when in 1638–1639 a group of Japanese Christians threw the Portuguese out of the area; by and large, however, only the Arab and Islamic Orient presented Europe with an unresolved challenge on the political, intellectual, and for a time, economic levels. For much of its history, then, Orientalism carries within it the stamp of a problematic European attitude towards Islam, and it is this acutely sensitive aspect of Orientalism around which my interest in this study turns.

Doubtless Islam was a real provocation in many ways. It lay uneasily close to Christianity, geographically and culturally. It drew on the Judeo-Hellenic traditions, it borrowed creatively from Christianity, it could boast of unrivaled military and political successes. Nor was this all. The Islamic lands sit adjacent to and even on top of the Biblical lands; moreover, the heart of the Islamic domain has always been the region closest to Europe, what has been called the Near Orient or Near East. Arabic and Hebrew are Semitic languages, and together they dispose and redispose of material that is urgently important to Christianity. From the end of the seventh century until the battle of Lepanto in 1571, Islam in either its Arab, Ottoman, or North African and Spanish form dominated or effectively threatened European Christianity. That Islam outstripped and outshone Rome cannot have been absent from the mind of any European past or present. Even Gibbon was no exception, as is evident in the following passage from the *Decline and Fall*:

> In the victorious days of the Roman republic it had been the aim of the senate to confine their councils and legions to a single war, and completely to suppress a first enemy before they provoked the hostilities of a second. These timid maxims of policy were disdained by the magnanimity or enthusiasm of the Arabian caliphs. With the same vigour and success they invaded the successors of Augustus and Artaxerxes; and the rival monarchies at the same instant became the prey of an enemy whom they had so long been accustomed to despise. In the ten years of the administration of Omar, the Saracens reduced to his obedience thirty-six thousand cities or castles, destroyed four thousand churches or temples of the unbelievers, and edified fourteen hundred moschs for the exercise of the religion of Mohammed. One hundred years after his flight from Mecca the arms and reign of his successors extended from India to the Atlantic Ocean, over the various and distant provinces. . . .[54]

When the term *Orient* was not simply a synonym for the Asiatic East as a whole, or taken as generally denoting the distant and exotic, it was most rigorously understood as applying to the Islamic

Orient. This "militant" Orient came to stand for what Henri Baudet has called "the Asiatic tidal wave."[55] Certainly this was the case in Europe through the middle of the eighteenth century, the point at which repositories of "Oriental" knowledge like d'Herbelot's *Bibliothèque orientale* stop meaning primarily Islam, the Arabs, or the Ottomans. Until that time cultural memory gave understandable prominence to such relatively distant events as the fall of Constantinople, the Crusades, and the conquest of Sicily and Spain, but if these signified the menacing Orient they did not at the same time efface what remained of Asia.

For there was always India, where, after Portugal pioneered the first bases of European presence in the early sixteenth century, Europe, and primarily England after a long period (from 1600 to 1758) of essentially commercial activity, dominated politically as an occupying force. Yet India itself never provided an indigenous threat to Europe. Rather it was because native authority crumbled there and opened the land to inter-European rivalry and to outright European political control that the Indian Orient could be treated by Europe with such proprietary hauteur—never with the sense of danger reserved for Islam.[56] Nevertheless, between this hauteur and anything like accurate positive knowledge there existed a vast disparity. D'Herbelot's entries for Indo-Persian subjects in the *Bibliothèque* were all based on Islamic sources, and it is true to say that until the early nineteenth century "Oriental languages" was considered a synonym for "Semitic languages." The Oriental renaissance of which Quinet spoke served the function of expanding some fairly narrow limits, in which Islam was the catchall Oriental example.[57] Sanskrit, Indian religion, and Indian history did not acquire the status of scientific knowledge until after Sir William Jones's efforts in the late eighteenth century, and even Jones's interest in India came to him by way of his prior interest in and knowledge of Islam.

It is not surprising, then, that the first major work of Oriental scholarship after d'Herbelot's *Bibliothèque* was Simon Ockley's *History of the Saracens*, whose first volume appeared in 1708. A recent historian of Orientalism has opined that Ockley's attitude towards the Muslims—that to them is owed what was first known of philosophy by European Christians—"shocked painfully" his European audience. For not only did Ockley make this Islamic pre-eminence clear in his work; he also "gave Europe its first authentic and substantial taste of the Arab viewpoint touching the wars with Byzantium and Persia."[58] However, Ockley was careful to dissociate himself from the infectious influence of Islam, and unlike his colleague William Whiston (Newton's successor at Cambridge), he always made it clear that Islam was an outrageous heresy. For his Islamic enthusiasm, on the other hand, Whiston was expelled from Cambridge in 1709.

Access to Indian (Oriental) riches had always to be made by first crossing the Islamic provinces and by withstanding the dangerous effect of Islam as a system of quasi-Arian belief. And at least for the larger segment of the eighteenth century, Britain and France were successful. The Ottoman Empire had long since settled into a (for Europe) comfortable senescence, to be inscribed in the nineteenth century as the "Eastern Question." Britain and France fought each other in India between 1744 and 1748 and again between 1756 and 1763, until, in 1769, the British emerged in practical economic and political control of the subcontinent. What was more inevitable than that Napoleon should choose to harass Britain's Oriental empire by first intercepting its Islamic throughway, Egypt?

Although it was almost immediately preceded by at least two major Orientalist projects, Napoleon's invasion of Egypt in 1798 and his foray into Syria have had by far the greater consequence for the modern history of Orientalism. Before Napoleon only two efforts (both by scholars) had been made to invade the Orient by stripping it of its veils and also by going beyond the comparative shelter of the Biblical Orient. The first was by Abraham-Hyacinthe Anquetil-Duperron (1731–1805), an eccentric theoretician of egalitarianism, a man who managed in his head to reconcile Jansenism with orthodox Catholicism and Brahmanism, and who traveled to Asia in order to prove the actual primitive existence of a Chosen People and of the Biblical genealogies. Instead he overshot his early goal and traveled as far east as Surat, there to find a cache of Avestan texts, there also to complete his translation of the Avesta. Raymond Schwab has said of the mysterious Avestan fragment that set Anquetil off on his voyages that whereas "the scholars looked at the famous fragment of Oxford and then returned to their studies, Anquetil looked, and then went to India." Schwab also remarks that Anquetil and Voltaire, though temperamentally and ideologically at hopeless odds with each other, had a similar interest in the Orient and the Bible, "the one to make the Bible more indisputable, the other to make it more unbelievable." Ironically, Anquetil's Avesta translations served Voltaire's purposes, since Anquetil's discoveries "soon led to criticism of the very [Biblical] texts which had hitherto been considered to be revealed texts." The net effect of Anquetil's expedition is well described by Schwab:

> In 1759, Anquetil finished his translation of the *Avesta* at Surat; in 1786 that of the *Upanishads* in Paris—he had dug a channel between the hemispheres of human genius, correcting and expanding the old humanism of the Mediterranean basin. Less than fifty years earlier, his compatriots were asked what it was like to be Persian, when he taught them how to compare the monuments of the Persians to those of the Greeks. Before him, one looked for information on the remote past of our planet exclusively among the great Latin, Greek, Jewish, and Arabic writers. The Bible was regarded as a lonely rock, an aerolite. A universe in writing was available, but scarcely anyone seemed to suspect the immensity of those unknown lands. The realization began with his translation of the *Avesta*, and reached dizzying heights owing to the exploration in Central Asia of the languages that multiplied after Babel. Into our schools, up to that time limited to the narrow Greco-Latin heritage of the Renaissance [of which much had been transmitted to Europe by Islam], he interjected a vision of innumerable civilizations from ages past, of an infinity of literatures; moreover the few European provinces were not the only places to have left their mark in history.[59]

For the first time, the Orient was revealed to Europe in the materiality of its texts, languages, and civilizations. Also for the first time, Asia acquired a precise intellectual and historical dimension with which to buttress the myths of its geographic distance and vastness. By one of those inevitable contracting compensations for a sudden cultural expansion, Anquetil's Oriental labors were succeeded by William Jones's, the second of the pre-Napoleonic projects I mentioned above. Whereas Anquetil opened large vistas, Jones closed them down, codifying, tabulating, comparing. Before he left England for India in 1783, Jones was already a master of Arabic, Hebrew, and Persian. These seemed perhaps the least of his accomplishments: he was also a poet, a jurist, a polyhistor, a classicist, and an indefatigable scholar whose powers would recommend him to such as Benjamin Franklin, Edmund Burke, William Pitt, and Samuel Johnson. In due course he was appointed to "an honorable and profitable place in the Indies," and immediately upon his arrival there to take up a post with the East India Company began the course of personal study that was to gather in, to rope off, to domesticate the Orient and thereby turn it into a province of European learning. For his personal work, entitled "Objects of Enquiry During My Residence in Asia" he enumerated among the topics of his investigation "the Laws of the Hindus and Moham- medans, Modern Politics and Geography of Hindustan, Best Mode of Governing Bengal, Arithmetic and Geometry, and Mixed Sciences of the Asiaticks, Medicine, Chemistry, Surgery, and Anatomy of the Indians, Natural Productions of India, Poetry, Rhetoric and Morality of Asia, Music of the Eastern Nations, Trade, Manufacture, Agriculture, and Commerce of India," and so forth. On August 17, 1787, he wrote unassumingly to Lord Althorp that "it is my ambition to know *India* better than any other European ever knew it." Here is where Balfour in 1910 could find the first adumbration of his claim as an Englishman to know the Orient more and better than anyone else.

Jones's official work was the law, an occupation with symbolic significance for the history of Orientalism. Seven years before Jones arrived in India, Warren Hastings had decided that Indians were to be ruled by their own laws, a more enterprising project than it appears at first glance since the Sanskrit code of laws existed then for practical use only in a Persian translation, and no Englishman at the time knew Sanskrit well enough to consult the original texts. A company official, Charles Wilkins, first mastered Sanskrit, then began to translate the *Institutes* of Manu; in this labor he was soon to be assisted by Jones. (Wilkins, incidentally, was the first trans- lator of the Bhagavad-Gita.) In January 1784 Jones convened the inaugural meeting of the Asiatic Society of Bengal, which was to be for India what the Royal Society was for England. As first president of the society and as magistrate, Jones acquired the effec- tive knowledge of the Orient and of Orientals that was later to make him the undisputed founder (the phrase is A. J. Arberry's) of Orientalism. To rule and to learn, then to compare Orient with Occident: these were Jones's goals, which, with an irresistible im- pulse always to codify, to subdue the infinite variety of the Orient to "a complete digest" of laws, figures, customs, and works, he is believed to have achieved. His most famous pronouncement indi- cates the extent to which modern Orientalism, even in its philo- sophical beginnings, was a comparative discipline having for its principal goal the grounding of the European languages in a distant, and harmless, Oriental source:

The *Sanscrit* language, whatever be its antiquity, is of a wonderful structure; more perfect than the *Greek*, more copious than the *Latin*, and more exquisitely refined than either, yet bearing to both of them a stronger affinity, both in the roots of verbs and in the forms of grammar, than could possibly have been produced by accident; so strong indeed, that no philologer could examine them all three without believing them to have sprung from some common source.[60]

Many of the early English Orientalists in India were, like Jones, legal scholars, or else, interestingly enough, they were medical men with strong missionary leanings. So far as one can tell, most of them were imbued with the dual purpose of investigating "the sciences and the arts of Asia, with the hope of facilitating ameliorations there and of advancing knowledge and improving the arts at home":[61] so the common Orientalist goal was stated in the *Centenary Volume* of the Royal Asiatic Society founded in 1823 by Henry Thomas Colebrooke. In their dealings with the modern Orientals, the early professional Orientalists like Jones had only two roles to fulfill, yet we cannot today fault them for strictures placed on their humanity by the official *Occidental* character of their presence in the Orient. They were either judges or they were doctors. Even Edgar Quinet, writing more metaphysically than realistically, was dimly aware of this therapeutic relationship. "L'Asie a les prophètes," he said in *Le Génie des religions*; "L'Europe a les docteurs."[62] Proper knowledge of the Orient proceeded from a thorough study of the classical texts, and only after that to an application of those texts to the modern Orient. Faced with the obvious decrepitude and political impotence of the modern Oriental, the European Orientalist found it his duty to rescue some portion of a lost, past classical Oriental grandeur in order to "facilitate ameliorations" in the present Orient. What the European took from the classical Oriental past was a vision (and thousands of facts and artifacts) which only he could employ to the best advantage; to the modern Oriental he gave facilitation and amelioration—and, too, the benefit of his judgment as to what was best for the modern Orient.

It was characteristic of all Orientalist projects before Napoleon's that very little could be done in advance of the project to prepare for its success. Anquetil and Jones, for example, learned what they did about the Orient only after they got there. They were confronting, as it were, the whole Orient, and only after a while and after considerable improvising could they whittle it down to a smaller province. Napoleon, on the other hand, wanted nothing less than to take the whole of Egypt, and his advance preparations were of unparalleled magnitude and thoroughness. Even so, these preparations were almost fanatically schematic and—if I may use the word—textual, which are features that will bear some analysis here. Three things above all else seem to have been in Napoleon's mind as he readied himself while in Italy in 1797 for his next military move. First, aside from the still threatening power of England, his military successes that had culminated in the Treaty of Campo Formio left him no other place to turn for additional glory than the East. Moreover, Talleyrand had recently animadverted on "les avantages à retirer de colonies nouvelles dans les circonstances présentes," and this notion, along with the appealing prospect of hurting Britain, drew him eastwards. Secondly, Napoleon had been attracted to the Orient since his adolescence; his youthful manuscripts, for example, contain a summary he made of Marigny's *Histoire des Arabes*, and it is evident from all of his writing and conversation that he was steeped, as Jean Thiry has put it, in the memories and glories that were attached to Alexander's Orient generally and to Egypt in particular.[63] Thus the idea of reconquering Egypt as a new Alexander proposed itself to him, allied with the additional benefit of acquiring a new Islamic colony at England's expense. Thirdly, Napoleon considered Egypt a likely project precisely because he knew it tactically, strategically, historically, and—not to be underestimated—textually, that is, as something one read about and knew through the writings of recent as well as classical European authorities. The point in all this is that for Napoleon Egypt was a project that acquired reality in his mind, and later in his preparations for its conquest, through experiences that belong to the realm of ideas and myths culled from texts, not empirical reality. His plans for Egypt therefore became the first in a long series of European encounters with the Orient in which the Orientalist's special expertise was put directly to functional colonial use; for at the crucial instant when an Orientalist had to decide whether his loyalties and sympathies lay with the Orient or with the conquering West, he always chose the latter, from Napoleon's time on. As for the emperor himself, he saw the Orient only as it had been encoded first by classical texts and then by Orientalist experts, whose vision, based on classical texts, seemed a useful substitute for any actual encounter with the real Orient.

Napoleon's enlistment of several dozen "savants" for his Egyptian Expedition is too well known to require detail here. His idea was to build a sort of living archive for the expedition, in the form of studies conducted on all topics by the members of the Institut d'Égypte, which he founded. What is perhaps less well known is Napoleon's prior reliance upon the work of the Comte de Volney, a French traveler whose *Voyage en Égypte et en Syrie* appeared in two volumes in 1787. Aside from a short personal preface inform- ing the reader that the sudden acquisition of some money (his inheritance) made it possible for him to take the trip east in 1783, Volney's *Voyage* is an almost oppressively impersonal document. Volney evidently saw himself as a scientist, whose job it was always to record the "état" of something he saw. The climax of the *Voyage* occurs in the second volume, an account of Islam as a religion.[64] Volney's views were canonically hostile to Islam as a religion and as a system of political institutions; nevertheless Napoleon found this work and Volney's *Considérations sur la guerre actuel de Turcs* (1788) of particular importance. For Volney after all was a canny Frenchman, and—like Chateaubriand and Lamartine a quarter- century after him—he eyed the Near Orient as a likely place for the realization of French colonial ambition. What Napoleon profited from in Volney was the enumeration, in ascending order of difficulty, of the obstacles to be faced in the Orient by any French expeditionary force.

Napoleon refers explicitly to Volney in his reflections on the Egyptian expedition, the *Campagnes d'Égypte et de Syrie, 1798– 1799*, which he dictated to General Bertrand on Saint Helena. Volney, he said, considered that there were three barriers to French hegemony in the Orient and that any French force would therefore have to fight three wars: one against England, a second against the Ottoman Porte, and a third, the most difficult, against the Muslims.[65] Volney's assessment was both shrewd and hard to fault since it was clear to Napoleon, as it would be to anyone who read Volney, that his *Voyage* and the *Considérations* were effective texts to be used by any European wishing to win in the Orient. In other words, Volney's work constituted a handbook for attenuating the human shock a European might feel as he directly experienced the Orient: Read the books, seems to have been Volney's thesis, and far from being disoriented by the Orient, you will compel it to you.

Napoleon took Volney almost literally, but in a characteristically subtle way. From the first moment that the Armée d'Égypte appeared on the Egyptian horizon, every effort was made to convince the Muslims that "nous sommes les vrais musulmans," as Bonaparte's proclamation of July 2, 1798, put it to the people of Alexandria.[66] Equipped with a team of Orientalists (and sitting on board a flagship called the *Orient*), Napoleon used Egyptian enmity towards the Mamelukes and appeals to the revolutionary idea of equal opportunity for all to wage a uniquely benign and selective war against Islam. What more than anything impressed the first Arab chronicler of the expedition, Abd-al-Rahman al-Jabarti, was Napoleon's use of scholars to manage his contacts with the natives —that and the impact of watching a modern European intellectual establishment at close quarters.[67] Napoleon tried everywhere to prove that he was fighting *for* Islam; everything he said was translated into Koranic Arabic, just as the French army was urged by its command always to remember the Islamic sensibility. (Compare, in this regard, Napoleon's tactics in Egypt with the tactics of the *Requerimiento*, a document drawn up in 1513—in Spanish—by the Spaniards to be read aloud to the Indians: "We shall take you and your wives and your children, and shall make slaves of them, and as such sell and dispose of them as their Highnesses [the King and Queen of Spain] may command; and we shall take away your goods, and shall do you all the mischief and damage that we can, as to vassals who do not obey," etc. etc.[68]) When it seemed obvious to Napoleon that his force was too small to impose itself on the Egyptians, he then tried to make the local imams, cadis, muftis, and ulemas interpret the Koran in favor of the Grande Armée. To this end, the sixty ulemas who taught at the Azhar were invited to his quarters, given full military honors, and then allowed to be flattered by Napoleon's admiration for Islam and Mohammed and by his obvious veneration for the Koran, with which he seemed perfectly familiar. This worked, and soon the population of Cairo seemed to have lost its distrust of the occupiers.[69] Napoleon later gave his deputy Kleber strict instructions after he left always to administer Egypt through the Orientalists and the religious Islamic leaders whom they could win over; any other politics was too expensive and foolish.[70] Hugo thought that he grasped the tactful glory of Napoleon's Oriental expedition in his poem "Lui":

> Au Nil je le retrouve encore.
> L'Égypte resplendit des feux de son aurore;
> Son astre impérial se lève à l'orient.

Vainqueur, enthousiaste, éclatant de prestiges,
Prodige, il étonna la terre des prodiges.
Les vieux scheiks vénéraient l'émir jeune et prudent;
Le peuple redoutait ses armes inouïes;
Sublime, il apparut aux tribus éblouies
Comme un Mahomet d'occident.[71]

(By the Nile, I find him once again.
Egypt shines with the fires of his dawn;
His imperial orb rises in the Orient.

Victor, enthusiast, bursting with achievements,
Prodigious, he stunned the land of prodigies.
The old sheikhs venerated the young and prudent emir.
The people dreaded his unprecedented arms;
Sublime, he appeared to the dazzled tribes
Like a Mahomet of the Occident.)

Such a triumph could only have been prepared *before* a military expedition, perhaps only by someone who had no prior experience of the Orient except what books and scholars told him. The idea of taking along a full-scale academy is very much an aspect of this textual attitude to the Orient. And this attitude in turn was bolstered by specific Revolutionary decrees (particularly the one of 10 Germinal An III—March 30, 1793—establishing an *école publique* in the Bibliothèque nationale to teach Arabic, Turkish, and Persian)[72] whose object was the rationalist one of dispelling mystery and institutionalizing even the most recondite knowledge. Thus many of Napoleon's Orientalist translators were students of Sylvestre de Sacy, who, beginning in June 1796, was the first and only teacher of Arabic at the École publique des langues orientales. Sacy later became the teacher of nearly every major Orientalist in Europe, where his students dominated the field for about three-quarters of a century. Many of them were politically useful, in the ways that several had been to Napoleon in Egypt.

But dealings with the Muslims were only a part of Napoleon's project to dominate Egypt. The other part was to render it completely open, to make it totally accessible to European scrutiny. From being a land of obscurity and a part of the Orient hitherto known at second hand through the exploits of earlier travelers, scholars, and conquerors, Egypt was to become a department of French learning. Here too the textual and schematic attitudes are evident. The Institut, with its teams of chemists, historians, biol-

ogists, archaeologists, surgeons, and antiquarians, was the learned
division of the army. Its job was no less aggressive: to put Egypt
into modern French; and unlike the Abbé Le Mascrier's 1735
Description de l'Égypte, Napoleon's was to be a universal undertaking. Almost from the first moments of the occupation Napoleon
saw to it that the Institut began its meetings, its experiments—
its fact-finding mission, as we would call it today. Most important,
everything said, seen, and studied was to be recorded, and indeed
was recorded in that great collective appropriation of one country
by another, the *Description de l'Égypte*, published in twenty-three
enormous volumes between 1809 and 1828.[73]

The *Description's* uniqueness is not only in its size, or even in the
intelligence of its contributors, but in its attitude to its subject
matter, and it is this attitude that makes it of great interest for the
study of modern Orientalist projects. The first few pages of its
préface historique, written by Jean-Baptiste-Joseph Fourier, the
Institut's secretary, make it clear that in "doing" Egypt the scholars
were also grappling directly with a kind of unadulterated cultural,
geographical, and historical significance. Egypt was the focal point
of the relationships between Africa and Asia, between Europe and
the East, between memory and actuality.

> Placed between Africa and Asia, and communicating easily with
> Europe, Egypt occupies the center of the ancient continent. This
> country presents only great memories; it is the homeland of the
> arts and conserves innumerable monuments; its principal temples
> and the palaces inhabited by its kings still exist, even though its
> least ancient edifices had already been built by the time of the
> Trojan War. Homer, Lycurgus, Solon, Pythagoras, and Plato all
> went to Egypt to study the sciences, religion, and the laws.
> Alexander founded an opulent city there, which for a long time
> enjoyed commercial supremacy and which witnessed Pompey,
> Caesar, Mark Antony, and Augustus deciding between them the
> fate of Rome and that of the entire world. It is therefore proper
> for this country to attract the attention of illustrious princes who
> rule the destiny of nations.
>
> No considerable power was ever amassed by any nation,
> whether in the West or in Asia, that did not also turn that nation
> toward Egypt, which was regarded in some measure as its natural
> lot.[74]

Because Egypt was saturated with meaning for the arts, sciences,
and government, its role was to be the stage on which actions of a

world-historical importance would take place. By taking Egypt, then, a modern power would naturally demonstrate its strength and justify history; Egypt's own destiny was to be annexed, to Europe preferably. In addition, this power would also enter a history whose common element was defined by figures no less great than Homer, Alexander, Caesar, Plato, Solon, and Pythagoras, who graced the Orient with their prior presence there. The Orient, in short, existed as a set of values attached, not to its modern realities, but to a series of valorized contacts it had had with a distant European past. This is a pure example of the textual, schematic attitude I have been referring to.

Fourier continues similarly for over a hundred pages (each page, incidentally, is a square meter in size, as if the project and the size of the page had been thought of as possessing comparable scale). Out of the free-floating past, however, he must justify the Napoleonic expedition as something that needed to be undertaken when it happened. The dramatic perspective is never abandoned. Conscious of his European audience and of the Oriental figures he was manipulating, he writes:

> One remembers the impression made on the whole of Europe by the astounding news that the French were in the Orient. . . . This great project was meditated in silence, and was prepared with such activity and secrecy that the worried vigilance of our enemies was deceived; only at the moment that it happened did they learn that it had been conceived, undertaken, and carried out successfully. . . .

So dramatic a *coup de théâtre* had its advantages for the Orient as well:

> This country, which has transmitted its knowledge to so many nations, is today plunged into barbarism.

Only a hero could bring all these factors together, which is what Fourier now describes:

> Napoleon appreciated the influence that this event would have on the relations between Europe, the Orient, and Africa, on Mediterranean shipping, and on Asia's destiny. . . . Napoleon wanted to offer a useful European example to the Orient, and finally also to make the inhabitants' lives more pleasant, as well as to procure for them all the advantages of a perfected civilization.
>
> None of this would be possible without a continuous application to the project of the arts and sciences.[75]

To restore a region from its present barbarism to its former classical greatness; to instruct (for its own benefit) the Orient in the ways of the modern West; to subordinate or underplay military power in order to aggrandize the project of glorious knowledge acquired in the process of political domination of the Orient; to formulate the Orient, to give it shape, identity, definition with full recognition of its place in memory, its importance to imperial strategy, and its "natural" role as an appendage to Europe; to dignify all the knowledge collected during colonial occupation with the title "contribution to modern learning" when the natives had neither been consulted nor treated as anything except as pretexts for a text whose usefulness was not to the natives; to feel oneself as a European in command, almost at will, of Oriental history, time, and geography; to institute new areas of specialization; to establish new disciplines; to divide, deploy, schematize, tabulate, index, and record everything in sight (and out of sight); to make out of every observable detail a generalization and out of every generalization an immutable law about the Oriental nature, temperament, mentality, custom, or type; and, above all, to transmute living reality into the stuff of texts, to possess (or think one possesses) actuality mainly because nothing in the Orient seems to resist one's powers: these are the features of Orientalist projection entirely realized in the *Description de l'Égypte*, itself enabled and reinforced by Napoleon's wholly Orientalist engulfment of Egypt by the instruments of Western knowledge and power. Thus Fourier concludes his preface by announcing that history will remember how "Égypte fut le théâtre de sa [Napoleon's] gloire, et préserve de l'oubli toutes les circonstances de cet évènement extraordinaire."[76]

The *Description* thereby displaces Egyptian or Oriental history as a history possessing its own coherence, identity, and sense. Instead, history as recorded in the *Description* supplants Egyptian or Oriental history by identifying itself directly and immediately with world history, a euphemism for European history. To save an event from oblivion is in the Orientalist's mind the equivalent of turning the Orient into a theater for his representations of the Orient: this is almost exactly what Fourier says. Moreover, the sheer power of having described the Orient in modern Occidental terms lifts the Orient from the realms of silent obscurity where it has lain neglected (except for the inchoate murmurings of a vast but undefined sense of its own past) into the clarity of modern European science. There this new Orient figures as—for instance, in Geoffroy Saint-Hilaire's biological theses in the *Description*—the confirmation of laws of zoological specialization formulated by Buffon.[77] Or it serves as a "contraste frappante avec les habitudes des nations Européennes,"[78] in which the "bizarre jouissances" of Orientals serve to highlight the sobriety and rationality of Occidental habits. Or, to cite one more use for the Orient, equivalents of those Oriental physiological characteristics that made possible the successful embalming of bodies are sought for in European bodies, so that chevaliers fallen on the field of honor can be preserved as lifelike relics of Napoleon's great Oriental campaign.[79]

Yet the military failure of Napoleon's occupation of Egypt did not also destroy the fertility of its over-all projection for Egypt or the rest of the Orient. Quite literally, the occupation gave birth to the entire modern experience of the Orient as interpreted from within the universe of discourse founded by Napoleon in Egypt, whose agencies of domination and dissemination included the Institut and the *Description*. The idea, as it has been characterized by Charles-Roux, was that Egypt "restored to prosperity, regenerated by wise and enlightened administration . . . would shed its civilizing rays upon all its Oriental neighbors."[80] True, the other European powers would seek to compete in this mission, none more than England. But what would happen as a continuing legacy of the common Occidental mission to the Orient—despite inter-European squabbling, indecent competition, or outright war—would be the creation of new projects, new visions, new enterprises combining additional parts of the old Orient with the conquering European spirit. After Napoleon, then, the very language of Orientalism changed radically. Its descriptive realism was upgraded and became not merely a style of representation but a language, indeed a means of *creation*. Along with the *langues mères*, as those forgotten dormant sources for the modern European demotics were entitled by Antoine Fabre d'Olivet, the Orient was reconstructed, reassembled, crafted, in short, *born* out of the Orientalists' efforts. The *Description* became the master type of all further efforts to bring the Orient closer to Europe, thereafter to absorb it entirely and—centrally important—to cancel, or at least subdue and reduce, its strangeness and, in the case of Islam, its hostility. For the Islamic Orient would henceforth appear as a category denoting the Orientalists' power and not the Islamic people as humans nor their history as history.

Thus out of the Napoleonic expedition there issued a whole

series of textual children, from Chateaubriand's *Itinéraire* to Lamartine's *Voyage en Orient* to Flaubert's *Salammbô*, and in the same
tradition, Lane's *Manners and Customs of the Modern Egyptians* and
Richard Burton's *Personal Narrative of a Pilgrimage to al-Madinah
and Meccah*. What binds them together is not only their common
background in Oriental legend and experience but also their learned
reliance on the Orient as a kind of womb out of which they were
brought forth. If paradoxically these creations turned out to be
highly stylized simulacra, elaborately wrought imitations of what
a live Orient might be thought to look like, that by no means
detracts either from the strength of their imaginative conception or
from the strength of European mastery of the Orient, whose
prototypes respectively were Cagliostro, the great European im-
personator of the Orient, and Napoleon, its first modern conqueror.

Artistic or textual work was not the only product of the
Napoleonic expedition. There were, in addition and certainly more
influential, the scientific project, whose chief instance is Ernest
Renan's *Système comparé et histoire générale des langues sémitiques*, completed in 1848 for—neatly enough—the Prix Volney,
and the geopolitical project, of which Ferdinand de Lesseps's Suez
Canal and England's occupation of Egypt in 1882 are prime instances. The difference between the two is not only in manifest
scale but also in quality of Orientalist conviction. Renan truly
believed that he had re-created the Orient, as it really was, in his
work. De Lesseps, on the other hand, always was somewhat awed
by the newness his project had released out of the old Orient, and
this sense communicated itself to everyone for whom the opening
of the canal in 1869 was no ordinary event. In his *Excursionist
and Tourist Advertiser* for July 1, 1869, Thomas Cook's enthusiasm
carries on de Lesseps's:

> On November the 17th, the greatest engineering feat of the present
> century is to have its success celebrated by a magnificent inaugura-
> tion fête, at which nearly every European royal family will have
> its special representative. Truly the occasion will be an exceptional
> one. The formation of a line of water communication between
> Europe and the East, has been the thought of centuries, occupying
> in turn the minds of Greeks, Roman, Saxon and Gaul, but it was
> not until within the last few years that modern civilization began
> seriously to set about emulating the labours of the ancient
> Pharaohs, who, many centuries since, constructed a canal between
> the two seas, traces of which remain to this day. . . . Everything

connected with [the modern] works are on the most gigantic scale, and a perusal of a little pamphlet, descriptive of the undertaking, from the pen of the Chevalier de St. Stoess, impresses us most forcibly with the genius of the great Master-mind—M. Ferdinand de Lesseps—to whose perseverance, calm daring and foresight, the dream of ages has at last become a real and tangible fact . . . the project for bringing more closely together the countries of the West and the East, and thus uniting the civilizations of different epochs.[81]

The combination of old ideas with new methods, the bringing together of cultures whose relations to the nineteenth century were different, the genuine imposition of the power of modern technology and intellectual will upon formerly stable and divided geographical entities like East and West: this is what Cook perceives and what, in his journals, speeches, prospectuses, and letters, de Lesseps advertises.

Genealogically, Ferdinand's start was auspicious. Mathieu de Lesseps, his father, had come to Egypt with Napoleon and remained there (as "unofficial French representative," Marlowe says[82]) for four years after the French evacuated it in 1801. Many of Ferdinand's later writings refer back to Napoleon's own interest in digging a canal, which, because he had been misinformed by experts, he never thought was a realizable goal. Infected by the erratic history of canal projects that included French schemes entertained by Richelieu and the Saint-Simonians, de Lesseps returned to Egypt in 1854, there to embark on the undertaking that was eventually completed fifteen years later. He had no real engineering background. Only a tremendous faith in his near-divine skills as builder, mover, and creator kept him going; as his diplomatic and financial talents gained him Egyptian and European support, he seems to have acquired the necessary knowledge to carry matters to completion. More useful, perhaps, he learned how to plant his potential contributors in the world-historical theater and make them see what his "pensée morale," as he called his project, really meant. "Vous envisagez," he told them in 1860, "les immenses services que le rapprochement de l'occident et de l'orient doit rendre à la civilization et au développement de la richesse générale. Le monde attend de vous un grand progrès et vous voulez répondre à l'attente du monde."[83] In accordance with such notions the name of the investment company formed by de Lesseps in 1858 was a charged one and reflected the grandiose plans he cherished: the Compagnie universelle. In 1862 the Académie française offered a prize for an epic on the canal. Bornier, the winner, delivered himself of such hyperbole as the following, none of it fundamentally contradicting de Lesseps's picture of what he was up to:

> Au travail! Ouvriers que notre France envoie,
> Tracez, pour l'univers, cette nouvelle voie!
> Vos pères, les héros, sont venus jusqu'ici;
> Soyez ferme comme aux intrepides,
> Comme eux vous combattez aux pieds des pyramides,
> Et leurs quatre mille ans vous contemplent aussi!
>
> Oui, c'est pour l'univers! Pour l'Asie et l'Europe,
> Pour ces climats lointain que la nuit enveloppe,
> Pour le Chinois perfide et l'Indien demi-nu;
> Pour les peuples heureux, libres, humains et braves,
> Pour les peuples méchants, pour les peuples esclaves,
> Pour ceux à qui le Christ est encore inconnu.[84]

De Lesseps was nowhere more eloquent and resourceful than when he was called upon to justify the enormous expense in money and men the canal would require. He could pour out statistics to enchant any ear; he would quote Herodotus and maritime statistics with equal fluency. In his journal entries for 1864 he cited with approbation Casimir Leconte's observation that an eccentric life would develop significant originality in men, and from originality would come great and unusual exploits.[85] Such exploits were their own justification. Despite its immemorial pedigree of failures, its outrageous cost, its astounding ambitions for altering the way Europe would handle the Orient, the canal was worth the effort. It was a project uniquely able to override the objections of those who were consulted and, in improving the Orient as a whole, to do what scheming Egyptians, perfidious Chinese, and half-naked Indians could never have done for themselves.

The opening ceremonies in November 1869 were an occasion which, no less than the whole history of de Lesseps's machinations, perfectly embodied his ideas. For years his speeches, letters, and pamphlets were laden with a vividly energetic and theatrical vocabulary. In the pursuit of success, he could be found saying of himself (always in the first person plural), we created, fought, disposed, achieved, acted, recognized, persevered, advanced; nothing, he repeated on many occasions, could stop us, nothing was impossible, nothing mattered finally except the realization of "le résultat final, le grand but," which he had conceived, defined, and finally executed. As the papal envoy to the ceremonies spoke on November 16 to the assembled dignitaries, his speech strove desperately to match the intellectual and imaginative spectacle offered by de Lesseps's canal:

> Il est permis d'affirmer que l'heure qui vient de sonner est non seulement une des plus solennelles de ce siècle, mais encore une des plus grandes et des plus décisives qu'ait vues l'humanité, depuis qu'elle a une histoire ci-bas. Ce lieu, où confinent—sans désormais y toucher—l'Afrique et l'Asie, cette grande fête du genre humain, cette assistance auguste et cosmopolite, toutes les races du globe, tous les drapeaux, tous les pavillons, flottant joyeusement sous ce ciel radieux et immense, la croix debout et respectée de tous en face du croissant, que de merveilles, que de contrastes saisissants, que de rêves réputés chimériques devenus de palpables réalités! et, dans cet assemblage de tant de prodiges, que de sujets de réflexions pour le penseur, que de joies dans l'heure présente et, dans les perspectives de l'avenir, que de glorieuses espérances! . . .
>
> Les deux extrémités du globe se rapprochent; en se rapprochant, elles se reconnaissent; en se reconnaissant, tous les hommes, enfants d'un seul et même Dieu, éprouvent le tressaillement joyeux de leur mutuelle fraternité! O Occident! O Orient! rapprochez, regardez, reconnaissez, saluez, étreignez-vous! . . .
>
> Mais derrière le phénomène matériel, le regard du penseur découvre des horizons plus vastes que les espaces mésurables, les horizons sans bornes où mouvent les plus hautes destinées, les plus glorieuses conquêtes, les plus immortelles certitudes du genre humain. . . .
>
> [Dieu] que votre souffle divin plane sur ces eaux! Qu'il y passe et repasse, de l'Occident à l'Orient, de l'Orient à l'Occident! O Dieu! Servez vous de cette voie pour rapprocher les hommes les uns des autres![86]

The whole world seemed crowded in to render homage to a scheme that God could only bless and make use of himself. Old distinctions and inhibitions were dissolved: the Cross faced down the Crescent, the West had come to the Orient never to leave it (until, in July 1956, Gamal Abdel Nasser would activate Egypt's taking over of the canal by pronouncing the name of de Lesseps).

In the Suez Canal idea we see the logical conclusion of Orientalist thought and, more interesting, of Orientalist effort. To the West, Asia had once represented silent distance and alienation; Islam was militant hostility to European Christianity. To overcome such redoubtable constants the Orient needed first to be known, then invaded and possessed, then re-created by scholars, soldiers, and judges who disinterred forgotten languages, histories, races, and cultures in order to posit them—beyond the modern Oriental's ken —as the true classical Orient that could be used to judge and rule the modern Orient. The obscurity faded to be replaced by hothouse entities; the Orient was a scholar's word, signifying what modern Europe had recently made of the still peculiar East. De Lesseps and his canal finally destroyed the Orient's distance, its cloistered intimacy *away* from the West, its perdurable exoticism. Just as a land barrier could be transmuted into a liquid artery, so too the Orient was transubstantiated from resistant hostility into obliging, and submissive, partnership. After de Lesseps no one could speak of the Orient as belonging to another world, strictly speaking. There was only "our" world, "one" world bound together because the Suez Canal had frustrated those last provincials who still believed in the difference between worlds. Thereafter the notion of "Oriental" is an administrative or executive one, and it is subordinate to demographic, economic, and sociological factors. For imperialists like Balfour, or for anti-imperialists like J. A. Hobson, the Oriental, like the African, is a member of a subject race and not exclusively an inhabitant of a geographical area. De Lesseps had melted away the Orient's geographical identity by (almost literally) dragging the Orient into the West and finally dispelling the threat of Islam. New categories and experiences, including the imperialist ones, would emerge, and in time Orientalism would adapt itself to them, but not without some difficulty.

IV
Crisis

It may appear strange to speak about something or someone as holding a *textual* attitude, but a student of literature will understand the phrase more easily if he will recall the kind of view attacked by Voltaire in *Candide*, or even the attitude to reality satirized by Cervantes in *Don Quixote*. What seems unexceptionable good sense to these writers is that it is a fallacy to assume that the swarming, unpredictable, and problematic mess in which human beings live can be understood on the basis of what books—texts—say; to apply what one learns out of a book literally to reality is to risk folly or ruin. One would no more think of using *Amadis of Gaul* to understand sixteenth-century (or present-day) Spain than one would use the Bible to understand, say, the House of Commons. But clearly people have tried and do try to use texts in so simple-minded a way, for otherwise *Candide* and *Don Quixote* would not still have the appeal for readers that they do today. It seems a common human failing to prefer the schematic authority of a text to the disorientations of direct encounters with the human. But is this failing constantly present, or are there circumstances that, more than others, make the textual attitude likely to prevail?

Two situations favor a textual attitude. One is when a human being confronts at close quarters something relatively unknown and threatening and previously distant. In such a case one has recourse not only to what in one's previous experience the novelty resembles but also to what one has read about it. Travel books or guidebooks are about as "natural" a kind of text, as logical in their composition and in their use, as any book one can think of, precisely because of this human tendency to fall back on a text when the uncertainties of travel in strange parts seem to threaten one's equanimity. Many travelers find themselves saying of an experience in a new country that it wasn't what they expected, meaning that it wasn't what a book said it would be. And of course many writers of travel books or guidebooks compose them in order to say that a country *is* like this, or better, that it *is* colorful, expensive, interesting, and so forth. The idea in either case is that people, places, and experiences can always be described by a book, so much so that the book (or text) acquires a greater authority, and use, even than the actuality it describes. The comedy of Fabrice del Dongo's search for the battle of Waterloo is not so much that he fails to find the battle, but that he looks for it as something texts have told him about.

A second situation favoring the textual attitude is the appearance of success. If one reads a book claiming that lions are fierce and then encounters a fierce lion (I simplify, of course), the chances are that one will be encouraged to read more books by that same author, and believe them. But if, in addition, the lion book instructs one how to deal with a fierce lion, and the instructions work perfectly, then not only will the author be greatly believed, he will also be impelled to try his hand at other kinds of written performance. There is a rather complex dialectic of reinforcement by which the experiences of readers in reality are determined by what they have read, and this in turn influences writers to take up subjects defined in advance by readers' experiences. A book on how to handle a fierce lion might then cause a series of books to be produced on such subjects as the fierceness of lions, the origins of fierceness, and so forth. Similarly, as the focus of the text centers more narrowly on the subject—no longer lions but their fierceness —we might expect that the ways by which it is recommended that a lion's fierceness be handled will actually *increase* its fierceness, force it to be fierce since that is what it is, and that is what in essence we know or can *only* know about it.

A text purporting to contain knowledge about something actual, and arising out of circumstances similar to the ones I have just described, is not easily dismissed. Expertise is attributed to it. The authority of academics, institutions, and governments can accrue to it, surrounding it with still greater prestige than its practical successes warrant. Most important, such texts can *create* not only knowledge but also the very reality they appear to describe. In time such knowledge and reality produce a tradition, or what Michel Foucault calls a discourse, whose material presence or weight, not the originality of a given author, is really responsible for the texts produced out of it. This kind of text is composed out of those preexisting units of information deposited by Flaubert in the catalogue of *idées reçues*.

In the light of all this, consider Napoleon and de Lesseps. Everything they knew, more or less, about the Orient came from books written in the tradition of Orientalism, placed in its library of *idées reçues*; for them the Orient, like the fierce lion, was something to be encountered and dealt with to a certain extent *because* the texts made that Orient possible. Such an Orient was silent, available to Europe for the realization of projects that involved but were never directly responsible to the native inhabitants, and unable to resist the projects, images, or mere descriptions devised for it. Earlier in this chapter I called such a relation between Western writing (and its consequences) and Oriental silence the result of and the sign of the West's great cultural strength, its will to power over the Orient. But there is another side to the strength, a side whose existence depends on the pressures of the Orientalist tradition and its textual attitude to the Orient; this side lives its own life, as books about fierce lions will do until lions can talk back. The perspective rarely drawn on Napoleon and de Lesseps—to take two among the many projectors who hatched plans for the Orient—is the one that sees them carrying on in the dimensionless silence of the Orient mainly because the discourse of Orientalism, over and above the Orient's powerlessness to do anything about them, suffused their activity with meaning, intelligibility, and reality. The discourse of Orientalism and what made it possible—in Napoleon's case, a West far more powerful militarily than the Orient—gave them Orientals who could be described in such works as the *Description de l'Égypte* and an Orient that could be cut across as de Lesseps cut across Suez. Moreover, Orientalism gave them their success—at least from their point of view, which had nothing to do with that of the Oriental. Success, in other words, had all the actual human interchange between Oriental and Westerner of the Judge's "said I to myself, said I" in *Trial by Jury*.

Once we begin to think of Orientalism as a kind of Western projection onto and will to govern over the Orient, we will encounter few surprises. For if it is true that historians like Michelet, Ranke, Toqueville, and Burckhardt *emplot* their narratives "as a story of a particular kind,"[87] the same is also true of Orientalists who plotted Oriental history, character, and destiny for hundreds of years. During the nineteenth and twentieth centuries the Orientalists became a more serious quantity, because by then the reaches of imaginative and actual geography had shrunk, because the Oriental-European relationship was determined by an unstoppable European expansion in search of markets, resources, and colonies, and finally, because Orientalism had accomplished its self-metamorphosis from a scholarly discourse to an imperial institution. Evidence of this metamorphosis is already apparent in what I have said of Napoleon, de Lesseps, Balfour, and Cromer. Their projects in the Orient are understandable on only the most rudimentary level as the efforts of men of vision and genius, heroes in Carlyle's sense. In fact Napoleon, de Lesseps, Cromer, and Balfour are far more *regular*, far less unusual, if we recall the schemata of d'Herbelot and Dante and add to them both a modernized, efficient engine (like the nineteenth-century European empire) and a positive twist: since one cannot ontologically obliterate the Orient (as d'Herbelot and Dante perhaps realized), one does have the means to capture it, treat it, describe it, improve it, radically alter it.

The point I am trying to make here is that the transition from a merely textual apprehension, formulation, or definition of the Orient to the putting of all this into practice in the Orient did take place, and that Orientalism had much to do with that—if I may use the word in a literal sense—*preposterous* transition. So far as its strictly scholarly work was concerned (and I find the idea of strictly scholarly work as disinterested and abstract hard to understand: still, we can allow it intellectually), Orientalism did a great many things. During its great age in the nineteenth century it produced scholars; it increased the number of languages taught in the West and the quantity of manuscripts edited, translated, and commented on; in many cases, it provided the Orient with sympathetic European students, genuinely interested in such matters as Sanskrit grammar, Phoenician numismatics, and Arabic poetry. Yet—and here we must be very clear—Orientalism overrode the Orient. As a system of thought about the Orient, it always rose from the specifically human detail to the general transhuman one; an observation about a tenth-century Arab poet multiplied itself into a policy towards (and about) the Oriental mentality in Egypt, Iraq, or Arabia. Similarly a verse from the Koran would be considered the best evidence of an ineradicable Muslim sensuality. Orientalism assumed an unchanging Orient, absolutely different (the reasons change from epoch to epoch) from the West. And Orientalism, in its post-eighteenth-century form, could never revise itself. All this makes Cromer and Balfour, as observers and administrators of the Orient, inevitable.

The closeness between politics and Orientalism, or to put it more circumspectly, the great likelihood that ideas about the Orient drawn from Orientalism can be put to political use, is an important yet extremely sensitive truth. It raises questions about the predisposition towards innocence or guilt, scholarly disinterest or pressure-group complicity, in such fields as black or women's studies. It necessarily provokes unrest in one's conscience about cultural, racial, or historical generalizations, their uses, value, degree of objectivity, and fundamental intent. More than anything else, the political and cultural circumstances in which Western Orientalism has flourished draw attention to the debased position of the Orient or Oriental as an object of study. Can any other than a political master-slave relation produce the Orientalized Orient perfectly characterized by Anwar Abdel Malek?

a) On the level of the *position of the problem*, and the problematic . . . the Orient and Orientals [are considered by Orientalism] as an "object" of study, stamped with an otherness —as all that is different, whether it be "subject" or "object"—but of a constitutive otherness, of an essentialist character. . . . This "object" of study will be, as is customary, passive, non-participating, endowed with a "historical" subjectivity, above all, non-active, non-autonomous, non-sovereign with regard to itself: the only Orient or Oriental or "subject" which could be admitted, at the extreme limit, is the alienated being, philosophically, that is, other than itself in relationship to itself, posed, understood, defined— and acted—by others.

b) On the level of the *thematic*, [the Orientalists] adopt an essentialist conception of the countries, nations and peoples of the Orient under study, a conception which expresses itself through a characterized ethnist typology . . . and will soon proceed with it towards racism.

According to the traditional orientalists, an essence should exist —sometimes even clearly described in metaphysical terms—which constitutes the inalienable and common basis of all the beings considered; this essence is both "historical," since it goes back to the dawn of history, and fundamentally a-historical, since it transfixes the being, "the object" of study, within its inalienable and non-evolutive specificity, instead of defining it as all other beings, states, nations, peoples, and cultures—as a product, a resultant of the vection of the forces operating in the field of historical evolution.

Thus one ends with a typology—based on a real specificity, but detached from history, and, consequently, conceived as being intangible, essential—which makes of the studied "object" another being with regard to whom the studying subject is transcendent; we will have a homo Sinicus, a homo Arabicus (and why not a homo Aegypticus, etc.), a homo Africanus, the man—the "normal man," it is understood—being the European man of the historical period, that is, since Greek antiquity. One sees how much, from the eighteenth to the twentieth century, the hegemonism of possessing minorities, unveiled by Marx and Engels, and the anthropocentrism dismantled by Freud are accompanied by europocentrism in the area of human and social sciences, and more particularly in those in direct relationship with non-European peoples.[88]

Abdel Malek sees Orientalism as having a history which, according to the "Oriental" of the late twentieth century, led it to the impasse described above. Let us now briefly outline that history as

it proceeded through the nineteenth century to accumulate weight
and power, "the hegemonism of possessing minorities," and
anthropocentrism in alliance with Europocentrism. From the last
decades of the eighteenth century and for at least a century and a
half, Britain and France dominated Orientalism as a discipline. The
great philological discoveries in comparative grammar made by
Jones, Franz Bopp, Jakob Grimm, and others were originally indebted to manuscripts brought from the East to Paris and London.
Almost without exception, every Orientalist began his career as a
philologist, and the revolution in philology that produced Bopp,
Sacy, Burnouf, and their students was a comparative science based
on the premise that languages belong to families, of which the Indo-
European and the Semitic are two great instances. From the outset,
then, Orientalism carried forward two traits: (1) a newly found
scientific self-consciousness based on the linguistic importance of
the Orient to Europe, and (2) a proclivity to divide, subdivide, and
redivide its subject matter without ever changing its mind about
the Orient as being always the same, unchanging, uniform, and
radically peculiar object.

Friedrich Schlegel, who learned his Sanskrit in Paris, illustrates
these traits together. Although by the time he published his *Über
die Sprache und Weisheit der Indier* in 1808 Schlegel had prac-
tically renounced his Orientalism, he still held that Sanskrit and
Persian on the one hand and Greek and German on the other had
more affinities with each other than with the Semitic, Chinese,
American, or African languages. Moreover, the Indo-European
family was artistically simple and satisfactory in a way the Semitic,
for one, was not. Such abstractions as this did not trouble Schlegel,
for whom nations, races, minds, and peoples as things one could
talk about passionately—in the ever-narrowing perspective of
populism first adumbrated by Herder—held a lifelong fascination.
Yet nowhere does Schlegel talk about the living, contemporary
Orient. When he said in 1800, "It is in the Orient that we must
search for the highest Romanticism," he meant the Orient of the
Sakuntala, the Zend-Avesta, and the Upanishads. As for the Semites,
whose language was agglutinative, unaesthetic, and mechanical,
they were different, inferior, backward. Schlegel's lectures on
language and on life, history, and literature are full of these discriminations, which he made without the slightest qualification.
Hebrew, he said, was made for prophetic utterance and divination;

the Muslims, however, espoused a "dead empty Theism, a merely negative Unitarian faith."[89]

Much of the racism in Schlegel's strictures upon the Semites and other "low" Orientals was widely diffused in European culture. But nowhere else, unless it be later in the nineteenth century among Darwinian anthropologists and phrenologists, was it made the basis of a scientific subject matter as it was in comparative linguistics or philology. Language and race seemed inextricably tied, and the "good" Orient was invariably a classical period somewhere in a long-gone India, whereas the "bad" Orient lingered in present-day Asia, parts of North Africa, and Islam everywhere. "Aryans" were confined to Europe and the ancient Orient; as Léon Poliakov has shown (without once remarking, however, that "Semites" were not only the Jews but the Muslims as well[90]), the Aryan myth dominated historical and cultural anthropology at the expense of the "lesser" peoples.

The official intellectual genealogy of Orientalism would certainly include Gobineau, Renan, Humboldt, Steinthal, Burnouf, Remusat, Palmer, Weil, Dozy, Muir, to mention a few famous names almost at random from the nineteenth century. It would also include the diffusive capacity of learned societies: the Société asiatique, founded in 1822; the Royal Asiatic Society, founded in 1823; the American Oriental Society, founded in 1842; and so on. But it might perforce neglect the great contribution of imaginative and travel literature, which strengthened the divisions established by Orientalists between the various geographical, temporal, and racial departments of the Orient. Such neglect would be incorrect, since for the Islamic Orient this literature is especially rich and makes a significant contribution to building the Orientalist discourse. It includes work by Goethe, Hugo, Lamartine, Chateaubriand, Kinglake, Nerval, Flaubert, Lane, Burton, Scott, Byron, Vigny, Disraeli, George Eliot, Gautier. Later, in the late nineteenth and early twentieth centuries, we could add Doughty, Barrès, Loti, T. E. Lawrence, Forster. All these writers give a bolder outline to Disraeli's "great Asiatic mystery." In this enterprise there is considerable support not only from the unearthing of dead Oriental civilizations (by European excavators) in Mesopotamia, Egypt, Syria, and Turkey, but also from major geographical surveys done all through the Orient.

By the end of the nineteenth century these achievements were materially abetted by the European occupation of the entire Near

Orient (with the exception of parts of the Ottoman Empire, which was swallowed up after 1918). The principal colonial powers once again were Britain and France, although Russia and Germany played some role as well.[91] To colonize meant at first the identification—indeed, the creation—of interests; these could be commercial, communicational, religious, military, cultural. With regard to Islam and the Islamic territories, for example, Britain felt that it had legitimate interests, as a Christian power, to safeguard. A complex apparatus for tending these interests developed. Such early organizations as the Society for Promoting Christian Knowledge (1698) and the Society for the Propagation of the Gospel in Foreign Parts (1701) were succeeded and later abetted by the Baptist Missionary Society (1792), the Church Missionary Society (1799), the British and Foreign Bible Society (1804), the London Society for Promoting Christianity Among the Jews (1808). These missions "openly joined the expansion of Europe."[92] Add to these the trading societies, learned societies, geographical exploration funds, translation funds, the implantation in the Orient of schools, missions, consular offices, factories, and sometimes large European communities, and the notion of an "interest" will acquire a good deal of sense. Thereafter interests were defended with much zeal and expense.

So far my outline is a gross one. What of the typical experiences and emotions that accompany both the scholarly advances of Orientalism and the political conquests aided by Orientalism? First, there is disappointment that the modern Orient is not at all like the texts. Here is Gérard de Nerval writing to Théophile Gautier at the end of August 1843:

> I have already lost, Kingdom after Kingdom, province after province, the more beautiful half of the universe, and soon I will know of no place in which I can find a refuge for my dreams; but it is Egypt that I most regret having driven out of my imagination, now that I have sadly placed it in my memory.[93]

This is by the author of a great *Voyage en Orient*. Nerval's lament is a common topic of Romanticism (the betrayed dream, as described by Albert Béguin in *L'Ame romantique et le rêve*) and of travelers in the Biblical Orient, from Chateaubriand to Mark Twain. Any direct experience of the mundane Orient ironically comments on such valorizations of it as were to be found in Goethe's "Mahometsgesang" or Hugo's "Adieu de l'hôtesse arabe." Memory of the modern Orient disputes imagination, sends one back to the imagination as a place preferable, for the European sensibility, to the real Orient. For a person who has never seen the Orient, Nerval once said to Gautier, a lotus is still a lotus; for me it is only a kind of onion. To write about the modern Orient is either to reveal an upsetting demystification of images culled from texts, or to confine oneself to the Orient of which Hugo spoke in his original preface to *Les Orientales*, the Orient as "image" or "pensée," symbols of "une sorte de préoccupation générale."[94]

If personal disenchantment and general preoccupation fairly map the Orientalist sensibility at first, they entail certain other more familiar habits of thought, feeling, and perception. The mind learns to separate a general apprehension of the Orient from a specific experience of it; each goes its separate way, so to speak. In Scott's novel *The Talisman* (1825), Sir Kenneth (of the Crouching Leopard) battles a single Saracen to a standoff somewhere in the Palestinian desert; as the Crusader and his opponent, who is Saladin in disguise, later engage in conversation, the Christian discovers his Muslim antagonist to be not so bad a fellow after all. Yet he remarks:

> I well thought . . . that your blinded race had their descent from the foul fiend, without whose aid you would never have been able to maintain this blessed land of Palestine against so many valiant soldiers of God. I speak not thus of thee in particular, Saracen, but generally of thy people and religion. Strange is it to me, however, not that you should have the descent from the Evil One, but that you should boast of it.[95]

For indeed the Saracen does boast of tracing his race's line back to Eblis, the Muslim Lucifer. But what is truly curious is not the feeble historicism by which Scott makes the scene "medieval," letting Christian attack Muslim theologically in a way nineteenth-century Europeans would not (they would, though); rather, it is the airy condescension of damning a whole people "generally" while mitigating the offense with a cool "I don't mean you in particular."

Scott, however, was no expert on Islam (although H. A. R. Gibb, who was, praised *The Talisman* for its insight into Islam and Saladin[96]), and he was taking enormous liberties with Eblis's role by turning him into a hero for the faithful. Scott's knowledge probably came from Byron and Beckford, but it is enough for us

here to note how strongly the general character ascribed to things
Oriental could withstand both the rhetorical and the existential
force of obvious exceptions. It is as if, on the one hand, a bin
called "Oriental" existed into which all the authoritative, anonymous, and traditional Western attitudes to the East were dumped
unthinkingly, while on the other, true to the anecdotal tradition
of storytelling, one could nevertheless tell of experiences with or
in the Orient that had little to do with the generally serviceable bin.
But the very structure of Scott's prose shows a closer intertwining
of the two than that. For the general category in advance offers the
specific instance a limited terrain in which to operate: no matter
how deep the specific exception, no matter how much a single
Oriental can escape the fences placed around him, he is *first* an
Oriental, *second* a human being, and *last* again an Oriental.

So general a category as "Oriental" is capable of quite interesting
variations. Disraeli's enthusiasm for the Orient appeared first during a trip East in 1831. In Cairo he wrote, "My eyes and mind yet
ache with a grandeur so little in unison with our own likeness."[97]
General grandeur and passion inspired a transcendent sense of
things and little patience for actual reality. His novel *Tancred* is
steeped in racial and geographical platitudes; everything is a matter
of race, Sidonia states, so much so that salvation can only be found
in the Orient and amongst its races. There, as a case in point,
Druzes, Christians, Muslims, and Jews hobnob easily because—
someone quips—Arabs are simply Jews on horseback, and all are
Orientals at heart. The unisons are made between general categories, not between categories and what they contain. An Oriental
lives in the Orient, he lives a life of Oriental ease, in a state of
Oriental despotism and sensuality, imbued with a feeling of
Oriental fatalism. Writers as different as Marx, Disraeli, Burton,
and Nerval could carry on a lengthy discussion between themselves,
as it were, using all those generalities unquestioningly and yet
intelligibly.

With disenchantment and a generalized—not to say schizo-
phrenic—view of the Orient, there is usually another peculiarity.
Because it is made into a general object, the whole Orient can be
made to serve as an illustration of a particular form of eccentricity.
Although the individual Oriental cannot shake or disturb the
general categories that make sense of his oddness, his oddness can
nevertheless be enjoyed for its own sake. Here, for example, is
Flaubert describing the spectacle of the Orient:

To amuse the crowd, Mohammed Ali's jester took a woman in a Cairo bazaar one day, set her on the counter of a shop, and coupled with her publicly while the shopkeeper calmly smoked his pipe.

On the road from Cairo to Shubra some time ago a young fellow had himself publicly buggered by a large monkey—as in the story above, to create a good opinion of himself and make people laugh.

A marabout died a while ago—an idiot—who had long passed as a saint marked by God; all the Moslem women came to see him and masturbated him—in the end he died of exhaustion—from morning to night it was a perpetual jacking-off. . . .

Quid dicis of the following fact: some time ago a *santon* (ascetic priest) used to walk through the streets of Cairo completely naked except for a cap on his head and another on his prick. To piss he would doff the prick-cap, and sterile women who wanted children would run up, put themselves under the parabola of his urine and rub themselves with it.[98]

Flaubert frankly acknowledges that this is grotesquerie of a special kind. "All the old comic business"—by which Flaubert meant the well-known conventions of "the cudgeled slave . . . the coarse trafficker in women . . . the thieving merchant"—acquire a new, "fresh . . . genuine and charming" meaning in the Orient. This meaning cannot be reproduced; it can only be enjoyed on the spot and "brought back" very approximately. The Orient is *watched*, since its almost (but never quite) offensive behavior issues out of a reservoir of infinite peculiarity; the European, whose sensibility tours the Orient, is a watcher, never involved, always detached, always ready for new examples of what the *Description de l'Égypte* called "bizarre jouissance." The Orient becomes a living tableau of queerness.

And this tableau quite logically becomes a special topic for texts. Thus the circle is completed; from being exposed as what texts do not prepare one for, the Orient can return as something one writes about in a disciplined way. Its foreignness can be translated, its meanings decoded, its hostility tamed; yet the *generality* assigned to the Orient, the disenchantment that one feels after encountering it, the unresolved eccentricity it displays, are all redistributed in what is said or written about it. Islam, for example, was typically Oriental for Orientalists of the late nineteenth and early twentieth centuries. Carl Becker argued that although "Islam" (note the vast generality) inherited the Hellenic tradition, it could neither grasp

nor employ the Greek, humanistic tradition; moreover, to understand Islam one needed above all else to see it, not as an "original"
religion, but as a sort of failed Oriental attempt to employ Greek
philosophy without the creative inspiration that we find in
Renaissance Europe.[99] For Louis Massignon, perhaps the most
renowned and influential of modern French Orientalists, Islam was
a systematic rejection of the Christian incarnation, and its greatest
hero was not Mohammed or Averroës but al-Hallaj, a Muslim
saint who was crucified by the orthodox Muslims for having dared
to personalize Islam.[100] What Becker and Massignon explicitly left
out of their studies was the eccentricity of the Orient, which they
backhandedly acknowledged by trying so hard to regularize it in
Western terms. Mohammed was thrown out, but al-Hallaj was made
prominent because he took himself to be a Christ-figure.

As a judge of the Orient, the modern Orientalist does not, as he
believes and even says, stand apart from it objectively. His human
detachment, whose sign is the absence of sympathy covered by
professional knowledge, is weighted heavily with all the orthodox
attitudes, perspectives, and moods of Orientalism that I have been
describing. His Orient is not the Orient as it is, but the Orient as
it has been Orientalized. An unbroken arc of knowledge and power
connects the European or Western statesman and the Western
Orientalists; it forms the rim of the stage containing the Orient.
By the end of World War I both Africa and the Orient formed not
so much an intellectual spectacle for the West as a privileged
terrain for it. The scope of Orientalism exactly matched the scope
of empire, and it was this absolute unanimity between the two that
provoked the only crisis in the history of Western thought about
and dealings with the Orient. And this crisis continues now.

Beginning in the twenties, and from one end of the Third World
to the other, the response to empire and imperialism has been
dialectical. By the time of the Bandung Conference in 1955 the
entire Orient had gained its political independence from the Western
empires and confronted a new configuration of imperial powers,
the United States and the Soviet Union. Unable to recognize "its"
Orient in the new Third World, Orientalism now faced a challenging and politically armed Orient. Two alternatives opened before
Orientalism. One was to carry on as if nothing had happened. The
second was to adapt the old ways to the new. But to the Orientalist,
who believes the Orient never changes, the new is simply the old
betrayed by new, misunderstanding *dis-Orientals* (we can permit

ourselves the neologism). A third, revisionist alternative, to dispense with Orientalism altogether, was considered by only a tiny minority.

One index of the crisis, according to Abdel Malek, was not simply that "national liberation movements in the ex-colonial" Orient worked havoc with Orientalist conceptions of passive, fatalistic "subject races"; there was in addition the fact that "specialists and the public at large became aware of the time-lag, not only between orientalist science and the material under study, but also—and this was to be determining—between the conceptions, the methods and the instruments of work in the human and social sciences and those of orientalism."[101] The Orientalists—from Renan to Goldziher to Macdonald to von Grunebaum, Gibb, and Bernard Lewis—saw Islam, for example, as a "cultural synthesis" (the phrase is P. M. Holt's) that could be studied apart from the economics, sociology, and politics of the Islamic peoples. For Orientalism, Islam had a meaning which, if one were to look for its most succinct formulation, could be found in Renan's first treatise: in order best to be understood Islam had to be reduced to "tent and tribe." The impact of colonialism, of worldly circumstances, of historical development: all these were to Orientalists as flies to wanton boys, killed—or disregarded—for their sport, never taken seriously enough to complicate the essential Islam.

The career of H. A. R. Gibb illustrates within itself the two alternative approaches by which Orientalism has responded to the modern Orient. In 1945 Gibb delivered the Haskell Lectures at the University of Chicago. The world he surveyed was not the same one Balfour and Cromer knew before World War I. Several revolutions, two world wars, and innumerable economic, political, and social changes made the realities of 1945 an unmistakably, even cataclysmically, new object. Yet we find Gibb opening the lectures he called *Modern Trends in Islam* as follows:

> The student of Arabic civilization is constantly brought up against the striking contrast between the imaginative power displayed, for example, in certain branches of Arabic literature and the literalism, the pedantry, displayed in reasoning and exposition, even when it is devoted to these same productions. It is true that there have been great philosophers among the Muslim peoples and that some of them were Arabs, but they were rare exceptions. The Arab mind, whether in relation to the outer world or in relation to the processes of thought, cannot throw off its intense feeling for the separateness and the individuality of the concrete events. This

is, I believe, one of the main factors lying behind that "lack of a sense of law" which Professor Macdonald regarded as the characteristic difference in the Oriental.

It is this, too, which explains—what is so difficult for the Western student to grasp [until it is explained to him by the Orientalist]—the aversion of the Muslims from the thought-processes of rationalism. . . . The rejection of rationalist modes of thought and of the utilitarian ethic which is inseparable from them has its roots, therefore, not in the so-called "obscurantism" of the Muslim theologians but in the atomism and discreteness of the Arab imagination.[102]

This is pure Orientalism, of course, but even if one acknowledges the exceeding knowledge of institutional Islam that characterizes the rest of the book, Gibb's inaugural biases remain a formidable obstacle for anyone hoping to understand modern Islam. What is the meaning of "difference" when the preposition "from" has dropped from sight altogether? Are we not once again being asked to inspect the Oriental Muslim as if his world, unlike ours—"differently" from it—had never ventured beyond the seventh century? As for modern Islam itself, despite the complexities of his otherwise magisterial understanding of it, why must it be regarded with so implacable a hostility as Gibb's? If Islam is flawed from the start by virtue of its permanent disabilities, the Orientalist will find himself opposing any Islamic attempts to reform Islam, because, according to his views, reform is a betrayal of Islam: this is exactly Gibb's argument. How can an Oriental slip out from these manacles into the modern world except by repeating with the Fool in *King Lear*, "They'll have me whipp'd for speaking true, thou'lt have me whipp'd for lying; and sometimes I am whipp'd for holding my peace."

Eighteen years later Gibb faced an audience of English compatriots, only now he was speaking as the director of the Center for Middle Eastern Studies at Harvard. His topic was "Area Studies Reconsidered," in which, among other *aperçus*, he agreed that "the Orient is much too important to be left to the Orientalists." The new, or second alternative, approach open to Orientalists was being announced, just as *Modern Trends* exemplified the first, or traditional, approach. Gibb's formula is well-intentioned in "Area Studies Reconsidered," so far, of course, as the Western experts on the Orient are concerned, whose job it is to prepare students for careers "in public life and business." What we now need, said Gibb, is the traditional Orientalist *plus* a good social scientist working together: between them the two will do "interdisciplinary" work. Yet the traditional Orientalist will not bring outdated knowledge to bear on the Orient; no, his expertise will serve to remind his uninitiated colleagues in area studies that "to apply the psychology and mechanics of Western political institutions to Asian or Arab situations is pure Walt Disney."[103]

In practice this notion has meant that when Orientals struggle against colonial occupation, you must say (in order not to risk a Disneyism) that Orientals have never understood the meaning of self-government the way "we" do. When some Orientals oppose racial discrimination while others practice it, you say "they're all Orientals at bottom" and class interest, political circumstances, economic factors are totally irrelevant. Or with Bernard Lewis, you say that if Arab Palestinians oppose Israeli settlement and occupation of their lands, then that is merely "the return of Islam," or, as a renowned contemporary Orientalist defines it, Islamic opposition to non-Islamic peoples,[104] a principle of Islam enshrined in the seventh century. History, politics, and economics do not matter. Islam is Islam, the Orient is the Orient, and please take all your ideas about a left and a right wing, revolutions, and change back to Disneyland.

If such tautologies, claims, and dismissals have not sounded familiar to historians, sociologists, economists, and humanists in any other field except Orientalism, the reason is patently obvious. For like its putative subject matter, Orientalism has not allowed ideas to violate its profound serenity. But modern Orientalists—or area experts, to give them their new name—have not passively sequestered themselves in language departments. On the contrary, they have profited from Gibb's advice. Most of them today are indistinguishable from other "experts" and "advisers" in what Harold Lasswell has called the policy sciences.[105] Thus the military–national-security possibilities of an alliance, say, between a specialist in "national character analysis" and an expert in Islamic institutions were soon recognized, for expediency's sake if for nothing else. After all, the "West" since World War II had faced a clever totalitarian enemy who collected allies for itself among gullible Oriental (African, Asian, undeveloped) nations. What better way of outflanking that enemy than by playing to the Oriental's illogical mind in ways only an Orientalist could devise? Thus emerged such masterful ploys as the stick-and-carrot technique, the Alliance for

Progress, SEATO, and so forth, all of them based on traditional "knowledge" retooled for better manipulation of its supposed object.

Thus as revolutionary turmoil grips the Islamic Orient, sociologists remind us that Arabs are addicted to "oral functions,"[106] while economists—recycled Orientalists—observe that for modern Islam neither capitalism nor socialism is an adequate rubric.[107] As anticolonialism sweeps and indeed unifies the entire Oriental world, the Orientalist damns the whole business not only as a nuisance but as an insult to the Western democracies. As momentous, generally important issues face the world—issues involving nuclear destruction, catastrophically scarce resources, unprecedented human demands for equality, justice, and economic parity—popular caricatures of the Orient are exploited by politicians whose source of ideological supply is not only the half-literate technocrat but the superliterate Orientalist. The legendary Arabists in the State Department warn of Arab plans to take over the world. The perfidious Chinese, half-naked Indians, and passive Muslims are described as vultures for "our" largesse and are damned when "we lose them" to communism, or to their unregenerate Oriental instincts: the difference is scarcely significant.

These contemporary Orientalist attitudes flood the press and the popular mind. Arabs, for example, are thought of as camel-riding, terroristic, hook-nosed, venal lechers whose undeserved wealth is an affront to real civilization. Always there lurks the assumption that although the Western consumer belongs to a numerical minority, he is entitled either to own or to expend (or both) the majority of the world resources. Why? Because he, unlike the Oriental, is a true human being. No better instance exists today of what Anwar Abdel Malek calls "the hegemonism of possessing minorities" and anthropocentrism allied with Europocentrism: a white middle-class Westerner believes it his human prerogative not only to manage the nonwhite world but also to own it, just because by definition "it" is not quite as human as "we" are. There is no purer example than this of dehumanized thought.

In a sense the limitations of Orientalism are, as I said earlier, the limitations that follow upon disregarding, essentializing, denuding the humanity of another culture, people, or geographical region. But Orientalism has taken a further step than that: it views the Orient as something whose existence is not only displayed but has remained fixed in time and place for the West. So impressive have the descriptive and textual successes of Orientalism been that

entire periods of the Orient's cultural, political, and social history
are considered mere responses to the West. The West is the actor,
the Orient a passive reactor. The West is the spectator, the judge and
jury, of every facet of Oriental behavior. Yet if history during
the twentieth century has provoked intrinsic change in and for the
Orient, the Orientalist is stunned: he cannot realize that to some
extent

> the new [Oriental] leaders, intellectuals or policy-makers, have
> learned many lessons from the travail of their predecessors. They
> have also been aided by the structural and institutional transforma-
> tions accomplished in the intervening period and by the fact that
> they are to a great extent more at liberty to fashion the future of
> their countries. They are also much more confident and perhaps
> slightly aggressive. No longer do they have to function hoping to
> obtain a favorable verdict from the invisible jury of the West.
> Their dialogue is not with the West, it is with their fellow-
> citizens.[108]

Moreover, the Orientalist assumes that what his texts have not prepared him for is the result either of outside agitation in the Orient
or of the Orient's misguided inanity. None of the innumerable
Orientalist texts on Islam, including their summa, *The Cambridge
History of Islam*, can prepare their reader for what has taken place
since 1948 in Egypt, Palestine, Iraq, Syria, Lebanon, or the
Yemens. When the dogmas about Islam cannot serve, not even for
the most Panglossian Orientalist, there is recourse to an Orientalized
social-science jargon, to such marketable abstractions as elites,
political stability, modernization, and institutional development, all
stamped with the cachet of Orientalist wisdom. In the meantime a
growing, more and more dangerous rift separates Orient and
Occident.

The present crisis dramatizes the disparity between texts and
reality. Yet in this study of Orientalism I wish not only to expose
the sources of Orientalism's views but also to reflect on its importance, for the contemporary intellectual rightly feels that to
ignore a part of the world now demonstrably encroaching upon
him is to avoid reality. Humanists have too often confined their
attention to departmentalized topics of research. They have neither
watched nor learned from disciplines like Orientalism whose un-
remitting ambition was to master *all* of a world, not some easily
delimited part of it such as an author or a collection of texts. However, along with such academic security-blankets as "history,"

"literature," or "the humanities," and despite its overreaching aspirations, Orientalism is involved in worldly, historical circumstances which it has tried to conceal behind an often pompous scientism and appeals to rationalism. The contemporary intellectual can learn from Orientalism how, on the one hand, either to limit or to enlarge realistically the scope of his discipline's claims, and on the other, to see the human ground (the foul-rag-and-bone shop of the heart, Yeats called it) in which texts, visions, methods, and disciplines begin, grow, thrive, and degenerate. To investigate Orientalism is also to propose intellectual ways for handling the methodological problems that history has brought forward, so to speak, in its subject matter, the Orient. But before that we must virtually see the humanistic values that Orientalism, by its scope, experiences, and structures, has all but eliminated.

2

Orientalist Structures
and Restructures

When the seyyid 'Omar, the Nakeeb el-Ashráf (or chief of the descendants of the Prophet) . . . married a daughter, about forty-five years since, there walked before the procession a young man who had made an incision in his abdomen, and drawn out a large portion of his intestines, which he carried before him on a silver tray. After the procession, he restored them to their proper place, and remained in bed many days before he recovered from the effects of this foolish and disgusting act.

—Edward William Lane, *An Account of the Manners and Customs of the Modern Egyptians*

. . . dans le cas de la chute de cet empire, soit par une révolution à Constantinople, soit par un démembrement successif, les puissances européennes prendront chacune, à titre de protectorat, la partie de l'empire qui lui sera assignée par les stipulations du congrès; que ces protectorats, définis et limités, quant aux territoires, selon les voisinages, la sûreté des frontières, l'analogie de religions, de moeurs et d'intérêts . . . ne consacreront que la suzeraineté des puissances. Cette sorte de suzeraineté définie ainsi, et consacrée comme droit européen, consistera principalement dans le droit d'occuper telle partie du territoire ou des côtes, pour y fonder, soit des villes libres, soit des colonies européennes, soit des ports et des échelles de commerce. . . . Ce n'est qu'une tutelle armée et civilisatrice que chaque puissance exercera sur son protectorat; elle garantira son existence et ses éléments de nationalité, sous le drapeau d'une nationalité plus forte. . . .

—Alphonse de Lamartine, *Voyage en Orient*

I

Redrawn Frontiers, Redefined Issues, Secularized Religion

Gustave Flaubert died in 1880 without having finished *Bouvard et Pécuchet*, his comic encyclopedic novel on the degeneration of knowledge and the inanity of human effort. Nevertheless the essential outlines of his vision are clear, and are clearly supported by the ample detail of his novel. The two clerks are members of the bourgeoisie who, because one of them is the unexpected beneficiary of a handsome will, retire from the city to spend their lives on a country estate doing what they please ("nous ferons tout ce que nous plaira!"). As Flaubert portrays their experience, doing as they please involves Bouvard and Pécuchet in a practical and theoretical jaunt through agriculture, history, chemistry, education, archaeology, literature, always with less than successful results; they move through fields of learning like travelers in time and knowledge, experiencing the disappointments, disasters, and letdowns of uninspired amateurs. What they move through, in fact, is the whole disillusioning experience of the nineteenth century, whereby—in Charles Morazé's phrase—"les bourgeois conquerants" turn out to be the bumbling victims of their own leveling incompetence and mediocrity. Every enthusiasm resolves itself into a boring cliché, and every discipline or type of knowledge changes from hope and power into disorder, ruin, and sorrow.

Among Flaubert's sketches for the conclusion of this panorama of despair are two items of special interest to us here. The two men debate the future of mankind. Pécuchet sees "the future of Humanity through a glass darkly," whereas Bouvard sees it "brightly!"

> Modern man is progressing, Europe will be regenerated by Asia.
> The historical law that civilization moves from Orient to Occident
> . . . the two forms of humanity will at last be soldered together.[1]

This obvious echo of Quinet represents the start of still another of the cycles of enthusiasm and disillusionment through which the two men will pass. Flaubert's notes indicate that like all his others, this anticipated project of Bouvard's is rudely interrupted by reality—this time by the sudden appearance of gendarmes who accuse him of debauchery. A few lines later, however, the second item of interest turns up. The two men simultaneously confess to each other that their secret desire is once again to become copyists. They have a double desk made for them, they buy books, pencils, erasers, and—as Flaubert concludes the sketch— "ils s'y mettent": they turn to. From trying to live through and apply knowledge more or less directly, Bouvard and Pécuchet are reduced finally to transcribing it uncritically from one text to another.

Although Bouvard's vision of Europe regenerated by Asia is not fully spelled out, it (and what it comes to on the copyist's desk) can be glossed in several important ways. Like many of the two men's other visions, this one is *global* and it is *reconstructive*; it represents what Flaubert felt to be the nineteenth-century predilection for the rebuilding of the world according to an imaginative vision, sometimes accompanied by a special scientific technique. Among the visions Flaubert has in mind are the utopias of Saint-Simon and Fourier, the scientific regenerations of mankind envisioned by Comte, and all the technical or secular religions promoted by ideologues, positivists, eclectics, occultists, traditionalists, and idealists such as Destutt de Tracy, Cabanis, Michelet, Cousin, Proudhon, Cournot, Cabet, Janet, and Lamennais.[2] Throughout the novel Bouvard and Pécuchet espouse the various causes of such figures; then, having ruined them, they move on looking for newer ones, but with no better results.

The roots of such revisionist ambitions as these are Romantic in a very specific way. We must remember the extent to which a major part of the spiritual and intellectual project of the late eighteenth century was a reconstituted theology—natural supernaturalism, as M. H. Abrams has called it; this type of thought is carried forward by the typical nineteenth-century attitudes Flaubert satirizes in *Bouvard et Pécuchet*. The notion of regeneration therefore harks back to

a conspicuous Romantic tendency, after the rationalism and decorum of the Enlightenment . . . [to revert] to the stark drama and suprarational mysteries of the Christian story and doctrines and to the violent conflicts and abrupt reversals of the Christian inner life, turning on the extremes of destruction and creation, hell and heaven, exile and reunion, death and rebirth, dejection and joy, paradise lost and paradise regained. . . . But since they lived, inescapably, after the Enlightenment, Romantic writers revived these ancient matters with a difference: they undertook to save the overview of human history and destiny, the existential paradigms, and the cardinal values of their religious heritage, by reconstituting them in a way that would make them intellectually acceptable, as well as emotionally pertinent, for the time being.[3]

What Bouvard has in mind—the regeneration of Europe by Asia —was a very influential Romantic idea. Friedrich Schlegel and Novalis, for example, urged upon their countrymen, and upon Europeans in general, a detailed study of India because, they said, it was Indian culture and religion that could defeat the materialism and mechanism (and republicanism) of Occidental culture. And from this defeat would arise a new, revitalized Europe: the Biblical imagery of death, rebirth, and redemption is evident in this prescription. Moreover, the Romantic Orientalist project was not merely a specific instance of a general tendency; it was a powerful shaper of the tendency itself, as Raymond Schwab has so convincingly argued in *La Renaissance orientale*. But what mattered was not Asia so much as Asia's *use to* modern Europe. Thus anyone who, like Schlegel or Franz Bopp, mastered an Oriental language was a spiritual hero, a knight-errant bringing back to Europe a sense of the holy mission it had now lost. It is precisely this sense that the later secular religions portrayed by Flaubert carry on in the nineteenth century. No less than Schlegel, Wordsworth, and Chateaubriand, Auguste Comte—like Bouvard—was the adherent and proponent of a secular post-Enlightenment myth whose outlines are unmistakably Christian.

In regularly allowing Bouvard and Pécuchet to go through revisionist notions from start to comically debased finish, Flaubert drew attention to the human flaw common to all projects. He saw perfectly well that underneath the *idée reçue* "Europe-regenerated-by-Asia" lurked a very insidious hubris. Neither "Europe" nor "Asia" was anything without the visionaries' technique for turning vast geographical domains into treatable, and manageable, entities. At bottom, therefore, Europe and Asia were *our* Europe and *our* Asia— our *will* and *representation*, as Schopenhauer had said. Historical laws were in reality *historians*' laws, just as "the two forms of humanity" drew attention less to actuality than to a European capacity for lending man-made distinctions an air of inevitability. As for the other half of the phrase—"will at last be soldered together"— there Flaubert mocked the blithe indifference of science to actuality,

a science which anatomized and melted human entities as if they were
so much inert matter. But it was not just any science he mocked: it
was enthusiastic, even messianic European science, whose victories
included failed revolutions, wars, oppression, and an unteachable
appetite for putting grand, bookish ideas quixotically to work
immediately. What such science or knowledge never reckoned with
was its own deeply ingrained and unself-conscious bad innocence
and the resistance to it of reality. When Bouvard plays the scientist
he naively assumes that science merely is, that reality is as the
scientist says it is, that it does not matter whether the scientist is a
fool or a visionary; he (or anyone who thinks like him) cannot see
that the Orient may not wish to regenerate Europe, or that Europe
was not about to fuse itself democratically with yellow or brown
Asians. In short, such a scientist does not recognize in his science
the egoistic will to power that feeds his endeavors and corrupts his
ambitions.

Flaubert, of course, sees to it that his poor fools are made to
rub their noses in these difficulties. Bouvard and Pécuchet have
learned that it is better not to traffic in ideas and in reality together.
The novel's conclusion is a picture of the two of them now perfectly
content to copy their favorite ideas faithfully from book onto paper.
Knowledge no longer requires application to reality; knowledge is
what gets passed on silently, without comment, from one text to
another. Ideas are propagated and disseminated anonymously, they
are repeated without attribution; they have literally become *idées
reçues*: what matters is that they are *there*, to be repeated, echoed,
and re-echoed uncritically.

In a highly compressed form this brief episode, taken out of
Flaubert's notes for *Bouvard et Pécuchet*, frames the specifically
modern structures of Orientalism, which after all is one discipline
among the secular (and quasi-religious) faiths of nineteenth-century
European thought. We have already characterized the general scope
of thought about the Orient that was handed on through the
medieval and Renaissance periods, for which Islam was the
essential Orient. During the eighteenth century, however, there
were a number of new, interlocking elements that hinted at the coming evangelical phase, whose outlines Flaubert was later to re-create.

For one, the Orient was being opened out considerably beyond
the Islamic lands. This quantitative change was to a large degree
the result of continuing, and expanding, European exploration of

the rest of the world. The increasing influence of travel literature, imaginary utopias, moral voyages, and scientific reporting brought the Orient into sharper and more extended focus. If Orientalism is indebted principally to the fruitful Eastern discoveries of Anquetil and Jones during the latter third of the century, these must be seen in the wider context created by Cook and Bougainville, the voyages of Tournefort and Adanson, by the Président de Brosses's *Histoire des navigations aux terres australes*, by French traders in the Pacific, by Jesuit missionaries in China and the Americas, by William Dampier's explorations and reports, by innumerable speculations on giants, Patagonians, savages, natives, and monsters supposedly residing to the far east, west, south, and north of Europe. But all such widening horizons had Europe firmly in the privileged center, as main observer (or mainly observed, as in Goldsmith's *Citizen of the World*). For even as Europe moved itself outwards, its sense of cultural strength was fortified. From travelers' tales, and not only from great institutions like the various India companies, colonies were created and ethnocentric perspectives secured.[4]

For another, a more knowledgeable attitude towards the alien and exotic was abetted not only by travelers and explorers but also by historians for whom European experience could profitably be compared with other, as well as older, civilizations. That powerful current in eighteenth-century historical anthropology, described by scholars as the confrontation of the gods, meant that Gibbon could read the lessons of Rome's decline in the rise of Islam, just as Vico could understand modern civilization in terms of the barbaric, poetic splendor of their earliest beginnings. Whereas Renaissance historians judged the Orient inflexibly as an enemy, those of the eighteenth century confronted the Orient's peculiarities with some detachment and with some attempt at dealing directly with Oriental source material, perhaps because such a technique helped a European to know himself better. George Sale's translation of the Koran and his accompanying preliminary discourse illustrate the change. Unlike his predecessors, Sale tried to deal with Arab history in terms of Arab sources; moreover, he let Muslim commentators on the sacred text speak for themselves.[5] In Sale, as throughout the eighteenth century, simple comparatism was the early phase of the comparative disciplines (philology, anatomy, jurisprudence, religion) which were to become the boast of nineteenth-century method.

But there was a tendency among some thinkers to exceed comparative study, and its judicious surveys of mankind from "China to
Peru," by sympathetic identification. This is a third eighteenth-
century element preparing the way for modern Orientalism. What
today we call historicism is an eighteenth-century idea; Vico,
Herder, and Hamann, among others, believed that all cultures were
organically and internally coherent, bound together by a spirit,
genius, *Klima*, or national idea which an outsider could penetrate
only by an act of historical sympathy. Thus Herder's *Ideen zur
Philosophie der Geschichte der Menschheit* (1784–1791) was a
panoramic display of various cultures, each permeated by an
inimical creative spirit, each accessible only to an observer who
sacrificed his prejudices to *Einfühlung*. Imbued with the populist
and pluralist sense of history advocated by Herder and others,[6] an
eighteenth-century mind could breach the doctrinal walls erected
between the West and Islam and see hidden elements of kinship
between himself and the Orient. Napoleon is a famous instance of
this (usually selective) identification by sympathy. Mozart is
another; *The Magic Flute* (in which Masonic codes intermingle
with visions of a benign Orient) and *The Abduction from the
Seraglio* locate a particularly magnanimous form of humanity in
the Orient. And this, much more than the modish habits of "Turkish" music, drew Mozart sympathetically eastwards.

It is very difficult nonetheless to separate such intuitions of the
Orient as Mozart's from the entire range of pre-Romantic and
Romantic representations of the Orient as exotic locale. Popular
Orientalism during the late eighteenth century and the early
nineteenth attained a vogue of considerable intensity. But even this
vogue, easily identifiable in William Beckford, Byron, Thomas
Moore, and Goethe, cannot be simply detached from the interest
taken in Gothic tales, pseudomedieval idylls, visions of barbaric
splendor and cruelty. Thus in some cases the Oriental representation
can be associated with Piranesi's prisons, in others with Tiepolo's
luxurious ambiences, in still others with the exotic sublimity of late-
eighteenth-century paintings.[7] Later in the nineteenth century, in
the works of Delacroix and literally dozens of other French and
British painters, the Oriental genre tableau carried representation
into visual expression and a life of its own (which this book un-
fortunately must scant). Sensuality, promise, terror, sublimity,
idyllic pleasure, intense energy: the Orient as a figure in the pre-

Romantic, pretechnical Orientalist imagination of late-eighteenth-century Europe was really a chameleonlike quality called (adjectivally) "Oriental."[8] But this free-floating Orient would be severely curtailed with the advent of academic Orientalism.

A fourth element preparing the way for modern Orientalist structures was the whole impulse to classify nature and man into types. The greatest names are, of course, Linnaeus and Buffon, but the intellectual process by which bodily (and soon moral, intellectual, and spiritual) extension—the typical materiality of an object—could be transformed from mere spectacle to the precise measurement of characteristic elements was very widespread. Linnaeus said that every note made about a natural type "should be a product of number, of form, of proportion, of situation," and indeed, if one looks in Kant or Diderot or Johnson, there is everywhere a similar penchant for dramatizing general features, for reducing vast numbers of objects to a smaller number of orderable and describable *types*. In natural history, in anthropology, in cultural generalization, a type had a particular *character* which provided the observer with a designation and, as Foucault says, "a controlled derivation." These types and characters belonged to a system, a network of related generalizations. Thus,

> all designation must be accomplished by means of a certain relation to all other possible designations. To know what properly appertains to one individual is to have before one the classification—or the possibility of classifying—all others.[9]

In the writing of philosophers, historians, encyclopedists, and essayists we find character-as-designation appearing as physiological-moral classification: there are, for example, the wild men, the Europeans, the Asiatics, and so forth. These appear of course in Linnaeus, but also in Montesquieu, in Johnson, in Blumenbach, in Soemmerring, in Kant. Physiological and moral characteristics are distributed more or less equally: the American is "red, choleric, erect," the Asiatic is "yellow, melancholy, rigid," the African is "black, phlegmatic, lax."[10] But such designations gather power when, later in the nineteenth century, they are allied with character as derivation, as genetic type. In Vico and Rousseau, for example, the force of moral generalization is enhanced by the precision with which dramatic, almost archetypal figures—primitive man, giants, heroes—are shown to be the genesis of current moral, philosophic, even linguistic issues. Thus when an Oriental was referred to, it was in terms of such genetic universals as his "primitive" state, his primary characteristics, his particular spiritual background.

The four elements I have described—expansion, historical confrontation, sympathy, classification—are the currents in eighteenth-century thought on. whose presence the specific intellectual and institutional structures of modern Orientalism depend. Without them Orientalism, as we shall see presently, could not have occurred. Moreover, these elements had the effect of releasing the Orient generally, and Islam in particular, from the narrowly religious scrutiny by which it had hitherto been examined (and judged) by the Christian West. In other words, modern Orientalism derives from secularizing elements in eighteenth-century European culture. One, the expansion of the Orient further east geographically and further back temporally loosened, even dissolved, the Biblical framework considerably. Reference points were no longer Christianity and Judaism, with their fairly modest calendars and maps, but India, China, Japan, and Sumer, Buddhism, Sanskrit, Zoroastrianism, and Manu. Two, the capacity for dealing historically (and not reductively, as a topic of ecclesiastical politics) with non-European and non-Judeo-Christian cultures was strengthened as history itself was conceived of more radically than before; to understand Europe properly meant also understanding the objective relations between Europe and its own previously unreachable temporal and cultural frontiers. In a sense, John of Segovia's idea of *contraferentia* between Orient and Europe was realized, but in a wholly secular way; Gibbon could treat Mohammed as a historical figure who influenced Europe and not as a diabolical miscreant hovering somewhere between magic and false prophecy. Three, a selective identification with regions and cultures not one's own wore down the obduracy of self and identity, which had been polarized into a community of embattled believers facing barbarian hordes. The borders of Christian Europe no longer served as a kind of custom house; the notions of human association and of human possibility acquired a very wide general—as opposed to parochial—legitimacy. Four, the classifications of mankind were systematically multiplied as the possibilities of designation and derivation were refined beyond the categories of what Vico called gentile and sacred nations; race, color, origin, temperament, character, and types overwhelmed the distinction between Christians and everyone else.

But if these interconnected elements represent a secularizing tendency, this is not to say that the old religious patterns of human history and destiny and "the existential paradigms" were simply removed. Far from it: they were reconstituted, redeployed, redistributed in the secular frameworks just enumerated. For anyone who studied the Orient a secular vocabulary in keeping with these frameworks was required. Yet if Orientalism provided the vocabulary, the conceptual repertoire, the techniques—for this is what, from the end of the eighteenth century on, Orientalism *did* and what Orientalism *was*—it also retained, as an undislodged current in its discourse, a reconstructed religious impulse, a naturalized supernaturalism. What I shall try to show is that this impulse in Orientalism resided in the Orientalist's conception of himself, of the Orient, and of his discipline.

The modern Orientalist was, in his view, a hero rescuing the Orient from the obscurity, alienation, and strangeness which he himself had properly distinguished. His research reconstructed the Orient's lost languages, mores, even mentalities, as Champollion reconstructed Egyptian hieroglyphics out of the Rosetta Stone. The specific Orientalist techniques—lexicography, grammar, translation, cultural decoding—restored, fleshed out, reasserted the values both of an ancient, classical Orient and of the traditional disciplines of philology, history, rhetoric, and doctrinal polemic. But in the process, the Orient and Orientalist disciplines changed dialectically, for they could not survive in their original form. The Orient, even in the "classic" form which the Orientalist usually studied, was modernized, restored to the present; the traditional disciplines too were brought into contemporary culture. Yet both bore the traces of *power*— power to have resurrected, indeed created, the Orient, power that dwelt in the new, scientifically advanced techniques of philology and of anthropological generalization. In short, having transported the Orient into modernity, the Orientalist could celebrate his method, and his position, as that of a secular creator, a man who made new worlds as God had once made the old. As for carrying on such methods and such positions beyond the life-span of any individual Orientalist, there would be a secular tradition of continuity, a lay order of disciplined methodologists, whose brotherhood would be based, not on blood lineage, but upon a common discourse, a praxis, a library, a set of received ideas, in short, a doxology, common to everyone who entered the ranks. Flaubert was prescient enough to see that in time the modern Orientalist would become a copyist, like Bouvard and Pécuchet; but during the early days, in

the careers of Silvestre de Sacy and Ernest Renan, no such danger
was apparent.

My thesis is that the essential aspects of modern Orientalist
theory and praxis (from which present-day Orientalism derives)
can be understood, not as a sudden access of objective knowledge
about the Orient, but as a set of structures inherited from the past,
secularized, redisposed, and re-formed by such disciplines as
philology, which in turn were naturalized, modernized, and laicized
substitutes for (or versions of) Christian supernaturalism. In the
form of new texts and ideas, the East was accommodated to these
structures. Linguists and explorers like Jones and Anquetil were
contributors to modern Orientalism, certainly, but what distinguishes modern Orientalism as a field, a group of ideas, a discourse,
is the work of a later generation than theirs. If we use the Napoleonic
expedition (1798–1801) as a sort of first enabling experience for
modern Orientalism, we can consider its inaugural heroes—in
Islamic studies, Sacy and Renan and Lane—to be builders of the
field, creators of a tradition, progenitors of the Orientalist brotherhood. What Sacy, Renan, and Lane did was to place Orientalism
on a scientific and rational basis. This entailed not only their own
exemplary work but also the creation of a vocabulary and ideas
that could be used impersonally by anyone who wished to become
an Orientalist. Their inauguration of Orientalism was a considerable
feat. It made possible a scientific terminology; it banished obscurity
and instated a special form of illumination for the Orient; it established the figure of the Orientalist as central authority *for* the Orient;
it legitimized a special kind of specifically coherent Orientalist work;
it put into cultural circulation a form of discursive currency by
whose presence the Orient henceforth would be *spoken for*; above
all, the work of the inaugurators carved out a field of study and a
family of ideas which in turn could form a community of scholars
whose lineage, traditions, and ambitions were at once internal to
the field and external enough for general prestige. The more Europe
encroached upon the Orient during the nineteenth century, the
more Orientalism gained in public confidence. Yet if this gain
coincided with a loss in originality, we should not be entirely
surprised, since its mode, from the beginning, was reconstruction
and repetition.

One final observation: The late-eighteenth-century and nineteenth-century ideas, institutions, and figures I shall deal with in
this chapter are an important part, a crucial elaboration, of the first

phase of the greatest age of territorial acquisition ever known. By the end of World War I Europe had colonized 85 percent of the earth. To say simply that modern Orientalism has been an aspect of both imperialism and colonialism is not to say anything very disputable. Yet it is not enough to say it; it needs to be worked through analytically and historically. I am interested in showing how modern Orientalism, unlike the precolonial awareness of Dante and d'Herbelot, embodies a systematic discipline of *accumulation*. And far from this being exclusively an intellectual or theoretical feature, it made Orientalism fatally tend towards the systematic accumulation of human beings and territories. To reconstruct a dead or lost Oriental language meant ultimately to reconstruct a dead or neglected Orient; it also meant that reconstructive precision, science, even imagination could prepare the way for what armies, administrations, and bureaucracies would later do on the ground, in the Orient. In a sense, the vindication of Orientalism was not only its intellectual or artistic successes but its later effectiveness, its usefulness, its authority. Surely it deserves serious attention on all those counts.

II

Silvestre de Sacy
and Ernest Renan:
Rational Anthropology and
Philological Laboratory

The two great themes of Silvestre de Sacy's life are heroic effort and a dedicated sense of pedagogic and rational utility. Born in 1757 into a Jansenist family whose occupation was traditionally that of *notaire*, Antoine-Isaac-Silvestre was privately tutored at a Benedictine abbey, first in Arabic, Syriac, and Chaldean, then in Hebrew. Arabic in particular was the language that opened the Orient to him since it was in Arabic, according to Joseph Reinaud, that Oriental material, both sacred and profane, was then to be found in its oldest and most instructive form.[11] Although a legitimist, in 1769 he was appointed the first teacher of Arabic at the newly created school of *langues orientales vivantes*, of which he became director in 1824. In 1806 he was named professor at the Collège de France, although from 1805 on he was the resident Orientalist at the French Foreign Ministry. There his work (unpaid until 1811) at first was to translate the bulletins of the Grande Armée and Napoleon's *Manifesto* of 1806, in which it was hoped that "Muslim fanaticism" could be excited against Russian Orthodoxy. But for many years thereafter Sacy created interpreters for the French Oriental dragomanate, as well as future scholars. When the French occupied Algiers in 1830, it was Sacy who translated the proclamation to the Algerians; he was regularly consulted on all diplomatic matters relating to the Orient by the foreign minister, and on occasion by the minister of war. At the age of seventy-five he replaced Dacier as secretary of the Académie des Inscriptions, and also became curator of Oriental manuscripts at the Bibliothèque royale. Throughout his long and distinguished career his name was rightly associated with the restructuring and re-forming of education (particularly in Oriental studies) in post-Revolutionary France.[12] With Cuvier, Sacy in 1832 was made a new peer of France.

It was not only because he was the first president of the Société asiatique (founded in 1822) that Sacy's name is associated with the beginning of modern Orientalism; it is because his work virtually put before the profession an entire systematic body of texts, a pedagogic practice, a scholarly tradition, and an important link between Oriental scholarship and public policy. In Sacy's work, for the first time in Europe since the Council of Vienne, there was a self-conscious methodological principle at work as a coeval with scholarly discipline. No less important, Sacy always felt himself to be a man standing at the beginning of an important revisionist project. He was a self-aware inaugurator, and more to the point of our general thesis, he acted in his writing like a secularized ecclesiastic for whom his Orient and his students were doctrine and parishioners respectively. The Duc de Broglie, an admiring contemporary, said of Sacy's work that it reconciled the manner of a scientist with that of a Biblical teacher, and that Sacy was the one man able to reconcile "the goals of Leibniz with the efforts of Bossuet."[13] Consequently everything he wrote was addressed specifically to students (in the case of his first work, his *Principes de grammaire générale* of 1799, the student was his own son) and presented, not as a novelty, but as a revised extract of the best that had already been done, said, or written.

These two characteristics—the didactic presentation to students and the avowed intention of repeating by revision and extract—are crucial. Sacy's writing always conveys the tone of a voice speaking; his prose is dotted with first-person pronouns, with personal qualifications, with rhetorical presence. Even at his most recondite—as in a scholarly note on third-century Sassanid numismatics—one senses not so much a pen writing as a voice pronouncing. The keynote of his work is contained in the opening lines of the dedication to his son of the *Principes de grammaire générale*: "C'est à toi, mon cher Fils, que ce petit ouvrage a été entrepris"—which is to say, I am writing (or speaking) to you because you need to know these things, and since they don't exist in any serviceable form, I have done the work myself for you. Direct address: utility: effort: immediate and beneficent rationality. For Sacy believed that everything could be made clear and reasonable, no matter how difficult the task and how obscure the subject. Here are Bossuet's sternness and Leibniz's abstract humanism, as well as the *tone* of Rousseau, all together in the same style.

The effect of Sacy's tone is to form a circle sealing off him and his audience from the world at large, the way a teacher and his pupils together in a closed classroom also form a sealed space. Unlike the matter of physics, philosophy, or classical literature, the matter of Oriental studies is arcane; it is of import to people who already have an interest in the Orient but want to know the Orient better, in a more orderly way, and here the pedagogical discipline is more effective than it is attractive. The didactic speaker, therefore, *displays* his material to the disciples, whose role it is to receive what is given to them in the form of carefully selected and arranged topics. Since the Orient is old and distant, the teacher's display is a restoration, a re-vision of what has disappeared from the wider ken. And since also the vastly rich (in space, time, and cultures) Orient cannot be totally exposed, only its most representative parts need be. Thus Sacy's focus is the anthology, the chrestomathy, the tableau, the survey of general principles, in which a relatively small set of powerful examples delivers the Orient to the student. Such examples are powerful for two reasons: one, because they reflect Sacy's powers as a Western authority deliberately taking from the Orient what its distance and eccentricity have hitherto kept hidden, and two, because these examples have the semiotical power in them (or imparted to them by the Orientalist) to signify the Orient.

All of Sacy's work is essentially compilatory; it is thus ceremoniously didactic and painstakingly revisionist. Aside from the *Principes de grammaire générale*, he produced a *Chrestomathie arabe* in three volumes (1806 and 1827), an anthology of Arab grammatical writing (1825), an Arabic grammar of 1810 (*à l'usage des élèves de l'École spéciale*), treatises on Arabic prosody and the Druze religion, and numerous short works on Oriental numismatics, onomastics, epigraphy, geography, history, and weights and measures. He did a fair number of translations and two extended commentaries on *Calila and Dumna* and the *Maqamat* of al-Hariri. As editor, memorialist, and historian of modern learning Sacy was similarly energetic. There was very little of note in other related disciplines with which he was not *au courant*, although his own writing was single-minded and, in its non-Orientalist respects, of a narrow positivist range.

Yet when in 1802 the Institut de France was commissioned by Napoleon to form a *tableau générale* on the state and progress of the arts and sciences since 1789, Sacy was chosen to be one of the team of writers: he was the most rigorous of specialists and the most historical-minded of generalists. Dacier's report, as it was known informally, embodied many of Sacy's predilections as well as containing his contributions on the state of Oriental learning. Its title —*Tableau historique de l'érudition française*—announces the new historical (as opposed to sacred) consciousness. Such consciousness is dramatic: learning can be arranged on a stage set, as it were, where its totality can be readily surveyed. Addressed to the king, Dacier's preface stated the theme perfectly. Such a survey as this made it possible to do something no other sovereign had attempted, namely to take in, with one *coup d'oeil*, the whole of human knowledge. Had such a *tableau historique* been undertaken in former times, Dacier continued, we might today have possessed many masterpieces now either lost or destroyed; the interest and utility of the tableau were that it preserved knowledge and made it immediately accessible. Dacier intimated that such a task was simplified by Napoleon's Oriental expedition, one of whose results was to heighten the degree of modern geographical knowledge.[14]

(At no point more than in Dacier's entire *discours* do we see how the dramatic form of a *tableau historique* has its use-equivalent in the arcades and counters of a modern department store.)

The importance of the *Tableau historique* for an understanding of Orientalism's inaugural phase is that it exteriorizes the form of Orientalist knowledge and its features, as it also describes the Orientalist's relationship to his subject matter. In Sacy's pages on Orientalism—as elsewhere in his writing—he speaks of his own work as having *uncovered, brought to light, rescued* a vast amount of obscure matter. Why? In order *to place it before* the student. For like all his learned contemporaries Sacy considered a learned work a positive addition to an edifice that all scholars erected together. Knowledge was essentially the *making visible* of material, and the aim of a tableau was the construction of a sort of Benthamite Panopticon. Scholarly discipline was therefore a specific technology of power: it gained for its user (and his students) tools and knowledge which (if he was a historian) had hitherto been lost.[15] And indeed the vocabulary of specialized power and acquisition is particularly associated with Sacy's reputation as a pioneer Orientalist. His heroism as a scholar was to have dealt successfully with insurmountable difficulties; he acquired the means to present a field to his students where there was none. He *made* the books, the precepts, the examples, said the Duc de Broglie of Sacy. The result was the production of material about the Orient, methods for studying it, and exempla that even Orientals did not have.[16]

Compared with the labors of a Hellenist or a Latinist working on the Institut team, Sacy's labors were awesome. They had the texts, the conventions, the schools; he did not, and consequently had to go about making them. The dynamic of primary loss and subsequent gain in Sacy's writing is obsessional; his investment in it was truly heavy. Like his colleagues in other fields he believed that knowledge is seeing—pan-optically, so to speak—but unlike them he not only had to identify the knowledge, he had to decipher it, interpret it, and most difficult, make it available. Sacy's achievement was to have produced a whole field. As a European he ransacked the Oriental archives, and he could do so without leaving France. What texts he isolated, he then brought back; he doctored them; then he annotated, codified, arranged, and commented on them. In time, the Orient as such became less important than what the Orientalist made of it; thus, drawn by Sacy into the sealed discursive place of a pedagogical tableau, the Orientalist's Orient was thereafter reluctant to emerge into reality.

Sacy was much too intelligent to let his views and his practice stand without supporting argument. First of all, he always made it plain why the "Orient" on its own could not survive a European's taste, intelligence, or patience. Sacy defended the utility and interest of such things as Arabic poetry, but what he was really saying was that Arabic poetry had to be properly transformed by the Orientalist before it could begin to be appreciated. The reasons were broadly epistemological, but they also contained an Orientalistic self-justification. Arabic poetry was produced by a completely strange (to Europeans) people, under hugely different climatic, social, and historical conditions from those a European knows; in addition, such poetry as this was nourished by "opinions, prejudices, beliefs, superstitions which we can acquire only after long and painful study." Even if one does go through the rigors of specialized training, much of the description in the poetry will not be accessible to Europeans "who have attained to a higher degree of civilization." Yet what we can master is of great value to us as Europeans accustomed to disguise our exterior attributes, our bodily activity, and our relationship to nature. Therefore, the Orientalist's use is to make available to his compatriots a considerable range of unusual experience, and still more valuable, a kind of literature capable of helping us understand the "truly divine" poetry of the Hebrews.[17]

So if the Orientalist is necessary because he fishes some useful gems out of the distant Oriental deep, and since the Orient cannot be known without his mediation, it is also true that Oriental writing itself ought not to be taken in whole. This is Sacy's introduction to his theory of fragments, a common Romantic concern. Not only are Oriental literary productions essentially alien to the European; they also do not contain a sustained enough interest, nor are they written with enough "taste and critical spirit," to merit publication except as extracts (*pour mériter d'être publiés autrement que par extrait*).[18] Therefore the Orientalist is required to *present* the Orient by a series of representative fragments, fragments republished, explicated, annotated, and surrounded with still more fragments. For such a presentation a special genre is required: the chrestomathy, which is where in Sacy's case the usefulness and interest of Orientalism are most directly and profitably displayed. Sacy's most famous production was the three-volume *Chrestomathie arabe*, which was sealed at the outset, so to speak, with an internally rhyming Arabic couplet: "Kitab al-anis al-mufid lil-Taleb al-mustafid;/wa gam'i al shathur min manṭhoum wa manthur" (A book pleasant and profitable for the studious pupil;/it collects fragments of both poetry and prose).

Sacy's anthologies were used very widely in Europe for several generations. Although what they contain was claimed as typical, they submerge and cover the censorship of the Orient exercised by the Orientalist. Moreover, the internal order of their contents, the arrangement of their parts, the choice of fragments, never reveal their secret; one has the impression that if fragments were not chosen for their importance, or for their chronological development, or for their aesthetic beauty (as Sacy's were not), they must nevertheless embody a certain Oriental naturalness, or typical inevitability. But this too is never said. Sacy claims simply to have exerted himself on behalf of his students, to make it unnecessary for them to purchase (or read) a grotesquely large library of Oriental stuff. In time, the reader forgets the Orientalist's effort and takes the restructuring of the Orient signified by a chrestomathy as the Orient *tout court*. Objective structure (designation of Orient) and subjective restructure (representation of Orient by Orientalist) become interchangeable. The Orient is overlaid with the Orientalist's rationality; its principles become his. From being distant, it becomes available; from being unsustainable on its own, it becomes pedagogically useful; from being lost, it is found, even if its missing parts have been made to drop away from it in the process. Sacy's anthologies not only supplement the Orient; they supply it as Oriental presence to the West.[19] Sacy's work canonizes the Orient; it begets a canon of textual objects passed on from one generation of students to the next.

And the living legacy of Sacy's disciples was astounding. Every major Arabist in Europe during the nineteenth century traced his intellectual authority back to him. Universities and academies in France, Spain, Norway, Sweden, Denmark, and especially Germany were dotted with the students who formed themselves at his feet and through the anthological tableaux provided by his work.[20] As with all intellectual patrimonies, however, enrichments and restrictions were passed on simultaneously. Sacy's genealogical originality was to have treated the Orient as something to be restored not only because of but also despite the modern Orient's disorderly and elusive presence. Sacy *placed* the Arabs *in* the Orient, which was itself placed in the general tableau of modern learning. Orientalism belonged therefore to European scholarship, but its material had to be re-created by the Orientalist before it could enter the arcades alongside Latinism and Hellenism. Each Orientalist re-created his own Orient according to the fundamental epistemological rules of loss and gain first supplied and enacted by Sacy. Just as he was the father of Orientalism, he was also the discipline's first sacrifice, for in translating new texts, fragments, and extracts subsequent Orientalists entirely displaced Sacy's work by supplying their own restored Orient. Nevertheless the process he started would continue, as philology in particular developed systematic and institutional powers Sacy had never exploited. This was Renan's accomplishment: to have associated the Orient with the most recent comparative disciplines, of which philology was one of the most eminent.

The difference between Sacy and Renan is the difference between inauguration and continuity. Sacy is the originator, whose work represents the field's emergence and its status as a nineteenth-century discipline with roots in revolutionary Romanticism. Renan derives from Orientalism's second generation: it was his task to solidify the official discourse of Orientalism, to systematize its insights, and to establish its intellectual and worldly institutions. For Sacy, it was his personal efforts that launched and vitalized the field and its structures; for Renan, it was his adaptation of Orientalism to philology and both of them to the intellectual culture of his time that perpetuated the Orientalist structures intellectually and gave them greater visibility.

Renan was a figure in his own right neither of total originality nor of absolute derivativeness. Therefore as a cultural force or as an important Orientalist he cannot be reduced simply to his personality nor to a set of schematic ideas in which he believed. Rather, Renan is best grasped as a dynamic force whose opportunities were already created for him by pioneers like Sacy, yet who brought their achievements into the culture as a kind of currency which he circulated and recirculated with (to force the image a little further) his own unmistakable re-currency. Renan is a figure who must be grasped, in short, as a type of cultural and intellectual praxis, as a style for making Orientalist statements within what Michel Foucault would call the archive of his time.[21] What matters is not only the things that Renan said but also how he said them, what, given his background and training, he chose to use as his subject matter, what to combine with what, and so forth. Renan's relations with his Oriental subject matter, with his time and audience, even with his own work, can be described, then, without resorting to formulae that depend on an unexamined assumption of ontological stability (e.g., the *Zeitgeist*, the history of ideas, life-and-times). Instead we are able to read Renan as a writer doing something describable, in a place defined temporally, spatially, and culturally (hence archivally), for an audience and, no less important, for the furtherance of his own position in the Orientalism of his era.

Renan came to Orientalism from philology, and it is the extraordinarily rich and celebrated cultural position of that discipline that endowed Orientalism with its most important technical characteristics. For anyone to whom the word *philology* suggests dry-as-dust and inconsequential word-study, however, Nietzsche's proclamation that along with the greatest minds of the nineteenth century he is a philologist will come as a surprise—though not if Balzac's *Louis Lambert* is recalled:

> What a marvelous book one would write by narrating the life and adventures of a word! Undoubtedly a word has received various impressions of the events for which it was used; depending on the places it was used, a word has awakened different kinds of impressions in different people; but is it not more grand still to consider a word in its triple aspect of soul, body, and movement?[22]

What is the category, Nietzsche will ask later, that includes himself, Wagner, Schopenhauer, Leopardi, all as philologists? The term seems to include both a gift for exceptional spiritual insight into language and the ability to produce work whose articulation is of aesthetic and historical power. Although the profession of philology was born the day in 1777 "when F. A. Wolf invented for himself the name of *stud. philol.*," Nietzsche is nevertheless at pains to show that professional students of the Greek and Roman classics are commonly incapable of understanding their discipline: "they never reach the *roots of the matter*: they never adduce philology as a problem." For simply "as knowledge of the ancient world philology cannot, of course, last forever; its material is exhaustible."[23] It is this that the herd of philologists cannot understand. But what distinguishes the few exceptional spirits whom Nietzsche deems worthy of praise—not unambiguously, and not in the cursory way that I am now describing—is their profound relation to modernity, a relation that is given them by their practice of philology.

Philology problematizes—itself, its practitioner, the present. It embodies a peculiar condition of being modern and European, since neither of those two categories has true meaning without being related to an earlier alien culture and time. What Nietzsche also sees is philology as something *born*, *made* in the Viconian sense as a sign of human enterprise, created as a category of human discovery, self-discovery, and originality. Philology is a way of historically setting oneself off, as great artists do, from one's time and an immediate past even as, paradoxically and antinomically, one actually characterizes one's modernity by so doing.

Between the Friedrich August Wolf of 1777 and the Friedrich Nietzsche of 1875 there is Ernest Renan, an Oriental philologist, also a man with a complex and interesting sense of the way philology and modern culture are involved in each other. In *L'Avenir de la science* (written in 1848 but not published till 1890) he wrote that "the founders of modern mind are philologists." And what is modern mind, he said in the preceding sentence, if not "rationalism, criticism, liberalism, [all of which] were founded on the same day as philology?" Philology, he goes on to say, is both a comparative discipline possessed only by moderns and a symbol of modern (and European) superiority; every advance made by humanity since the fifteenth century can be attributed to minds we should call philological. The job of philology in modern culture (a culture Renan calls philological) is to continue to see reality and nature clearly, thus driving out supernaturalism, and to continue to keep pace with discoveries in the physical sciences. But more than all this, philology enables a general view of human life and of the system of things: "Me, being there at the center, inhaling the perfume of everything, judging, comparing, combining, inducing—in this way I shall arrive at the very system of things." There is an unmistakable aura of power about the philologist. And Renan makes his point about philology and the natural sciences:

> To do philosophy is to know things; following Cuvier's nice phrase, philosophy is *instructing the world in theory*. Like Kant I believe that every purely speculative demonstration has no more validity than a mathematical demonstration, and can teach us nothing about existing reality. Philology is the *exact science* of mental objects [*La philologie est la science exacte des choses de*

l'esprit]. It is to the sciences of humanity what physics and chemistry are to the philosophic sciences of bodies.[24]

I shall return to Renan's citation from Cuvier, as well as to the constant references to natural science, a little later. For the time being, we should remark that the whole middle section of *L'Avenir de la science* is taken up with Renan's admiring accounts of philology, a science he depicts as being at once the most difficult of all human endeavors to characterize and the most precise of all disciplines. In the aspirations of philology to a veritable science of humanity, Renan associates himself explicitly with Vico, Herder, Wolf, and Montesquieu as well as with such philological near-contemporaries as Wilhelm von Humboldt, Bopp, and the great Orientalist Eugène Burnouf (to whom the volume is dedicated). Renan locates philology centrally within what he everywhere refers to as the march of knowledge, and indeed the book itself is a manifesto of humanistic meliorism, which, considering its subtitle ("Pensées de 1848") and other books of 1848 like *Bouvard et Pécuchet* and *The Eighteenth Brumaire of Louis Bonaparte*, is no mean irony. In a sense, then, the manifesto generally and Renan's accounts of philology particularly—he had by then already written the massive philological treatise on Semitic languages that had earned him the Prix Volney—were designed to place Renan as an intellectual in a clearly perceptible relationship to the great social issues raised by 1848. That he should choose to fashion such a relationship on the basis of the *least* immediate of all intellectual disciplines (philology), the one with the least degree of apparent *popular* relevance, the most conservative and the most traditional, suggests the extreme deliberateness of Renan's position. For he did not really speak as one man to all men but rather as a reflective, specialized voice that took, as he put it in the 1890 preface, the inequality of races and the necessary domination of the many by the few for granted as an antidemocratic law of nature and society.[25]

But how was it possible for Renan to hold himself and what he was saying in such a paradoxical position? For what was philology on the one hand if not a science of all humanity, a science premised on the unity of the human species and the worth of every human detail, and yet what was the philologist on the other hand if not—as Renan himself proved with his notorious race prejudice against the very Oriental Semites whose study had made his professional name[26]—a harsh divider of men into superior and inferior races, a liberal critic whose work harbored the most esoteric notions of temporality, origins, development, relationship, and human worth? Part of the answer to this question is that, as his early letters of philological intent to Victor Cousin, Michelet, and Alexander von Humboldt show,[27] Renan had a strong guild sense as a professional scholar, a professional Orientalist, in fact, a sense that put distance between himself and the masses. But more important, I think, is Renan's own conception of his role as an Oriental philologist within philology's larger history, development, and objectives as he saw them. In other words, what may to us seem like paradox was the expected result of how Renan perceived his dynastic position within philology, its history and inaugural discoveries, and what he, Renan, did within it. Therefore Renan should be characterized, not as speaking *about* philology, but rather as *speaking philologically* with all the force of an initiate using the encoded language of a new prestigious science none of whose pronouncements about language itself could be construed either directly or naively.

As Renan understood, received, and was instructed in philology, the discipline imposed a set of doxological rules upon him. To be a philologist meant to be governed in one's activity first of all by a set of recent revaluative discoveries that effectively began the science of philology and gave it a distinctive epistemology of its own: I am speaking here of the period roughly from the 1780s to the mid-1830s, the latter part of which coincides with the period of Renan's beginning his education. His memoirs record how the crisis of religious faith that culminated in the loss of that faith led him in 1845 into a life of scholarship: this was his initiation into philology, its world-view, crises, and style. He believed that on a personal level his life reflected the institutional life of philology. In his life, however, he determined to be as Christian as he once was, only now without Christianity and with what he called "la science laïque" (lay science).[28]

The best example of what a lay science could and could not do was provided years later by Renan in a lecture given at the Sorbonne in 1878, "On the Services Rendered by Philology to the Historical Sciences." What is revealing about this text is the way Renan clearly had religion in mind when he spoke about philology—for example, what philology, like religion, teaches us about the origins of humanity, civilization, and language—only to make it evident to his hearers that philology could deliver a far less coherent, less

knitted together and positive message than religion.[29] Since Renan
was irremediably historical and, as he once put it, morphological in
his outlook, it stood to reason that the only way in which, as a very
young man, he could move out of religion into philological scholarship was to retain in the new lay science the historical world-view
he had gained from religion. Hence, "one occupation alone seemed
to me to be worthy of filling my life; and that was to pursue my
critical research into Christianity [an allusion to Renan's major
scholarly project on the history and origins of Christianity] using
those far ampler means offered me by lay science."[30] Renan had
assimilated himself to philology according to his own post-
Christian fashion.

The difference between the history offered internally by Christianity and the history offered by philology, a relatively new discipline,
is precisely what made modern philology possible, and this Renan
knew perfectly. For whenever "philology" is spoken of around the
end of the eighteenth century and the beginning of the nineteenth,
we are to understand the *new* philology, whose major successes
include comparative grammar, the reclassification of languages into
families, and the final rejection of the divine origins of language. It
is no exaggeration to say that these accomplishments were a more
or less direct consequence of the view that held language to be an
entirely human phenomenon. And this view became current once
it was discovered empirically that the so-called sacred languages
(Hebrew, primarily) were neither of primordial antiquity nor of
divine provenance. What Foucault has called the discovery of language was therefore a secular event that displaced a religious conception of how God delivered language to man in Eden.[31] Indeed,
one of the consequences of this change, by which an etymological,
dynastic notion of linguistic filiation was pushed aside by the view
of language as a domain all of its own held together with jagged
internal structures and coherences, is the dramatic subsidence of
interest in the problem of the origins of language. Whereas in the
1770s, which is when Herder's essay on the origins of language
won the 1772 medal from the Berlin Academy, it was all the rage
to discuss that problem, by the first decade of the new century it was
all but banned as a topic for learned dispute in Europe.

On all sides, and in many different ways, what William Jones
stated in his *Anniversary Discourses* (1785–1792), or what Franz
Bopp put forward in his *Vergleichende Grammatik* (1832), is that

the divine dynasty of language was ruptured definitively and discredited as an idea. A new historical conception, in short, was needed, since Christianity seemed unable to survive the empirical evidence that reduced the divine status of its major text. For some, as Chateaubriand put it, faith was unshakable despite new knowledge of how Sanskrit outdated Hebrew: "Hélas! il est arrivé qu'une connaissance plus approfondie de la langue savante de l'Inde a fait rentrer ces siècles innombrables dans le cercle étroit de la Bible. Bien m'en a pris d'être redevenue croyant, avant d'avoir éprouvé cette mortification."[32] (Alas! it has happened that a deeper knowledge of the learned language of India has forced innumerable centuries into the narrow circle of the Bible. How lucky for me that I have become a believer again before having had to experience this mortification.) For others, especially philologists like the pioneering Bopp himself, the study of language entailed its own history, philosophy, and learning, all of which did away with any notion of a primal language given by the Godhead to man in Eden. As the study of Sanskrit and the expansive mood of the later eighteenth century seemed to have moved the earliest beginnings of civilization very far east of the Biblical lands, so too language became less of a continuity between an outside power and the human speaker than an internal field created and accomplished by language users among themselves. There was no first language, just as—except by a method I shall discuss presently—there was no simple language.

The legacy of these first-generation philologists was, to Renan, of the highest importance, higher even than the work done by Sacy. Whenever he discussed language and philology, whether at the beginning, middle, or end of his long career, he repeated the lessons of the new philology, of which the antidynastic, anticontinuous tenets of a technical (as opposed to a divine) linguistic practice are the major pillar. For the linguist, language cannot be pictured as the result of force emanating unilaterally from God. As Coleridge put it, "Language is the armory of the human mind; and at once contains the trophies of its past and the weapons of its future conquests."[33] The idea of a first Edenic language gives way to the heuristic notion of a protolanguage (Indo-European, Semitic) whose existence is never a subject of debate, since it is acknowledged that such a language cannot be recaptured but can only be reconstituted in the philological process. To the extent that one language serves, again heuristically, as a touchstone for all the others, it is Sanskrit in its earliest Indo-European form. The terminology has also shifted: there are now *families* of languages (the analogy with species and anatomical classifications is marked), there is *perfect* linguistic form, which need not correspond to any "real" language, and there are original languages only as a function of the philological discourse, not because of nature.

But some writers shrewdly commented on how it was that Sanskrit and things Indian in general simply took the place of Hebrew and the Edenic fallacy. As early as 1804 Benjamin Constant noted in his *Journal intime* that he was not about to discuss India in his *De la religion* because the English who owned the place and the Germans who studied it indefatigably had made India the *fons et origo* of everything; and then there were the French who had decided after Napoleon and Champollion that everything originated in Egypt and the new Orient.[34] These teleological enthusiasms were fueled after 1808 by Friedrich Schlegel's celebrated *Über die Sprache und Weisheit der Indier*, which seemed to confirm his own pronouncement made in 1800 about the Orient being the purest form of Romanticism.

What Renan's generation—educated from the mid-1830s to the late 1840s—retained from all this enthusiasm about the Orient was the intellectual necessity of the Orient for the Occidental scholar of languages, cultures, and religions. Here the key text was Edgar Quinet's *Le Génie des religions* (1832), a work that announced the Oriental Renaissance and placed the Orient and the West in a functional relationship with each other. I have already referred to the vast meaning of this relationship as analyzed comprehensively by Raymond Schwab in *La Renaissance orientale*; my concern with it here is only to note specific aspects of it that bear upon Renan's vocation as a philologist and as an Orientalist. Quinet's association with Michelet, their interest in Herder and Vico, respectively, impressed on them the need for the scholar-historian to confront, almost in the manner of an audience seeing a dramatic event unfold, or a believer witnessing a revelation, the different, the strange, the distant. Quinet's formulation was that the Orient proposes and the West disposes: Asia has its prophets, Europe its doctors (its learned men, its scientists: the pun is intended). Out of this encounter, a new dogma or god is born, but Quinet's point is that both East and West fulfill their destinies and confirm their identities in the encounter. As a scholarly attitude the picture of a learned Westerner surveying as if from a peculiarly suited vantage point the passive, seminal, feminine, even silent and supine East, then going on to *articulate* the East, making the Orient deliver up its secrets under the learned authority of a philologist whose power derives from the ability to unlock secret, esoteric languages—this would persist in Renan. What did not persist in Renan during the 1840s, when he served his apprenticeship as a philologist, was the dramatic attitude: that was replaced by the scientific attitude.

For Quinet and Michelet, history was a drama. Quinet suggestively describes the whole world as a temple and human history as a sort of religious rite. Both Michelet and Quinet *saw* the world they discussed. The origin of human history was something they could describe in the same splendid and impassioned and dramatic terms used by Vico and Rousseau to portray life on earth in primitive times. For Michelet and Quinet there is no doubt that they belong to the communal European Romantic undertaking "either in epic or some other major genre—in drama, in prose romance, or in the visionary 'greater Ode'—radically to recast into terms appropriate to the historical and intellectual circumstances of their own age, the Christian pattern of the fall, the redemption, and the emergence of a new earth which will constitute a restored paradise."[85] I think that for Quinet the idea of a new god being born was tantamount to the filling of the place left by the old god; for Renan, however, being a philologist meant the severance of any and all connections with the old Christian god, so that instead a new doctrine—probably science—would stand free and in a new place, as it were. Renan's whole career was devoted to the fleshing out of this progress.

He put it very plainly at the end of his undistinguished essay on the origins of language: man is no longer an inventor, and the age of creation is definitely over.[36] There was a period, at which we can only guess, when man was literally *transported* from silence into words. After that there was language, and for the true scientist the task is to examine how language *is*, not how it came about. Yet if Renan dispels the passionate creation of primitive times (which had excited Herder, Vico, Rousseau, even Quinet and Michelet) he instates a new, and deliberate, type of artificial creation, one that is performed as a result of scientific analysis. In his *leçon inaugurale* at the College de France (February 21, 1862) Renan proclaimed his lectures open to the public so that it might see at first hand "le laboratoire même de la science philologique" (the very laboratory of philological science).[37] Any reader of Renan would have understood that such a statement was meant also to carry a typical if rather limp irony, one less intended to shock than passively to delight. For Renan was succeeding to the chair of Hebrew, and his lecture was on the contribution of the Semitic peoples to the history of civilization. What more subtle affront could there be to "sacred" history than the substitution of a philological laboratory for divine intervention in history; and what more telling way was there of declaring the Orient's contemporary relevance to be simply as material for European investigation?[38] Sacy's comparatively lifeless fragments arranged in tableaux were now being replaced with something new.

The stirring peroration with which Renan concluded his *leçon* had another function than simply to connect Oriental-Semitic philology with the future and with science. Étienne Quatremère, who immediately preceded Renan in the chair of Hebrew, was a scholar who seemed to exemplify the popular caricature of what a scholar was like. A man of prodigiously industrious and pedantic habits, he went about his work, Renan said in a relatively unfeeling memorial minute for the *Journal des débats* in October 1857, like a laborious worker who even in rendering immense services nevertheless could not see the whole edifice being constructed. The edifice was nothing less than "la science historique de l'esprit humain," now in the process of being built stone by stone.[39] Just as Quatremère was not of this age, so Renan in his work was determined to be of it. Moreover, if the Orient had been hitherto identified exclusively and indiscriminately with India and China, Renan's ambition was to carve out a new Oriental province for himself, in this case the Semitic Orient. He had no doubt remarked the casual, and surely current, confusion of Arabic with Sanskrit (as in Balzac's *La Peau de chagrin*, where the fateful talisman's Arabic script is described as Sanskrit), and he made it his job accordingly to do for the Semitic languages what Bopp had done for the Indo-European: so he said in the 1855 preface to the comparative Semitic treatise.[40] Therefore Renan's plans were to bring the Semitic languages into sharp and glamorous focus *à la* Bopp, and in addition to elevate the study of these neglected inferior languages to the level of a passionate new science of mind *à la* Louis Lambert.

On more than one occasion Renan was quite explicit in his asser-

tions that Semites and Semitic were *creations* of Orientalist philological study.[41] Since he was the man who did the study, there was
meant to be little ambiguity about the centrality of his role in this
new, artificial creation. But how did Renan mean the word *creation*
in these instances? And how was this creation connected with either
natural creation, or the creation ascribed by Renan and others to
the laboratory and to the classificatory and natural sciences,
principally what was called philosophical anatomy? Here we must
speculate a little. Throughout his career Renan seemed to imagine
the role of science in human life as (and I quote in translation as
literally as I can) "*telling* (speaking or articulating) definitively
to man the word [logos?] of things."[42] Science gives speech to
things; better yet, science brings out, causes to be pronounced, a
potential speech within things. The special value of linguistics (as
the new philology was then often called) is not that natural science
resembles it, but rather that it treats words as natural, otherwise
silent objects, which are made to give up their secrets. Remember
that the major breakthrough in the study of inscriptions and hiero-
glyphs was the discovery by Champollion that the symbols on the
Rosetta Stone had a *phonetic* as well as a semantic component.[43]
To make objects speak was like making words speak, giving them
circumstantial value, and a precise place in a rule-governed order
of regularity. In its first sense, *creation*, as Renan used the word,
signified the articulation by which an object like *Semitic* could be
seen as a creature of sorts. Second, creation also signified the setting
—in the case of Semitic it meant Oriental history, culture, race,
mind—illuminated and brought forward from its reticence by the
scientist. Finally, creation was the formulation of a system of classification by which it was possible to see the object in question
comparatively with other like objects; and by "comparatively"
Renan intended a complex network of paradigmatic relations that
obtained between Semitic and Indo-European languages.

If in what I have so far said I have insisted so much on Renan's
comparatively forgotten study of Semitic languages, it has been for
several important reasons. Semitic was the scientific study to which
Renan turned right after the loss of his Christian faith; I described
above how he came to see the study of Semitic as replacing his
faith and enabling a critical future relation with it. The study of
Semitic was Renan's first full-length Orientalist and scientific study
(finished in 1847, published first in 1855), and was as much a part
of his late major works on the origins of Christianity and the his-

tory of the Jews as it was a propaedeutic for them. In intention, if not perhaps in achievement—interestingly, few of the standard or contemporary works in either linguistic history or the history of Orientalism cite Renan with anything more than cursory attention[44] —his Semitic opus was proposed as a philological breakthrough, from which in later years he was always to draw retrospective authority for his positions (almost always bad ones) on religion, race, and nationalism.[45] Whenever Renan wished to make a statement about either the Jews or the Muslims, for example, it was always with his remarkably harsh (and unfounded, except according to the science he was practicing) strictures on the Semites in mind. Furthermore, Renan's Semitic was meant as a contribution both to the development of Indo-European linguistics and to the differentiation of Orientalisms. To the former Semitic was a degraded form, degraded in both the moral and the biological sense, whereas to the latter Semitic was a—if not the—stable form of cultural decadence. Lastly, Semitic was Renan's first creation, a fiction invented by him in the philological laboratory to satisfy his sense of public place and mission. It should by no means be lost on us that Semitic was for Renan's ego the symbol of European (and consequently his) dominion over the Orient and over his own era.

Therefore, as a branch of the Orient, Semitic was not fully a natural object—like a species of monkey, for instance—nor fully an unnatural or a divine object, as it had once been considered. Rather, Semitic occupied a median position, legitimated in its oddities (regularity being defined by Indo-European) by an inverse relation to normal languages, comprehended as an eccentric, quasi-monstrous phenomenon partly because libraries, laboratories, and museums could serve as its place of exhibition and analysis. In his treatise, Renan adopted a tone of voice and a method of exposition that drew the maximum from book-learning and from natural observation as practiced by men like Cuvier and the Geoffroy Saint-Hilaires *père et fils*. This is an important stylistic achievement, for it allowed Renan consistently to avail himself of the *library*, rather than either primitivity or divine fiat, as a conceptual framework in which to understand language, together with the *museum*, which is where the results of laboratory observation are delivered for exhibition, study, and teaching.[46] Everywhere Renan treats of normal human facts—language, history, culture, mind, imagination—as transformed into something else, as something peculiarly deviant, because they are Semitic and Oriental, and because they end up for analysis in the laboratory. Thus the Semites are rabid monotheists who produced no mythology, no art, no commerce, no civilization; their consciousness is a narrow and rigid one; all in all they represent "une combinaison inférieure de la nature humaine."[47] At the same time Renan wants it understood that he speaks of a prototype, not a real Semitic type with actual existence (although he violated this too by discussing present-day Jews and Muslims with less than scientific detachment in many places in his writings).[48] So on the one hand we have the transformation of the human into the specimen, and on the other the comparative judgment rendered by which the specimen remains a specimen and a subject for philological, scientific study.

Scattered throughout the *Histoire générale et système comparé des langues sémitiques* are reflections on the links between linguistics and anatomy, and—for Renan this is equally important—remarks on how these links could be employed to do human history (*les sciences historiques*). But first we should consider the implicit links. I do not think it wrong or an exaggeration to say that a typical page of Renan's Orientalist *Histoire générale* was constructed typographically and structurally with a page of comparative philosophical anatomy, in the style of Cuvier or Geoffroy Saint-Hilaire, kept in mind. Both linguists and anatomists purport to be speaking about matters not directly obtainable or observable in nature; a skeleton and a detailed line drawing of a muscle, as much as paradigms constituted by the linguists out of a purely hypothetical proto-Semitic or proto-Indo-European, are similarly products of the laboratory and of the library. The text of a linguistic or an anatomical work bears the same general relation to nature (or actuality) that a museum case exhibiting a specimen mammal or organ does. What is given on the page and in the museum case is a truncated exaggeration, like many of Sacy's Oriental extracts, whose purpose is to exhibit a relationship between the science (or scientist) and the object, not one between the object and nature. Read almost any page by Renan on Arabic, Hebrew, Aramaic, or proto-Semitic and you read a fact of power, by which the Orientalist philologist's authority summons out of the library at will examples of man's speech, and ranges them there surrounded by a suave European prose that points out defects, virtues, barbarisms, and shortcomings in the language, the people, and the civilization. The tone and the tense of the exhibition are cast almost uniformly in the contemporary present, so that one is given an impression of a

pedagogical demonstration during which the scholar-scientist stands
before us on a lecture-laboratory platform, creating, confining, and
judging the material he discusses.

This anxiety on Renan's part to convey the sense of a demonstration actually taking place is heightened when he remarks explicitly
that whereas anatomy employs stable and visible signs by which to
consign objects to classes, linguistics does not.[49] Therefore the
philologist must make a given linguistic fact correspond in some
way to a historical period: hence the possibility of a classification.
Yet, as Renan was often to say, linguistic temporality and history
are full of lacunae, enormous discontinuities, hypothetical periods.
Therefore linguistic events occur in a nonlinear and essentially dis-
continuous temporal dimension controlled by the linguist in a very
particular way. That way, as Renan's whole treatise on the Semitic
branch of the Oriental languages goes very far to show, is comparative: Indo-European is taken as the living, *organic* norm, and
Semitic Oriental languages are seen comparatively to be *inorganic*.[50] Time is transformed into the space of comparative classification, which at bottom is based on a rigid binary opposition
between organic and inorganic languages. So on the one hand there
is the organic, biologically generative process represented by Indo-
European, while on the other there is an inorganic, essentially un-
regenerative process, ossified into Semitic: most important, Renan
makes it absolutely clear that such an imperious judgment is made
by the Oriental philologist in his laboratory, for distinctions of the
kind he has been concerned with are neither possible nor available
for anyone except the trained professional. "Nous refusons donc
aux langues sémitiques la faculté de se régénérer, toute en recon-
naissant qu'elles n'échappent pas plus que les autres oeuvres de la
conscience humaine à la nécessité du changement et des modifications successives" (Therefore we refuse to allow that the Semitic
languages have the capacity to regenerate themselves, even while
recognizing that they do not escape—any more than other products
of human consciousness—the necessity of change or of successive
modifications).[51]

Yet behind even this radical opposition, there is another one
working in Renan's mind, and for several pages in the first chapter
of book 5 he exposes his position quite candidly to the reader. This
occurs when he introduces Saint-Hilaire's views on the "degradation of types."[52] Although Renan does not specify which Saint-
Hilaire he refers to, the reference is clear enough. For both Étienne

and his son Isidore were biological speculators of extraordinary fame and influence, particularly among literary intellectuals during the first half of the nineteenth century in France. Étienne, we recall, had been a member of the Napoleonic expedition, and Balzac dedicated an important section of the preface for *La Comédie humaine* to him; there is also much evidence that Flaubert read both the father and the son and used their views in his work.[53] Not only were Étienne and Isidore legatees of the tradition of "Romantic" biology, which included Goethe and Cuvier, with a strong interest in analogy, homology, and organic *ur*-form among species, but they were also specialists in the philosophy and anatomy of monstrosity—teratology, as Isidore called it—in which the most horrendous physiological aberrations were considered a result of internal degradation within the species-life.[54] I cannot here go into the intricacies (as well as the macabre fascination) of teratology, though it is enough to mention that both Étienne and Isidore exploited the theoretical power of the linguistic paradigm to explain the deviations possible within a biological system. Thus Étienne's notion was that a monster is an *anomaly*, in the same sense that in language words exist in analogical as well as anomalous relations with each other: in linguistics the idea is at least as old as Varro's *De Lingua Latina*. No anomaly can be considered simply as a gratuitous exception; rather anomalies confirm the regular structure binding together all members of the same class. Such a view is quite daring in anatomy. At one moment in the "Préliminaire" to his *Philosophie anatomique* Étienne says:

> And, indeed, such is the character of our epoch that it becomes impossible today to enclose oneself strictly within the framework of a simple monograph. Study an object in isolation and you will only be able to bring it back to itself; consequently you can never have perfect knowledge of it. But see it in the midst of beings who are connected with each other in many different ways, and which are isolated from each other in different ways, and you will discover for this object a wider scope of relationships. First of all, you will know it better, even in its specificity: but more important, by considering it in the very center of its own sphere of activity, you will know precisely how it behaves in its own exterior world, and you will also know how its own features are constituted in reaction to its surrounding milieu.[55]

Not only is Saint-Hilaire saying that it is the specific character of contemporary study (he was writing in 1822) to examine phenomena comparatively; he is also saying that for the scientist there is no such thing as a phenomenon, no matter how aberrant and exceptional, that cannot be explained with reference to other phenomena. Note also how Saint-Hilaire employs the metaphor of centrality (*le centre de sa sphère d'activité*) used later by Renan in *L'Avenir de la science* to describe the position occupied by any object in nature—including even the philologist—once the object is scientifically *placed* there by the examining scientist. Thereafter between the object and the scientist a bond of sympathy is established. Of course, this can only take place during the laboratory experience, and not elsewhere. The point being made is that a scientist has at his disposal a sort of leverage by which even the totally unusual occurrence can be seen naturally and known scientifically, which in this case means without recourse to the supernatural, and with recourse only to an enveloping environment constituted by the scientist. As a result nature itself can be reperceived as continuous, harmoniously coherent, and fundamentally intelligible.

Thus for Renan Semitic is a phenomenon of arrested development in comparison with the mature languages and cultures of the Indo-European group, and even with the other Semitic Oriental languages.[56] The paradox that Renan sustains, however, is that even as he encourages us to see languages as in some way corresponding to "êtres vivants de la nature," he is everywhere else proving that his Oriental languages, the Semitic languages, are inorganic, arrested, totally ossified, incapable of self-regeneration; in other words, he proves that Semitic is not a live language, and for that matter, neither are Semites live creatures. Moreover, Indo-European language and culture are alive and organic *because* of the laboratory, not despite it. But far from being a marginal issue in Renan's work, this paradox stands, I believe, at the very center of his entire work, his style, and his archival existence in the culture of his time, a culture to which—as people so unlike each other as Matthew Arnold, Oscar Wilde, James Frazer, and Marcel Proust concurred —he was a very important contributor. To be able to sustain a vision that incorporates and holds together life and quasi-living creatures (Indo-European, European culture) as well as quasi-monstrous, parallel inorganic phenomena (Semitic, Oriental culture) is precisely the achievement of the European scientist in his laboratory. He *constructs*, and the very act of construction is a sign of imperial power over recalcitrant phenomena, as well as a confirmation of the dominating culture and its "naturalization." Indeed, it is not too much to say that Renan's philological laboratory is the actual locale of his European ethnocentrism; but what needs emphasis here is that the philological laboratory has no existence outside the discourse, the writing by which it is constantly produced and experienced. Thus even the culture he calls organic and alive— Europe's—is also a *creature being created* in the laboratory and by philology.

Renan's entire later career was European and cultural. Its accomplishments were varied and celebrated. Whatever authority his style possessed can, I think, be traced back to his technique for constructing the inorganic (or the missing) and for giving it the appearance of life. He was most famous, of course, for his *Vie de Jésus*, the work that inaugurated his monumental histories of Christianity and the Jewish people. Yet we must realize that the *Vie* was exactly the same type of feat that the *Histoire générale* was, a construction enabled by the historian's capacity for skillfully crafting a dead (dead for Renan in the double sense of a dead faith and a lost, hence dead, historical period) Oriental biography —and the paradox is immediately apparent—*as if it were* the truthful narrative of a natural life. Whatever Renan said had first passed through the philological laboratory; when it appeared in print woven through the text, there was in it the life-giving force of a contemporary cultural signature, which drew from modernity all its scientific power and all its uncritical self-approbation. For that sort of culture such genealogies as dynasty, tradition, religion, ethnic communities were all simply functions of a theory whose job was to instruct the world. In borrowing this latter phrase from Cuvier, Renan was circumspectly placing scientific demonstration over experience; temporality was relegated to the scientifically useless realm of ordinary experience, while to the special periodicity of culture and cultural comparativism (which spawned ethnocentrism, racial theory, and economic oppression) were given powers far in advance of moral vision.

Renan's style, his career as Orientalist and man of letters, the circumstances of the meaning he communicates, his peculiarly intimate relationship with the European scholarly and general culture of his time—liberal, exclusivist, imperious, antihuman except in a very conditional sense—all these are what I would call *celibate* and scientific. Generation for him is consigned to the realm of *l'avenir*, which in his famous manifesto he associated with science. Although as a historian of culture he belongs to the school of men like Turgot, Condorcet, Guizot, Cousin, Jouffroy, and Ballanche, and in scholarship to the school of Sacy, Caussin de Perceval, Ozanam, Fauriel, and Burnouf, Renan's is a peculiarly ravaged, ragingly masculine world of history and learning; it is indeed the world, not of fathers, mothers, and children, but of men like his Jesus, his Marcus Aurelius, his Caliban, his solar god (the last as described in "Rêves" of the *Dialogues philosophiques*).[57] He cherished the power of science and Orientalist philology particularly; he sought its insights and its techniques; he used it to intervene, often with considerable effectiveness, in the life of his epoch. And yet his ideal role was that of spectator.

According to Renan, a philologist ought to prefer *bonheur* to *jouissance*: the preference expresses a choice of elevated, if sterile, happiness over sexual pleasure. Words belong to the realm of *bonheur*, as does the study of words, ideally speaking. To my knowledge, there are very few moments in all of Renan's public writing where a beneficent and instrumental role is assigned to women. One occurs when Renan opines that foreign women (nurses, maids) must have instructed the conquering Normans' children, and hence we can account for the changes that take place in language. Note how productivity and dissemination are not the functions aided, but rather internal change, and a subsidiary one at that. "Man," he says at the end of the same essay, "belongs neither to his language nor to his race; he belongs to himself before all, since before all he is a free being and a moral one."[58] Man was free and moral, but enchained by race, history, and science as Renan saw them, conditions imposed by the scholar on man.

The study of Oriental languages took Renan to the heart of these conditions, and philology made it concretely apparent that knowledge of man was—to paraphrase Ernst Cassirer—poetically transfiguring[59] only if it had been previously severed from raw actuality (as Sacy had necessarily severed his Arabic fragments from their actuality) and then put into a doxological straitjacket. By becoming *philology*, the study of words as once practiced by Vico, Herder, Rousseau, Michelet, and Quinet lost its plot and its dramatic presentational quality, as Schelling once called it. Instead, philology became epistemologically complex; *Sprachgefühl* was no longer enough since words themselves pertained less to the senses or the body (as they had for Vico) and more to a sightless, imageless, and abstract realm ruled over by such hothouse formulations as race, mind, culture, and nation. In that realm, which was discursively constructed and called the Orient, certain kinds of assertions could be made, all of them possessing the same powerful generality and cultural validity. For all of Renan's effort was to deny Oriental culture the right to be generated, except artificially in the philological laboratory. A man was not a child of the culture; that dynastic conception had been too effectively challenged by philology. Philology taught one how culture is a construct, an *articulation* (in the sense that Dickens used the word for Mr. Venus's profession in *Our Mutual Friend*), even a creation, but not anything more than a quasi-organic structure.

What is specially interesting in Renan is how much he knew himself to be a creature of his time and of his ethnocentric culture. On the occasion of an academic response to a speech made by Ferdinand de Lesseps in 1885, Renan averred as how "it was so sad to be a wiser man than one's nation. . . . One cannot feel bitterness towards one's homeland. Better to be mistaken along with the nation than to be too right with those who tell it hard truths."[60] The economy of such a statement is almost too perfect to be true. For does not the old Renan say that the best relationship is one of parity with one's own culture, its morality, and its ethos during one's time, that and not a dynastic relation by which one is either the child of his times or their parent? And here we return to the laboratory, for it is there—as Renan thought of it—that filial and ultimately social responsibilities cease and scientific and Orientalist ones take over. His laboratory was the platform from which as an Orientalist he addressed the world; it mediated the statements he made, gave them confidence and general precision, as well as continuity. Thus the philological laboratory as Renan understood it redefined not only his epoch and his culture, dating and shaping them in new ways; it gave his Oriental subject matter a scholarly coherence, and more, it made him (and later Orientalists in his tradition) into the Occidental *cultural* figure he then became. We may well wonder whether this new autonomy within the culture was the freedom Renan hoped his philological Orientalist science would bring or whether, so far as a critical historian of Orientalism is concerned, it set up a complex affiliation between Orientalism and its putative human subject matter that is based finally on power and not really on disinterested objectivity.

III

Oriental Residence
and Scholarship:
The Requirements of
Lexicography and Imagination

Renan's views of the Oriental Semites belong, of course, less to
the realm of popular prejudice and common anti-Semitism than
they do to the realm of scientific Oriental philology. When we read
Renan and Sacy, we readily observe the way cultural generalization
had begun to acquire the armor of scientific statement and the
ambience of corrective study. Like many academic specialties in
their early phases, modern Orientalism held its subject matter, which
it defined, in a viselike grip which it did almost everything in its
power to sustain. Thus a knowing vocabulary developed, and its
functions, as much as its style, located the Orient in a *comparative*
framework, of the sort employed and manipulated by Renan. Such
comparatism is rarely descriptive; most often, it is both evaluative
and expository. Here is Renan comparing typically:

> One sees that in all things the Semitic race appears to us to be
> an incomplete race, by virtue of its simplicity. This race—if I dare
> use the analogy—is to the Indo-European family what a pencil
> sketch is to painting; it lacks that variety, that amplitude, that
> abundance of life which is the condition of perfectibility. Like
> those individuals who possess so little fecundity that, after a
> gracious childhood, they attain only the most mediocre virility,
> the Semitic nations experienced their fullest flowering in their first
> age and have never been able to achieve true maturity.[61]

Indo-Europeans are the touchstone here, just as they are when
Renan says that the Semitic Oriental sensibility never reached the
heights attained by the Indo-Germanic races.

Whether this comparative attitude is principally a scholarly necessity or whether it is disguised ethnocentric race prejudice, we
cannot say with absolute certainty. What we can say is that the two

work together, in support of each other. What Renan and Sacy tried to do was to reduce the Orient to a kind of human flatness, which exposed its characteristics easily to scrutiny and removed from it its complicating humanity. In Renan's case, the legitimacy of his efforts was provided by philology, whose ideological tenets encourage the reduction of a language to its roots; thereafter, the philologist finds it possible to connect those linguistics roots, as Renan and others did, to race, mind, character, and temperament at their roots. The affinity between Renan and Gobineau, for example, was acknowledged by Renan to be a common philological and Orientalist perspective;[62] in subsequent editions of the *Histoire générale* he incorporated some of Gobineau's work within his own. Thus did comparatism in the study of the Orient and Orientals come to be synonymous with the apparent ontological inequality of Occident and Orient.

The main traits of this inequality are worth recapitulating briefly. I have already referred to Schlegel's enthusiasm for India, and then his subsequent revulsion from it and of course from Islam. Many of the earliest Oriental amateurs began by welcoming the Orient as a salutary *dérangement* of their European habits of mind and spirit. The Orient was overvalued for its pantheism, its spirituality, its stability, its longevity, its primitivity, and so forth. Schelling, for example, saw in Oriental polytheism a preparation of the way for Judeo-Christian monotheism: Abraham was prefigured in Brahma. Yet almost without exception such overesteem was followed by a counterresponse: the Orient suddenly appeared lamentably under-humanized, antidemocratic, backward, barbaric, and so forth. A swing of the pendulum in one direction caused an equal and opposite swing back: the Orient was undervalued. Orientalism as a profession grew out of these opposites, of compensations and corrections based on inequality, ideas nourished by and nourishing similar ideas in the culture at large. Indeed the very project of restriction and restructuring associated with Orientalism can be traced directly to the inequality by which the Orient's comparative poverty (or wealth) besought scholarly, scientific treatment of the kind to be found in disciplines like philology, biology, history, anthropology, philosophy, or economics.

And thus the actual profession of Orientalist enshrined this inequality and the special paradoxes it engendered. Most often an individual entered the profession as a way of reckoning with the Orient's claim on him; yet most often too his Orientalist training opened his eyes, so to speak, and what he was left with was a sort of debunking project, by which the Orient was reduced to considerably less than the eminence once seen in it. How else is one to explain the enormous labors represented by the work of William Muir (1819–1905), for example, or of Reinhart Dozy (1820–1883), and the impressive antipathy in that work to the Orient, Islam, and the Arabs? Characteristically, Renan was one of Dozy's supporters, just as in Dozy's four-volume *Histoire des Mussulmans d'Espagne, jusqu'à la conquête de l'Andalousie par les Almoravides* (1861) there appear many of Renan's anti-Semitic strictures, compounded in 1864 by a volume arguing that the Jews' primitive God was not Jahweh but Baal, proof for which was to be found in Mecca, of all places. Muir's *Life of Mahomet* (1858–1861) and his *The Caliphate, Its Rise, Decline and Fall* (1891) are still considered reliable monuments of scholarship, yet his attitude towards his subject matter was fairly put by him when he said that "the sword of Muhammed, and the Kor'ān, are the most stubborn enemies of Civilisation, Liberty, and the Truth which the world has yet known."[63] Many of the same notions are to be found in the work of Alfred Lyall, who was one of the authors cited approvingly by Cromer.

Even if the Orientalist does not explicitly judge his material as Dozy and Muir did, the principle of inequality exerts its influence nevertheless. It remains the professional Orientalist's job to piece together a portrait, a restored picture as it were, of the Orient or the Oriental; fragments, such as those unearthed by Sacy, supply the material, but the narrative shape, continuity, and figures are constructed by the scholar, for whom scholarship consists of circumventing the unruly (un-Occidental) nonhistory of the Orient with orderly chronicle, portraits, and plots. Caussin de Perceval's *Essai sur l'histoire des Arabes avant l'Islamisme, pendant l'époque de Mahomet* (three volumes, 1847–1848) is a wholly professional study, depending for its sources on documents made available *internally* to the field by other Orientalists (principally Sacy, of course) or documents—like the texts of ibn-Khaldun, upon whom Caussin relied very heavily—reposing in Orientalist libraries in Europe. Caussin's thesis is that the Arabs were made a people by Mohammed, Islam being essentially a political instrument, not by any means a spiritual one. What Caussin strives for is clarity amidst a huge mass of confusing detail. Thus what emerges out of the study of Islam is quite literally a one-dimensional portrait of Mohammed, who is made to appear at the end of the work (after his death has been described) in precise photographic detail.[64] Neither a demon, nor a prototype of Cagliostro, Caussin's Mohammed is a man appropriated to a history of Islam (the fittest version of it) as an exclusively political movement, centralized by the innumerable citations that thrust him up and, in a sense, out of the text. Caussin's intention was to leave nothing unsaid about Mohammed; the Prophet is thereby seen in a cold light, stripped both of his immense religious force and of any residual powers to frighten Europeans. The point here is that as a figure for his own time and place Mohammed is effaced, in order for a very slight human miniature of him to be left standing.

A nonprofessional analogue to Caussin's Mohammed is Carlyle's, a Mohammed forced to serve a thesis totally overlooking the historical and cultural circumstances of the Prophet's own time and place. Although Carlyle quotes Sacy, his essay is clearly the product of someone arguing for some general ideas on sincerity, heroism, and prophethood. His attitude is salutary: Mohammed is no legend, no shameful sensualist, no laughable petty sorcerer who trained pigeons to pick peas out of his ear. Rather he is a man of real vision and self-conviction, albeit an author of a book, the Koran, that is "a wearisome confused jumble, crude, incondite; endless iterations, long-windedness, entanglement; most crude, incondite— insupportable stupidity, in short."[65] Not a paragon of lucidity and stylistic grace himself, Carlyle asserts these things as a way of rescuing Mohammed from the Benthamite standards that would have condemned both Mohammed and him together. Yet Mohammed is a hero, transplanted into Europe out of the same barbaric Orient found wanting by Lord Macaulay in his famous "Minute" of 1835, in which it was asserted that "our native subjects" have more to learn from us than we do from them.[86]

Both Caussin and Carlyle, in other words, show us that the Orient need not cause us undue anxiety, so unequal are Oriental to European achievements. The Orientalist and non-Orientalist perspectives coincide here. For within the comparative field that Orientalism became after the philological revolution of the early nineteenth century, and outside it, either in popular stereotypes or in the figures made of the Orient by philosophers like Carlyle and stereotypes like those of Macaulay, the Orient in itself was subordinated intellectually to the West. As material for study or reflection the Orient acquired all the marks of an inherent weakness. It became subject to the vagaries of miscellaneous theories that used it for illustration. Cardinal Newman, no great Orientalist, used Oriental Islam as the basis of lectures in 1853 justifying British intervention in the Crimean War.[67] Cuvier found the Orient useful for his work *Le Règne animal* (1816). The Orient was usefully employed as conversation in the various salons of Paris.[68] The list of references, borrowings, and transformations that overtook the Oriental idea is immense, but at bottom what the early Orientalist achieved, and what the non-Orientalist in the West exploited, was a reduced model of the Orient suitable for the prevailing, dominant culture and its theoretical (and hard after the theoretical, the practical) exigencies.

Occasionally one comes across exceptions, or if not exceptions then interesting complications, to this unequal partnership between East and West. Karl Marx identified the notion of an Asiatic economic system in his 1853 analyses of British rule in India, and then put beside that immediately the human depredation introduced into this system by English colonial interference, rapacity, and outright cruelty. In article after article he returned with increasing conviction to the idea that even in destroying Asia, Britain was making possible there a real social revolution. Marx's style pushes us right up against the difficulty of reconciling our natural repugnance as fellow creatures to the sufferings of Orientals while their society is being violently transformed with the historical necessity of these transformations.

> Now, sickening as it must be to human feeling to witness those myriads of industrious patriarchal and inoffensive social organizations disorganized and dissolved into their units, thrown into a sea of woes, and their individual members losing at the same time their ancient form of civilization and their hereditary means of subsistence, we must not forget that these idyllic village communities, inoffensive though they may appear, had always been the solid foundation of Oriental despotism, that they restrained the human mind within the smallest possible compass, making it the unresisting tool of superstition, enslaving it beneath the traditional rules, depriving it of all grandeur and historical energies. . . .
>
> England, it is true, in causing a social revolution in Hindustan was actuated only by the vilest interests, and was stupid in her manner of enforcing them. But that is not the question. The question is, can mankind fulfil its destiny without a fundamental revolution in the social state of Asia? If not, whatever may have been the crimes of England she was the unconscious tool of history in bringing about that revolution.

Then, whatever bitterness the spectacle of the crumbling of an
ancient world may have for our personal feelings, we have the
right, in point of history, to exclaim with Goethe:

> Sollte diese Qual uns quälen
> Da sie unsere Lust vermehrt
> Hat nicht Myriaden Seelen
> Timurs Herrschaft aufgeziehrt?[69]
>
> (Should this torture then torment us
> Since it brings us greater pleasure?
> Were not through the rule of Timur
> Souls devoured without measure?)

The quotation, which supports Marx's argument about torment
producing pleasure, comes from the *Westöstlicher Diwan* and
identifies the sources of Marx's conceptions about the Orient. These
are Romantic and even messianic: as human material the Orient is
less important than as an element in a Romantic redemptive project.
Marx's economic analyses are perfectly fitted thus to a standard
Orientalist undertaking, even though Marx's humanity, his sympathy for the misery of people, are clearly engaged. Yet in the end
it is the Romantic Orientalist vision that wins out, as Marx's
theoretical socio-economic views become submerged in this class-
ically standard image:

> England has to fulfill a double mission in India: one destructive,
> the other regenerating—the annihilation of the Asiatic society,
> and the laying of the material foundations of Western society in
> Asia.[70]

The idea of regenerating a fundamentally lifeless Asia is a piece of
pure Romantic Orientalism, of course, but coming from the same
writer who could not easily forget the human suffering involved, the
statement is puzzling. It requires us first to ask how Marx's moral
equation of Asiatic loss with the British colonial rule he condemned
gets skewed back towards the old inequality between East and West
we have so far remarked. Second, it requires us to ask where the
human sympathy has gone, into what realm of thought it has disappeared while the Orientalist vision takes its place.

We are immediately brought back to the realization that Orientalists, like many other early-nineteenth-century thinkers, conceive
of humanity either in large collective terms or in abstract generalities. Orientalists are neither interested in nor capable of discussing individuals; instead artificial entities, perhaps with their

roots in Herderian populism, predominate. There are Orientals, Asiatics, Semites, Muslims, Arabs, Jews, races, mentalities, nations, and the like, some of them the product of learned operations of the type found in Renan's work. Similarly, the age-old distinction between "Europe" and "Asia" or "Occident" and "Orient" herds beneath very wide labels every possible variety of human plurality, reducing it in the process to one or two terminal, collective abstractions. Marx is no exception. The collective Orient was easier for him to use in illustration of a theory than existential human identities. For between Orient and Occident, as if in a self-fulfilling proclamation, only the vast anonymous collectivity mattered, or existed. No other type of exchange, severely constrained though it may have been, was at hand.

That Marx was still able to sense some fellow feeling, to identify even a little with poor Asia, suggests that something happened before the labels took over, before he was dispatched to Goethe as a source of wisdom on the Orient. It is as if the individual mind (Marx's, in this case) could find a precollective, preofficial individuality in Asia—find and give in to its pressures upon his emotions, feelings, senses—only to give it up when he confronted a more formidable censor in the very vocabulary he found himself forced to employ. What that censor did was to stop and then chase away the sympathy, and this was accompanied by a lapidary definition: Those people, it said, don't suffer—they are Orientals and hence have to be treated in other ways than the ones you've just been using. A wash of sentiment therefore disappeared as it encountered the unshakable definitions built up by Orientalist science, supported by "Oriental" lore (e.g., the *Diwan*) supposed to be appropriate for it. The vocabulary of emotion dissipated as it submitted to the lexicographical police action of Orientalist science and even Orientalist art. An experience was dislodged by a dictionary definition: one can almost see that happen in Marx's Indian essays, where what finally occurs is that something forces him to scurry back to Goethe, there to stand in his protective Orientalized Orient.

In part, of course, Marx was concerned with vindicating his own theses on socio-economic revolution; but in part also he seems to have had easy resource to a massed body of writing, both internally consolidated by Orientalism and put forward by it beyond the field, that controlled any statement made about the Orient. In Chapter One I tried to show how this control had had a general cultural

history in Europe since antiquity; in this chapter my concern has
been to show how in the nineteenth century a modern professional
terminology and practice were created whose existence dominated
discourse about the Orient, whether by Orientalists or non-Orien-
talists. Sacy and Renan were instances of the way Orientalism
fashioned, respectively, a body of texts and a philologically rooted
process by which the Orient took on a discursive identity that made
it unequal with the West. In using Marx as the case by which a
non-Orientalist's human engagements were first dissolved, then
usurped by Orientalist generalizations, we find ourselves having to
consider the process of lexicographical and institutional consolidation peculiar to Orientalism. What was this operation, by which
whenever you discussed the Orient a formidable mechanism of
omnicompetent definitions would present itself as the only one having suitable validity for your discussion? And since we must also
show how this mechanism operated specifically (and effectively)
upon personal human experiences that otherwise contradicted it, we
must also show where *they* went and what forms *they* took, while
they lasted.

All this is a very difficult and complex operation to describe, at
least as difficult and complex as the way any growing discipline
crowds out its competitors and acquires authority for its traditions,
methods, and institutions, as well as general cultural legitimacy for
its statements, personalities, and agencies. But we can simplify a
great deal of the sheer narrative complexity of the operation by
specifying the kinds of experiences that Orientalism typically employed for its own ends and represented for its wider-than-profes-
sional audience. In essence these experiences continue the ones I
described as having taken place in Sacy and Renan. But whereas
those two scholars represent a wholly bookish Orientalism, since
neither claimed any particular expertise with the Orient *in situ*,
there is another tradition that claimed its legitimacy from the
peculiarly compelling fact of residence in, actual existential contact
with, the Orient. Anquetil, Jones, the Napoleonic expedition define
the tradition's earliest contours, of course, and these will thereafter
retain an unshakable influence on all Orientalist residents. These
contours are the ones of European power: to reside in the Orient
is to live the privileged life, not of an ordinary citizen, but of a
representative European whose empire (French or British) *contains*
the Orient in its military, economic, and above all, cultural arms.
Oriental residence, and its scholarly fruits, are thereby fed into the

bookish tradition of the textual attitudes we found in Renan and Sacy: together the two experiences will constitute a formidable library against which no one, not even Marx, can rebel and which no one can avoid.

Residence in the Orient involves personal experience and personal testimony to a certain extent. Contributions to the library of Orientalism and to its consolidation depend on how experience and testimony get converted from a purely personal document into the enabling codes of Orientalist science. In other words, within a text there has to take place a metamorphosis from personal to official statement; the record of Oriental residence and experience by a European must shed, or at least minimize, its purely autobiographical and indulgent descriptions in favor of descriptions on which Orientalism in general and later Orientalists in particular can draw, build, and base further scientific observation and description. So one of the things we can watch for is a more explicit conversion than in Marx of personal sentiments about the Orient into official Orientalist statements.

Now the situation is enriched and complicated by the fact that during the entire nineteenth century the Orient, and especially the Near Orient, was a favorite place for Europeans to travel in and write about. Moreover, there developed a fairly large body of Oriental-style European literature very frequently based on personal experiences in the Orient. Flaubert comes to mind immediately as one prominent source of such literature; Disraeli, Mark Twain, and Kinglake are three other obvious examples. But what is of interest is the difference between writing that is converted from personal to professional Orientalism, and the second type, also based on residence and personal testimony, which remains "literature" and not science: it is this difference that I now want to explore.

To be a European in the Orient *always* involves being a consciousness set apart from, and unequal with, its surroundings. But the main thing to note is the intention of this consciousness: What is it in the Orient for? Why does it set itself there even if, as is the case with writers like Scott, Hugo, and Goethe, it travels to the Orient for a very concrete sort of experience without actually leaving Europe? A small number of intentional categories proposed themselves schematically. One: the writer who intends to use his residence for the specific task of providing professional Orientalism with scientific material, who considers his residence a form of scientific observation. Two: the writer who intends the same purpose but is less willing to sacrifice the eccentricity and style of his individual consciousness to impersonal Orientalist definitions. These latter do appear in his work, but they are disentangled from the personal vagaries of style only with difficulty. Three: the writer for whom a real or metaphorical trip to the Orient is the fulfillment of some deeply felt and urgent project. His text therefore is built on a personal aesthetic, fed and informed by the project. In categories two and three there is considerably more space than in one for the play of a personal—or at least non-Orientalist—consciousness; if we take Edward William Lane's *Manners and Customs of the Modern Egyptians* as the pre-eminent example of category one, Burton's *Pilgrimage to al-Madinah and Meccah* as belonging to category two, and Nerval's *Voyage en Orient* as representing category three, the relative spaces left in the text for the exercise and display of authorial presence will be clear.

Despite their differences, however, these three categories are not so separate from each other as one would imagine. Nor does each category contain "pure" representative types. For example, works in all three categories rely upon the sheer egoistic powers of the European consciousness at their center. In all cases the Orient is *for* the European observer, and what is more, in the category that contains Lane's *Egyptians*, the Orientalist ego is very much in evidence, however much his style tries for impartial impersonality. Moreover, certain motifs recur consistently in all three types. The Orient as a place of pilgrimage is one; so too is the vision of Orient as spectacle, or *tableau vivant*. Every work on the Orient in these categories tries to characterize the place, of course, but what is of greater interest is the extent to which the work's internal structure is in some measure synonymous with a comprehensive *interpretation* (or an attempt at it) of the Orient. Most of the time, not surprisingly, this interpretation is a form of Romantic restructuring of the Orient, a re-vision of it, which restores it redemptively to the present. Every interpretation, every structure created for the Orient, then, is a reinterpretation, a rebuilding of it.

Having said that, we return directly to differences between the categories. Lane's book on the Egyptians was influential, it was frequently read and cited (by Flaubert among others), and it established its author's reputation as an eminent figure in Orientalist scholarship. In other words, Lane's authority was gained, not by virtue simply of what he said, but by virtue of how what he said could be adapted to Orientalism. He is quoted as a source of knowledge about Egypt or Arabia, whereas Burton or Flaubert were and are read for what they tell us about Burton and Flaubert over and above their knowledge of the Orient. The author-function in Lane's *Modern Egyptians* is less strong than in the other categories because his work was disseminated into the profession, consolidated by it, institutionalized with it. The authorial identity in a work of professional discipline such as his is subordinated to the demands of the field, as well as to the demands of the subject matter. But this is not done simply, or without raising problems.

Lane's classic, *An Account of the Manners and Customs of the Modern Egyptians* (1836), was the self-conscious result of a series of works and of two periods of residence in Egypt (1825–1828 and 1833–1835). One uses the phrase "self-conscious" with some emphasis here because the impression Lane wished to give was that his study was a work of immediate and direct, unadorned and neutral, description, whereas in fact it was the product of considerable editing (the work he wrote was not the one he finally published) and also of a considerable variety of quite special efforts. Nothing in his birth or background seemed to destine him for the Orient, except his methodical studiousness and his capacity for classical studies and for mathematics, which somewhat explain the apparent internal neatness of his book. His preface offers a series of interesting clues about what it was that he did for the book. He went to Egypt originally to study Arabic. Then, after making some notes about modern Egypt, he was encouraged to produce a systematic work on the country and its inhabitants by a committee of the Society for the Diffusion of Useful Knowledge. From being a random set of observations the work was changed into a document of useful knowledge, knowledge arranged for and readily accessible to anyone wishing to know the essentials of a foreign society. The preface makes it clear that such knowledge must somehow dispose of pre-existing knowledge, as well as claim for itself a particularly effective character: here Lane is the subtle polemicist. He must show initially that he did what others before him either could not or did not do, and then, that he was able to acquire information both authentic and perfectly correct. And thus his peculiar authority begins to emerge.

While Lane dallies in his preface with a Dr. Russell's "account of the people of Aleppo" (a forgotten work), it is obvious that the *Description de l'Égypte* is his main antecedent competition. But that work, confined by Lane to a long footnote, is mentioned in contemptuous quotation marks as "the great French work" on

Egypt. *That* work was at once too philosophically general and too
careless, Lane says; and Jacob Burckhardt's famous study was
merely a collection of proverbial Egyptian wisdom, "bad tests of the
morality of a people." Unlike the French and Burckhardt, Lane
was able to submerge himself amongst the natives, to live as they
did, to conform to their habits, and "to escape exciting, in strangers,
any suspicion of . . . being a person who had no right to intrude
among them." Lest that imply Lane's having lost his objectivity, he
goes on to say that he conformed only to the *words* (his italics) of
the Koran, and that he was always aware of his difference from an
essentially alien culture.[71] Thus while one portion of Lane's identity
floats easily in the unsuspecting Muslim sea, a submerged part
retains its secret European power, to comment on, acquire, possess
everything around it.

The Orientalist can imitate the Orient without the opposite being
true. What he says about the Orient is therefore to be understood
as description obtained in a one-way exchange: as *they* spoke and
behaved, *he* observed and wrote down. His power was to have
existed amongst them as a native speaker, as it were, and also as a
secret writer. And what he wrote was intended as useful knowledge,
not for them, but for Europe and its various disseminative institutions. For that is one thing that Lane's prose never lets us forget:
that ego, the first-person pronoun moving through Egyptian customs, rituals, festivals, infancy, adulthood, and burial rites, is in
reality both an Oriental masquerade and an Orientalist device for
capturing and conveying valuable, otherwise inaccessible information. As narrator, Lane is both exhibit and exhibitor, winning two
confidences at once, displaying two appetites for experience: the
Oriental one for engaging companionship (or so it seems) and the
Western one for authoritative, useful knowledge.

Nothing illustrates this better than the last tripartite episode in
the preface. Lane there describes his principal informant and friend,
Sheikh Ahmed, as companion and as curiosity. Together the two
pretend that Lane is a Muslim; yet only after Ahmed conquers his
fear, inspired by Lane's audacious mimicry, can he go through the
motions of praying by his side in a mosque. This final achievement is preceded by two scenes in which Ahmed is portrayed as a
bizarre glass-eater and a polygamist. In all three portions of the
Sheikh Ahmed episode the distance between the Muslim and Lane
increases, even as in the action itself it decreases. As mediator and
translator, so to speak, of Muslim behavior, Lane ironically enters

the Muslim pattern only far enough to be able to describe it in a sedate English prose. His identity as counterfeit believer and privileged European is the very essence of bad faith, for the latter undercuts the former in no uncertain way. Thus what seems to be factual reporting of what *one* rather peculiar Muslim does is made to appear by Lane as the candidly exposed center of *all* Muslim faith. No mind is given by Lane to the betrayal of his friendship with Ahmed or with the others who provide him with information. What matters is that the report seem accurate, general, and dispassionate, that the English reader be convinced that Lane was never infected with heresy or apostasy, and finally, that Lane's text cancel the human content of its subject matter in favor of its scientific validity.

It is for all these ends that the book is organized, not simply as the narrative of Lane's residence in Egypt but as narrative structure overwhelmed by Orientalist restructuring and detail. This, I think, is the central achievement of Lane's work. In outline and shape *Modern Egyptians* follows the routine of an eighteenth-century novel, say one by Fielding. The book opens with an account of country and setting, followed by chapters on "Personal Characteristics" and "Infancy and Early Education." Twenty-five chapters on such things as festivals, laws, character, industry, magic, and domestic life precede the last section, "Death and Funeral Rites." On the face of it, Lane's argument is chronological and developmental. He writes about himself as the observer of scenes that follow the major divisions in the human lifetime: his model is the narrative pattern, as it is in *Tom Jones* with the hero's birth, adventures, marriage, and implied death. Only in Lane's text the narrative voice is ageless; his subject, however, the modern Egyptian, goes through the individual life-cycle. This reversal, by which a solitary individual endows himself with timeless faculties and imposes on a society and people a personal life-span, is but the first of several operations regulating what might have been the mere narration of travels in foreign parts, turning an artless text into an encyclopedia of exotic display and a playground for Orientalist scrutiny.

Lane's control of his material is not only established through his dramatized double presence (as fake Muslim and genuine Westerner) and his manipulation of narrative voice and subject, but also through his use of detail. Each major section in each chapter is invariably introduced with some unsurprising general observation. For example, "it is generally observed that many of the most remarkable peculiarities in the manners, customs, and character of a nation are attributable to the physical peculiarities of the country."[72] What follows confirms this easily—the Nile, Egypt's "remarkably salubrious" climate, the peasant's "precise" labor. Yet instead of this leading to the next episode in narrative order, the detail is added to, and consequently the narrative fulfillment expected on purely formal grounds is not given. In other words, although the gross outlines of Lane's text conform to the narrative and causal sequence of birth–life–death, the special detail introduced during the sequence itself foils narrative movement. From a general observation, to a delineation of some aspect of Egyptian character, to an account of Egyptian childhood, adolescence, maturity, and senescence, Lane is always there with great detail to *prevent* smooth transitions. Shortly after we hear about Egypt's salubrious climate, for instance, we are informed that few Egyptians live beyond a few years, because of fatal illness, the absence of medical aid, and oppressive summer weather. Thereafter we are told that the heat "excites the Egyptian [an unqualified generalization] to intemperance in sensual enjoyments," and soon are bogged down in descriptions, complete with charts and line drawings, of Cairene architecture, decoration, fountains, and locks. When a narrative strain re-emerges, it is clearly only as a formality.

What prevents narrative order, at the very same time that narrative order is the dominating fiction of Lane's text, is sheer, overpowering, monumental description. Lane's objective is to make Egypt and the Egyptians totally visible, to keep nothing hidden from his reader, to deliver the Egyptians without depth, in swollen detail. As rapporteur his propensity is for sadomasochistic colossal tidbits: the self-multilation of dervishes, the cruelty of judges, the blending of religion with licentiousness among Muslims, the excess of libidinous passions, and so on. Yet no matter how odd and perverse the event and how lost we become in its dizzying detail, Lane is ubiquitous, his job being to reassemble the pieces and enable us to move on, albeit jerkily. To a certain extent he does this by just being a European who can discursively control the passions and excitements to which the Muslims are unhappily subject. But to an even greater extent, Lane's capacity to rein in his profuse subject matter with an unyielding bridle of discipline and detachment depends on his cold distance from Egyptian life and Egyptian productivity.

The main symbolic moment occurs at the beginning of chapter 6,

"Domestic Life—Continued." By now Lane has adopted the narrative convention of taking a walk through Egyptian life, and having reached the end of his tour of the public rooms and habits of an Egyptian household (the social and spatial worlds are mixed together by him), he begins to discuss the intimate side of home life. Immediately, he "must give some account of marriage and the marriage-ceremonies." As usual, the account begins with a general observation: to abstain from marriage "when a man has attained a sufficient age, and when there is no just impediment, is esteemed by the Egyptians improper, and even disreputable." Without transition this observation is applied by Lane to himself, and he is found guilty. For one long paragraph he then recounts the pressures placed on him to get married, which he unflinchingly refuses. Finally, after a native friend even offers to arrange a *mariage de convenance*, also refused by Lane, the whole sequence is abruptly terminated with a period and a dash.[73] He resumes his general discussion with another general observation.

Not only do we have here a typical Lane-esque interruption of the main narrative with untidy detail, we have also a firm and literal disengagement of the author from the productive processes of Oriental society. The mini-narrative of his refusal to join the society he describes concludes with a dramatic hiatus: *his* story cannot continue, he seems to be saying, so long as he does not enter the intimacy of domestic life, and so he drops from sight as a candidate for it. He literally abolishes himself as a human subject by refusing to marry into human society. Thus he preserves his authoritative identity as a mock participant and bolsters the objectivity of his narrative. If we already knew that Lane was a non-Muslim, we now know too that in order for him to become an Orientalist—instead of an Oriental—he had to deny himself the sensual enjoyments of domestic life. Moreover, he had also to avoid dating himself by entering the human life-cycle. Only in this negative way could he retain his timeless authority as observer.

Lane's choice was between living without "inconvenience and discomfort" and accomplishing his study of the modern Egyptians. The result of his choice is plainly to have made possible his definition of the Egyptians, since had he become one of them, his perspective would no longer have been antiseptically and asexually lexicographical. In two important and urgent ways, therefore, Lane gains scholarly credibility and legitimacy. First, by interfering with the ordinary narrative course of human life: this is the function of

his colossal detail, in which the observing intelligence of a foreigner
can introduce and then piece together massive information. The
Egyptians are disemboweled for exposition, so to speak, then put
together admonishingly by Lane. Second, by disengaging from the
generation of Egyptian-Oriental life: this is the function of his
subduing his animal appetite in the interest of disseminating information, not in and for Egypt, but in and for European learning
at large. To have achieved both the imposition of a scholarly will
upon an untidy reality and an intentional shift away from the place
of his residence to the scene of his scholarly reputation is the source
of his great fame in the annals of Orientalism. Useful knowledge
such as his could only have been obtained, formulated, and diffused
by such denials.

Lane's two other major works, his never-completed Arabic
lexicon and his uninspired translation of the *Arabian Nights*, consolidated the system of knowledge inaugurated by *Modern Egyptians*. In both of his later works his individuality has disappeared
entirely as a creative presence, as of course has the very idea of a
narrative work. Lane the man appears only in the official persona
of annotator and retranslator (the *Nights*) and impersonal lexicog-
rapher. From being an author contemporary with his subject
matter, Lane became—as Orientalist scholar of classical Arabic
and classical Islam—its survivor. But it is the form of that survival
which is of interest. For Lane's legacy as a scholar mattered not to
the Orient, of course, but to the institutions and agencies of his
European society. And these were either academic—the official
Orientalist societies, institutions, and agencies—or they were extra-
academic in very particular ways, figuring in the work of later
Europeans resident in the Orient.

If we read Lane's *Modern Egyptians*, not as a source of Oriental
lore, but as a work directed towards the growing organization of
academic Orientalism, we will find it illuminating. The subordina-
tion of genetic ego to scholarly authority in Lane corresponds
exactly to the increased specialization and institutionalization of
knowledge about the Orient represented by the various Oriental
societies. The Royal Asiatic Society was founded a decade before
Lane's book appeared, but its committee of correspondence—whose
"objects were to receive intelligence and inquiries relating to the
arts, sciences, literature, history and antiquities" of the Orient[74]—
was the structural recipient of Lane's fund of information, processed
and formulated as it was. As for the diffusion of such work as

Lane's, there were not only the various societies of useful knowledge but also, in an age when the original Orientalist program of aiding commerce and trade with the Orient had become exhausted, the specialized learned societies whose products were works displaying the potential (if not actual) values of disinterested scholarship. Thus, a program of the Société asiatique states:

> To compose or to print grammars, dictionaries, and other elementary books recognized as useful or indispensable for the study of those languages taught by appointed professors [of Oriental languages]; by subscriptions or by other means to contribute to the publication of the same kind of work undertaken in France or abroad; to acquire manuscripts, or to copy either completely or in part those that are to be found in Europe, to translate or to make extracts from them, to multiply their number by reproducing them either by engraving or by lithography; to make it possible for the authors of useful works on geography, history, the arts, and the sciences to acquire the means for the public to enjoy the fruits of their nocturnal labors; to draw the attention of the public, by means of a periodic collection devoted to Asiatic literature, to the scientific, literary, or poetic productions of the Orient and those of the same sort that regularly are produced in Europe, to those facts about the Orient that could be relevant to Europe, to those discoveries and works of all kinds of which the Oriental peoples could become the subject: these are the objectives proposed for and by the Société asiatique.

Orientalism organized itself systematically as the acquisition of Oriental material and its regulated dissemination as a form of specialized knowledge. One copied and printed works of grammar, one acquired original texts, one multiplied their number and diffused them widely, even dispensed knowledge in periodic form. It was into and for this system that Lane wrote his work, and sacrificed his ego. The mode in which his work persisted in the archives of Orientalism was provided for also. There was to be a "museum," Sacy said,

> a vast depot of objects of all kinds, of drawings, of original books, maps, accounts of voyages, all offered to those who wish to give themselves to the study of [the Orient]; in such a way that each of these students would be able to feel himself transported as if by enchantment into the midst of, say, a Mongolian tribe or of the Chinese race, whichever he might have made the object of his studies. . . . It is possible to say . . . that after the publication of

elementary books on . . . the Oriental languages, nothing is more important than to lay the cornerstone of this museum, which I consider a living commentary upon and interpretation [*truchement*] of the dictionaries.[75]

Truchement derives nicely from the Arabic *turjaman*, meaning "interpreter," "intermediary," or "spokesman." On the one hand, Orientalism acquired the Orient as literally and as widely as possible; on the other, it domesticated this knowledge to the West, filtering it through regulatory codes, classifications, specimen cases, periodical reviews, dictionaries, grammars, commentaries, editions, translations, all of which together formed a simulacrum of the Orient and reproduced it materially in the West, for the West. The Orient, in short, would be converted from the personal, sometimes garbled testimony of intrepid voyagers and residents into impersonal definition by a whole array of scientific workers. It would be converted from the consecutive experience of individual research into a sort of imaginary museum without walls, where everything gathered from the huge distances and varieties of Oriental culture became categorically *Oriental*. It would be reconverted, restructured from the bundle of fragments brought back piecemeal by explorers, expeditions, commissions, armies, and merchants into lexicographical, bibliographical, departmentalized, and *textualized* Orientalist sense. By the middle of the nineteenth century the Orient had become, as Disraeli said, a career, one in which one could remake and restore not only the Orient but also oneself.

IV

Pilgrims and Pilgrimages, British and French

Every European traveler or resident in the Orient has had to protect himself from its unsettling influences. Someone like Lane ultimately rescheduled and resituated the Orient when he came to write about it. The eccentricities of Oriental life, with its odd calendars, its exotic spatial configurations, its hopelessly strange languages, its seemingly perverse morality, were reduced considerably when they appeared as a series of detailed items presented in a normative European prose style. It is correct to say that in Orientalizing the Orient, Lane not only defined but edited it; he excised from it what, in addition to his own human sympathies, might have ruffled the European sensibility. In most cases, the Orient seemed to have offended sexual propriety; everything about the Orient—or at least Lane's Orient-in-Egypt—exuded dangerous sex, threatened hygiene and domestic seemliness with an excessive "freedom of intercourse," as Lane put it more irrepressibly than usual.

But there were other sorts of threats than sex. All of them wore away the European discreteness and rationality of time, space, and personal identity. In the Orient one suddenly confronted unimaginable antiquity, inhuman beauty, boundless distance. These could be put to use more innocently, as it were, if they were thought and written about, not directly experienced. In Byron's "Giaour," in the *Westöstlicher Diwan*, in Hugo's *Orientales*, the Orient is a form of release, a place of original opportunity, whose keynote was struck in Goethe's "Hegire"—

> Nord und West Süd zersplittern,
> Throne bersten, Reiche zittern,
> Fluchte du, in reinen Osten
> Patriarchenluft zu kosten!

> (North, West, and South disintegrate,
> Thrones burst, empires tremble.
> Fly away, and in the pure East
> Taste the Patriarchs' air.)

One always *returned* to the Orient—"Dort, im Reinen und in Rechten/Will ich menschlichen Geschlechten/In des Ursprungs Tiefe dringen" (There in purity and righteousness will I go back to the profound origins of the human race)—seeing it as completion and confirmation of everything one had imagined:

> Gottes ist der Orient!
> Gottes ist der Okzident!
> Nord und südliches Gelände
> Ruht im Frieden seiner Hände.[76]

> (God's is the Orient!
> God's is the Occident!
> Northern and southern lands
> Repose in the peace of His hands.)

The Orient, with its poetry, its atmosphere, its possibilities, was represented by poets like Hafiz—*unbegrenzt*, boundless, Goethe said, older and younger than we Europeans. And for Hugo, in "Cri de guerre du mufti" and "La Douleur du pacha"[77] the fierceness and the inordinate melancholy of Orientals was mediated, not by actual fear for life or disoriented lostness, but by Volney and George Sale, whose learned work translated barbarous splendor into usable information for the sublimely talented poet.

What Orientalists like Lane, Sacy, Renan, Volney, Jones (not to mention the *Description de l'Égypte*), and other pioneers made available, the literary crowd exploited. We must recall now our earlier discussion of the three types of work dealing with the Orient and based upon actual residence there. The rigorous exigencies of knowledge purged from Orientalist writing an authorial sensibility: hence Lane's self-excision, and hence also the first kind of work we enumerated. As for types two and three, the self is there prominently, subservient to a voice whose job it is to dispense real knowledge (type two), or dominating and mediating everything we are told about the Orient (type three). Yet from one end of the nineteenth century to the other—after Napoleon, that is—the Orient was a place of pilgrimage, and every major work belonging to a genuine if not always to an academic Orientalism took its form, style, and intention from the idea of pilgrimage there. In this idea as in so many of the other forms of Orientalist writing we have been discussing, the Romantic idea of restorative reconstruction (natural supernaturalism) is the principal source.

Every pilgrim sees things his own way, but there are limits to what a pilgrimage can be for, to what shape and form it can take, to what truths it reveals. All pilgrimages to the Orient passed through, or had to pass through, the Biblical lands; most of them in fact were attempts either to relive or to liberate from the large, incredibly fecund Orient some portion of Judeo-Christian/Greco-Roman actuality. For these pilgrims the Orientalized Orient, the Orient of Orientalist scholars, was a gauntlet to be run, just as the Bible, the Crusades, Islam, Napoleon, and Alexander were redoubtable predecessors to be reckoned with. Not only does a learned Orient inhibit the pilgrim's musings and private fantasies; its very antecedence places barriers between the contemporary traveler and his writing, unless, as was the case with Nerval and Flaubert in their use of Lane, Orientalist work is severed from the library and caught in the aesthetic project. Another inhibition is that Orientalist

writing is too circumscribed by the official requirements of Orientalist learning. A pilgrim like Chateaubriand claimed insolently that
he undertook his voyages exclusively for his own sake: "j'allais
chercher des images: voilà tout."[78] Flaubert, Vigny, Nerval, Kinglake, Disraeli, Burton, all undertook their pilgrimages in order to
dispel the mustiness of the pre-existing Orientalist archive. Their
writing was to be a fresh new repository of Oriental experience—
but, as we shall see, even this project usually (but not always) resolved itself into the reductionism of the Orientalistic. The reasons
are complex, and they have very much to do with the nature of the
pilgrim, his mode of writing, and the intentional form of his work.

What was the Orient for the individual traveler in the nineteenth
century? Consider first the differences between an English speaker
and a French speaker. For the former the Orient was India, of
course, an actual British possession; to pass through the Near Orient
was therefore to pass en route to a major colony. Already, then,
the room available for imaginative play was limited by the realities
of administration, territorial legality, and executive power. Scott,
Kinglake, Disraeli, Warburton, Burton, and even George Eliot (in
whose *Daniel Deronda* the Orient has plans made for it) are writers,
like Lane himself and Jones before him, for whom the Orient was
defined by material possession, by a material imagination, as it were.
England had defeated Napoleon, evicted France: what the English
mind surveyed was an imperial domain which by the 1880s had
become an unbroken patch of British-held territory, from the
Mediterranean to India. To write about Egypt, Syria, or Turkey,
as much as traveling in them, was a matter of touring the realm
of political will, political management, political definition. The
territorial imperative was extremely compelling, even for so un-
restrained a writer as Disraeli, whose *Tancred* is not merely an
Oriental lark but an exercise in the astute political management of
actual forces on actual territories.

In contrast, the French pilgrim was imbued with a sense of acute
loss in the Orient. He came there to a place in which France, unlike
Britain, had no sovereign presence. The Mediterranean echoed
with the sounds of French defeats, from the Crusades to Napoleon.
What was to become known as "la mission civilisatrice" began in
the nineteenth century as a political second-best to Britain's
presence. Consequently French pilgrims from Volney on planned
and projected for, imagined, ruminated about places that were
principally *in their minds*; they constructed schemes for a typically

French, perhaps even a European, concert in the Orient, which of
course they supposed would be orchestrated by them. Theirs was
the Orient of memories, suggestive ruins, forgotten secrets, hidden
correspondences, and an almost virtuosic style of being, an Orient
whose highest literary forms would be found in Nerval and Flaubert,
both of whose work was solidly fixed in an imaginative, unrealiz-
able (except aesthetically) dimension.

This was also true to a certain extent of scholarly French travelers
in the Orient. Most of them were interested in the Biblical past or
in the Crusades, as Henri Bordeaux has argued in his *Voyageurs
d'Orient*.[79] To these names we must add (at Hassan al-Nouty's
suggestion) the names of Oriental Semiticists, including Quatremère; Saulcy, the explorer of the Dead Sea; Renan as Phoenician
archaeologist; Judas, the student of Phoenician languages; Catafago
and Défrémery, who studied the Ansarians, Ismailis, and Seljuks;
Clermont-Ganneau, who explored Judea; and the Marquis de
Vogüé, whose work centered on Palmyrian epigraphy. In addition
there was the whole school of Egyptologists descended from Champollion and Mariette, a school that would later include Maspero
and Legrain. As an index of the difference between British realities
and French fantasies, it is worthwhile recalling the words in Cairo
of the painter Ludovic Lepic, who commented sadly in 1884 (two
years after the British occupation had begun): "L'Orient est mort
au Caire." Only Renan, ever the realistic racist, condoned the
British suppression of Arabi's nationalist rebellion, which, out of his
greater wisdom, he said was a "disgrace to civilization."[80]

Unlike Volney and Napoleon, the nineteenth-century French
pilgrims did not seek a scientific so much as an exotic yet especially
attractive reality. This is obviously true of the literary pilgrims,
beginning with Chateaubriand, who found in the Orient a locale
sympathetic to their private myths, obsessions, and requirements.
Here we notice how all the pilgrims, but especially the French
ones, exploit the Orient in their work so as in some urgent way to
justify their existential vocation. Only when there is some additional
cognitive purpose in writing about the Orient does the outpouring
of self seem more under control. Lamartine, for instance, writes
about himself, and also about France as a power in the Orient;
that second enterprise mutes and finally controls imperatives heaped
upon his style by *his* soul, *his* memory, and *his* imagination. No
pilgrim, French or English, could so ruthlessly dominate his self
or his subject as Lane did. Even Burton and T. E. Lawrence, of

whom the former fashioned a deliberately Muslim pilgrimage and the latter what he called a reverse pilgrimage *away* from Mecca, delivered masses of historical, political, and social Orientalism that were never as free of their egos as Lane's were of his. This is why Burton, Lawrence, and Charles Doughty occupy a middle position between Lane and Chateaubriand.

Chateaubriand's *Itinéraire de Paris à Jérusalem, et de Jérusalem à Paris* (1810–1811) records the details of a journey undertaken in 1805–1806, after he had traveled in North America. Its many hundreds of pages bear witness to its author's admission that "je parle éternellement de moi," so much so that Stendhal, no self-abnegating writer himself, could find Chateaubriand's failure as a knowledgeable traveler to be the result of his "stinking egotism." He brought a very heavy load of personal objectives and suppositions to the Orient, unloaded them there, and proceeded thereafter to push people, places, and ideas around in the Orient as if nothing could resist his imperious imagination. Chateaubriand came to the Orient as a constructed *figure*, not as a true self. For him Bonaparte was the last Crusader; he in turn was "the last Frenchman who left his country to travel in the Holy Land with the ideas, the goals, and the sentiments of a pilgrim of former times." But there were other reasons. Symmetry: having been to the New World and seen its monuments of nature, he needed to complete his circle of studies by visiting the Orient and its monuments of knowledge: as he had studied Roman and Celtic antiquity, all that was left for him was the ruins of Athens, Memphis, and Carthage. Self-completion: he needed to replenish his stock of images. Confirmation of the importance of the religious spirit: "religion is a kind of universal language understood by all men," and where better to observe it than there in the Orient, even in lands where a comparatively low religion like Islam held sway. Above all, the need to see things, not as they were, but as Chateaubriand supposed they were: the Koran was "le livre de Mahomet"; it contained "ni principe de civilisation, ni précepte qui puisse élever le caractère." "This book," he continued, more or less freely inventing as he went along, "preaches neither hatred of tyranny nor love of liberty."[81]

To so preciously constituted a figure as Chateaubriand, the Orient was a decrepit canvas awaiting his restorative efforts. The Oriental Arab was "civilized man fallen again into a savage state": no wonder, then, that as he watched Arabs trying to speak French, Chateaubriand felt like Robinson Crusoe thrilled by hearing his parrot speak for the first time. True, there were places like Bethlehem (whose etymological meaning Chateaubriand got completely wrong) in which one found again some semblance of real —that is, European—civilization, but those were few and far between. Everywhere, one encountered Orientals, Arabs whose civilization, religion, and manners were so low, barbaric, and antithetical as to merit reconquest. The Crusades, he argued, were not aggression; they were a just Christian counterpart to Omar's arrival in Europe. Besides, he added, even if the Crusades in their modern or original form were aggression, the issue they raised transcended such questions of ordinary mortality:

> The Crusades were not only about the deliverance of the Holy Sepulchre, but more about knowing which would win on the earth, a cult that was civilization's enemy, systematically favorable to ignorance [this was Islam, of course], to despotism, to slavery, or a cult that had caused to reawaken in modern people the genius of a sage antiquity, and had abolished base servitude?[82]

This is the first significant mention of an idea that will acquire an almost unbearable, next to mindless authority in European writing: the theme of Europe teaching the Orient the meaning of liberty, which is an idea that Chateaubriand and everyone after him believed that Orientals, and especially Muslims, knew nothing about.

> Of liberty, they know nothing; of propriety, they have none: force is their God. When they go for long periods without seeing conquerors who do heavenly justice, they have the air of soldiers without a leader, citizens without legislators, and a family without a father.[83]

Already in 1810 we have a European talking like Cromer in 1910, arguing that Orientals require conquest, and finding it no paradox that a Western conquest of the Orient was not conquest after all, but liberty. Chateaubriand puts the whole idea in the Romantic redemptive terms of a Christian mission to revive a dead world, to quicken in it a sense of its own potential, one which only a European can discern underneath a lifeless and degenerate surface. For the traveler this means that he must use the Old Testament and the Gospels as his guide in Palestine;[84] only in this way can the apparent degeneration of the modern Orient be gotten beyond. Yet Chateaubriand senses no irony in the fact that his tour and his vision will reveal nothing to him about the modern Oriental and *his* destiny.

What matters about the Orient is what it lets happen to Chateaubriand, what it allows his spirit to do, what it permits him to reveal about himself, his ideas, his expectations. The liberty that so concerns him is no more than his own release from the Orient's hostile wastes.

Where his release allows him to go is directly back into the realm of imagination and imaginative interpretation. Description of the Orient is obliterated by the designs and patterns foisted upon it by the imperial ego, which makes no secret of its powers. If in Lane's prose we watch the ego disappear so that the Orient may appear in all its realistic detail, in Chateaubriand the ego dissolves itself in the contemplation of wonders it creates, and then is reborn, stronger than ever, more able to savor its powers and enjoy its interpretations.

> When one travels in Judea, at first a great ennui grips the heart; but when, passing from one solitary place to another, space stretches out without limits before you, slowly the ennui dissipates, and one feels a secret terror, which, far from depressing the soul, gives it courage and elevates one's native genius. Extraordinary things are disclosed from all parts of an earth worked over by miracles: the burning sun, the impetuous eagle, the sterile fig tree; all of poetry, all the scenes from Scripture are present there. Every name encloses a mystery; every grotto declares the future; every summit retains within it the accents of a prophet. God Himself has spoken from these shores: the arid torrents, the riven rocks, the open tombs attest to the prodigy; the desert still seems struck dumb with terror, and one would say that it has still not been able to break the silence since it heard the voice of the eternal.[85]

The process of thought in this passage is revealing. An experience of Pascalian terror does not merely reduce one's self-confidence, it miraculously stimulates it. The barren landscape stands forth like an illuminated text presenting itself to the scrutiny of a very strong, refortified ego. Chateaubriand has transcended the abject, if frightening, reality of the contemporary Orient so that he may stand in an original and creative relationship to it. By the end of the passage he is no longer a modern man but a visionary seer more or less contemporary with God; if the Judean desert has been silent since God spoke there, it is Chateaubriand who can hear the silence, understand its meaning, and—to his reader—make the desert speak again.

The great gifts of sympathetic intuition which had enabled Chateaubriand to represent and interpret North American mysteries in *René* and *Atala*, as well as Christianity in *Le Génie du Christianisme*, are aroused to even greater feats of interpretation during the *Itinéraire*. No longer is the author dealing with natural primitivity and romantic sentiment: here he is dealing with eternal creativity and divine originality themselves, for it is in the Biblical Orient that they were first deposited, and they have remained there in unmediated and latent form. Of course, they cannot be simply grasped; they must be aspired to and achieved by Chateaubriand. And it is this ambitious purpose that the *Itinéraire* is made to serve, just as in the text Chateaubriand's ego must be reconstructed radically enough to get the job done. Unlike Lane, Chateaubriand attempts to *consume* the Orient. He not only appropriates it, he represents and speaks for it, not in history but beyond history, in the timeless dimension of a completely healed world, where men and lands, God and men, are as one. In Jerusalem, therefore, at the center of his vision and at the ultimate end of his pilgrimage, he grants himself a sort of total reconciliation with the Orient, the Orient as Jewish, Christian, Muslim, Greek, Persian, Roman, and finally French. He is moved by the plight of the Jews, but he judges that they too serve to illuminate his general vision, and as a further benefit, they give the necessary poignance to his Christian vindictiveness. God, he says, has chosen a new people, and it is not the Jews.[86]

He makes some other concessions to terrestrial reality, however. If Jerusalem is booked into his itinerary as its final extraterrestrial goal, Egypt provides him with material for a political excursus. His ideas about Egypt supplement his pilgrimage nicely. The magnificent Nile Delta moves him to assert that

> I found only the memories of my glorious country worthy of those magnificent plains; I saw the remains of monuments of a new civilization, brought to the banks of the Nile by the genius of France.[87]

But these ideas are put in a nostalgic mode because in Egypt Chateaubriand believes he can equate the absence of France with the absence of a free government ruling a happy people. Besides, after Jerusalem, Egypt appears to be only a kind of spiritual anticlimax. After political commentary on its sorry state, Chateaubriand asks himself the routine question about "difference" as a result of historical development: how can this degenerate stupid mob of "Musulmans" have come to inhabit the same land whose vastly different owners so impressed Herodotus and Diodorus?

This is a fitting valedictory to Egypt, which he leaves for Tunis, Carthaginian ruins, and finally, home. Yet he does one last thing of note in Egypt: unable to do more than look at the Pyramids from a distance, he takes the trouble to send an emissary there, to have him inscribe his (Chateaubriand's) name on the stone, adding for our benefit, "one has to fulfill all the little obligations of a pious traveler." We would not ordinarily give much more than amused attention to this charming bit of touristic banality. As a preparation, however, for the very last page of the *Itinéraire*, it appears more important than at first glance. Reflecting on his twenty-year project to study "tous les hasards et tous les chagrins" as an exile, Chateaubriand notes elegiacally how every one of his books has been in fact a kind of prolongation of his existence. A man with neither a home nor the possibility of acquiring one, he finds himself now well past his youth. If heaven accords him eternal rest, he says, he promises to dedicate himself in silence to erecting a "monument à ma patrie." What he is left with on earth, however, is his writing, which, if his name will live, has been enough, and if it will not live, has been too much.[88]

These closing lines send us back to Chateaubriand's interest in getting his name inscribed on the Pyramids. We will have understood that his egoistic Oriental memoirs supply us with a constantly demonstrated, an indefatigably performed experience of self. Writing was an act of life for Chateaubriand, for whom nothing, not even a distant piece of stone, must remain scriptively untouched by him if he was to stay alive. If the order of Lane's narrative was to be violated by scientific authority and enormous detail, then Chateaubriand's was to be transformed into the asserted will of an egoistic, highly volatile individual. Whereas Lane would sacrifice his ego to the Orientalist canon, Chateaubriand would make everything he said about the Orient wholly dependent on his ego. Yet neither writer could conceive of his posterity as continuing on fruitfully after him. Lane entered the impersonality of a technical discipline: his work would be used, but not as a human document. Chateaubriand, on the other hand, saw that his writing, like the token inscription of his name on a Pyramid, would signify his self; if not, if he had not succeeded in prolonging his life by writing, it would be merely excessive, superfluous.

Even if all travelers to the Orient after Chateaubriand and Lane have taken their work into account (in some cases, even to the extent of copying from them verbatim), their legacy embodies the fate of Orientalism and the options to which it was limited. Either one wrote science like Lane or personal utterance like Chateaubriand. The problems with the former were its impersonal Western confidence that descriptions of general, collective phenomena were possible, and its tendency to make realities not so much out of the Orient as out of its own observations. The problem with personal utterance was that it inevitably retreated into a position equating the Orient with private fantasy, even if that fantasy was of a very high order indeed, aesthetically speaking. In both cases, of course, Orientalism enjoyed a powerful influence on how the Orient was described and characterized. But what that influence always prevented, even until today, was some sense of the Orient that was neither impossibly general nor imperturbably private. To look into Orientalism for a lively sense of an Oriental's human or even social reality—as a contemporary inhabitant of the modern world—is to look in vain.

The influence of the two options I have described, Lane's and Chateaubriand's, British and French, is a great deal of the reason for this omission. The growth of knowledge, particularly specialized knowledge, is a very slow process. Far from being merely additive or cumulative, the growth of knowledge is a process of selective accumulation, displacement, deletion, rearrangement, and insistence within what has been called a research consensus. The legitimacy of such knowledge as Orientalism was during the nineteenth century stemmed not from religious authority, as had been the case before the Enlightenment, but from what we can call the restorative citation of antecedent authority. Beginning with Sacy, the learned Orientalist's attitude was that of a scientist who surveyed a series of textual fragments, which he thereafter edited and arranged as a restorer of old sketches might put a series of them together for the cumulative picture they implicitly represent. Consequently, amongst themselves Orientalists treat each other's work in the same citationary way. Burton, for example, would deal with the *Arabian Nights* or with Egypt indirectly, *through* Lane's work, by citing his predecessor, challenging him even though he was granting him very great authority. Nerval's own voyage to the Orient was by way of Lamartine's, and the latter's by way of Chateaubriand. In short, as a form of growing knowledge Orientalism resorted mainly to citations of predecessor scholars in the field for its nutriment. Even when new materials came his way, the Orientalist judged them by borrowing from predecessors (as scholars so often do) their perspectives, ideologies, and guiding theses. In a fairly strict way, then, Orientalists after Sacy and Lane rewrote Sacy and Lane; after Chateaubriand, pilgrims rewrote him. From these complex rewritings the actualities of the modern Orient were systematically excluded, especially when gifted pilgrims like Nerval and Flaubert preferred Lane's descriptions to what their eyes and minds showed them immediately.

In the system of knowledge about the Orient, the Orient is less a place than a *topos*, a set of references, a congeries of characteristics, that seems to have its origin in a quotation, or a fragment of a text, or a citation from someone's work on the Orient, or some bit of previous imagining, or an amalgam of all these. Direct observation or circumstantial description of the Orient are the fictions presented by writing on the Orient, yet invariably these are totally secondary to systematic tasks of another sort. In Lamartine, Nerval, and Flaubert, the Orient is a re-presentation of canonical material guided by an aesthetic and executive will capable of producing interest in the reader. Yet in all three writers, Orientalism or some aspect of it is asserted, even though, as I said earlier, the narrative consciousness is given a very large role to play. What we shall see is that for all its eccentric individuality, this narrative consciousness will end up by being aware, like Bouvard and Pécuchet, that pilgrimage is after all a form of copying.

When he began his trip to the Orient in 1833, Lamartine did so, he said, as something he had always dreamed about: "un voyage en Orient [était] comme un grand acte de ma vie intérieure." He is a bundle of predispositions, sympathies, biases: he hates the Romans and Carthage, and loves Jews, Egyptians, and Hindus, whose Dante he claims he will become. Armed with a formal verse "Adieu" to France, in which he lists everything that he plans to do in the Orient, he embarks for the East. At first everything he encounters either confirms his poetic predictions or realizes his propensity for analogy. Lady Hester Stanhope is the Circe of the desert; the Orient is the "patrie de mon imagination"; the Arabs are a primitive people; Biblical poetry is engraved on the land of Lebanon; the Orient testifies to the attractive largeness of Asia and to Greece's comparative smallness. Soon after he reaches Palestine, however, he becomes the incorrigible maker of an imaginary Orient. He alleges that the plains of Canaan appear to best advantage in the works of Poussin and Lorrain. From being a "translation," as he called it earlier, his voyage is now turned into a prayer, which exercises his memory, soul, and heart more than it does his eyes, mind, or spirit.[89]

This candid announcement completely unlooses Lamartine's analogic and reconstructive (and undisciplined) zeal. Christianity is a religion of imagination and recollection, and since Lamartine considers that he typifies the pious believer, he indulges himself accordingly. A catalogue of his tendentious "observations" would be interminable: a woman he sees reminds him of Haidée in *Don Juan*; the relationship between Jesus and Palestine is like that between Rousseau and Geneva; the actual river Jordan is less important than the "mysteries" it gives rise to in one's soul; Orientals, and Muslims in particular, are lazy, their politics are capricious, passionate, and futureless; another woman reminds him of a passage in *Atala*; neither Tasso nor Chateaubriand (whose antecedent travels seem often to harass Lamartine's otherwise heedless egoism) got the Holy Land right—and on and on. His pages on Arabic poetry, about which he discourses with supreme confidence, betray no discomfort at his total ignorance of the language. All that matters to him is that his travels in the Orient reveal to him how the Orient is "la terre des cultes, des prodiges," and that he is its appointed poet in the West. With no trace of self-irony he announces:

> This Arab land is the land of prodigies; everything sprouts there, and every credulous or fanatical man can become a prophet there in his turn.[90]

He has become a prophet merely by the fact of residence in the Orient.

By the end of his narrative Lamartine has achieved the purpose of his pilgrimage to the Holy Sepulchre, that beginning and end point of all time and space. He has internalized reality enough to want to retreat from it back into pure contemplation, solitude, philosophy, and poetry.[91]

Rising above the merely geographical Orient, he is transformed into a latter-day Chateaubriand, surveying the East as if it were a personal (or at the very least a French) province ready to be disposed of by European powers. From being a traveler and pilgrim in real time and space, Lamartine has become a transpersonal ego identifying itself in power and consciousness with the whole of Europe. What he sees before him is the Orient in the process of its inevitable future dismemberment, being taken over and consecrated by European suzerainty. Thus in Lamartine's climactic vision the Orient is reborn as European right-to-power over it:

> This sort of suzerainty thus defined, and consecrated as a European right, will consist principally in the right to occupy one or another territory, as well as the coasts, in order to found there either free cities, or European colonies, or commercial ports of call. . . .

Nor does Lamartine stop at this. He climbs still higher to the point where the Orient, what he has just seen and where he has just been, is reduced to "nations without territory, *patrie*, rights, laws or security . . . waiting anxiously for the shelter" of European occupation.[92]

In all the visions of the Orient fabricated by Orientalism there is no recapitulation, literally, as entire as this one. For Lamartine a pilgrimage to the Orient has involved not only the penetration of the Orient by an imperious consciousness but also the virtual elimination of that consciousness as a result of its accession to a kind of impersonal and continental control over the Orient. The Orient's actual identity is withered away into a set of consecutive fragments, Lamartine's recollective observations, which are later to be gathered up and brought forth as a restated Napoleonic dream of world hegemony. Whereas Lane's human identity disappeared into the scientific grid of his Egyptian classifications, Lamartine's consciousness transgresses its normal bounds completely. In so doing, it repeats Chateaubriand's journey and his visions only to move on beyond them, into the sphere of the Shelleyan and Napoleonic abstract, by which worlds and populations are moved about like so many cards on a table. What remains of the Orient in Lamartine's prose is not very substantial at all. Its geopolitical reality has been overlaid with his plans for it; the sites he has visited, the people he has met, the experiences he has had, are reduced to a few echoes in his pompous generalizations. The last traces of particularity have been rubbed out in the "résumé politique" with which the *Voyage en Orient* concludes.

Against the transcendent quasi-national egoism of Lamartine we must place Nerval and Flaubert in contrast. Their Oriental works play a substantial role in their total *oeuvre*, a much greater one than Lamartine's imperialist *Voyage* in his *oeuvre*. Yet both of them, like Lamartine, came to the Orient prepared for it by voluminous reading in the classics, modern literature, and academic Oriental-ism; about this preparation Flaubert was much more candid than Nerval, who in *Les Filles du feu* says disingenuously that all he knew about the Orient was a half-forgotten memory from his school education.[93] The evidence of his *Voyage en Orient* flatly contradicts this, although it shows a much less systematic and disciplined knowledge of Orientalia than Flaubert's. More important, however, is the fact that both writers (Nerval in 1842–1843 and Flaubert in 1849–1850) had greater personal and aesthetic uses for their visits to the Orient than any other nineteenth-century travelers. It is not inconsequential that both were geniuses to begin with, and that both were thoroughly steeped in aspects of European culture that encouraged a sympathetic, if perverse, vision of the Orient. Nerval and Flaubert belonged to that community of thought and feeling described by Mario Praz in *The Romantic Agony*, a com-munity for which the imagery of exotic places, the cultivation of sadomasochistic tastes (what Praz calls *algolagnia*), a fascination with the macabre, with the notion of a Fatal Woman, with secrecy and occultism, all combined to enable literary work of the sort produced by Gautier (himself fascinated by the Orient), Swinburne, Baudelaire, and Huysmans.[94] For Nerval and Flaubert, such female figures as Cleopatra, Salomé, and Isis have a special significance; and it was by no means accidental that in their work on the Orient, as well as in their visits to it, they pre-eminently valorized and enhanced female types of this legendary, richly suggestive, and associative sort.

In addition to their general cultural attitudes, Nerval and Flaubert brought to the Orient a personal mythology whose con-cerns and even structure required the Orient. Both men were touched by the Oriental renaissance as Quinet and others had de-fined it: they sought the invigoration provided by the fabulously antique and the exotic. For each, however, the Oriental pilgrimage was a quest for something relatively personal: Flaubert seeking a "homeland," as Jean Bruneau has called it,[95] in the locales of the origin of religions, visions, and classical antiquity; Nerval seeking —or rather following—the traces of his personal sentiments and dreams, like Sterne's Yorick before him. For both writers the Orient was a place therefore of *déjà vu*, and for both, with the artistic economy typical of all major aesthetic imaginations, it was a place often returned to after the actual voyage had been completed. For neither of them was the Orient exhausted by their uses of it, even if there is often a quality of disappointment, disenchantment, or demystification to be found in their Oriental writings.

The paramount importance of Nerval and Flaubert to a study such as this of the Orientalist mind in the nineteenth century is that they produced work that is connected to and depends upon the kind of Orientalism we have so far discussed, yet remains independent from it. First there is the matter of their work's scope. Nerval produced his *Voyage en Orient* as a collection of travel notes, sketches, stories, and fragments; his preoccupation with the Orient is to be found as well in *Les Chimères*, in his letters, in some of his fiction and other prose writings. Flaubert's writing both before and after his visit is soaked in the Orient. The Orient appears in the *Carnets de Voyage* and in the first version of *La Tentation de Saint Antoine* (and in the two later versions), as well as in *Hérodias*, *Salammbô*, and the numerous reading notes, scenarios, and unfinished stories still available to us, which have been very intelligently studied by Bruneau.[96] There are echoes of Orientalism in Flaubert's other major novels, too. In all, both Nerval and Flaubert continually elaborated their Oriental material and absorbed it variously into the special structures of their personal aesthetic projects. This is not to say, however, that the Orient is incidental to their work. Rather—by contrast with such writers as Lane (from whom both men borrowed shamelessly), Chateaubriand, Lamartine, Renan, Sacy—their Orient was not so much grasped, appropriated, reduced, or codified as lived in, exploited aesthetically and imaginatively as a roomy place full of possibility. What mattered to them was the structure of their work as an independent, aesthetic, and personal fact, and not the ways by which, if one wanted to, one could effectively dominate or set down the Orient graphically. Their egos never absorbed the Orient, nor totally identified the Orient with documentary and textual knowledge of it (with official Orientalism, in short).

On the one hand, therefore, the scope of their Oriental work exceeds the limitations imposed by orthodox Orientalism. On the other hand, the subject of their work is more than Oriental or Orientalistic (even though they do their own Orientalizing of the Orient); it quite consciously plays with the limitations and the challenges presented to them by the Orient and by knowledge about it. Nerval, for example, believes that he has to infuse what he sees with vitality since, he says,

Le ciel et la mer sont toujours là; le ciel d'Orient, la mer d'Ionie se donnent chaque matin le saint baiser d'amour; mais la terre est morte, morte sous la main de l'homme, et les dieux se sont envolés!

(The sky and the sea are still there; the Oriental sky and the Ionian sky give each other the sacred kiss of love each morning; but the earth is dead, dead because man has killed it, and the gods have fled.)

If the Orient is to live at all, now that its gods have fled, it must be through his fertile efforts. In the *Voyage en Orient* the narrative consciousness is a constantly energetic voice, moving through the labyrinths of Oriental existence armed—Nerval tells us—with two Arabic words, *tayeb*, the word for assent, and *mafisch*, the word for rejection. These two words enable him selectively to confront the antithetical Oriental world, to confront it and draw out from it its secret principles. He is predisposed to recognize that the Orient is "le pays des rêves et de l'illusion," which, like the veils he sees everywhere in Cairo, conceal a deep, rich fund of female sexuality. Nerval repeats Lane's experience of discovering the necessity for marriage in an Islamic society, but unlike Lane he does attach himself to a woman. His liaison with Zaynab is more than socially obligatory:

I must unite with a guileless young girl who is of this sacred soil, which is our first homeland; I must bathe myself in the vivifying springs of humanity, from which poetry and the faith of our fathers flowed forth! . . . I would like to lead my life like a novel, and I willingly place myself in the situation of one of those active and resolute heroes who wish at all costs to create a drama around them, a knot of complexity, in a word, action.[97]

Nerval invests himself in the Orient, producing not so much a novelistic narrative as an everlasting intention—never fully realized —to fuse mind with physical action. This antinarrative, this para-pilgrimage, is a swerving away from discursive finality of the sort envisioned by previous writers on the Orient.

Connected physically and sympathetically to the Orient, Nerval wanders informally through its riches and its cultural (and principally feminine) ambience, locating in Egypt especially that maternal "center, at once mysterious and accessible" from which all wisdom derives.[98] His impressions, dreams, and memories alternate with sections of ornate, mannered narrative done in the Oriental style; the hard realities of travel—in Egypt, Lebanon,

Turkey—mingle with the design of a deliberate digression, as if Nerval were repeating Chateaubriand's *Itinéraire* using an underground, though far less imperial and obvious, route. Michel Butor puts it beautifully:

> To Nerval's eyes, Chateaubriand's journey remains a voyage along the surface, while his own is calculated, utilizing annex centers, lobbies of ellipses englobing the principal centers; this allows him to place in evidence, by parallax, all the dimensions of the snare harbored by the normal centers. Wandering the streets or environs of Cairo, Beirut, or Constantinople, Nerval is always lying in wait for anything that will allow him to sense a cavern extending beneath Rome, Athens, and Jerusalem [the principal cities of Chateaubriand's *Itinéraire*]. . . .
>   Just as the three cities of Chateaubriand are in communication —Rome, with its emperors and popes, reassembling the heritage, the testament, of Athens and Jerusalem—the caverns of Nerval . . . become engaged in intercourse.[99]

Even the two large plotted episodes, "The Tale of the Caliph Hakim" and "The Tale of the Queen of the Morning," that will supposedly convey a durable, solid narrative discourse seem to push Nerval away from "overground" finality, edging him further and further into a haunting internal world of paradox and dream. Both tales deal with multiple identity, one of whose motifs—explicitly stated—is incest, and both return us to Nerval's quintessential Oriental world of uncertain, fluid dreams infinitely multiplying themselves past resolution, definiteness, materiality. When the journey is completed and Nerval arrives in Malta on his way back to the European mainland, he realizes that he is now in "le pays du froid et des orages, et déjà l'Orient n'est plus pour moi qu'un de ses rêves du matin auxquels viennent bientôt succéder les ennuis du jour."[100] His *Voyage* incorporates numerous pages copied out of Lane's *Modern Egyptians*, but even their lucid confidence seems to dissolve in the endlessly decomposing, cavernous element which is Nerval's Orient.

His *carnet* for the *Voyage* supplies us, I think, with two perfect texts for understanding how his Orient untied itself from anything resembling an Orientalist conception of the Orient, even though his work depends on Orientalism to a certain extent. First, his appetites strive to gather in experience and memory indiscriminately: "Je sens le besoin de m'assimiler toute la nature (femmes étrangères). Souvenirs d'y avoir vécu." The second elaborates a bit on the first: "Les rêves et la folie . . . Le désir de l'*Orient*. L'Europe s'élève. Le rêve se réalise . . . Elle. Je l'avais fuie, je l'avais perdue . . . Vaisseau d'Orient."[101] The Orient symbolizes Nerval's dream-quest and the fugitive woman central to it, both as desire and as loss. "Vaisseau d'Orient"—vessel of the Orient—refers enigmatically either to the woman as the vessel carrying the Orient, or possibly, to Nerval's own vessel for the Orient, his prose *voyage*. In either case, the Orient is identified with commemorative *absence*.

How else can we explain in the *Voyage*, a work of so original and individual a mind, the lazy use of large swatches of Lane, incorporated without a murmur by Nerval as *his* descriptions of the Orient? It is as if having failed both in his search for a stable Oriental reality and in his intent to give systematic order to his re-presentation of the Orient, Nerval was employing the borrowed authority of a canonized Orientalist text. After his voyage the earth remained dead, and aside from its brilliantly crafted but fragmented embodiments in the *Voyage*, his self was no less drugged and worn out than before. Therefore the Orient seemed retrospectively to belong to a negative realm, in which failed narratives, disordered chronicles, mere transcription of scholarly texts, were its only possible vessel. At least Nerval did not try to save his project by wholeheartedly giving himself up to French designs on the Orient, although he did resort to Orientalism to make some of his points.

In contrast to Nerval's negative vision of an emptied Orient, Flaubert's is eminently corporeal. His travel notes and letters reveal a man scrupulously reporting events, persons, and settings, delighting in their *bizarreries*, never attempting to reduce the incongruities before him. In what he writes (or perhaps because he writes), the premium is on the eye-catching, translated into self-consciously worked-out phrases: for example, "Inscriptions and birddroppings are the only two things in Egypt that give any indication of life."[102] His tastes run to the perverse, whose form is often a combination of extreme animality, even of grotesque nastiness, with extreme and sometimes intellectual refinement. Yet this particular kind of perversity was not something merely observed, it was also studied, and came to represent an essential element in Flaubert's fiction. The familiar oppositions, or ambivalences, as Harry Levin has called them, that roam through Flaubert's writing—flesh versus mind, Salomé versus Saint John, Salammbô versus Saint Anthony[103]—are powerfully validated by what he saw in the Orient, what, given his eclectic learning, he could see there of the partnership between knowledge and carnal grossness. In Upper Egypt he was taken with ancient Egyptian art, its preciosity and deliberate lubricity: "so dirty pictures existed even so far back in antiquity?" How much more the Orient really answered questions than it raised them is evident in the following:

> You [Flaubert's mother] ask me whether the Orient is up to what I imagined it to be. Yes, it is; and more than that, it extends far beyond the narrow idea I had of it. I have found, clearly delineated, everything that was hazy in my mind. Facts have taken the place of suppositions—so excellently so that it is often as though I were suddenly coming upon old forgotten dreams.[104]

Flaubert's work is so complex and so vast as to make any simple account of his Oriental writing very sketchy and hopelessly incomplete. Nevertheless, in the context created by other writers on the Orient, a certain number of main features in Flaubert's Orientalism can fairly be described. Making allowances for the difference between candidly personal writing (letters, travel notes, diary jottings) and formally aesthetic writing (novels and tales), we can still remark that Flaubert's Oriental perspective is rooted in an eastward and southward search for a "visionary alternative," which "meant gorgeous color, in contrast to the greyish tonality of the French provincial landscape. It meant exciting spectacle instead of humdrum routine, the perennially mysterious in place of the all too familiar."[105] When he actually visited it, however, this Orient impressed him with its decrepitude and senescence. Like every other Orientalism, then, Flaubert's is revivalist: *he* must bring the Orient to life, he must deliver it to himself and to his readers, and it is his experience of it in books and on the spot, and his language for it, that will do the trick. His novels of the Orient accordingly were labored historical and learned reconstructions. Carthage in *Salammbô* and the products of Saint Anthony's fevered imagination were authentic fruits of Flaubert's wide reading in the (mainly Western) sources of Oriental religion, warfare, ritual, and societies.

What the formal aesthetic work retains, over and above the marks of Flaubert's voracious readings and recensions, are memories of Oriental travel. The *Bibliothèque des idées reçues* has it that an Orientalist is "un homme qui a beaucoup voyagé,"[106] only unlike most other such travelers Flaubert put his voyages to ingenious use. Most of his experiences are conveyed in theatrical form. He is

interested not only in the content of what he sees but—like Renan
—in *how* he sees, the way by which the Orient, sometimes horribly
but always attractively, seems to present itself to him. Flaubert is its
best audience:

> . . . Kasr el-'Aini Hospital. Well maintained. The work of Clot
> Bey—his hand is still to be seen. Pretty cases of syphilis; in the
> ward of Abbas's Mamelukes, several have it in the arse. At a sign
> from the doctor, they all stood up on their beds, undid their
> trouserbelts (it was like army drill), and opened their anuses with
> their fingers to show their chancres. Enormous infundibula; one
> had a growth of hair inside his anus. One old man's prick entirely
> devoid of skin; I recoiled from the stench. A rachitic: hands
> curved backward, nails as long as claws; one could see the bone
> structure of his torso as clearly as a skeleton; the rest of his body,
> too, was fantastically thin, and his head was ringed with whitish
> leprosy.
> Dissecting room: . . . On the table an Arab cadaver, wide
> open; beautiful black hair. . . .[107]

The lurid detail of this scene is related to many scenes in Flaubert's
novels, in which illness is presented to us as if in a clinical theater.
His fascination with dissection and beauty recalls, for instance, the
final scene of *Salammbô*, culminating in Mâtho's ceremonial death.
In such scenes, sentiments of repulsion or sympathy are repressed
entirely; what matters is the correct rendering of exact detail.

The most celebrated moments in Flaubert's Oriental travel have
to do with Kuchuk Hanem, a famous Egyptian dancer and courtesan
he encountered in Wadi Halfa. He had read in Lane about the
almehs and the *khawals*, dancing girls and boys respectively, but it
was his imagination rather than Lane's that could immediately
grasp as well as enjoy the almost metaphysical paradox of the
almeh's profession and the meaning of her name. (In *Victory*,
Joseph Conrad was to repeat Flaubert's observation by making his
musician heroine—Alma—irresistibly attractive and dangerous to
Axel Heyst.) *Alemah* in Arabic means a learned woman. It was
the name given to women in conservative eighteenth-century
Egyptian society who were accomplished reciters of poetry. By the
mid-nineteenth century the title was used as a sort of guild name
for dancers who were also prostitutes, and such was Kuchuk
Hanem, whose dance "L'Abeille" Flaubert watched before he slept
with her. She was surely the prototype of several of his novels'
female characters in her learned sensuality, delicacy, and (accord-

ing to Flaubert) mindless coarseness. What he especially liked about her was that she seemed to place no demands on him, while the "nauseating odor" of her bedbugs mingled enchantingly with "the scent of her skin, which was dripping with sandalwood." After his voyage, he had written Louise Colet reassuringly that "the oriental woman is no more than a machine: she makes no distinction between one man and another man." Kuchuk's dumb and irreducible sexuality allowed Flaubert's mind to wander in ruminations whose haunting power over him reminds us somewhat of Deslauriers and Frédéric Moreau at the end of *l'Education sentimentale*:

> As for me, I scarcely shut my eyes. Watching that beautiful creature asleep (she snored, her head against my arm: I had slipped my forefinger under her necklace), my night was one long, infinitely intense reverie—that was why I stayed. I thought of my nights in Paris brothels—a whole series of old memories came back—and I thought of her, of her dance, of her voice as she sang songs that for me were without meaning and even without distinguishable words.[108]

The Oriental woman is an occasion and an opportunity for Flaubert's musings; he is entranced by her self-sufficiency, by her emotional carelessness, and also by what, lying next to him, she allows him to think. Less a woman than a display of impressive but verbally inexpressive femininity, Kuchuk is the prototype of Flaubert's Salammbô and Salomé, as well as of all the versions of carnal female temptation to which his Saint Anthony is subject. Like the Queen of Sheba (who also danced "The Bee") she could say—were she able to speak—"Je ne suis pas une femme, je suis un monde."[109] Looked at from another angle Kuchuk is a disturbing symbol of fecundity, peculiarly Oriental in her luxuriant and seemingly unbounded sexuality. Her home near the upper reaches of the Nile occupied a position structurally similar to the place where the veil of Tanit— the goddess described as *Omniféconde*—is concealed in *Salammbô*.[110] Yet like Tanit, Salomé, and Salammbô herself, Kuchuk was doomed to remain barren, corrupting, without issue. How much she and the Oriental world she lived in came to intensify for Flaubert his own sense of barrenness is indicated in the following:

> We have a large orchestra, a rich palette, a variety of resources. We know many more tricks and dodges, probably, than were ever known before. No, what we lack is the intrinsic principle, the soul

of the thing, the very idea of the subject. We take notes, we make
journeys: emptiness! emptiness! We become scholars, archaeologists, historians, doctors, cobblers, people of taste. What is the
good of all that? Where is the heart, the verve, the sap? Where to
start from? Where to go? We're good at sucking, we play a lot of
tongue-games, we pet for hours: but the real thing! To ejaculate,
beget the child![111]

Woven through all of Flaubert's Oriental experiences, exciting or
disappointing, is an almost uniform association between the Orient
and sex. In making this association Flaubert was neither the first
nor the most exaggerated instance of a remarkably persistent motif
in Western attitudes to the Orient. And indeed, the motif itself is
singularly unvaried, although Flaubert's genius may have done more
than anyone else's could have to give it artistic dignity. Why the
Orient seems still to suggest not only fecundity but sexual promise
(and threat), untiring sensuality, unlimited desire, deep generative
energies, is something on which one could speculate: it is not the
province of my analysis here, alas, despite its frequently noted
appearance. Nevertheless one must acknowledge its importance as
something eliciting complex responses, sometimes even a frightening self-discovery, in the Orientalists, and Flaubert was an
interesting case in point.

The Orient threw him back on his own human and technical
resources. It did not respond, just as Kuchuk did not, to his
presence. Standing before its ongoing life Flaubert, like Lane before
him, felt his detached powerlessness, perhaps also his self-induced
unwillingness, to enter and become part of what he saw. This of
course was Flaubert's perennial problem; it had existed before he
went East, and it remained after the visit. Flaubert admitted the
difficulty, the antidote to which was in his work (especially in an
Oriental work like *La Tentation de Saint Antoine*) to stress the
form of encyclopedic presentation of material at the expense of
human engagement in life. Indeed, Saint Anthony is nothing if not
a man for whom reality is a series of books, spectacles, and pageants
unrolling temptingly and at a distance before his eyes. All of
Flaubert's immense learning is structured—as Michel Foucault has
tellingly noted—like a theatrical, fantastic library, parading before
the anchorite's gaze;[112] residually, the parade carries in its form
Flaubert's memories of Kasr el'Aini (the syphilitics' army drill) and
Kuchuk's dance. More to the point, however, is that Saint Anthony

is a celibate to whom temptations are primarily sexual. After putting up with every sort of dangerous charm, he is finally given a glimpse into the biological processes of life; he is delirious at being able to see life being born, a scene for which Flaubert felt himself to be incompetent during his Oriental sojourn. Yet because Anthony is delirious, we are meant to read the scene ironically. What is granted to him at the end, the desire to *become* matter, to become life, is at best a desire—whether realizable and fulfillable or not, we cannot know.

Despite the energy of his intelligence and his enormous power of intellectual absorption, Flaubert felt in the Orient, first, that "the more you concentrate on it [in detail] the less you grasp the whole," and then, second, that "the pieces fall into place of themselves."[113] At best, this produces a *spectacular* form, but it remains barred to the Westerner's full participation in it. On one level this was a personal predicament for Flaubert, and he devised means, some of which we have discussed, for dealing with it. On a more general level, this was an *epistemological* difficulty for which, of course, the discipline of Orientalism existed. At one moment during his Oriental tour he considered what the epistemological challenge could give rise to. Without what he called spirit and style, the mind could "get lost in archaeology": he was referring to a sort of regimented antiquarianism by which the exotic and the strange would get formulated into lexicons, codes, and finally clichés of the kind he was to ridicule in the *Dictionnaire des idées reçues*. Under the influence of such an attitude the world would be "regulated like a college. Teachers will be the law. Everyone will be in uniform."[114] As against such an imposed discipline, he no doubt felt that his own treatments of exotic material, notably the Oriental material he had both experienced and read about for years, were infinitely preferable. In those at least there was room for a sense of immediacy, imagination, and flair, whereas in the ranks of archaeological tomes everything but "learning" had been squeezed out. And more than most novelists Flaubert was acquainted with organized learning, its products, and its results: these products are clearly evident in the misfortunes of Bouvard and Pécuchet, but they would have been as comically apparent in fields like Orientalism, whose textual attitudes belonged to the world of *idées reçues*. Therefore one could either construct the world with verve and style, or one could copy it tirelessly according to impersonal academic rules of procedure.

In both cases, with regard to the Orient, there was a frank acknowledgment that it was a world elsewhere, apart from the ordinary
attachments, sentiments, and values of *our* world in the West.

In all of his novels Flaubert associates the Orient with the escap-
ism of sexual fantasy. Emma Bovary and Frédéric Moreau pine for
what in their drab (or harried) bourgeois lives they do not have,
and what they realize they want comes easily to their daydreams
packed inside Oriental clichés: harems, princesses, princes, slaves,
veils, dancing girls and boys, sherbets, ointments, and so on. The
repertoire is familiar, not so much because it reminds us of Flaubert's own voyages in and obsession with the Orient, but because,
once again, the association is clearly made between the Orient and
the freedom of licentious sex. We may as well recognize that for
nineteenth-century Europe, with its increasing *embourgeoisement,*
sex had been institutionalized to a very considerable degree. On
the one hand, there was no such thing as "free" sex, and on the
other, sex in society entailed a web of legal, moral, even political
and economic obligations of a detailed and certainly encumbering
sort. Just as the various colonial possessions—quite apart from
their economic benefit to metropolitan Europe—were useful as
places to send wayward sons, superfluous populations of delinquents, poor people, and other undesirables, so the Orient was a
place where one could look for sexual experience unobtainable in
Europe. Virtually no European writer who wrote on or traveled to
the Orient in the period after 1800 exempted himself or herself
from this quest: Flaubert, Nerval, "Dirty Dick" Burton, and Lane
are only the most notable. In the twentieth century one thinks of
Gide, Conrad, Maugham, and dozens of others. What they looked
for often—correctly, I think—was a different type of sexuality,
perhaps more libertine and less guilt-ridden; but even that quest, if
repeated by enough people, could (and did) become as regulated
and uniform as learning itself. In time "Oriental sex" was as
standard a commodity as any other available in the mass culture,
with the result that readers and writers could have it if they wished
without necessarily going to the Orient.

It was certainly true that by the middle of the nineteenth century
France, no less than England and the rest of Europe, had a flourishing knowledge industry of the sort that Flaubert feared. Great numbers of texts were being produced, and more important, the agencies
and institutions for their dissemination and propagation were everywhere to be found. As historians of science and knowledge have

observed, the organization of scientific and learned fields that took place during the nineteenth century was both rigorous and all-encompassing. Research became a regular activity; there was a regulated exchange of information, and agreement on what the problems were as well as consensus on the appropriate paradigms for research and its results.[115] The apparatus serving Oriental studies was part of the scene, and this was one thing that Flaubert surely had in mind when he proclaimed that "everyone will be in uniform." An Orientalist was no longer a gifted amateur enthusiast, or if he was, he would have trouble being taken seriously as a scholar. To be an Orientalist meant university training in Oriental studies (by 1850 every major European university had a fully developed curriculum in one or another of the Orientalist disciplines), it meant subvention for one's travel (perhaps by one of the Asiatic societies or a geographical exploration fund or a government grant), it meant publication in accredited form (perhaps under the imprint of a learned society or an Oriental translation fund). And both within the guild of Orientalist scholars and to the public at large, such uniform accreditation as clothed the work of Orientalist scholarship, not personal testimony nor subjective impressionism, meant Science.

Added to the oppressive regulation of Oriental matters was the accelerated attention paid by the Powers (as the European empires were called) to the Orient, and to the Levant in particular. Ever since the Treaty of Chanak of 1806 between the Ottoman Empire and Great Britain, the Eastern Question had hovered ever more prominently on Europe's Mediterranean horizons. Britain's interests were more substantial in the East than France's, but we must not forget Russia's movements into the Orient (Samarkand and Bokhara were taken in 1868; the Transcaspian Railroad was being extended systematically), nor Germany's and Austria-Hungary's. France's North African interventions, however, were not the only components of its Islamic policy. In 1860, during the clashes between Maronites and Druzes in Lebanon (already predicted by Lamartine and Nerval), France supported the Christians, England the Druzes. For standing near the center of all European politics in the East was the question of minorities, whose "interests" the Powers, each in its own way, claimed to protect and represent. Jews, Greek and Russian Orthodox, Druzes, Circassians, Armenians, Kurds, the various small Christian sects: all these were studied, planned for, designed upon by European Powers improvising as well as constructing their Oriental policy.

I mention such matters simply as a way of keeping vivid the sense of layer upon layer of interests, official learning, institutional pressure, that covered the Orient as a subject matter and as a territory during the latter half of the nineteenth century. Even the most innocuous travel book—and there were literally hundreds written after mid-century[116]—contributed to the density of public awareness of the Orient; a heavily marked dividing line separated the delights, miscellaneous exploits, and testimonial portentousness of individual pilgrims in the East (which included some American voyagers, among them Mark Twain and Herman Melville[117]) from the authoritative reports of scholarly travelers, missionaries, governmental functionaries, and other expert witnesses. This dividing line existed clearly in Flaubert's mind, as it must have for any individual consciousness that did not have an innocent perspective on the Orient as a terrain for literary exploitation.

English writers on the whole had a more pronounced and harder sense of what Oriental pilgrimages might entail than the French. India was a valuably real constant in this sense, and therefore all the territory between the Mediterranean and India acquired a correspondingly weighty importance. Romantic writers like Byron and Scott consequently had a political vision of the Near Orient and a very combative awareness of how relations between the Orient and Europe would have to be conducted. Scott's historical sense in *The Talisman* and *Count Robert of Paris* allowed him to set these novels in Crusader Palestine and eleventh-century Byzantium, respectively, without at the same time detracting from his canny political appreciation of the way powers act abroad. The failure of Disraeli's *Tancred* can easily be ascribed to its author's perhaps overdeveloped knowledge of Oriental politics and the British Establishment's network of interests; Tancred's ingenuous desire to go to Jerusalem very soon mires Disraeli in ludicrously complex descriptions of how a Lebanese tribal chieftain tries to manage Druzes, Muslims, Jews, and Europeans to his political advantage. By the end of the novel Tancred's Eastern quest has more or less disappeared because there is nothing in Disraeli's material vision of Oriental realities to nourish the pilgrim's somewhat capricious impulses. Even George Eliot, who never visited the Orient herself, could not sustain the Jewish equivalent of an Oriental pilgrimage in *Daniel Deronda* (1876) without straying into the complexities of British realities as they decisively affected the Eastern project.

Thus whenever the Oriental motif for the English writer was not principally a stylistic matter (as in FitzGerald's *Rubáiyát* or in Morier's *Adventures of Hajji Baba of Ispahan*), it forced him to confront a set of imposing resistances to his individual fantasy. There are no English equivalents to the Oriental works by Chateaubriand, Lamartine, Nerval, and Flaubert, just as Lane's early Orientalist counterparts—Sacy and Renan—were considerably more aware than he was of how much they were creating what they wrote about. The form of such works as Kinglake's *Eothen* (1844) and Burton's *Personal Narrative of a Pilgrimage to Al-Madinah and Meccah* (1855–1856) is rigidly chronological and dutifully linear, as if what the authors were describing was a shopping trip to an Oriental bazaar rather than an adventure. Kinglake's undeservedly famous and popular work is a pathetic catalogue of pompous ethnocentrisms and tiringly nondescript accounts of the Englishman's East. His ostensible purpose in the book is to prove that travel in the Orient is important to "moulding of your character—that is, your very identity," but in fact this turns out to be little more than solidifying "your" anti-Semitism, xenophobia, and general allpurpose race prejudice. We are told, for instance, that the *Arabian Nights* is too lively and inventive a work to have been created by a "mere Oriental, who, for creative purposes, is a thing dead and dry—a mental mummy." Although Kinglake blithely confesses to no knowledge of any Oriental language, he is not constrained by ignorance from making sweeping generalizations about the Orient, its culture, mentality, and society. Many of the attitudes he repeats are canonical, of course, but it is interesting how little the experience of actually seeing the Orient affected his opinions. Like many other travelers he is more interested in remaking himself and the Orient (dead and dry—a mental mummy) than he is in seeing what there is to be seen. Every being he encounters merely corroborates his belief that Easterners are best dealt with when intimidated, and what better instrument of intimidation than a sovereign Western ego? En route to Suez across the desert, alone, he glories in his self-sufficiency and power: "I was here in this African desert, and I *myself, and no other, had charge of my life*."[118] It is for the comparatively useless purpose of letting Kinglake take hold of himself that the Orient serves him.

Like Lamartine before him, Kinglake comfortably identified his superior consciousness with his nation's, the difference being that in the Englishman's case his government was closer to settling in the rest of the Orient than France was—for the time being. Flaubert saw this with perfect accuracy:

> It seems to me almost impossible that within a short time England won't become mistress of Egypt. She already keeps Aden full of her troops, the crossing of Suez will make it very easy for the redcoats to arrive in Cairo one fine morning—the news will reach France two weeks later and everyone will be very surprised! Remember my prediction: at the first sign of trouble in Europe, England will take Egypt, Russia will take Constantinople, and we, in retaliation, will get ourselves massacred in the mountains of Syria.[119]

For all their vaunted individuality Kinglake's views express a public and national will over the Orient; his ego is the instrument of this will's expression, not by any means its master. There is no evidence in his writing that he struggled to create a novel opinion of the Orient; neither his knowledge nor his personality was adequate for that, and this is the great difference between him and Richard Burton. As a traveler, Burton was a real adventurer; as a scholar, he could hold his own with any academic Orientalist in Europe; as a character, he was fully aware of the necessity of combat between himself and the uniformed teachers who ran Europe and European knowledge with such precise anonymity and scientific firmness. Everything Burton wrote testifies to this combativeness, rarely with more candid contempt for his opponents than in the preface to his translation of the *Arabian Nights*. He seems to have taken a special sort of infantile pleasure in demonstrating that he knew more than any professional scholar, that he had acquired many more details than they had, that he could handle the material with more wit and tact and freshness than they.

As I said earlier, Burton's work based on his personal experience occupies a median position between Orientalist genres represented on the one hand by Lane and on the other by the French writers I have discussed. His Oriental narratives are structured as pilgrimages and, in the case of *The Land of Midian Revisited*, pilgrimages for a second time to sites of sometimes religious, sometimes political and economic significance. He is present as the principal character of these works, as much the center of fantastic adventure and even fantasy (like the French writers) as the authoritative commentator and detached Westerner on Oriental society and customs (like Lane). He has been rightly considered the first in a series of fiercely individualistic Victorian travelers in the East (the others being Blunt and Doughty) by Thomas Assad, who bases his work on the distance in tone and intelligence between his writers' work and such works as Austen Layard's *Discoveries in the Ruins of Nineveh and Babylon* (1851), Eliot Warburton's celebrated *The Crescent and the Cross* (1844), Robert Curzon's *Visit to the Monasteries of the Levant* (1849), and (a work he does not mention) Thackeray's moderately amusing *Notes of a Journey from Cornhill to Grand Cairo* (1845).[120] Yet Burton's legacy is more complex than individualism precisely because in his writing we can find exemplified the struggle between individualism and a strong feeling of national identification with Europe (specifically England) as an imperial power in the East. Assad sensitively points out that Burton was an imperialist, for all his sympathetic self-association with the Arabs; but what is more relevant is that Burton thought of himself both as a rebel against authority (hence his identification with the East as a place of free-dom from Victorian moral authority) and as a potential agent of authority in the East. It is the *manner* of that coexistence, between two antagonistic roles for himself, that is of interest.

The problem finally reduces itself to the problem of knowledge of the Orient, which is why a consideration of Burton's Orientalism ought to conclude our account of Orientalist structures and re-structures in most of the nineteenth century. As a traveling ad-venturer Burton conceived of himself as sharing the life of the people in whose lands he lived. Far more successfully than T. E. Lawrence, he was able to become an Oriental; he not only spoke the language flawlessly, he was able to penetrate to the heart of Islam and, disguised as an Indian Muslim doctor, accomplish the pilgrimage to Mecca. Yet Burton's most extraordinary characteristic is, I believe, that he was preternaturally knowledgeable about the degree to which human life in society was governed by rules and codes. All of his vast information about the Orient, which dots every page he wrote, reveals that he knew that the Orient in general and Islam in particular were systems of information, behavior, and belief, that to be an Oriental or a Muslim was to know certain things in a certain way, and that these were of course subject to history, geography, and the development of society in circumstances specific to it. Thus his accounts of travel in the East reveal to us a consciousness aware of these things and able to steer a narrative course through them: no man who did not know Arabic and Islam as well as Burton could have gone as far as he did in actually becom-

ing a pilgrim to Mecca and Medina. So what we read in his prose
is the history of a consciousness negotiating its way through an alien
culture by virtue of having successfully absorbed its systems of
information and behavior. Burton's freedom was in having shaken
himself loose of his European origins enough to be able to live as
an Oriental. Every scene in the *Pilgrimage* reveals him as winning
out over the obstacles confronting him, a foreigner, in a strange
place. He was able to do this because he had sufficient knowledge
of an alien society for this purpose.

In no writer on the Orient so much as in Burton do we feel that
generalizations about the Oriental—for example, the pages on the
notion of *Kayf* for the Arab or on how education is suited to the
Oriental mind (pages that are clearly meant as a rebuttal to
Macaulay's simple-minded assertions)[121]—are the result of knowledge acquired about the Orient by living there, actually seeing it
firsthand, truly trying to see Oriental life from the viewpoint of a
person immersed in it. Yet what is never far from the surface of
Burton's prose is another sense it radiates, a sense of assertion and
domination over all the complexities of Oriental life. Every one of
Burton's footnotes, whether in the *Pilgrimage* or in his translation
of the *Arabian Nights* (the same is true of his "Terminal Essay"
for it[122]) was meant to be testimony to his victory over the sometimes scandalous system of Oriental knowledge, a system he had
mastered by himself. For even in Burton's prose we are never
directly *given* the Orient; everything about it is presented to us by
way of Burton's knowledgeable (and often prurient) interventions,
which remind us repeatedly how he had taken over the management
of Oriental life for the purposes of his narrative. And it is this fact
—for in the *Pilgrimage* it is a fact—that elevates Burton's consciousness to a position of supremacy over the Orient. In that position his individuality perforce encounters, and indeed merges with,
the voice of Empire, which is itself a system of rules, codes, and
concrete epistemological habits. Thus when Burton tells us in the
Pilgrimage that "Egypt is a treasure to be won," that it "is the
most tempting prize which the East holds out to the ambition of
Europe, not excepted even the Golden Horn,"[123] we must recognize
how the voice of the highly idiosyncratic master of Oriental knowledge informs, feeds into the voice of European ambition for rule
over the Orient.

Burton's two voices blending into one presage the work of
Orientalists–*cum*–imperial agents like T. E. Lawrence, Edward

Henry Palmer, D. G. Hogarth, Gertrude Bell, Ronald Storrs, St. John Philby, and William Gifford Palgrave, to name only some English writers. The double-pronged intention of Burton's work is at the same time to use his Oriental residence for scientific observation *and* not easily to sacrifice his individuality to that end. The second of these two intentions leads him inevitably to submit to the first because, as will appear increasingly obvious, he is a European for whom such knowledge of Oriental society as he has is possible only for a European, with a European's self-awareness of society as a collection of rules and practices. In other words, to be a European in the Orient, and to be one knowledgeably, one must see and know the Orient as a domain ruled over by Europe. Orientalism, which is the system of European or Western knowledge about the Orient, thus becomes synonymous with European domination of the Orient, and this domination effectively overrules even the eccentricities of Burton's personal style.

Burton took the assertion of personal, authentic, sympathetic, and humanistic knowledge of the Orient as far as it would go in its struggle with the archive of official European knowledge about the Orient. In the history of nineteenth-century attempts to restore, restructure, and redeem all the various provinces of knowledge and life, Orientalism—like all the other Romantically inspired learned disciplines—contributed an important share. For not only did the field evolve from a system of inspired observation into what Flaubert called a regulated college of learning, it also reduced the personalities of even its most redoubtable individualists like Burton to the role of imperial scribe. From being a place, the Orient became a domain of actual scholarly rule and potential imperial sway. The role of the early Orientalists like Renan, Sacy, and Lane was to provide their work and the Orient together with a *mise en scène*; later Orientalists, scholarly or imaginative, took firm hold of the scene. Still later, as the scene required management, it became clear that institutions and governments were better at the game of management than individuals. This is the legacy of nineteenth-century Orientalism to which the twentieth century has become inheritor. We must now investigate as exactly as possible the way twentieth-century Orientalism—inaugurated by the long process of the West's occupation of the Orient from the 1880s on—successfully controlled freedom and knowledge; in short, the way Orientalism was fully formalized into a repeatedly produced copy of itself.

3

Orientalism Now

On les apercevait tenant leurs idoles entre leurs bras comme de grands
enfants paralytiques.

—Gustave Flaubert, *La Tentation de Saint Antoine*

The conquest of the earth, which mostly means the taking it away
from those who have a different complexion or slightly flatter noses
than ourselves, is not a pretty thing when you look into it too much.
What redeems it is the idea only. An idea at the back of it; not a
sentimental pretence but an idea; and an unselfish belief in the idea—
something you can set up, and bow down before, and offer a sacrifice
to. . . .

—Joseph Conrad, *Heart of Darkness*

I

Latent and Manifest
Orientalism

In Chapter One, I tried to indicate the scope of thought and action covered by the word *Orientalism*, using as privileged types the British and French experiences of and with the Near Orient, Islam, and the Arabs. In those experiences I discerned an intimate, perhaps even the most intimate, and rich relationship between Occident and Orient. Those experiences were part of a much wider European or Western relationship with the Orient, but what seems to have influenced Orientalism most was a fairly constant sense of confrontation felt by Westerners dealing with the East. The boundary notion of East and West, the varying degrees of projected inferiority and strength, the range of work done, the kinds of characteristic features ascribed to the Orient: all these testify to a willed imaginative and geographic division made between East and West, and lived through during many centuries. In Chapter Two my focus narrowed a good deal. I was interested in the earliest phases of what I call modern Orientalism, which began during the latter part of the eighteenth century and the early years of the nineteenth. Since I did not intend my study to become a narrative chronicle of the development of Oriental studies in the modern West, I proposed instead an account of the rise, development, and institutions of Orientalism as they were formed against a background of intellectual, cultural, and political history until about 1870 or 1880. Although my interest in Orientalism there included a decently ample variety of scholars and imaginative writers, I cannot claim by any means to have presented more than a portrait of the typical structures (and their ideological tendencies) constituting the field, its associations with other fields, and the work of some of its most influential scholars. My principal operating assumptions were—and continue to be—that fields of learning, as much as the works of even the most eccentric artist, are constrained and acted upon by society, by cultural traditions, by worldly circumstance, and by stabilizing influences like schools, libraries, and governments; moreover, that both learned and imaginative writing are never free, but are limited in their imagery, assumptions, and intentions; and finally, that the advances made by a "science" like Orientalism in its academic form are less objectively true than we often like to think. In short, my study hitherto has tried to describe the *economy* that makes Orientalism a coherent subject matter, even while allowing that as an idea, concept, or image the word *Orient* has a considerable and interesting cultural resonance in the West.

I realize that such assumptions are not without their controversial side. Most of us assume in a general way that learning and scholarship move forward; they get better, we feel, as time passes and as more information is accumulated, methods are refined, and later generations of scholars improve upon earlier ones. In addition, we entertain a mythology of creation, in which it is believed that artistic genius, an original talent, or a powerful intellect can leap beyond the confines of its own time and place in order to put before the world a new work. It would be pointless to deny that such ideas as these carry some truth. Nevertheless the possibilities for work present in the culture to a great and original mind are never unlimited, just as it is also true that a great talent has a very healthy respect for what others have done before it and for what the field already contains. The work of predecessors, the institutional life of a scholarly field, the collective nature of any learned enterprise: these, to say nothing of economic and social circumstances, tend to diminish the effects of the individual scholar's production. A field like Orientalism has a cumulative and corporate identity, one that is particularly strong given its associations with traditional learning (the classics, the Bible, philology), public institutions (governments, trading companies, geographical societies, universities), and generically determined writing (travel books, books of exploration, fantasy, exotic description). The result for Orientalism has been a sort of consensus: certain things, certain types of statement, certain types of work have seemed for the Orientalist correct. He has built his work and research upon them, and they in turn have pressed hard upon new writers and scholars. Orientalism can thus be regarded as a manner of regularized (or Orientalized) writing, vision, and study, dominated by imperatives, perspectives, and ideological biases ostensibly suited to the Orient. The Orient is taught, researched, administered, and pronounced upon in certain discrete ways.

The Orient that appears in Orientalism, then, is a system of representations framed by a whole set of forces that brought the Orient into Western learning, Western consciousness, and later, Western empire. If this definition of Orientalism seems more political than not, that is simply because I think Orientalism was itself a product of certain political forces and activities. Orientalism is a school of interpretation whose material happens to be the Orient, its civilizations, peoples, and localities. Its objective discoveries—the work of innumerable devoted scholars who edited texts and translated them, codified grammars, wrote dictionaries, reconstructed dead epochs, produced positivistically verifiable learning—are and always have been conditioned by the fact that its truths, like any truths delivered by language, are embodied in language, and what is the truth of language, Nietzsche once said, but

> a mobile army of metaphors, metonyms, and anthropomorphisms —in short, a sum of human relations, which have been enhanced, transposed, and embellished poetically and rhetorically, and which after long use seem firm, canonical, and obligatory to a people: truths are illusions about which one has forgotten that this is what they are.[1]

Perhaps such a view as Nietzsche's will strike us as too nihilistic, but at least it will draw attention to the fact that so far as it existed in the West's awareness, the Orient was a word which later accrued to it a wide field of meanings, associations, and connotations, and that these did not necessarily refer to the real Orient but to the field surrounding the word.

Thus Orientalism is not only a positive doctrine about the Orient that exists at any one time in the West; it is also an influential academic tradition (when one refers to an academic specialist who is called an Orientalist), as well as an area of concern defined by travelers, commercial enterprises, governments, military expeditions, readers of novels and accounts of exotic adventure, natural historians, and pilgrims to whom the Orient is a specific kind of knowledge about specific places, peoples, and civilizations. For the Orient idioms became frequent, and these idioms took firm hold in European discourse. Beneath the idioms there was a layer of doctrine about the Orient; this doctrine was fashioned out of the experiences of many Europeans, all of them converging upon such essential aspects of the Orient as the Oriental character, Oriental despotism, Oriental sensuality, and the like. For any European during the nineteenth century—and I think one can say this almost without qualification—Orientalism was such a system of truths, truths in Nietzsche's sense of the word. It is therefore correct that every European, in what he could say about the Orient, was consequently a racist, an imperialist, and almost totally ethnocentric. Some of the immediate sting will be taken out of these labels if we recall additionally that human societies, at least the more advanced cultures, have rarely offered the individual anything but imperialism, racism, and ethnocentrism for dealing with "other" cultures. So Orientalism aided and was aided by general cultural pressures that tended to make more rigid the sense of difference between the European and Asiatic parts of the world. My contention is that Orientalism is fundamentally a political doctrine willed over the Orient because the Orient was weaker than the West, which elided the Orient's difference with its weakness.

This proposition was introduced early in Chapter One, and nearly everything in the pages that followed was intended in part as a corroboration of it. The very presence of a "field" such as Orientalism, with no corresponding equivalent in the Orient itself, suggests the relative strength of Orient and Occident. A vast number of pages on the Orient exist, and they of course signify a degree and quantity of interaction with the Orient that are quite formidable; but the crucial index of Western strength is that there is no possibility of comparing the movement of Westerners eastwards (since the end of the eighteenth century) with the movement of Easterners westwards. Leaving aside the fact that Western armies, consular corps, merchants, and scientific and archaeological expeditions were always going East, the number of travelers from the Islamic East to Europe between 1800 and 1900 is minuscule when compared with the number in the other direction.[2] Moreover, the Eastern travelers in the West were there to learn from and to gape at an advanced culture; the purposes of the Western travelers in the Orient were, as we have seen, of quite a different order. In addition, it has been estimated that around 60,000 books dealing with the Near Orient were written between 1800 and 1950; there is no remotely comparable figure for Oriental books about the West. As a cultural apparatus Orientalism is all aggression, activity, judgment, will-to-truth, and knowledge. The Orient existed for the West, or so it seemed to countless Orientalists, whose attitude to what they worked on was either paternalistic or candidly condescending—unless, of course, they were antiquarians, in which case the "classical" Orient was a credit to *them* and not to the lamentable modern Orient.

And then, beefing up the Western scholars' work, there were numerous agencies and institutions with no parallels in Oriental society.

Such an imbalance between East and West is obviously a function of changing historical patterns. During its political and military heyday from the eighth century to the sixteenth, Islam dominated both East and West. Then the center of power shifted westwards, and now in the late twentieth century it seems to be directing itself back towards the East again. My account of nineteenth-century Orientalism in Chapter Two stopped at a particularly charged period in the latter part of the century, when the often dilatory, abstract, and projective aspects of Orientalism were about to take on a new sense of worldly mission in the service of formal colonialism. It is this project and this moment that I want now to describe, especially since it will furnish us with some important background for the twentieth-century crises of Orientalism and the resurgence of political and cultural strength in the East.

On several occasions I have alluded to the connections between Orientalism as a body of ideas, beliefs, clichés, or learning about the East, and other schools of thought at large in the culture. Now one of the important developments in nineteenth-century Orientalism was the distillation of essential ideas about the Orient—its sensuality, its tendency to despotism, its aberrant mentality, its habits of inaccuracy, its backwardness—into a separate and unchallenged coherence; thus for a writer to use the word *Oriental* was a reference for the reader sufficient to identify a specific body of information about the Orient. This information seemed to be morally neutral and objectively valid; it seemed to have an epistemological status equal to that of historical chronology or geographical location. In its most basic form, then, Oriental material could not really be violated by anyone's discoveries, nor did it seem ever to be revaluated completely. Instead, the work of various nineteenth-century scholars and of imaginative writers made this essential body of knowledge more clear, more detailed, more substantial—and more distinct from "Occidentalism." Yet Orientalist ideas could enter into alliance with general philosophical theories (such as those about the history of mankind and civilization) and diffuse world-hypotheses, as philosophers sometimes call them; and in many ways the professional contributors to Oriental knowledge were anxious to couch their formulations and ideas, their scholarly work, their considered contemporary observations, in language and terminology whose cultural validity derived from other sciences and systems of thought.

The distinction I am making is really between an almost unconscious (and certainly an untouchable) positívity, which I shall call *latent* Orientalism, and the various stated views about Oriental society, languages, literatures, history, sociology, and so forth, which I shall call *manifest* Orientalism. Whatever change occurs in knowledge of the Orient is found almost exclusively in manifest Orientalism; the unanimity, stability, and durability of latent Orientalism are more or less constant. In the nineteenth-century writers I analyzed in Chapter Two, the differences in their ideas about the Orient can be characterized as exclusively manifest differences, differences in form and personal style, rarely in basic content. Every one of them kept intact the separateness of the Orient, its eccentricity, its backwardness, its silent indifference, its feminine penetrability, its supine malleability; this is why every writer on the Orient, from Renan to Marx (ideologically speaking), or from the most rigorous scholars (Lane and Sacy) to the most powerful imaginations (Flaubert and Nerval), saw the Orient as a locale requiring Western attention, reconstruction, even redemption. The Orient existed as a place isolated from the mainstream of European progress in the sciences, arts, and commerce. Thus whatever good or bad values were imputed to the Orient appeared to be functions of some highly specialized Western interest in the Orient. This was the situation from about the 1870s on through the early part of the twentieth century—but let me give some examples that illustrate what I mean.

Theses of Oriental backwardness, degeneracy, and inequality with the West most easily associated themselves early in the nineteenth century with ideas about the biological bases of racial inequality. Thus the racial classifications found in Cuvier's *Le Règne animal*, Gobineau's *Essai sur l'inégalité des races humaines*, and Robert Knox's *The Dark Races of Man* found a willing partner in latent Orientalism. To these ideas was added second-order Darwinism, which seemed to accentuate the "scientific" validity of the division of races into advanced and backward, or European-Aryan and Oriental-African. Thus the whole question of imperialism, as it was debated in the late nineteenth century by pro-imperialists and anti-imperialists alike, carried forward the binary typology of advanced and backward (or subject) races, cultures, and societies. John Westlake's *Chapters on the Principles of International Law* (1894) argues, for example, that regions of the earth designated as "uncivilized" (a word carrying the freight of Orientalist assumptions, among others) ought to be annexed or occupied by advanced powers. Similarly, the ideas of such writers as Carl Peters, Leopold de Saussure, and Charles Temple draw on the advanced/backward binarism[3] so centrally advocated in late-nineteenth-century Orientalism.

Along with all other peoples variously designated as backward, degenerate, uncivilized, and retarded, the Orientals were viewed in a framework constructed out of biological determinism and moral-political admonishment. The Oriental was linked thus to elements in Western society (delinquents, the insane, women, the poor) having in common an identity best described as lamentably alien. Orientals were rarely seen or looked at; they were seen through, analyzed not as citizens, or even people, but as problems to be solved or confined or—as the colonial powers openly coveted their territory—taken over. The point is that the very designation of something as Oriental involved an already pronounced evaluative judgment, and in the case of the peoples inhabiting the decayed Ottoman Empire, an implicit program of action. Since the Oriental was a member of a subject race, he had to be subjected: it was that simple. The *locus classicus* for such judgment and action is to be found in Gustave Le Bon's *Les Lois psychologiques de l'évolution des peuples* (1894).

But there were other uses for latent Orientalism. If that group of ideas allowed one to separate Orientals from advanced, civilizing powers, and if the "classical" Orient served to justify both the Orientalist and his disregard of modern Orientals, latent Orientalism also encouraged a peculiarly (not to say invidiously) male conception of the world. I have already referred to this in passing during my discussion of Renan. The Oriental male was considered in isolation from the total community in which he lived and which many Orientalists, following Lane, have viewed with something resembling contempt and fear. Orientalism itself, furthermore, was an exclusively male province; like so many professional guilds during the modern period, it viewed itself and its subject matter with sexist blinders. This is especially evident in the writing of travelers and novelists: women are usually the creatures of a male power-fantasy. They express unlimited sensuality, they are more or less stupid, and above all they are willing. Flaubert's Kuchuk Hanem is the prototype of such caricatures, which were common enough in pornographic novels (e.g., Pierre Louÿs's *Aphrodite*) whose novelty draws on the Orient for their interest. Moreover the male conception of the world, in its effect upon the practicing Orientalist, tends to be static, frozen, fixed eternally. The very possibility of development, transformation, human movement— in the deepest sense of the word—is denied the Orient and the Oriental. As a known and ultimately an immobilized or unproductive quality, they come to be identified with a bad sort of eternality: hence, when the Orient is being approved, such phrases as "the wisdom of the East."

Transferred from an implicit social evaluation to a grandly cultural one, this static male Orientalism took on a variety of forms in the late nineteenth century, especially when Islam was being discussed. General cultural historians as respected as Leopold von Ranke and Jacob Burckhardt assailed Islam as if they were dealing not so much with an anthropomorphic abstraction as with a religio-political culture about which deep generalizations were possible and warranted: in his *Weltgeschichte* (1881–1888) Ranke spoke of Islam as defeated by the Germanic-Romanic peoples, and in his "Historische Fragmente" (unpublished notes, 1893) Burckhardt spoke of Islam as wretched, bare, and trivial.[4] Such intellectual operations were carried out with considerably more flair and enthusiasm by Oswald Spengler, whose ideas about a Magian personality (typified by the Muslim Oriental) infuse *Der Untergang des Abendlandes* (1918–1922) and the "morphology" of cultures it advocates.

What these widely diffused notions of the Orient depended on was the almost total absence in contemporary Western culture of the Orient as a genuinely felt and experienced force. For a number of evident reasons the Orient was always in the position both of outsider and of incorporated weak partner for the West. To the extent that Western scholars were aware of contemporary Orientals or Oriental movements of thought and culture, these were perceived either as silent shadows to be animated by the Orientalist, brought into reality by him, or as a kind of cultural and intellectual proletariat useful for the Orientalist's grander interpretative activity, necessary for his performance as superior judge, learned man, powerful cultural will. I mean to say that in discussions of the Orient, the Orient is all absence, whereas one feels the Orientalist and what he says as presence; yet we must not forget that the Orientalist's presence is enabled by the Orient's effective absence.

This fact of substitution and displacement, as we must call it, clearly places on the Orientalist himself a certain pressure to reduce the Orient in his work, even after he has devoted a good deal of time to elucidating and exposing it. How else can one explain major scholarly production of the type we associate with Julius Wellhausen and Theodor Nöldeke and, overriding it, those bare, sweeping statements that almost totally denigrate their chosen subject matter? Thus Nöldeke could declare in 1887 that the sum total of his work as an Orientalist was to confirm his "low opinion" of the Eastern peoples.[5] And like Carl Becker, Nöldeke was a philhellenist, who showed his love of Greece curiously by displaying a positive dislike of the Orient, which after all was what he studied as a scholar.

A very valuable and intelligent study of Orientalism—Jacques Waardenburg's *L'Islam dans le miroir de l'Occident*—examines five important experts as makers of an image of Islam. Waardenburg's mirror-image metaphor for late-nineteenth- and early-twentieth-century Orientalism is apt. In the work of each of his eminent Orientalists there is a highly tendentious—in four cases out of the five, even hostile—vision of Islam, as if each man saw Islam as a reflection of his own chosen weakness. Each scholar was profoundly learned, and the style of his contribution was unique. The five Orientalists among them exemplify what was best and strongest in the tradition during the period roughly from the 1880s to the interwar years. Yet Ignaz Goldziher's appreciation of Islam's tolerance towards other religions was undercut by his dislike of Mohammed's anthropomorphisms and Islam's too-exterior theology and jurisprudence; Duncan Black Macdonald's interest in Islamic piety and orthodoxy was vitiated by his perception of what he considered Islam's heretical Christianity; Carl Becker's understanding of Islamic civilization made him see it as a sadly undeveloped one; C. Snouck Hurgronje's highly refined studies of Islamic mysticism (which he considered the essential part of Islam) led him to a harsh judgment of its crippling limitations; and Louis Massignon's extraordinary identification with Muslim theology, mystical passion, and poetic art kept him curiously unforgiving to Islam for what he regarded as its unregenerate revolt against the idea of incarnation. The manifest differences in their methods emerge as less important than their Orientalist consensus on Islam: latent inferiority.[6]

Waardenburg's study has the additional virtue of showing how these five scholars shared a common intellectual and methodological tradition whose unity was truly international. Ever since the first Orientalist congress in 1873, scholars in the field have known each other's work and felt each other's presence very directly. What Waardenburg does not stress enough is that most of the late-nineteenth-century Orientalists were bound to each other politically as well. Snouck Hurgronje went directly from his studies of Islam to being an adviser to the Dutch government on handling its Muslim Indonesian colonies; Macdonald and Massignon were widely sought after as experts on Islamic matters by colonial administrators from North Africa to Pakistan; and, as Waardenburg says (all too briefly) at one point, all five scholars shaped a coherent vision of Islam that had a wide influence on government circles throughout the Western world.[7] What we must add to Waardenburg's observation is that these scholars were completing, bringing to an ultimate concrete refinement, the tendency since the sixteenth and seventeenth centuries to treat the Orient not only as a vague literary problem but—according to Masson-Oursel—as "un ferme propos d'assimiler adéquatement la valeur des langues pour pénétrer les moeurs et les pensées, pour forcer même des secrets de l'histoire."[8]

I spoke earlier of incorporation and assimilation of the Orient, as these activities were practiced by writers as different from each other as Dante and d'Herbelot. Clearly there is a difference between those efforts and what, by the end of the nineteenth century, had become a truly formidable European cultural, political, and material enterprise. The nineteenth-century colonial "scramble for Africa" was by no means limited to Africa, of course. Neither was the penetration of the Orient entirely a sudden, dramatic afterthought following years of scholarly study of Asia. What we must reckon with is a long and slow process of appropriation by which Europe, or the European awareness of the Orient, transformed itself from being textual and contemplative into being administrative, economic, and even military. The fundamental change was a spatial and geographical one, or rather it was a change in the quality of geographical and spatial apprehension so far as the Orient was concerned. The centuries-old designation of geographical space to the east of Europe as "Oriental" was partly political, partly doctrinal, and partly imaginative; it implied no necessary connection between actual experience of the Orient and knowledge of what is

Oriental, and certainly Dante and d'Herbelot made no claims about
their Oriental ideas except that they were corroborated by a long
learned (and not existential) tradition. But when Lane, Renan,
Burton, and the many hundreds of nineteenth-century European
travelers and scholars discuss the Orient, we can immediately note
a far more intimate and even proprietary attitude towards the
Orient and things Oriental. In the classical and often temporally
remote form in which it was reconstructed by the Orientalist, in
the precisely actual form in which the modern Orient was lived in,
studied, or imagined, the *geographical space* of the Orient was penetrated, worked over, taken hold of. The cumulative effect of decades
of so sovereign a Western handling turned the Orient from alien into
colonial space. What was important in the latter nineteenth century
was not *whether* the West had penetrated and possessed the Orient,
but rather *how* the British and French felt that they had done it.

The British writer on the Orient, and even more so the British
colonial administrator, was dealing with territory about which there
could be no doubt that English power was truly in the ascendant,
even if the natives were on the face of it attracted to France and
French modes of thought. So far as the actual space of the Orient
was concerned, however, England was really there, France was
not, except as a flighty temptress of the Oriental yokels. There is
no better indication of this qualitative difference in spatial attitudes
than to look at what Lord Cromer had to say on the subject, one
that was especially dear to his heart:

> The reasons why French civilisation presents a special degree
> of attraction to Asiatics and Levantines are plain. It is, as a
> matter of fact, more attractive than the civilisations of England
> and Germany, and, moreover, it is more easy of imitation. Com-
> pare the undemonstrative, shy Englishman, with his social ex-
> clusiveness and insular habits, with the vivacious and cosmopolitan
> Frenchman, who does not know what the word shyness means,
> and who in ten minutes is apparently on terms of intimate friend-
> ship with any casual acquaintance he may chance to make. The
> semi-educated Oriental does not recognise that the former has,
> at all events, the merit of sincerity, whilst the latter is often
> merely acting a part. He looks coldly on the Englishman, and
> rushes into the arms of the Frenchman.

The sexual innuendoes develop more or less naturally thereafter.
The Frenchman is all smiles, wit, grace, and fashion; the English-

man is plodding, industrious, Baconian, precise. Cromer's case is
of course based on British solidity as opposed to a French seductive-
ness without any real presence in Egyptian reality.

> Can it be any matter for surprise [Cromer continues] that the
> Egyptian, with his light intellectual ballast, fails to see that some
> fallacy often lies at the bottom of the Frenchman's reasoning, or
> that he prefers the rather superficial brilliancy of the Frenchman to
> the plodding, unattractive industry of the Englishman or the
> German? Look, again, at the theoretical perfection of French
> administrative systems, at their elaborate detail, and at the pro-
> vision which is apparently made to meet every possible contingency
> which may arise. Compare these features with the Englishman's
> practical systems, which lay down rules as to a few main points,
> and leave a mass of detail to individual discretion. The half-
> educated Egyptian naturally prefers the Frenchman's system, for
> it is to all outward appearance more perfect and more easy of
> application. He fails, moreover, to see that the Englishman desires
> to elaborate a system which will suit the facts with which he has
> to deal, whereas the main objection to applying French adminis-
> trative procedures to Egypt is that the facts have but too often
> to conform to the ready-made system.

Since there is a real British presence in Egypt, and since that
presence—according to Cromer—is there not so much to train the
Egyptian's mind as to "form his character," it follows therefore that
the ephemeral attractions of the French are those of a pretty damsel
with "somewhat artificial charms," whereas those of the British
belong to "a sober, elderly matron of perhaps somewhat greater
moral worth, but of less pleasing outward appearance."[9]

Underlying Cromer's contrast between the solid British nanny
and the French coquette is the sheer privilege of British emplace-
ment in the Orient. "The facts with which he [the Englishman] has
to deal" are altogether more complex and interesting, by virtue of
their possession by England, than anything the mercurial French
could point to. Two years after the publication of his *Modern Egypt*
(1908), Cromer expatiated philosophically in *Ancient and Modern
Imperialism*. Compared with Roman imperialism, with its frankly
assimilationist, exploitative, and repressive policies, British imperialism seemed to Cromer to be preferable, if somewhat more wishy-
washy. On certain points, however, the British were clear enough,
even if "after a rather dim, slipshod, but characteristically Anglo-

Saxon fashion," their Empire seemed undecided between "one of two bases—an extensive military occupation or the principle of nationality [for subject races]." But this indecision was academic finally, for in practice Cromer and Britain itself had opted against "the principle of nationality." And then there were other things to be noted. One point was that the Empire was not going to be given up. Another was that intermarriage between natives and English men and women was undesirable. Third—and most important, I think—Cromer conceived of British imperial presence in the Eastern colonies as having had a lasting, not to say cataclysmic, effect on the minds and societies of the East. His metaphor for expressing this effect is almost theological, so powerful in Cromer's mind was the idea of Western penetration of Oriental expanses. "The country," he says, "over which the breath of the West, heavily charged with scientific thought, has once passed, and has, in passing, left an enduring mark, can never be the same as it was before."[10]

In such respects as these, nonetheless, Cromer's was far from an original intelligence. What he saw and how he expressed it were common currency among his colleagues both in the imperial Establishment and in the intellectual community. This consensus is notably true in the case of Cromer's viceregal colleagues, Curzon, Swettenham, and Lugard. Lord Curzon in particular always spoke the imperial lingua franca, and more obtrusively even than Cromer he delineated the relationship between Britain and the Orient in terms of possession, in terms of a large geographical space wholly owned by an efficient colonial master. For him, he said on one occasion, the Empire was not an "object of ambition" but "first and foremost, a great historical and political and sociological fact." In 1909 he reminded delegates to the Imperial Press Conference meeting at Oxford that "we train here and we send out to you your governors and administrators and judges, your teachers and preachers and lawyers." And this almost pedagogical view of empire had, for Curzon, a specific setting in Asia, which as he once put it, made "one pause and think."

> I sometimes like to picture to myself this great Imperial fabric as a huge structure like some Tennysonian "Palace of Art," of which the foundations are in this country, where they have been laid and must be maintained by British hands, but of which the Colonies are the pillars, and high above all floats the vastness of an Asiatic dome.[11]

With such a Tennysonian Palace of Art in mind, Curzon and Cromer were enthusiastic members together of a departmental committee formed in 1909 to press for the creation of a school of Oriental studies. Aside from remarking wistfully that had he known the vernacular he would have been helped during his "famine tours" in India, Curzon argued for Oriental studies as part of the British responsibility to the Orient. On September 27, 1909, he told the House of Lords that

> our familiarity, not merely with the languages of the people of the East but with their customs, their feelings, their traditions, their history and religion, our capacity to understand what may be called the genius of the East, is the sole basis upon which we are likely to be able to maintain in the future the position we have won, and no step that can be taken to strengthen that position can be considered undeserving of the attention of His Majesty's Government or of a debate in the House of Lords.

At a Mansion House conference on the subject five years later, Curzon finally dotted the i's. Oriental studies were no intellectual luxury; they were, he said,

> a great Imperial obligation. In my view the creation of a school [of Oriental studies—later to become the London University School of Oriental and African Studies] like this in London is part of the necessary furniture of Empire. Those of us who, in one way or another, have spent a number of years in the East, who regard that as the happiest portion of our lives, and who think that the work that we did there, be it great or small, was the highest responsibility that can be placed upon the shoulders of Englishmen, feel that there is a gap in our national equipment which ought emphatically to be filled, and that those in the City of London who, by financial support or by any other form of active and practical assistance, take their part in filling that gap, will be rendering a patriotic duty to the Empire and promoting the cause and goodwill among mankind.[12]

To a very great extent Curzon's ideas about Oriental studies derive logically from a good century of British utilitarian administration of and philosophy about the Eastern colonies. The influence of Bentham and the Mills on British rule in the Orient (and India particularly) was· considerable, and was effective in doing away with too much regulation and innovation; instead, as Eric Stokes has convincingly shown, utilitarianism combined with the legacies of liberalism and evangelicalism as philosophies of British rule in the East stressed the rational importance of a strong executive armed with various legal and penal codes, a system of doctrines on such matters as frontiers and land rents, and everywhere an irreducible supervisory imperial authority.[13] The cornerstone of the whole system was a constantly refined knowledge of the Orient, so that as traditional societies hastened forward and became modern commercial societies, there would be no loss of paternal British control, and no loss of revenue either. However, when Curzon referred somewhat inelegantly to Oriental studies as "the necessary furniture of Empire," he was putting into a static image the transactions by which Englishmen and natives conducted their business and kept their places. From the days of Sir William Jones the Orient had been both what Britain ruled and what Britain knew about it: the coincidence between geography, knowledge, and power, with Britain always in the master's place, was complete. To have said, as Curzon once did, that "the East is a University in which the scholar never takes his degree" was another way of saying that the East required one's presence there more or less forever.[14]

But then there were the other European powers, France and Russia among them, that made the British presence always a (perhaps marginally) threatened one. Curzon was certainly aware that all the major Western powers felt towards the world as Britain did. The transformation of geography from "dull and pedantic"—Curzon's phrase for what had now dropped out of geography as an academic subject—into "the most cosmopolitan of all sciences" argued *exactly* that new Western and widespread predilection. Not for nothing did Curzon in 1912 tell the Geographical Society, of which he was president, that

> an absolute revolution has occurred, not merely in the manner and methods of teaching geography, but in the estimation in which it is held by public opinion. Nowadays we regard geographical knowledge as an essential part of knowledge in general. By the aid of geography, and in no other way, do we understand the action of great natural forces, the distribution of population, the growth of commerce, the expansion of frontiers, the development of States, the splendid achievements of human energy in its various manifestations.
>
> We recognize geography as the handmaid of history. . . . Geography, too, is a sister science to economics and politics; and

to any of us who have attempted to study geography it is known that the moment you diverge from the geographical field you find yourself crossing the frontiers of geology, zoology, ethnology, chemistry, physics, and almost all the kindred sciences. Therefore we are justified in saying that geography is one of the first and foremost of the sciences: that it is part of the equipment that is necessary for a proper conception of citizenship, and is an indispensable adjunct to the production of a public man.[15]

Geography was essentially the material underpinning for knowledge about the Orient. All the latent and unchanging characteristics of the Orient stood upon, were rooted in, its geography. Thus on the one hand the geographical Orient nourished its inhabitants, guaranteed their characteristics, and defined their specificity; on the other hand, the geographical Orient solicited the West's attention, even as —by one of those paradoxes revealed so frequently by organized knowledge—East was East and West was West. The cosmopolitanism of geography was, in Curzon's mind, its universal importance to the whole of the West, whose relationship to the rest of the world was one of frank covetousness. Yet geographical appetite could also take on the moral neutrality of an epistemological impulse to find out, to settle upon, to uncover—as when in *Heart of Darkness* Marlow confesses to having a passion for maps.

I would look for hours at South America, or Africa, or Australia, and lose myself in all the glories of exploration. At that time there were many blank spaces on the earth, and when I saw one that looked particularly inviting on a map (but they all look that) I would put my finger on it and say, When I grow up I will go there.[16]

Seventy years or so before Marlow said this, it did not trouble Lamartine that what on a map was a blank space was inhabited by natives; nor, theoretically, had there been any reservation in the mind of Emer de Vattel, the Swiss-Prussian authority on international law, when in 1758 he invited European states to take possession of territory inhabited only by mere wandering tribes.[17] The important thing was to dignify simple conquest with an idea, to turn the appetite for more geographical space into a theory about the special relationship between geography on the one hand and civilized or uncivilized peoples on the other. But to these rationalizations there was also a distinctively French contribution.

By the end of the nineteenth century, political and intellectual circumstances coincided sufficiently in France to make geography, and geographical speculation (in both senses of that word), an attractive national pastime. The general climate of opinion in Europe was propitious; certainly the successes of British imperialism spoke loudly enough for themselves. However, Britain always seemed to France and to French thinkers on the subject to block even a relatively successful French imperial role in the Orient. Before the Franco-Prussian War there was a good deal of wishful political thinking about the Orient, and it was not confined to poets and novelists. Here, for instance, is Saint-Marc Girardin writing in the *Revue des Deux Mondes* on March 15, 1862:

> La France a beaucoup à faire en Orient, parce que l'Orient attend beaucoup d'elle. Il lui demande même plus qu'elle ne peut faire; il lui remettrait volontiers le soin entier de son avenir, ce qui serait pour la France et pour l'Orient un grand danger: pour la France, parce que, disposée a prendre en mains la cause des populations souffrantes, elle se charge le plus souvent de plus d'obligations qu'elle n'en peut remplir; pour l'Orient, parce que tout peuple qui attend sa destinée de l'étranger n'a jamais qu'une condition précaire et qu'il n'y a de salut pour les nations que celui qu'elles se font elles-mêmes.[18]

Of such views as this Disraeli would doubtless have said, as he often did, that France had only "sentimental interests" in Syria (which is the "Orient" of which Girardin was writing). The fiction of "populations souffrantes" had of course been used by Napoleon when he appealed to the Egyptians on their behalf against the Turks and for Islam. During the thirties, forties, fifties, and sixties the suffering populations of the Orient were limited to the Christian minorities in Syria. And there was no record of "l'Orient" appealing to France for its salvation. It would have been altogether more truthful to say that Britain stood in France's way in the Orient, for even if France genuinely felt a sense of obligation to the Orient (and there were some Frenchmen who did), there was very little France could do to get between Britain and the huge land mass it commanded from India to the Mediterranean.

Among the most remarkable consequences of the War of 1870 in France were a tremendous efflorescence of geographical societies and a powerfully renewed demand for territorial acquisition. At the end of 1871 the Société de géographie de Paris declared itself

no longer confined to "scientific speculation." It urged the citizenry
not to "forget that our former preponderance was contested from
the day we ceased to compete . . . in the conquests of civilization
over barbarism." Guillaume Depping, a leader of what has come to
be called the geographical movement, asserted in 1881 that during
the 1870 war "it was the schoolmaster who triumphed," meaning
that the real triumphs were those of Prussian scientific geography
over French strategic sloppiness. The government's *Journal officiel*
sponsored issue after issue centered on the virtues (and profits) of
geographical exploration and colonial adventure; a citizen could
learn in one issue from de Lesseps of "the opportunities in Africa"
and from Garnier of "the exploration of the Blue River." Scientific
geography soon gave way to "commercial geography," as the connection between national pride in scientific and civilizational
achievement and the fairly rudimentary profit motive was urged, to
be channeled into support for colonial acquisition. In the words
of one enthusiast, "The geographical societies are formed to break
the fatal charm that holds us enchained to our shores." In aid of
this liberating quest all sorts of schemes were spun out, including
the enlisting of Jules Verne—whose "unbelievable success," as it
was called, ostensibly displayed the scientific mind at a very high
peak of ratiocination—to head "a round-the-world campaign of
scientific exploration," and a plan for creating a vast new sea just
south of the North African coast, as well as a project for "binding"
Algeria to Senegal by railroad—"a ribbon of steel," as the projectors
called it.[19]

Much of the expansionist fervor in France during the last third
of the nineteenth century was generated out of an explicit wish to
compensate for the Prussian victory in 1870–1871 and, no less
important, the desire to match British imperial achievements. So
powerful was the latter desire, and out of so long a tradition of
Anglo-French rivalry in the Orient did it derive, that France seemed
literally haunted by Britain, anxious in all things connected with
the Orient to catch up with and emulate the British. When in the
late 1870s, the Société académique indo-chinoise reformulated its
goals, it found it important to "bring Indochina into the domain
of Orientalism." Why? In order to turn Cochin China into a "French
India." The absence of substantial colonial holdings was blamed
by military men for that combination of military and commercial
weakness in the war with Prussia, to say nothing of long-standing
and pronounced colonial inferiority compared with Britain. The

"power of expansion of the Western races," argued a leading geographer, La Roncière Le Noury, "its superior causes, its elements, its influences on human destinies, will be a beautiful study for future historians." Yet only if the white races indulged their taste for voyaging—a mark of their intellectual supremacy—could colonial expansion occur.[20]

From such theses as this came the commonly held view of the Orient as a geographical space to be cultivated, harvested, and guarded. The images of agricultural care for and those of frank sexual attention to the Orient proliferated accordingly. Here is a typical effusion by Gabriel Charmes, writing in 1880:

> On that day when we shall be no longer in the Orient, and when other great European powers will be there, all will be at an end for our commerce in the Mediterranean, for our future in Asia, for the traffic of our southern ports. *One of the most fruitful sources of our national wealth will be dried up.* (Emphasis added)

Another thinker, Leroy-Beaulieu, elaborated this philosophy still further:

> A society colonizes, when itself having reached a high degree of maturity and of strength, it procreates, it protects, it places in good conditions of development, and it brings to virility a new society to which it has given birth. Colonization is one of the most complex and delicate phenomena of social physiology.

This equation of self-reproduction with colonization led Leroy-Beaulieu to the somewhat sinister idea that whatever is lively in a modern society is "magnified by this pouring out of its exuberant activity on the outside." Therefore, he said,

> Colonization is the expansive force of a people; it is its power of reproduction; *it is its enlargement and its multiplication through space*; it is the subjection of the universe or a vast part of it to that people's language, customs, ideas, and laws.[21]

The point here is that the space of weaker or underdeveloped regions like the Orient was viewed as something inviting French interest, penetration, insemination—in short, colonization. Geographical conceptions, literally and figuratively, did away with the discrete entities held in by borders and frontiers. No less than entrepreneurial visionaries like de Lesseps, whose plan was to liberate the Orient and the Occident from their geographical bonds,

French scholars, administrators, geographers, and commercial agents poured out their exuberant activity onto the fairly supine, feminine Orient. There were the geographical societies, whose number and membership outdid those of all Europe by a factor of two; there were such powerful organizations as the Comité de l'Asie française and the Comité d'Orient; there were the learned societies, chief among them the Société asiatique, with its organization and membership firmly embedded in the universities, the institutes, and the government. Each in its own way made French interests in the Orient more real, more substantial. Almost an entire century of what now seemed passive study of the Orient had had to end, as France faced up to its transnational responsibilities during the last two decades of the nineteenth century.

In the only part of the Orient where British and French interests literally overlapped, the territory of the now hopelessly ill Ottoman Empire, the two antagonists managed their conflict with an almost perfect and characteristic consistency. Britain was *in* Egypt and Mesopotamia; through a series of quasi-fictional treaties with local (and powerless) chiefs it controlled the Red Sea, the Persian Gulf, and the Suez Canal, as well as most of the intervening land mass between the Mediterranean and India. France, on the other hand, seemed fated to hover over the Orient, descending once in a while to carry out schemes that repeated de Lesseps's success with the canal; for the most part these schemes were railroad projects, such as the one planned across more or less British territory, the Syrian-Mesopotamian line. In addition France saw itself as the protector of Christian minorities—Maronites, Chaldeans, Nestorians. Yet together, Britain and France were agreed in principle on the necessity, when the time came, for the partition of Asiatic Turkey. Both before and during World War I secret diplomacy was bent on carving up the Near Orient first into spheres of influence, then into mandated (or occupied) territories. In France, much of the expansionist sentiment formed during the heyday of the geographical movement focused itself on plans to partition Asiatic Turkey, so much so that in Paris in 1914 "a spectacular press campaign was launched" to this end.[22] In England numerous committees were empowered to study and recommend policy on the best ways of dividing up the Orient. Out of such commissions as the Bunsen Committee would come the joint Anglo-French teams of which the most famous was the one headed by Mark Sykes and Georges Picot. Equitable division of geographical space was the rule of these plans, which were deliberate attempts also at calming Anglo-French rivalry. For, as Sykes put it in a memorandum,

> it was clear . . . that an Arab rising was sooner or later to take place, and that the French and ourselves ought to be on better terms if the rising was not to be a curse instead of a blessing. . . .[23]

The animosities remained. And to them was added the irritant provided by the Wilsonian program for national self-determination, which, as Sykes himself was to note, seemed to invalidate the whole skeleton of colonial and partitionary schemes arrived at jointly between the Powers. It would be out of place here to discuss the entire labyrinthine and deeply controversial history of the Near Orient in the early twentieth century, as its fate was being decided between the Powers, the native dynasties, the various nationalist parties and movements, the Zionists. What matters more immediately is the peculiar epistemological framework through which the Orient was seen, and out of which the Powers acted. For despite their differences, the British and the French saw the Orient as a geographical—and cultural, political, demographical, sociological, and historical—entity over whose destiny they believed themselves to have traditional entitlement. The Orient to them was no sudden discovery, no mere historical accident, but an area to the east of Europe whose principal worth was uniformly defined in terms of Europe, more particularly in terms specifically claiming for Europe—European science, scholarship, understanding, and administration—the credit for having made the Orient what it was now. And this had been the achievement—inadvertent or not is beside the point—of modern Orientalism.

There were two principal methods by which Orientalism delivered the Orient to the West in the early twentieth century. One was by means of the disseminative capacities of modern learning, its diffusive apparatus in the learned professions, the universities, the professional societies, the explorational and geographical organizations, the publishing industry. All these, as we have seen, built upon the prestigious authority of the pioneering scholars, travelers, and poets, whose cumulative vision had shaped a quintessential Orient; the doctrinal—or doxological—manifestation of such an Orient is what I have been calling here latent Orientalism. So far as anyone wishing to make a statement of any consequence about the Orient was concerned, latent Orientalism supplied him with an enunciative capacity that could be used, or rather mobilized, and turned into sensible discourse for the concrete occasion at hand. Thus when Balfour spoke about the Oriental to the House of Commons in 1910, he must surely have had in mind those enunciative capacities in the current and acceptably rational language of his time, by which something called an "Oriental" could be named and talked about without danger of too much obscurity. But like all enunciative capacities and the discourses they enable, latent Orientalism was profoundly conservative—dedicated, that is, to its self-preservation. Transmitted from one generation to another, it was a part of the culture, as much a language about a part of reality as geometry or physics. Orientalism staked its existence, not upon its openness, its receptivity to the Orient, but rather on its internal, repetitious consistency about its constitutive will-to-power over the Orient. In such a way Orientalism was able to survive revolutions, world wars, and the literal dismemberment of empires.

The second method by which Orientalism delivered the Orient to the West was the result of an important convergence. For decades the Orientalists had spoken about the Orient, they had translated texts, they had explained civilizations, religions, dynasties, cultures, mentalities—as academic objects, screened off from Europe by virtue of their inimitable foreignness. The Orientalist was an expert, like Renan or Lane, whose job in society was to interpret the Orient for his compatriots. The relation between Orientalist and Orient was essentially hermeneutical: standing before a distant, barely intelligible civilization or cultural monument, the Orientalist scholar reduced the obscurity by translating, sympathetically portraying, inwardly grasping the hard-to-reach object. Yet the Orientalist remained outside the Orient, which, however much it was made to appear intelligible, remained beyond the Occident. This cultural, temporal, and geographical distance was expressed in metaphors of depth, secrecy, and sexual promise: phrases like "the veils of an Eastern bride" or "the inscrutable Orient" passed into the common language.

Yet the distance between Orient and Occident was, almost paradoxically, in the process of being reduced throughout the nineteenth century. As the commercial, political, and other existential encounters between East and West increased (in ways we have been discussing all along), a tension developed between the dogmas of latent Orientalism, with its support in studies of the "classical" Orient, and the descriptions of a present, modern, manifest Orient articulated by travelers, pilgrims, statesmen, and the like. At some moment impossible to determine precisely, the tension caused a convergence of the two types of Orientalism. Probably—and this is only a speculation—the convergence occurred when Orientalists, beginning with Sacy, undertook to advise governments on what the modern Orient was all about. Here the role of the specially trained and equipped expert took on an added dimension: the Orientalist could be regarded as the special agent of Western power as it attempted policy vis-à-vis the Orient. Every learned (and not so learned) European traveler in the Orient felt himself to be a representative Westerner who had gotten beneath the films of obscurity. This is obviously true of Burton, Lane, Doughty, Flaubert, and the other major figures I have been discussing.

The discoveries of Westerners about the manifest and modern Orient acquired a pressing urgency as Western territorial acquisition in the Orient increased. Thus what the scholarly Orientalist defined as the "essential" Orient was sometimes contradicted, but in many cases was confirmed, when the Orient became an actual administrative obligation. Certainly Cromer's theories about the Oriental—theories acquired from the traditional Orientalist archive —were vindicated plentifully as he ruled millions of Orientals in actual fact. This was no less true of the French experience in Syria, North Africa, and elsewhere in the French colonies, such as they were. But at no time did the convergence between latent Orientalist doctrine and manifest Orientalist experience occur more dramatically than when, as a result of World War I, Asiatic Turkey was being surveyed by Britain and France for its dismemberment. There, laid out on an operating table for surgery, was the Sick Man of Europe, revealed in all his weakness, characteristics, and topographical outline.

The Orientalist, with his special knowledge, played an inestimably important part in this surgery. Already there had been intimations of his crucial role as a kind of secret agent *inside* the Orient when the British scholar Edward Henry Palmer was sent to the Sinai in 1882 to gauge anti-British sentiment and its possible enlistment on behalf of the Arabi revolt. Palmer was killed in the process, but he was only the most unsuccessful of the many who performed similar services for the Empire, now a serious and exacting business entrusted in part to the regional "expert." Not for nothing was another Orientalist, D. G. Hogarth, author of the famous account of the exploration of Arabia aptly titled *The Pene-tration of Arabia* (1904),[24] made the head of the Arab Bureau in Cairo during World War I. And neither was it by accident that men and women like Gertrude Bell, T. E. Lawrence, and St. John Philby, Oriental experts all, posted to the Orient as agents of empire, friends of the Orient, formulators of policy alternatives be-cause of their intimate and expert knowledge of the Orient and of Orientals. They formed a "band"—as Lawrence called it once—bound together by contradictory notions and personal similarities: great individuality, sympathy and intuitive identification with the Orient, a jealously preserved sense of personal mission in the Orient, cultivated eccentricity, a final disapproval of the Orient. For them all the Orient was their direct, peculiar experience of it. In them Orientalism and an effective praxis for handling the Orient received their final European form, before the Empire disappeared and passed its legacy to other candidates for the role of dominant power.

Such individualists as these were not academics. We shall soon see that they were the beneficiaries of the academic study of the Orient, without in any sense belonging to the official and pro-fessional company of Orientalist scholars. Their role, however, was not to scant academic Orientalism, nor to subvert it, but rather to make it effective. In their genealogy were people like Lane and Burton, as much for their encyclopedic autodidacticism as for the accurate, the quasi-scholarly knowledge of the Orient they had obviously deployed when dealing with or writing about Orientals. For the curricular study of the Orient they substituted a sort of elaboration of latent Orientalism, which was easily available to them in the imperial culture of their epoch. Their scholarly frame of reference, such as it was, was fashioned by people like William Muir, Anthony Bevan, D. S. Margoliouth, Charles Lyall, E. G. Browne, R. A. Nicholson, Guy Le Strange, E. D. Ross, and Thomas Arnold, who also followed directly in the line of descent from Lane. Their imaginative perspectives were provided principally by their illustrious contemporary Rudyard Kipling, who had sung so memorably of holding "dominion over palm and pine."

The difference between Britain and France in such matters was perfectly consistent with the history of each nation in the Orient: the British were there; the French lamented the loss of India and the intervening territories. By the end of the century, Syria had become the main focus of French activity, but even there it was a matter of common consensus that the French could not match the British either in quality of personnel or in degree of political influence. The Anglo–French competition over the Ottoman spoils was felt even on the field of battle in the Hejaz, in Syria, in Mesopotamia—but in all these places, as astute men like Edmond Bremond noted, the French Orientalists and local experts were outclassed in brilliance and tactical maneuvering by their British counterparts.[25] Except for an occasional genius like Louis Massignon, there were no French Lawrences or Sykeses or Bells. But there were determined imperialists like Étienne Flandin and Franklin-Bouillon. Lecturing to the Paris Alliance française in 1913, the Comte de Cressaty, a vociferous imperialist, proclaimed Syria as France's own Orient, the site of French political, moral, and economic interests—interests, he added, that had to be defended during this "âge des envahissants impérialistes"; and yet Cressaty noted that even with French commercial and industrial firms in the Orient, with by far the largest number of native students enrolled in French schools, France was invariably being pushed around in the Orient, threatened not only by Britain but by Austria, Germany, and Russia. If France was to continue to prevent "le retour de l'Islam," it had better take hold of the Orient: this was an argument proposed by Cressaty and seconded by Senator Paul Doumer.[26] These views were repeated on numerous occasions, and indeed France did well by itself in North Africa and in Syria after World War I, but the special, concrete management of emerging Oriental populations and theoretically independent territories with which the British always credited themselves was something the French felt had eluded them. Ultimately, perhaps, the difference one always feels between modern British and modern French Orientalism is a stylistic one; the import of the generalizations about Orient and Orientals, the sense of distinction preserved between Orient and Occident, the desirability of Occidental dominance over the Orient—all these are the same in both traditions. For of the many elements making up what we customarily call "expertise," style, which is the result of specific worldly circumstances being molded by tradition, institutions, will, and intelligence into formal articulation, is one of the most manifest. It is to this determinant, to this perceptible and modernized refinement in early-twentieth-century Orientalism in Britain and France, that we must now turn.

II

Style, Expertise, Vision:
Orientalism's Worldliness

As he appears in several poems, in novels like *Kim*, and in too
many catchphrases to be an ironic fiction, Kipling's White Man, as
an idea, a persona, a style of being, seems to have served many Brit-
ishers while they were abroad. The actual color of their skin set
them off dramatically and reassuringly from the sea of natives, but
for the Britisher who circulated amongst Indians, Africans, or
Arabs there was also the certain knowledge that he belonged to,
and could draw upon the empirical and spiritual reserves of, a long
tradition of executive responsibility towards the colored races. It
was of this tradition, its glories and difficulties, that Kipling wrote
when he celebrated the "road" taken by White Men in the colonies:

> Now, this is the road that the White Men tread
> When they go to clean a land—
> Iron underfoot and the vine overhead
> And the deep on either hand.
> We have trod that road—and a wet and windy road—
> Our chosen star for guide.
> Oh, well for the world when the White Men tread
> Their highway side by side![27]

"Cleaning a land" is best done by White Men in delicate concert
with each other, an allusion to the present dangers of European
rivalry in the colonies; for failing in the attempt to coordinate
policy, Kipling's White Men are quite prepared to go to war: "Freedom for ourselves and freedom for our sons/And, failing freedom,
War." Behind the White Man's mask of amiable leadership there is
always the express willingness to use force, to kill and be killed.
What dignifies his mission is some sense of intellectual dedication; he
is a White Man, but not for mere profit, since his "chosen star" presumably sits far above earthly gain. Certainly many White Men
often wondered what it was they fought for on that "wet and
windy road," and certainly a great number of them must have been
puzzled as to how the color of their skins gave them superior
ontological status plus great power over much of the inhabited

world. Yet in the end, being a White Man, for Kipling and for
those whose perceptions and rhetoric he influenced, was a self-
confirming business. One became a White Man because one *was*
a White Man; more important, "drinking that cup," living that
unalterable destiny in "the White Man's day," left one little time
for idle speculation on origins, causes, historical logic.

Being a White Man was therefore an idea and a reality. It
involved a reasoned position towards both the white and the nonwhite worlds. It meant—in the colonies—speaking in a certain
way, behaving according to a code of regulations, and even feeling
certain things and not others. It meant specific judgments, evalua-
tions, gestures. It was a form of authority before which nonwhites,
and even whites themselves, were expected to bend. In the institutional forms it took (colonial governments, consular corps, commercial establishments) it was an agency for the expression, diffusion, and implementation of policy towards the world, and within
this agency, although a certain personal latitude was allowed, the
impersonal communal idea of being a White Man ruled. Being a
White Man, in short, was a very concrete manner of being-in-the-
world, a way of taking hold of reality, language, and thought. It
made a specific style possible.

Kipling himself could not merely have happened; the same is
true of his White Man. Such ideas and their authors emerge out of
complex historical and cultural circumstances, at least two of which
have much in common with the history of Orientalism in the nineteenth century. One of them is the culturally sanctioned habit of
deploying large generalizations by which reality is divided into
various collectives: languages, races, types, colors, mentalities,
each category being not so much a neutral designation as an
evaluative interpretation. Underlying these categories is the rigidly
binomial opposition of "ours" and "theirs," with the former always
encroaching upon the latter (even to the point of making "theirs"
exclusively a function of "ours"). This opposition was reinforced
not only by anthropology, linguistics, and history but also, of course,
by the Darwinian theses on survival and natural selection, and—no
less decisive—by the rhetoric of high cultural humanism. What gave
writers like Renan and Arnold the right to generalities about race
was the official character of their formed cultural literacy. "Our"
values were (let us say) liberal, humane, correct; they were supported by the tradition of belles-lettres, informed scholarship,
rational inquiry; as Europeans (and white men) "we" shared in

them every time their virtues were extolled. Nevertheless, the human partnerships formed by reiterated cultural values excluded as much as they included. For every idea about "our" art spoken for by Arnold, Ruskin, Mill, Newman, Carlyle, Renan, Gobineau, or Comte, another link in the chain binding "us" together was formed while another outsider was banished. Even if this is always the result of such rhetoric, wherever and whenever it occurs, we must remember that for nineteenth-century Europe an imposing edifice of learning and culture was built, so to speak, in the face of actual outsiders (the colonies, the poor, the delinquent), whose role in the culture was to give definition to what *they* were constitutionally unsuited for.[28]

The other circumstance common to the creation of the White Man and Orientalism is the "field" commanded by each, as well as the sense that such a field entails peculiar modes, even rituals, of behavior, learning, and possession. Only an Occidental could speak of Orientals, for example, just as it was the White Man who could designate and name the coloreds, or nonwhites. Every statement made by Orientalists or White Men (who were usually interchangeable) conveyed a sense of the irreducible distance separating white from colored, or Occidental from Oriental; moreover, behind each statement there resonated the tradition of experience, learning, and education that kept the Oriental-colored to his position of *object studied by the Occidental-white*, instead of vice versa. Where one was in a position of power—as Cromer was, for example—the Oriental belonged to the system of rule whose principle was simply to make sure that no Oriental was ever allowed to be independent and rule himself. The premise there was that since the Orientals were ignorant of self-government, they had better be kept that way for their own good.

Since the White Man, like the Orientalist, lived very close to the line of tension keeping the coloreds at bay, he felt it incumbent on him readily to define and redefine the domain he surveyed. Passages of narrative description regularly alternate with passages of re-articulated definition and judgment that disrupt the narrative; this is a characteristic style of the writing produced by Oriental experts who operated using Kipling's White Man as a mask. Here is T. E. Lawrence, writing to V. W. Richards in 1918:

> . . . the Arab appealed to my imagination. It is the old, old civilisation, which has refined itself clear of household gods, and

half the trappings which ours hastens to assume. The gospel of
bareness in materials is a good one, and it involves apparently a
sort of moral bareness too. They think for the moment, and endeavour to slip through life without turning corners or climbing
hills. In part it is a mental and moral fatigue, a race trained out,
and to avoid difficulties they have to jettison so much that we
think honorable and grave: and yet without in any way sharing
their point of view, I think I can understand it enough to look at
myself and other foreigners from their direction, and without
condemning it. I know I am a stranger to them, and always will
be; but I cannot believe them worse, any more than I could
change to their ways.[29]

A similar perspective, however different the subject under discussion may seem to be, is found in these remarks by Gertrude Bell:

How many thousand years this state of things has lasted [namely,
that Arabs live in "a state of war"], those who shall read the
earliest records of the inner desert will tell us, for it goes back to
the first of them, but in all the centuries the Arab has bought no
wisdom from experience. He is never safe, and yet he behaves as
though security were his daily bread.[30]

To which, as a gloss, we should add her further observation, this
time about life in Damascus:

I begin to see dimly what the civilisation of a great Eastern city
means, how they live, what they think; and I have got on to
terms with them. I believe the fact of my being English is a great
help. . . . We have gone up in the world since five years ago. The
difference is very marked. I think it is due to the success of our
government in Egypt to a great extent. . . . The defeat of Russia
stands for a great deal, and my impression is that the vigorous
policy of Lord Curzon in the Persian Gulf and on the India
frontier stands for a great deal more. No one who does not know
the East can realise how it all hangs together. It is scarcely an
exaggeration to say that if the English mission had been turned
back from the gates of Kabul, the English tourist would be
frowned upon in the streets of Damascus.[31]

In such statements as these, we note immediately that "the Arab"
or "Arabs" have an aura of apartness, definiteness, and collective
self-consistency such as to wipe out any traces of individual Arabs
with narratable life histories. What appealed to Lawrence's imagination was the clarity of the Arab, both as an image and as a supposed philosophy (or attitude) towards life: in both cases what

Lawrence fastens on is the Arab as if seen from the cleansing perspective of one not an Arab, and one for whom such un-self-conscious primitive simplicity as the Arab possesses is something defined by the observer, in this case the White Man. Yet Arab refinement, which in its essentials corresponds to Yeats's visions of Byzantium where

> Flames that no faggot feeds, flint nor steel has lit,
> Nor storm disturbs, flames begotten of flame,
> Where blood-begotten spirits come
> And all complexities of fury leave[32]

is associated with Arab perdurability, as if the Arab had not been subject to the ordinary processes of history. Paradoxically, the Arab seems to Lawrence to have exhausted himself in his very temporal persistence. The enormous age of Arab civilization has thus served to refine the Arab down to his quintessential attributes, and to tire him out morally in the process. What we are left with is Bell's Arab: centuries of experience and no wisdom. As a collective entity, then, the Arab accumulates no existential or even semantical thickness. He remains the same, except for the exhausting refinements mentioned by Lawrence, from one end to the other of "the records of the inner desert." We are to assume that if *an* Arab feels joy, if he is sad at the death of his child or parent, if he has a sense of the injustices of political tyranny, then those experiences are necessarily subordinate to the sheer, unadorned, and persistent fact of being an Arab.

The primitiveness of such a state exists simultaneously on at least two levels: one, *in the definition*, which is reductive; and two (according to Lawrence and Bell), *in reality*. This absolute coincidence was itself no simple coincidence. For one, it could only have been made from the outside by virtue of a vocabulary and epistemological instruments designed both to get to the heart of things and to avoid the distractions of accident, circumstance, or experience. For another, the coincidence was a fact uniquely the result of method, tradition, and politics all working together. Each in a sense obliterated the distinctions between the type—*the* Oriental, *the* Semite, *the* Arab, *the* Orient—and ordinary human reality, Yeats's "uncontrollable mystery on the bestial floor," in which all human beings live. The scholarly investigator took a type marked "Oriental" for the same thing as any individual Oriental he might encounter. Years of tradition had encrusted discourse about such matters as the Semitic or Oriental spirit with some legitimacy. And political good sense taught, in Bell's marvelous phrase, that in the East "it all hangs together." Primitiveness therefore inhered in the Orient, *was* the Orient, an idea to which anyone dealing with or writing about the Orient had to return, as if to a touchstone outlasting time or experience.

There is an excellent way of understanding all this as it applied to the white agents, experts, and advisers for the Orient. What mattered to Lawrence and Bell was that their references to Arabs or Orientals belonged to a recognizable, and authoritative, convention of formulation, one that was able to subordinate detail to it. But from where, more particularly, did "the Arab," "the Semite," or "the Oriental" come?

We have remarked how, during the nineteenth century in such writers as Renan, Lane, Flaubert, Caussin de Perceval, Marx, and Lamartine, a generalization about "the Orient" drew its power from the presumed representativeness of everything Oriental; each particle of the Orient told of its Orientalness, so much so that the attribute of being Oriental overrode any countervailing instance. An Oriental man was first an Oriental and only second a man. Such radical typing was naturally reinforced by sciences (or discourses, as I prefer to call them) that took a backward and downward direction towards the species category, which was supposed also to be an ontogenetic explanation for every member of the species. Thus within broad, semipopular designations such as "Oriental" there were some more scientifically valid distinctions being made; most of these were based principally on language types—e.g., Semitic, Dravidic, Hamitic—but they were quickly able to acquire anthropological, psychological, biological, and cultural evidence in their support. Renan's "Semitic," as an instance, was a linguistic generalization which in Renan's hands could add to itself all sorts of parallel ideas from anatomy, history, anthropology, and even geology. "Semitic" could then be employed not only as a simple description or designation; it could be applied to any complex of historical and political events in order to pare them down to a nucleus both antecedent to and inherent in them. "Semitic," therefore, was a transtemporal, transindividual category, purporting to predict every discrete act of "Semitic" behavior on the basis of some pre-existing "Semitic" essence, and aiming as well to interpret all aspects of human life and activity in terms of some common "Semitic" element.

The peculiar hold on late-nineteenth-century liberal European culture of such relatively punitive ideas will seem mysterious unless it is remembered that the appeal of sciences like linguistics, anthropology, and biology was that they were empirical, and by no means speculative or idealistic. Renan's Semitic, like Bopp's Indo-European, was a constructed object, it is true, but it was considered logical and inevitable as a protoform, given the scientifically apprehendable and empirically analyzable data of specific Semitic languages. Thus, in trying to formulate a prototypical and primitive linguistic type (as well as a cultural, psychological, and historical one), there was also an "attempt to define a primary human potential,"[33] out of which completely specific instances of behavior uniformly derived. Now this attempt would have been impossible had it not also been believed—in classical empiricist terms—that mind and body were interdependent realities, both determined originally by a given set of geographical, biological, and quasi-historical conditions.[34] From this set, which was not available to the native for discovery or introspection, there was no subsequent escape. The antiquarian bias of Orientalists was supported by these empiricist ideas. In all their studies of "classical" Islam, Buddhism, or Zoroastrianism they felt themselves, as George Eliot's Dr. Casaubon confesses, to be acting "like the ghost of an ancient, wandering about the world and trying mentally to construct it as it used to be, in spite of ruin and confusing changes."[35]

Were these theses about linguistic, civilizational, and finally racial characteristics merely one side of an academic debate amongst European scientists and scholars, we might dismiss them as furnishing material for an unimportant closet drama. The point is, however, that both the terms of the debate and the debate itself had very wide circulation; in late-nineteenth-century culture, as Lionel Trilling has said, "racial theory, stimulated by a rising nationalism and a spreading imperialism, supported by an incomplete and mal-assimilated science, was almost undisputed."[36] Race theory, ideas about primitive origins and primitive classifications, modern decadence, the progress of civilization, the destiny of the white (or Aryan) races, the need for colonial territories—all these were elements in the peculiar amalgam of science, politics, and culture whose drift, almost without exception, was always to raise Europe or a European race to dominion over non-European portions of mankind. There was general agreement too that, according to a strangely transformed variety of Darwinism sanctioned by Darwin himself, the modern Orientals were degraded remnants of a former greatness; the ancient, or "classical," civilizations of the Orient were perceivable through the disorders of present decadence, but only (*a*) because a white specialist with highly refined scientific techniques could do the sifting and reconstructing, and (*b*) because a vocabulary of sweeping generalities (the Semites, the Aryans, the Orientals) referred not to a set of fictions but rather to a whole array of seemingly objective and agreed-upon distinctions. Thus a remark about what Orientals were and were not capable of was supported by biological "truths" such as those spelled out in P. Charles Michel's "A Biological View of Our Foreign Policy" (1896), in Thomas Henry Huxley's *The Struggle for Existence in Human Society* (1888), Benjamin Kidd's *Social Evolution* (1894), John B. Crozier's *History of Intellectual Development on the Lines of Modern Evolution* (1897–1901), and Charles Harvey's *The Biology of British Politics* (1904).[37] It was assumed that if languages were as distinct from each other as the linguists said they were, then too the language users—their minds, cultures, potentials, and even their bodies—were different in similar ways. And these distinctions had the force of ontological, empirical truth behind them, together with the convincing demonstration of such truth in studies of origins, development, character, and destiny.

The point to be emphasized is that this truth about the distinctive differences between races, civilizations, and languages was (or pretended to be) radical and ineradicable. It went to the bottom of things, it asserted that there was no escape from origins and the types these origins enabled; it set the real boundaries between human beings, on which races, nations, and civilizations were constructed; it forced vision away from common, as well as plural, human realities like joy, suffering, political organization, forcing attention instead in the downward and backward direction of immutable origins. A scientist could no more escape such origins in his research than an Oriental could escape "the Semites" or "the Arabs" or "the Indians" from which his present reality—debased, colonized, backward—excluded him, except for the white researcher's didactic presentation.

The profession of specialized research conferred unique privileges. We recall that Lane could appear to be an Oriental and yet retain his scholarly detachment. The Orientals he studied became in fact *his* Orientals, for he saw them not only as actual people but as monumentalized objects in his account of them. This double perspective encouraged a sort of structured irony. On the one hand, there was a collection of people living in the present; on the other hand, these people—as the subject of study—became "the Egyptians," "the Muslims," or "the Orientals." Only the scholar could see, and manipulate, the discrepancy between the two levels. The tendency of the former was always towards greater variety, yet this variety was always being restrained, compressed downwards and backwards to the *radical* terminal of the generality. Every modern, native instance of behavior became an effusion to be sent back to the original terminal, which was strengthened in the process. This kind of "dispatching" was precisely the *discipline* of Orientalism.

Lane's ability to deal with the Egyptians as present beings and as validations of *sui generis* labels was a function both of Orientalist discipline and of generally held views about the Near Oriental Muslim or Semite. In no people more than in the Oriental Semites was it possible to see the present and the origin together. The Jews and the Muslims, as subjects of Orientalist study, were readily understandable in view of their primitive origins: this was (and to a certain extent still is) the cornerstone of modern Orientalism. Renan had called the Semites an instance of arrested development, and functionally speaking this came to mean that for the Orientalist no modern Semite, however much he may have believed himself to be modern, could ever outdistance the organizing claims on him of his origins. This functional rule worked on the temporal and spatial levels together. No Semite advanced in time beyond the development of a "classical" period; no Semite could ever shake loose the pastoral, desert environment of his tent and tribe. Every manifestation of actual "Semitic" life could be, and ought to be, referred back to the primitive explanatory category of "the Semitic."

The executive power of such a system of reference, by which each discrete instance of real behavior could be reduced down and back to a small number of explanatory "original" categories, was considerable by the end of the nineteenth century. In Orientalism it was the equivalent of bureaucracy in public administration. The department was more useful than the individual file, and certainly the human being was significant principally as the occasion for a file. We must imagine the Orientalist at work in the role of a clerk putting together a very wide assortment of files in a large cabinet marked "the Semites." Aided by recent discoveries in comparative and primitive anthropology, a scholar like William Robertson Smith could group together the inhabitants of the Near Orient and write on their kinship and marriage customs, on the form and content of their religious practice. The power of Smith's work is its plainly radical demythologizing of the Semites. The nominal barriers presented to the world by Islam or Judaism are swept aside; Smith uses Semitic philology, mythology, and Orientalist scholarship "to construct . . . a hypothetical picture of the development of the social systems, consistent with all the Arabian facts." If this picture succeeds in revealing the antecedent, and still influential, roots of monotheism in totemism or animal worship, then the scholar has been successful. And this, Smith says, despite the fact that "our Mohammedan sources draw a veil, as far as they can, over all details of the old heathenism."[38]

Smith's work on the Semites covered such areas as theology, literature, and history; it was done with a full awareness of work done by Orientalists (see, for instance, Smith's savage attack in 1887 on Renan's *Histoire du peuple d'Israël*), and more important, was intended as an aid to the understanding of the modern Semites. For Smith, I think, was a crucial link in the intellectual chain connecting the White-Man-as-expert to the modern Orient. None of the encapsulated wisdom delivered as Oriental expertise by Lawrence, Hogarth, Bell, and the others would have been possible without Smith. And even Smith the antiquarian scholar would not have had half the authority without his additional and direct experience of "the Arabian facts." It was the combination in Smith of the "grasp" of primitive categories with the ability to see general truths behind the empirical vagaries of contemporary Oriental behavior that gave weight to his writing. Moreover, it was this special combination that adumbrated the style of expertise upon which Lawrence, Bell, and Philby built their reputation.

Like Burton and Charles Doughty before him, Smith voyaged in the Hejaz, between 1880 and 1881. Arabia has been an especially privileged place for the Orientalist, not only because Muslims treat Islam as Arabia's *genius loci*, but also because the Hejaz appears historically as barren and retarded as it is geographically; the Arabian desert is thus considered to be a locale about which one can make statements regarding the past in exactly the same form (and with the same content) that one makes them regarding the present. In the Hejaz you can speak about Muslims, modern Islam, and primitive Islam without bothering to make distinctions. To this vocabulary devoid of historical grounding, Smith was able to bring the cachet of additional authority provided by his Semitic studies.

What we hear in his comments is the standpoint of a scholar commanding *all* the antecedents for Islam, the Arabs, and Arabia. Hence:

> It is characteristic of Mohammedanism that all national feeling assumes a religious aspect, inasmuch as the whole polity and social forms of a Moslem country are clothed in a religious dress. But it would be a mistake to suppose that genuine religious feeling is at the bottom of everything that justifies itself by taking a religious shape. The prejudices of the Arab have their roots in a conservatism which lies deeper than his belief in Islam. It is, indeed, a great fault of the religion of the Prophet that it lends itself so easily to the prejudices of the race among whom it was first promulgated, and that it has taken under its protection so many barbarous and obsolete ideas, which even Mohammed must have seen to have no religious worth, but which he carried over into his system in order to facilitate the propagation of his reformed doctrines. Yet many of the prejudices which seem to us most distinctively Mohammedan have no basis in the Koran.[39]

The "us" in the last sentence of this amazing piece of logic defines the White Man's vantage point explicitly. This allows "us" to say in the first sentence that all political and social life are "clothed" in religious dress (Islam can thus be characterized as totalitarian), then to say in the second that religion is only a cover used by Muslims (in other words, all Muslims are hypocrites essentially). In the third sentence, the claim is made that Islam—even while laying hold upon the Arab's faith—has not really reformed the Arab's basic pre-Islamic conservatism. Nor is this all. For if Islam was successful as a religion it was because it fecklessly allowed these "authentic" Arab prejudices to creep in; for such a tactic (now we see that it was a tactic on Islam's behalf) we must blame Mohammed, who was after all a ruthless crypto-Jesuit. But all this is more or less wiped out in the last sentence, when Smith assures "us" that everything he has said about Islam is invalid, since the quintessential aspects of Islam known to the West are not "Mohammedan" after all.

The principles of identity and noncontradiction clearly do not bind the Orientalist. What overrides them is Orientalist expertise, which is based on an irrefutable collective verity entirely within the Orientalist's philosophical and rhetorical grasp. Smith is able without the slightest trepidation to speak about "the jejune, prac-

tical and . . . constitutionally irreligious habit of the Arabic mind,"
Islam as a system of "organized hypocrisy," the impossibility of
"feeling any respect for Moslem devotion, in which formalism and
vain repetition are reduced to a system." His attacks on Islam are
not relativist, for it is clear to him that Europe's and Christianity's
superiority is actual, not imagined. At bottom, Smith's vision of
the world is binary, as is evident in such passages as the following:

> The Arabian traveller is quite different from ourselves. The
> labour of moving from place to place is a mere nuisance to him,
> he has no enjoyment in effort [as "we" do], and grumbles at
> hunger or fatigue with all his might [as "we" do not]. You will
> never persuade the Oriental that, when you get off your camel,
> you can have any other wish than immediately to squat on a rug
> and take your rest (*isterih*), smoking and drinking. Moreover
> the Arab is little impressed by scenery [but "we" are].[40]

"We" are this, "they" are that. Which Arab, which Islam, when,
how, according to what tests: these appear to be distinctions
irrelevant to Smith's scrutiny of and experience in the Hejaz. The
crucial point is that everything one can know or learn about
"Semites" and "Orientals" receives immediate corroboration, not
merely in the archives, but directly on the ground.

Out of such a coercive framework, by which a modern "colored"
man is chained irrevocably to the general truths formulated about
his prototypical linguistic, anthropological, and doctrinal forebears
by a white European scholar, the work of the great twentieth-
century Oriental experts in England and France derived. To this
framework these experts also brought their private mythology and
obsessions, which in writers like Doughty and Lawrence have been
studied with considerable energy. Each—Wilfrid Scawen Blunt,
Doughty, Lawrence, Bell, Hogarth, Philby, Sykes, Storrs—believed
his vision of things Oriental was individual, self-created out of some
intensely personal encounter with the Orient, Islam, or the Arabs;
each expressed general contempt for official knowledge held about
the East. "The sun made me an Arab," Doughty wrote in *Arabia
Deserta*, "but never warped me to Orientalism." Yet in the final
analysis they all (except Blunt) expressed the traditional Western
hostility to and fear of the Orient. Their views refined and gave a
personal twist to the academic style of modern Orientalism, with
its repertoire of grand generalizations, tendentious "science" from
which there was no appeal, reductive formulae. (Doughty again,

on the same page as his sneer at Orientalism: "The Semites are like to a man sitting in a cloaca to the eyes, and whose brows touch heaven."[41]) They acted, they promised, they recommended public policy on the basis of such generalizations; and, by a remarkable irony, they acquired the identity of White Orientals in their natal cultures—even as, in the instances of Doughty, Lawrence, Hogarth, and Bell, their professional involvement with the East (like Smith's) did not prevent them from despising it thoroughly. The main issue for them was preserving the Orient and Islam under the control of the White Man.

A new dialectic emerges out of this project. What is required of the Oriental expert is no longer simply "understanding": now the Orient must be made to perform, its power must be enlisted on the side of "our" values, civilization, interests, goals. Knowledge of the Orient is directly translated into activity, and the results give rise to new currents of thought and action in the Orient. But these in turn will require from the White Man a new assertion of control, this time not as the author of a scholarly work on the Orient but as the maker of contemporary history, of the Orient as urgent actuality (which, because he began it, only the expert can understand adequately). The Orientalist has now become a figure of Oriental history, indistinguishable from it, its shaper, its characteristic *sign* for the West. Here is the dialectic in brief:

> Some Englishmen, of whom Kitchener was chief, believed that a rebellion of Arabs against Turks would enable England, while fighting Germany, simultaneously to defeat her ally Turkey. Their knowledge of the nature and power and country of the Arabic-speaking peoples made them think that the issue of such a rebellion would be happy: and indicated its character and method. So they allowed it to begin, having obtained formal assurances of help for it from the British Government. Yet none the less the rebellion of the Sherif of Mecca came to most as a surprise, and found the Allies unready. It aroused mixed feelings and made strong friends and enemies, amid whose clashing jealousies its affairs began to miscarry.[42]

This is Lawrence's own synopsis of chapter 1 of *The Seven Pillars of Wisdom*. The "knowledge" of "some Englishmen" authors a movement in the Orient whose "affairs" create a mixed progeny; the ambiguities, the half-imagined, tragicomic results of this new, revived Orient become the subject of expert writing, a new form of Orientalist discourse that presents a vision of the contemporary

Orient, not as narrative, but as all complexity, problematics, betrayed hope—with the White Orientalist author as its prophetic,
articulate definition.

The defeat of narrative by vision—which is true even in so
patently storylike a work as *The Seven Pillars*—is something we
have already encountered in Lane's *Modern Egyptians*. A conflict
between a holistic view of the Orient (description, monumental
record) and a narrative of events in the Orient is a conflict on
several levels, involving several different issues. As the conflict is
frequently renewed in the discourse of Orientalism, it is worthwhile
analyzing it here briefly. The Orientalist surveys the Orient from
above, with the aim of getting hold of the whole sprawling panorama before him—culture, religion, mind, history, society. To do
this he must see every detail through the device of a set of reductive categories (the Semites, the Muslim mind, the Orient, and so
forth). Since these categories are primarily schematic and efficient
ones, and since it is more or less assumed that no Oriental can
know himself the way an Orientalist can, any vision of the Orient
ultimately comes to rely for its coherence and force on the person,
institution, or discourse whose property it is. Any comprehensive
vision is fundamentally conservative, and we have noted how in the
history of ideas about the Near Orient in the West these ideas have
maintained themselves regardless of any evidence disputing them.
(Indeed, we can argue that these ideas produce evidence that proves
their validity.)

The Orientalist is principally a kind of agent of such comprehensive visions; Lane is a typical instance of the way an individual believes himself to have subordinated his ideas, or even what he sees,
to the exigencies of some "scientific" view of the whole phenomenon
known collectively as the Orient, or the Oriental nation. A vision
therefore is static, just as the scientific categories informing late-
nineteenth-century Orientalism are static: there is no recourse
beyond "the Semites" or "the Oriental mind"; these are final
terminals holding every variety of Oriental behavior within a general view of the whole field. As a discipline, as a profession, as
specialized language or discourse, Orientalism is staked upon the
permanence of the whole Orient, for without "the Orient" there can
be no consistent, intelligible, and articulated knowledge called
"Orientalism." Thus the Orient belongs to Orientalism, just as it is
assumed that there is pertinent information belonging to (or about)
the Orient.

Against this static system of "synchronic essentialism"[43] I have called vision because it presumes that the whole Orient can be seen panoptically, there is a constant pressure. The source of pressure is narrative, in that if any Oriental detail can be shown to move, or to develop, diachrony is introduced into the system. What seemed stable—and the Orient is synonymous with stability and unchanging eternality—now appears unstable. Instability suggests that history, with its disruptive detail, its currents of change, its tendency towards growth, decline, or dramatic movement, is possible in the Orient and for the Orient. History and the narrative by which history is represented argue that vision is insufficient, that "the Orient" as an unconditional ontological category does an injustice to the potential of reality for change.

Moreover, narrative is the specific form taken by written history to counter the permanence of vision. Lane sensed the dangers of narrative when he refused to give linear shape to himself and to his information, preferring instead the monumental form of encyclopedic or lexicographical vision. Narrative asserts the power of men to be born, develop, and die, the tendency of institutions and actualities to change, the likelihood that modernity and contemporaneity will finally overtake "classical" civilizations; above all, it asserts that the domination of reality by vision is no more than a will to power, a will to truth and interpretation, and not an objective condition of history. Narrative, in short, introduces an opposing point of view, perspective, consciousness to the unitary web of vision; it violates the serene Apollonian fictions asserted by vision.

When as a result of World War I the Orient was made to enter history, it was the Orientalist-as-agent who did the work. Hannah Arendt has made the brilliant observation that the counterpart of the bureaucracy is the imperial agent,[44] which is to say that if the collective academic endeavor called Orientalism was a bureaucratic institution based on a certain conservative vision of the Orient, then the servants of such a vision in the Orient were imperial agents like T. E. Lawrence. In his work we can see most clearly the conflict between narrative history and vision, as—in his words—the "new Imperialism" attempted "an active tide of imposing responsibility on the local peoples [of the Orient]."[45] The competition between the European Powers now caused them to prod the Orient into active life, to press the Orient into service, to turn the Orient from unchanging "Oriental" passivity into militant modern life. It would be important, nevertheless, never to let the Orient go its own way or get out of hand, the canonical view being that Orientals had no tradition of freedom.

The great drama of Lawrence's work is that it symbolizes the struggle, first, to stimulate the Orient (lifeless, timeless, forceless) into movement; second, to impose upon that movement an essentially Western shape; third, to contain the new and aroused Orient in a personal vision, whose retrospective mode includes a powerful sense of failure and betrayal.

> I meant to make a new nation, to restore a lost influence, to give twenty millions of Semites the foundation on which to build an inspired dream-palace of their national thoughts. . . . All the subject provinces of the Empire to me were not worth one dead English boy. If I have restored to the East some self-respect, a goal, ideals: if I have made the standard rule of white over red more exigent, I have fitted those peoples in a degree for the new commonwealth in which the dominant races will forget their brute achievements, and white and red and yellow and brown and black will stand up together without side-glances in the service of the world.[46]

None of this, whether as intention, as an actual undertaking, or as a failed project, would have been remotely possible without the White Orientalist perspective at the outset:

> The Jew in the Metropole at Brighton, the miser, the worshipper of Adonis, the lecher in the stews of Damascus were alike signs of the Semitic capacity for enjoyment, and expressions of the same nerve which gave us at the other pole the self-denial of the Essenes, or the early Christians, or the first Khalifas, finding the ways to heaven fairest for the poor in spirit. The Semite hovered between lust and self-denial.

Lawrence is backed in such statements by a respectable tradition stretching like a lighthouse beam through the whole nineteenth century; at its light-emanating center, of course, is "the Orient," and that is powerful enough to light up both the gross and the refined topographies within its range. The Jew, the worshipper of Adonis, the Damascene lecher, are signs not so much of humanity, let us say, as of a semiotic field called Semitic and built into coherence by the Semitic branch of Orientalism. Inside this field, certain things were possible:

> Arabs could be swung on an idea as on a cord; for the unpledged allegiance of their minds made them obedient servants. None of

them would escape the bond till success had come, and with it
responsibility and duty and engagement. Then the idea was gone
and the work ended—in ruins. Without a creed they could be
taken to the four corners of the world (but not to heaven) by
being shown the riches of the earth and the pleasures of it; but if
on the road . . . they met the prophet of an idea, who had nowhere to lay his head and who depended for his food on charity
or birds, then they would all leave their wealth for his inspiration. . . . They were as unstable as water, and like water would
perhaps finally prevail. Since the dawn of life, in successive waves
they had been dashing themselves against the coasts of flesh. Each
wave was broken. . . . One such wave (and not the least) I
raised and rolled before the breath of an idea, till it reached its
crest, and toppled over and fell at Damascus. The wash of that
wave, thrown back by the resistance of vested things, will provide
the matter of the following wave, when in fullness of time the sea
shall be raised once more.

"Could," "would," and "if" are Lawrence's way inserting himself
in the field, as it were. Thus the possibility is prepared for the last
sentence, in which as manipulator of the Arabs Lawrence puts
himself at their head. Like Conrad's Kurtz, Lawrence has cut
himself loose from the earth so as to become identified with a new
reality in order—he says later—that he might be responsible for
"hustling into form . . . the new Asia which time was inexorably
bringing upon us."[47]

The Arab Revolt acquires meaning only as Lawrence designs
meaning for it; his meaning imparted thus to Asia was a triumph,
"a mood of enlargement . . . in that we felt that we had assumed
another's pain or experience, his personality." The Orientalist has
become now the representative Oriental, unlike earlier participant
observers such as Lane, for whom the Orient was something kept
carefully at bay. But there is an unresolvable conflict in Lawrence
between the White Man and the Oriental, and although he does not
explicitly say so, this conflict essentially restages in his mind the
historical conflict between East and West. Conscious of his power
over the Orient, conscious also of his duplicity, unconscious of anything in the Orient that would suggest to him that history, after all,
is history and that even without him the Arabs would finally attend
to their quarrel with the Turks, Lawrence reduces the entire narrative of the revolt (its momentary successes and its bitter failure) to
his vision of himself as an unresolved, "standing civil war":

Yet in reality we had borne the vicarious for our own sakes, or at least because it was pointed for our benefit: and could escape from this knowledge only by a make-belief in sense as well as in motive. . . .

There seemed no straight walking for us leaders in this crooked lane of conduct, ring within ring of unknown, shamefaced motives cancelling or double-charging their precedents.[48]

To this intimate sense of defeat Lawrence was later to add a theory about "the old men" who stole the triumph from him. In any event, what matters to Lawrence is that as a white expert, the legatee of years of academic and popular wisdom about the Orient, he is able to subordinate his style of being to theirs, thereafter to assume the role of Oriental prophet giving shape to a movement in "the new Asia." And when, for whatever reason, the movement fails (it is taken over by others, its aims are betrayed, its dream of independence invalidated), it is *Lawrence*'s disappointment that counts. So far from being a mere man lost in the great rush of confusing events, Lawrence equates himself fully with the struggle of the new Asia to be born.

Whereas Aeschylus had represented Asia mourning its losses, and Nerval had espressed his disappointment in the Orient for not being more glamorous than he had wanted, Lawrence *becomes* both the mourning continent and a subjective consciousness expressing an almost cosmic disenchantment. In the end Lawrence— and thanks not only to Lowell Thomas and Robert Graves—and Lawrence's vision became the very symbol of Oriental trouble: Lawrence, in short, had assumed responsibility for the Orient by interspersing his knowing experience between the reader and history. Indeed what Lawrence presents to the reader is an unmediated expert power—the power to be, for a brief time, the Orient. All the events putatively ascribed to the historical Arab Revolt are reduced finally to Lawrence's experiences on its behalf.

In such a case, therefore, style is not only the power to symbolize such enormous generalities as Asia, the Orient, or the Arabs; it is also a form of displacement and incorporation by which one voice becomes a whole history, and—for the white Westerner, as reader or writer—the only kind of Orient it is possible to know. Just as Renan had mapped the field of possibility open to the Semites in culture, thought, and language, so too Lawrence charts the space (and indeed, appropriates that space) and time of modern Asia.

The effect of this style is that it brings Asia tantalizingly close to the West, but only for a brief moment. We are left at the end with a sense of the pathetic distance still separating "us" from an Orient destined to bear its foreignness as a mark of its permanent estrangement from the West. This is the disappointing conclusion corroborated (contemporaneously) by the ending of E. M. Forster's *A Passage to India*, where Aziz and Fielding attempt, and fail at, reconciliation:

> "Why can't we be friends now?" said the other, holding him affectionately. "It's what I want. It's what you want."
> But the horses didn't want it—they swerved apart; the earth didn't want it, sending up rocks through which riders must pass single file; the temples, the tank, the jail, the palace, the birds, the carrion, the Guest House, that came into view as they issued from the gap and saw Mau beneath: they didn't want it, they said in their hundred voices, "No, not yet," and the sky said, "No, not there."[49]

This style, this compact definition, is what the Orient will always come up against.

Despite its pessimism, there is a positive political message behind its phrases. The gulf between East and West can be modulated, as Cromer and Balfour knew well, by superior Western knowledge and power. Lawrence's vision is complemented in France by Maurice Barrès's *Une Enquête aux pays du Levant*, the record of a journey through the Near Orient in 1914. Like so many works before it, the *Enquête* is a work of recapitulation whose author not only searches out sources and origins of Western culture in the Orient but also redoes Nerval, Flaubert, and Lamartine in their voyages to the Orient. For Barrès, however, there is an additional political dimension to his journey: he seeks proof, and conclusive evidence, for a constructive French role in the East. Yet the difference between French and British expertise remains: the former manages an actual conjunction of peoples and territory, whereas the latter deals with a realm of spiritual possibility. For Barrès the French presence is best seen in French schools where, as he says of a school in Alexandria, "It is ravishing to see those little Oriental girls welcoming and so wonderfully reproducing the *fantaisie* and the melody [in their spoken French] of the Ile-de-France." If France does not actually have any colonies there, she is not entirely without possessions:

There is, there in the Orient, a feeling about France which is so religious and strong that it is capable of absorbing and reconciling all our most diverse aspirations. In the Orient we represent spirituality, justice, and the category of the ideal. England is powerful there; Germany is all-powerful; but we possess Oriental souls.

Arguing vociferously with Jaurès, this celebrated European doctor proposes to vaccinate Asia against its own illnesses, to occidentalize the Orientals, to bring them into salubrious contact with France. Yet even in these projects Barrès's vision preserves the very distinction between East and West he claims to be mitigating.

How will we be able to form for ourselves an intellectual elite with which we can work, made out of Orientals who would not be deracinated, who would continue to evolve according to their own norms, who would remain penetrated by family traditions, and who would thus form a link between us and the mass of natives? How will we create relationships with a view towards preparing the way for agreements and treaties which would be the desirable form taken by our political future [in the Orient]? All these things are finally all about soliciting in these strange peoples the taste for maintaining contact with our intelligence, *even though this taste may in fact come out of their own sense of their national destiny.*[50]

The emphasis in the last sentence is Barrès's own. Since unlike Lawrence and Hogarth (whose book *The Wandering Scholar* is the wholly informative and unromantic record of two trips to the Levant in 1896 and 1910[51]) he writes of a world of distant probabilities; he is more prepared to imagine the Orient as going its own way. Yet the bond (or leash) between East and West that he advocates is designed to permit a constant variety of intellectual pressure going from West to East. Barrès sees things, not in terms of waves, battles, spiritual adventures, but in terms of the cultivation of intellectual imperialism, as ineradicable as it is subtle. The British vision, exemplified by Lawrence, is of the mainstream Orient, of peoples, political organizations, and movements guided and held in check by the White Man's expert tutelage; the Orient is "our" Orient, "our" people, "our" dominions. Discriminations between elites and the masses are less likely to be made by the British than by the French, whose perceptions and policy were always based on minorities and on the insidious pressures of spiritual community between France and its colonial children. The

British agent-Orientalist—Lawrence, Bell, Philby, Storrs, Hogarth —during and after World War I took over both the role of expert-adventurer-eccentric (created in the nineteenth century by Lane, Burton, Hester Stanhope) and the role of colonial authority, whose position is in a central place next to the indigenous ruler: Lawrence with the Hashimites, Philby with the house of Saud, are the two best-known instances. British Oriental expertise fashioned itself around consensus and orthodoxy and sovereign authority; French Oriental expertise between the wars concerned itself with heterodoxy, spiritual ties, eccentrics. It is no accident, then, that the two major scholarly careers of this period, one British, one French, were H. A. R. Gibb's and Louis Massignon's, one whose interest was defined by the notion of Sunna (or orthodoxy) in Islam, the other whose focus was on the quasi-Christlike, theosophical Sufi figure, Mansur al-Hallaj. I shall return to these two major Orientalists a little later.

If I have concentrated so much on imperial agents and policy-makers instead of scholars in this section, it was to accentuate the major shift in Orientalism, knowledge about the Orient, intercourse with it, from an academic to an *instrumental* attitude. What accompanies the shift is a change in the attitude as well of the individual Orientalist, who need no longer see himself—as Lane, Sacy, Renan, Caussin, Müller, and others did—as belonging to a sort of guild community with its own internal traditions and rituals. Now the Orientalist has become the representative man of his Western culture, a man who compresses within his own work a major duality of which that work (regardless of its specific form) is the symbolic expression: Occidental consciousness, knowledge, science taking hold of the furthest Oriental reaches as well as the most minute Oriental particulars. Formally the Orientalist sees himself as accomplishing the union of Orient and Occident, but mainly by reasserting the technological, political, and cultural supremacy of the West. History, in such a union, is radically attentuated if not banished. Viewed as a current of development, as a narrative strand, or as a dynamic force unfolding systematically and materially in time and space, human history—of the East or the West —is subordinated to an essentialist, idealist conception of Occident and Orient. Because he feels himself to be standing at the very rim of the East-West divide, the Orientalist not only speaks in vast generalities; he also seeks to convert each aspect of Oriental or

Occidental life into an unmediated sign of one or the other geographical half.

The interchange in the Orientalist's writing between his expert
self and his testimonial, beholding self as Western representative is
pre-eminently worked out in visual terms. Here is a typical passage
(quoted by Gibb) from Duncan Macdonald's classic work *The
Religious Attitude and Life in Islam* (1909):

> The Arabs show themselves not as especially easy of belief, but
> as hard-headed, materialistic, questioning, doubting, scoffing at
> their own superstitions and usages, fond of tests of the super-
> natural—and all this in a curiously light-minded, almost childish
> fashion.[52]

The governing verb is *show*, which here gives us to understand that
the Arabs display themselves (willingly or unwillingly) to and for
expert scrutiny. The number of attributes ascribed to them, by its
crowded set of sheer appositions, causes "the Arabs" to acquire a
sort of existential weightlessness; thereby, "the Arabs" are made to
rejoin the very broad designation, common to modern anthropological thought, of "the childish primitive." What Macdonald also
implies is that for such descriptions there is a peculiarly privileged
position occupied by the Western Orientalist, whose representative
function is precisely *to show* what needs to be seen. All specific
history is capable of being seen thus at the apex, or the sensitive
frontier, of Orient and Occident together. The complex dynamics of
human life—what I have been calling history as narrative—
becomes either irrelevant or trivial in comparison with the circular
vision by which the details of Oriental life serve merely to reassert
the Orientalness of the subject and the Westernness of the observer.

If such a vision in some ways recalls Dante's, we should by no
means fail to notice what an enormous difference there is between
this Orient and Dante's. Evidence here is meant to be (and probably
is considered) scientific; its pedigree, genealogically speaking, is
European intellectual and human science during the nineteenth
century. Moreover, the Orient is no simple marvel, or an enemy, or
a branch of exotica; it is a political actuality of great and significant
moment. Like Lawrence, Macdonald cannot really detach his
representative characteristics as a Westerner from his role as a
scholar. Thus his vision of Islam, as much as Lawrence's of the
Arabs, implicates *definition* of the object with the *identity* of the

person defining. All Arab Orientals must be accommodated to a
vision of an Oriental type as constructed by the Western scholar, as
well as to a specific encounter with the Orient in which the
Westerner regrasps the Orient's essence as a consequence of his
intimate estrangement from it. For Lawrence as for Forster, this
latter sensation produces the despondency as well of personal failure;
for such scholars as Macdonald, it strengthens the Orientalist discourse itself.

And it puts that discourse abroad in the world of culture,
politics, and actuality. In the period between the wars, as we can
easily judge from, say, Malraux's novels, the relations between East
and West assumed a currency that was both widespread and
anxious. The signs of Oriental claims for political independence
were everywhere; certainly in the dismembered Ottoman Empire
they were encouraged by the Allies and, as is perfectly evident in
the whole Arab Revolt and its aftermath, quickly became problematic. The Orient now appeared to constitute a challenge, not just
to the West in general, but to the West's spirit, knowledge, and
imperium. After a good century of constant intervention in (and
study of) the Orient, the West's role in an East itself responding
to the crises of modernity seemed considerably more delicate. There
was the issue of outright occupation; there was the issue of the
mandated territories; there was the issue of European competition
in the Orient; there was the issue of dealing with native elites, native
popular movements, and native demands for self-government and
independence; there was the issue of civilizational contacts between
Orient and Occident. Such issues forced reconsideration of Western
knowledge of the Orient. No less a personage than Sylvain Lévi,
president of the Société asiatique between 1928 and 1935, professor
of Sanskrit at the Collège de France, reflected seriously in 1925 on
the urgency of the East-West problem:

> Our duty is to understand Oriental civilization. The humanistic
> problem, which consists, on an intellectual level, in making a
> sympathetic and intelligent effort to understand foreign civiliza-
> tions in both their past and their future forms, is specifically posed
> for us Frenchmen [although similar sentiments could have been
> expressed by an Englishman: the problem was a *European* one]
> in a practical way with regard to our great Asiatic colonies. . . .
> These peoples are the inheritors of a long tradition of history,
> of art, and of religion, the sense of which they have not entirely
> lost and which they are probably anxious to prolong. We have

assumed the responsibility of intervening in their development, sometimes without consulting them, sometimes in answer to their request. . . . We claim, rightly or wrongly, to represent a superior civilization, and because of the right given us by virtue of this superiority, which we regularly affirm with such assurance as makes it seem incontestable to the natives, we have called in question all their native traditions. . . .

In a general way, then, wherever the European has intervened, the native has perceived himself with a sort of general despair which was really poignant since he felt that the sum of his well-being, in the moral sphere more than in sheer material terms, instead of increasing had in fact diminished. All of which has made the foundation of his social life seem to be flimsy and to crumble under him, and the golden pillars on which he had thought to rebuild his life now seem no more than tinseled cardboard.

This disappointment has been translated into rancor from one end to the other of the Orient, and this rancor is very close now to turning to hate, and hate only waits for the right moment in order to turn into action.

If because of laziness or incomprehension Europe does not make the effort that its interests alone require from it, *then the Asiatic drama will approach the crisis point.*

It is here that that science which is a form of life and an instrument of policy—that is, wherever our interests are at stake—owes it to itself to penetrate native civilization and life in their intimacy in order to discover their fundamental values and durable characteristics rather than to smother native life with the incoherent threat of European civilizational imports. We must offer ourselves to these civilizations as we do our other products, that is, on the local exchange market. [Emphasis in original][53]

Lévi has no difficulty in connecting Orientalism with politics, for the long—or rather, the prolonged—Western intervention in the East cannot be denied either in its consequences for knowledge or in its effect upon the hapless native; together the two add up to what could be a menacing future. For all his expressed humanism, his admirable concern for fellow creatures, Lévi conceives the present juncture in unpleasantly constricted terms. The Oriental is imagined to feel his world threatened by a superior civilization; yet his motives are impelled, not by some positive desire for freedom, political independence, or cultural achievement *on their own terms*, but instead by rancor or jealous malice. The panacea offered for this potentially ugly turn of affairs is that the Orient be marketed for a Western consumer, be put before him as one among numerous

wares beseeching his attention. By a single stroke you will defuse
the Orient (by letting it think itself to be an "equal" quantity on
the Occidental marketplace of ideas), and you will appease
Western fears of an Oriental tidal wave. At bottom, of course,
Lévi's principal point—and his most telling confession—is that
unless something is done about the Orient, "the Asiatic drama will
approach the crisis point."

Asia suffers, yet in its suffering it threatens Europe: the eternal,
bristling frontier endures between East and West, almost unchanged
since classical antiquity. What Lévi says as the most august of
modern Orientalists is echoed with less subtlety by cultural humanists. Item: in 1925 the French periodical *Les Cahiers du mois*
conducted a survey among notable intellectual figures; the writers
canvassed included Orientalists (Lévi, Émile Senart) as well as
literary men like André Gide, Paul Valéry, and Edmond Jaloux.
The questions dealt with relations between Orient and Occident in
a timely, not to say brazenly provocative, way, and this already
indicates something about the cultural ambience of the period.
We will immediately recognize how ideas of the sort promulgated in
Orientalist scholarship have now reached the level of accepted truth.
One question asks whether Orient and Occident are mutually im-
penetrable (the idea was Maeterlinck's) or not; another asks
whether or not Oriental influence represented "un peril grave"—
Henri Massis's words—to French thought; a third asks about those
values in Occidental culture to which its superiority over the Orient
can be ascribed. Valéry's response seems to me worth quoting from,
so forthright are the lines of its argument and so time-honored, at
least in the early twentieth century:

From the cultural point of view, I do not think that we have much
to fear *now* from the Oriental influence. It is not unknown to us.
We owe to the Orient all the beginnings of our arts and of a great
deal of our knowledge. We can very well welcome what now
comes out of the Orient, if something new is coming out of there
—which I very much doubt. This doubt is precisely our guarantee
and our European weapon.

Besides, the real question in such matters is to *digest*. But that
has always been, just as precisely, the great specialty of the European mind through the ages. Our role is therefore to maintain this
power of choice, of universal comprehension, of the transformation of everything into our own substance, powers which have
made us what we are. The Greeks and the Romans showed us

how to deal with the monsters of Asia, how to treat them by analysis, how to extract from them their quintessence. . . . The Mediterranean basin seems to me to be like a closed vessel where the essences of the vast Orient have always come in order to be condensed. [Emphasis and ellipses in original][54]

If European culture generally has digested the Orient, certainly Valéry was aware that one specific agency for doing the job has been Orientalism. In the world of Wilsonian principles of national self-determination, Valéry relies confidently on analyzing the Orient's threat away. "The power of choice" is mainly for Europe first to acknowledge the Orient as the origin of European science, then to treat it as a superseded origin. Thus, in another context, Balfour could regard the native inhabitants of Palestine as having priority on the land, but nowhere near the subsequent authority to keep it; the mere wishes of 700,000 Arabs, he said, were of no moment compared to the destiny of an essentially European colonial movement.[55]

Asia represented, then, the unpleasant likelihood of a sudden eruption that would destroy "our" world; as John Buchan put it in 1922:

The earth is seething with incoherent power and unorganized intelligence. Have you ever reflected on the case of China? There you have millions of quick brains stifled in trumpery crafts. They have no direction, no driving power, so the sum of their efforts is futile, and the world laughs at China.[56]

But if China organized itself (as it would), it would be no laughing matter. Europe's effort therefore was to maintain itself as what Valéry called "une machine puissante,"[57] absorbing what it could from outside Europe, converting everything to its use, intellectually and materially, keeping the Orient selectively organized (or disorganized). Yet this could be done only through clarity of vision and analysis. Unless the Orient was seen for what it was, its power —military, material, spiritual—would sooner or later overwhelm Europe. The great colonial empires, great systems of systematic repression, existed to fend off the feared eventuality. Colonial subjects, as George Orwell saw them in Marrakech in 1939, must not be seen except as a kind of continental emanation, African, Asian, Oriental:

When you walk through a town like this—two hundred thousand inhabitants, of whom at least twenty thousand own literally nothing except the rags they stand up in—when you see how the people live, and still more, how easily they die, it is always difficult to believe that you are walking among human beings. All colonial empires are in reality founded upon that fact. The people have brown faces—besides they have so many of them! Are they really the same flesh as yourself? Do they even have names? Or are they merely a kind of undifferentiated brown stuff, about as individual as bees or coral insects? They arise out of the earth, they sweat and starve for a few years, and then they sink back into the nameless mounds of the graveyard and nobody notices that they are gone. And even the graves themselves soon fade back into the soil.[58]

Aside from the picturesque characters offered European readers in the exotic fiction of minor writers (Pierre Loti, Marmaduke Pick-thall, and the like), the non-European known to Europeans is precisely what Orwell says about him. He is either a figure of fun, or an atom in a vast collectivity designated in ordinary or cultivated discourse as an undifferentiated type called Oriental, African, yellow, brown, or Muslim. To such abstractions Orientalism had contributed its power of generalization, converting instances of a civilization into ideal bearers of its values, ideas, and positions, which in turn the Orientalists had found in "the Orient" and trans-formed into common cultural currency.

If we reflect that Raymond Schwab brought out his brilliant biography of Anquetil-Duperron in 1934—and began those studies which were to put Orientalism in its proper cultural context—we must also remark that what he did was in stark contrast to his fellow artists and intellectuals, for whom Orient and Occident were still the secondhand abstractions they were for Valéry. Not that Pound, Eliot, Yeats, Arthur Waley, Fenollosa, Paul Claudel(in his *Connaissance de l'est*), Victor Ségalen, and others were ignoring "the wisdom of the East," as Max Müller had called it a few generations earlier. Rather the culture viewed the Orient, and Islam in particular, with the mistrust with which its learned attitude to the Orient had always been freighted. A suitable instance of this contemporary attitude at its most explicit is to be found in a series of lectures given at the University of Chicago in 1924 on "The Occident and the Orient" by Valentine Chirol, a well-known European newspaperman of great experience in the East; his purpose was to make clear to educated Americans that the Orient was not as far off as perhaps they believed. His line is a simple one: that Orient and Occident are irreducibly opposed to each other, and that the Orient—in particular "Mohammedanism"—is one of "the great world-forces" responsible for "the deepest lines of cleavage" in the world.[59] Chirol's sweeping generalizations are, I think, adequately represented by the titles of his six lectures: "Their Ancient Battleground"; "The Passing of the Ottoman Empire, the Peculiar Case of Egypt"; "The Great British Experiment in Egypt"; "Protectorates and Mandates"; "The New Factor of Bolshevism"; and "Some General Conclusions."

To such relatively popular accounts of the Orient as Chirol's, we can add a testimonial by Élie Faure, who in his ruminations draws, like Chirol, on history, cultural expertise, and the familiar contrast between White Occidentalism and colored Orientalism. While delivering himself of paradoxes like "le carnage permanent de l'indifférence orientale" (for, unlike "us," "they" have no conception of peace), Faure goes on to show that the Orientals' bodies are lazy, that the Orient has no conception of history, of the nation, or of *patrie*, that the Orient is essentially mystical—and so on. Faure argues that unless the Oriental learns to be rational, to develop techniques of knowledge and positivity, there can be no *rapprochement* between East and West.[60] A far more subtle and learned account of the East-West dilemma can be found in Fernand Baldensperger's essay "Où s'affrontent l'Orient et l'Occident intellectuels," but he too speaks of an inherent Oriental disdain for the idea, for mental discipline, for rational interpretation.[61]

Spoken as they are out of the depths of European culture, by writers who actually believe themselves to be speaking on behalf of that culture, such commonplaces (for they are perfect *idées reçues*) cannot be explained simply as examples of provincial chauvinism. They are not that, and—as will be evident to anyone who knows anything about Faure's and Baldensperger's other work—are the more paradoxical for not being that. Their background is the transformation of the exacting, professional science of Orientalism, whose function in nineteenth-century culture had been the restoration to Europe of a lost portion of humanity, but which had become in the twentieth century both an instrument of policy and, more important, a code by which Europe could interpret both itself and the Orient to itself. For reasons discussed earlier in this book, modern Orientalism already carried within itself the imprint of the great European fear of Islam, and this was aggravated by the political challenges of the *entre-deux-guerres*. My point is that the metamorphosis of a relatively innocuous philological subspecialty into a capacity for managing political movements, administering colonies, making nearly apocalyptic statements representing the White Man's difficult civilizing mission—all this is something at work within a purportedly liberal culture, one full of concern for its vaunted norms of catholicity, plurality, and open-mindedness. In fact, what took place was the very opposite of liberal: the hardening of doctrine and meaning, imparted by "science," into "truth." For if such truth reserved for itself the right to judge the Orient as immutably Oriental in the ways I have indicated, then liberality was no more than a form of oppression and mentalistic prejudice.

The extent of such illiberality was not—and is not—often recognized from within the culture, for reasons that this book is trying to explore. It is heartening, nevertheless, that such illiberality has occasionally been challenged. Here is an instance from I. A. Richards's foreword to his *Mencius on the Mind* (1932); we can quite easily substitute "Oriental" for "Chinese" in what follows.

> As to the effects of an increased knowledge of Chinese thought upon the West, it is interesting to notice that a writer so unlikely to be thought either ignorant or careless as M. Etienne Gilson can yet, in the English Preface of his *The Philosophy of St. Thomas Aquinas*, speak of Thomistic Philosophy as "accepting and gathering up the whole of human tradition." This is how we all think, to us the Western world is still the World [or the part of the World that counts]; but an impartial observer would perhaps say that such provincialism is dangerous. And we are not yet so happy in the West that we can be sure that we are not suffering from its effects.[62]

Richards's argument advances claims for the exercise of what he calls Multiple Definition, a genuine type of pluralism, with the combativeness of systems of definition eliminated. Whether or not we accept his counter to Gilson's provincialism, we can accept the proposition that liberal humanism, of which Orientalism has historically been one department, *retards* the process of enlarged and enlarging meaning through which true understanding can be attained. What took the place of enlarged meaning in twentieth-century Orientalism—that is, within the technical field—is the subject most immediately at hand.

III

Modern Anglo-French Orientalism in Fullest Flower

Because we have become accustomed to think of a contemporary expert on some branch of the Orient, or some aspect of its life, as a specialist in "area studies," we have lost a vivid sense of how, until around World War II, the Orientalist was considered to be a generalist (with a great deal of specific knowledge, of course) who had highly developed skills for making summational statements. By summational statements I mean that in formulating a relatively uncomplicated idea, say, about Arabic grammar or Indian religion, the Orientalist would be understood (and would understand himself) as also making a statement about the Orient as a whole, thereby summing it up. Thus every discrete study of one bit of Oriental material would also confirm in a summary way the profound Orientality of the material. And since it was commonly believed that the whole Orient hung together in some profoundly organic way, it made perfectly good hermeneutical sense for the Orientalist scholar to regard the material evidence he dealt with as ultimately leading to a better understanding of such things as the Oriental character, mind, ethos, or world-spirit.

Most of the first two chapters of this book have made similar arguments about earlier periods in the history of Orientalist thought. The differentiation in its later history that concerns us here, however, is the one between the periods immediately before and after World War I. In both instances, as with the earlier periods, the Orient is Oriental no matter the specific case, and no matter the style or technique used to describe it; the difference between the two periods in question is the *reason* given by the Orientalist for seeing the essential Orientality of the Orient. A good example of the prewar rationale can be found in the following passage by Snouck Hurgronje, taken from his 1899 review of Eduard Sachau's *Muhammedanisches Recht*:

> . . . the law, which in practice had to make ever greater concessions to the use and customs of the people and the arbitrariness of

their rulers, nevertheless retained a considerable influence on the intellectual life of the Muslims. Therefore it remains, and still is for us too, an important subject of study, not only for abstract reasons connected with the history of law, civilization and religion, but also for practical purposes. The more intimate the relations of Europe with the Muslim East become, the more Muslim countries fall under European suzerainty, the more important it is for us Europeans to become acquainted with the intellectual life, the religious law, and the conceptual background of Islam.[63]

Although Hurgronje allows that something so abstract as "Islamic law" did occasionally yield to the pressure of history and society, he is more interested than not in retaining the abstraction for intellectual use because in its broad outline "Islamic law" confirms the disparity between East and West. For Hurgronje the distinction between Orient and Occident was no mere academic or popular cliché: quite the contrary. For him it signified the essential, historical power relationship between the two. Knowledge of the Orient either proves, enhances, or deepens the difference by which European suzerainty (the phrase has a venerable nineteenth-century pedigree) is extended effectively over Asia. To know the Orient as a whole, then, is to know it because it is entrusted to one's keeping, if one is a Westerner.

An almost symmetrical passage to Hurgronje's is to be found in the concluding paragraph of Gibb's article "Literature" in *The Legacy of Islam*, published in 1931. After having described the three casual contacts between East and West up till the eighteenth century, Gibb then proceeds to the nineteenth century:

Following on these three moments of casual contact, the German romantics turned again to the East, and for the first time made it their conscious aim to open a way for the real heritage of oriental poetry to enter into the poetry of Europe. The nineteenth century, with its new sense of power and superiority, seemed to clang the gate decisively in the face of their design. Today, on the other hand, there are signs of a change. Oriental literature has begun to be studied again for its own sake, and a new understanding of the East is being gained. As this knowledge spreads and the East recovers its rightful place in the life of humanity, oriental literature may once again perform its historic function, and assist us to liberate ourselves from the narrow and oppressive conceptions which would limit all that is significant in literature, thought, and history to our own segment of the globe.[64]

Gibb's phrase "for its own sake" is in diametrical opposition to the string of reasons subordinated to Hurgronje's declaration about European suzerainty over the East. What remains, nevertheless, is that seemingly inviolable over-all identity of something called "the East" and something else called "the West." Such entities have a use for each other, and it is plainly Gibb's laudable intention to show that the influence on Western of Oriental literature need not be (in its results) what Brunetière had called "a national disgrace." Rather, the East could be confronted as a sort of humanistic challenge to the local confines of Western ethnocentricity.

His earlier solicitation of Goethe's idea of *Weltliteratur* notwithstanding, Gibb's call for humanistic interinanimation between East and West reflects the changed political and cultural realities of the postwar era. European suzerainty over the Orient had not passed; but it had evolved—in British Egypt—from a more or less placid acceptance by the natives into a more and more contested political issue compounded by fractious native demands for independence. These were the years of constant British trouble with Zaghlul, the Wafd party, and the like.[65] Moreover, since 1925 there had been a worldwide economic recession, and this too increased the sense of tension that Gibb's prose reflects. But the specifically cultural message in what he says is the most compelling. Heed the Orient, he seems to be telling his reader, for its use to the Western mind in the struggle to overcome narrowness, oppressive specialization, and limited perspectives.

The ground had shifted considerably from Hurgronje to Gibb, as had the priorities. No longer did it go without much controversy that Europe's domination over the Orient was almost a fact of nature; nor was it assumed that the Orient was in need of Western enlightenment. What mattered during the interwar years was a cultural self-definition that transcended the provincial and the xenophobic. For Gibb, the West has need of the Orient as something to be studied because it releases the spirit from sterile specialization, it eases the affliction of excessive parochial and nationalistic self-centeredness, it increases one's grasp of the really central issues in the study of culture. If the Orient appears more a partner in this new rising dialectic of cultural self-consciousness, it is, first, because the Orient is more of a challenge now than it was before, and second, because the West is entering a relatively new phase of cultural crisis, caused in part by the diminishment of Western suzerainty over the rest of the world.

Therefore, in the best Orientalist work done during the interwar
period—represented in the impressive careers of Massignon and
Gibb himself—we will find elements in common with the best
humanistic scholarship of the period. Thus the summational attitude of which I spoke earlier can be regarded as the Orientalist
equivalent of attempts in the purely Western humanities to understand culture *as a whole*, antipositivistically, intuitively, sympathetically. Both the Orientalist and the non-Orientalist begin with
the sense that Western culture is passing through an important
phase, whose main feature is the crisis imposed on it by such threats
as barbarism, narrow technical concerns, moral aridity, strident
nationalism, and so forth. The idea of using specific texts, for instance, to work from the specific to the general (to understand
the whole life of a period and consequently of a culture) is common
to those humanists in the West inspired by the work of Wilhelm
Dilthey, as well as to towering Orientalist scholars like Massignon
and Gibb. The project of revitalizing philology—as it is found in
the work of Curtius, Vossler, Auerbach, Spitzer, Gundolf, Hofmannsthal[66]—has its counterpart therefore in the invigorations provided to strictly technical Orientalist philology by Massignon's
studies of what he called the mystical lexicon, the vocabulary of
Islamic devotion, and so on.

But there is another, more interesting conjunction between
Orientalism in this phase of its history and the European sciences
of man (*sciences de l'homme*), the *Geisteswissenschaften* contemporary with it. We must note, first, that non-Orientalist cultural
studies were perforce more immediately responsive to the threats
to humanistic culture of a self-aggrandizing, amoral technical
specialization represented, in part at least, by the rise of fascism in
Europe. This response extended the concerns of the interwar
period into the period following World War II as well. An eloquent
scholarly and personal testimonial to this response can be found
in Erich Auerbach's magisterial *Mimesis*, and in his last methodological reflections as a *Philolog*.[67] He tells us that *Mimesis* was
written during his exile in Turkey and was meant to be in large
measure an attempt virtually *to see* the development of Western
culture at almost the last moment when that culture still had its
integrity and civilizational coherence; therefore, he set himself
the task of writing a general work based on specific textual analyses
in such a way as to lay out the principles of Western literary performance in all their variety, richness, and fertility. The aim was a

synthesis of Western culture in which the synthesis itself was matched in importance by the very gesture of doing it, which Auerbach believed was made possible by what he called "late bourgeois humanism."[68] The discrete particular was thus converted into a highly mediated symbol of the world-historical process.

No less important for Auerbach—and this fact is of immediate relevance to Orientalism—was the humanistic tradition of involvement in a national culture or literature not one's own. Auerbach's example was Curtius, whose prodigious output testified to his deliberate choice as a German to dedicate himself professionally to the Romance literatures. Not for nothing, then, did Auerbach end his autumnal reflections with a significant quotation from Hugo of St. Victor's *Didascalicon*: "The man who finds his homeland sweet is still a tender beginner; he to whom every soil is as his native one is already strong; but he is perfect to whom the entire world is as a foreign land."[69] The more one is able to leave one's cultural home, the more easily is one able to judge it, and the whole world as well, with the spiritual detachment *and* generosity necessary for true vision. The more easily, too, does one assess oneself and alien cultures with the same combination of intimacy and distance.

No less important and methodologically formative a cultural force was the use in the social sciences of "types" both as an analytical device and as a way of seeing familiar things in a new way. The precise history of the "type" as it is to be found in early-twentieth-century thinkers like Weber, Durkheim, Lukacs, Mannheim, and the other sociologists of knowledge has been examined often enough:[70] yet it has not been remarked, I think, that Weber's studies of Protestantism, Judaism, and Buddhism blew him (perhaps unwittingly) into the very territory originally charted and claimed by the Orientalists. There he found encouragement amongst all those nineteenth-century thinkers who believed that there was a sort of ontological difference between Eastern and Western economic (as well as religious) "mentalities." Although he never thoroughly studied Islam, Weber nevertheless influenced the field considerably, mainly because his notions of type were simply an "outside" confirmation of many of the canonical theses held by Orientalists, whose economic ideas never extended beyond asserting the Oriental's fundamental incapacity for trade, commerce, and economic rationality. In the Islamic field those clichés held good for literally hundreds of years—until Maxime Rodinson's important study *Islam and Capitalism* appeared in 1966. Still, the notion of a type—

Oriental, Islamic, Arab, or whatever—endures and is nourished by similar kinds of abstractions or paradigms or types as they emerge out of the modern social sciences.

I have often spoken in this book of the sense of estrangement experienced by Orientalists as they dealt with or lived in a culture so profoundly different from their own. Now one of the striking differences between Orientalism in its Islamic version and all the other humanistic disciplines where Auerbach's notions on the necessity of estrangement have some validity is that Islamic Orientalists never saw their estrangement from Islam either as salutary or as an attitude with implications for the better understanding of their own culture. Rather, their estrangement from Islam simply intensified their feelings of superiority about European culture, even as their antipathy spread to include the entire Orient, of which Islam was considered a degraded (and usually, a virulently dangerous) representative. Such tendencies—it has also been my argument—became built into the very traditions of Orientalist study throughout the nineteenth century, and in time became a standard component of most Orientalist training, handed on from generation to generation. In addition, I think, the likelihood was very great that European scholars would continue to see the Near Orient through the perspective of its Biblical "origins," that is, as a place of unshakably influential religious primacy. Given its special relationship to both Christianity and Judaism, Islam remained forever the Orientalist's idea (or type) of *original* cultural effrontery, aggravated naturally by the fear that Islamic civilization originally (as well as contemporaneously) continued to stand somehow opposed to the Christian West.

For these reasons, Islamic Orientalism between the wars shared in the general sense of cultural crisis adumbrated by Auerbach and the others I have spoken of briefly, without at the same time developing in the same way as the other human sciences. Because Islamic Orientalism also preserved within it the peculiarly polemical *religious* attitude it had had from the beginning, it remained fixed in certain methodological tracks, so to speak. Its cultural alienation, for one, needed to be preserved from modern history and sociopolitical circumstance, as well as from the necessary revisions imposed on any theoretical or historical "type" by new data. For another, the abstractions offered by Orientalism (or rather, the opportunity for making abstractions) in the case of Islamic civilization were considered to have acquired a new validity; since it was assumed that Islam worked the way Orientalists said it did (without reference to actuality, but only to a set of "classical" principles), it was also assumed that modern Islam would be nothing more than a reasserted version of the old, especially since it was also supposed that modernity for Islam was less of a challenge than an insult. (The very large number of assumptions and suppositions in this description, incidentally, are intended to portray the rather eccentric twists and turns necessary for Orientalism to have maintained its peculiar way of seeing human reality.) Finally, if the synthesizing ambition in philology (as conceived by Auerbach or Curtius) was to lead to an enlargement of the scholar's awareness, of his sense of the brotherhood of man, of the universality of certain principles of human behavior, in Islamic Orientalism synthesis led to a sharpened sense of difference between Orient and Occident as reflected in Islam.

What I am describing, then, is something that will characterize Islamic Orientalism until the present day: its retrogressive position when compared with the other human sciences (and even with the other branches of Orientalism), its general methodological and ideological backwardness, and its comparative insularity from developments both in the other humanities and in the real world of historical, economic, social, and political circumstances.[71] Some awareness of this lag in Islamic (or Semitic) Orientalism was already present towards the end of the nineteenth century, perhaps because it was beginning to be apparent to some observers how very little either Semitic or Islamic Orientalism had shaken itself loose from the religious background from which it originally derived. The first Orientalist congress was organized and held in Paris in 1873, and almost from the outset it was evident to other scholars that the Semiticists and Islamicists were in intellectual arrears, generally speaking. Writing a survey of all the congresses that had been held between 1873 and 1897, the English scholar R. N. Cust had this to say about the Semitic-Islamic subfield:

> Such meetings [as those held in the ancient-Semitic field], indeed, advance Oriental learning.
>   The same cannot be said with regard to the modern-Semitic section; it was crowded, but the subjects discussed were of the smallest literary interest, such as would occupy the minds of the dilettanti scholars of the old school, not the great class of "indicatores" of the nineteenth century. I am forced to go back to Pliny to find a word. There was an absence from this section both

of the modern philological and archeological spirit, and the report
reads more like that of a congress of University tutors of the last
century met to discuss the reading of a passage in a Greek play,
or the accentuation of a vowel, before the dawn of Comparative
Philology had swept away the cobwebs of the Scholiasts. Was it
worth while to discuss whether Mahomet could hold a pen or
write?[72]

To some extent the polemical antiquarianism that Cust described was a scholarly version of European anti-Semitism. Even the
designation "modern-Semitic," which was meant to include both
Muslims and Jews (and which had its origin in the so-called
ancient-Semitic field pioneered by Renan), carried its racist banner
with what was doubtless meant to be a decent ostentation. A little
later in his report Cust comments on how in the same meeting
" 'the Aryan' supplied much material for reflection." Clearly "the
Aryan" is a counterabstraction to "the Semite," but for some of the
reasons I listed earlier, such atavistic labels were felt to be especially
pertinent to Semites—with what expensive moral and human consequences for the human community as a whole, the history of the
twentieth century amply demonstrates. Yet what has not been
sufficiently stressed in histories of modern anti-Semitism has been
the legitimation of such atavistic designations by Orientalism, and
more important for my purposes here, the way this academic and
intellectual legitimation has persisted right through the modern
age in discussions of Islam, the Arabs, or the Near Orient. For
whereas it is no longer possible to write learned (or even popular)
disquisitions on either "the Negro mind" or "the Jewish personality," it is perfectly possible to engage in such research as "the
Islamic mind," or "the Arab character"—but of this subject more
later.

Thus, in order properly to understand the intellectual genealogy
of interwar Islamic Orientalism—as it is most interestingly and
satisfyingly seen (no irony intended) in the careers of Massignon
and Gibb—we must be able to understand the differences between
the Orientalist's summational attitude towards his material and the
kind of attitude to which it bears a strong cultural resemblance,
that in the work of philologists such as Auerbach and Curtius. The
intellectual crisis in Islamic Orientalism was another aspect of the
spiritual crisis of "late bourgeois humanism"; in its form and style,
however, Islamic Orientalism viewed the problems of mankind as

separable into the categories called "Oriental" or "Occidental." It was believed, then, that for the Oriental, liberation, self-expression, and self-enlargement were not the issues that they were for the Occidental. Instead, the Islamic Orientalist expressed his ideas about Islam in such a way as to emphasize his, as well as putatively the Muslim's, *resistance* to change, to mutual comprehension between East and West, to the development of men and women out of archaic, primitive classical institutions and into modernity. Indeed, so fierce was this sense of resistance to change, and so universal were the powers ascribed to it, that in reading the Orientalists one understands that the apocalypse to be feared was not the destruction of Western civilization but rather the destruction of the barriers that kept East and West from each other. When Gibb opposed nationalism in the modern Islamic states, he did so because he felt that nationalism would corrode the inner structures keeping Islam Oriental; the net result of secular nationalism would be to make the Orient no different from the West. Yet it is a tribute to Gibb's extraordinarily sympathetic powers of identification with an alien religion that he put his disapproval in such a way as to seem to be *speaking for* the Islamic orthodox community. How much such pleading was a reversion to the old Orientalist habit of speaking for the natives and how much it was a sincere attempt at speaking in Islam's best interests is a question whose answer lies somewhere between the two alternatives.

No scholar or thinker, of course, is a perfect representative of some ideal type or school in which, by virtue of national origin or the accidents of history, he participates. Yet in so relatively insulated and specialized a tradition as Orientalism, I think there is in each scholar some awareness, partly conscious and partly nonconscious, of national tradition, if not of national ideology. This is particularly true in Orientalism, additionally so because of the direct political involvement of European nations in the affairs of one or another Oriental country: the case of Snouck Hurgronje, to cite a non-British and non-French instance where the scholar's sense of national identity is simple and clear, comes to mind immediately.[73] Yet even after making all the proper qualifications about the difference between an individual and a type (or between an individual and a tradition), it is nevertheless striking to note the extent to which Gibb and Massignon *were* representative types. Perhaps it would be better to say that Gibb and Massignon fulfilled all the expectations created for them by their national traditions, by the politics of their nations, by the internal history of their national "schools" of Orientalism.

Sylvain Lévi put the distinction between the two schools trenchantly:

> The political interest that ties England to India holds British work to a sustained contact with concrete realities, and maintains the cohesion between representations of the past and the spectacle of the present.
>
> Nourished by classical traditions, France seeks out the human mind as it manifests itself in India in the same way that it is interested in China.[74]

It would be too easy to say that this polarity results, on the one hand, in work that is sober, efficient, concrete, and on the other, in work that is universalistic, speculative, brilliant. Yet the polarity serves to illuminate two long and extremely distinguished careers that between them dominated French and Anglo–American Islamic Orientalism until the 1960s; if the domination makes any sense at all, it is because each scholar derived from and worked in a self-conscious tradition whose constraints (or limits, intellectually and politically speaking) can be described as Lévi describes them above.

Gibb was born in Egypt, Massignon in France. Both were to become deeply religious men, students not so much of society as of the religious life in society. Both were also profoundly worldly; one of their greatest achievements was putting traditional scholarship to use in the modern political world. Yet the range of their work— the texture of it, almost—is vastly different, even allowing for the obvious disparities in their schooling and religious education. In his lifelong devotion to the work of al-Hallaj—"whose traces," Gibb said in his obituary notice for Massignon in 1962, he "never ceased to seek out in later Islamic literature and devotion"—Massignon's almost unrestricted range of research would lead him virtually everywhere, finding evidence for "l'esprit humaine à travers l'espace et le temps." In an *oeuvre* that took "in every aspect and region of contemporary Muslim life and thought," Massignon's presence in Orientalism was a constant challenge to his colleagues. Certainly Gibb for one admired—but finally drew back from—the way Massignon pursued themes that in some way linked the spiritual life of Muslims and Catholics [and enabled him to find] a congenial element in the veneration of Fatima, and consequently a special field of interest in the study of Shi'ite thought in many of its manifestations, or again in the community of Abrahamanic origins and such themes as the Seven Sleepers. His writings on these subjects have acquired from the qualities that he brought to them a permanent significance in Islamic studies. But just because of these qualities they are composed, as it were, in two registers. One was at the ordinary level of objective scholarship, seeking to elucidate the nature of the given phenomenon by a masterly use of established tools of academic research. The other was at a level on which objective data and understanding were absorbed and transformed by an individual intuition of spiritual dimensions. It was not always easy to draw a dividing line between the former and the transfiguration that resulted from the outpouring of the riches of his own personality.

There is a hint here that Catholics are more likely to be drawn to a study of "the veneration of Fatima" than Protestants, but there is no mistaking Gibb's suspicion of anyone who blurred the distinction between "objective" scholarship and one based on (even an elaborate) "individual intuition of spiritual dimensions." Gibb was right, however, in the next paragraph of the obituary to acknowledge Massignon's "fertility" of mind in such diverse fields as "the symbolism of Muslim art, the structure of Muslim logic, the intricacies of medieval finance, and the organization of artisan corporations"; and he was right also, immediately after, to characterize Massignon's early interest in the Semitic languages as giving rise to "elliptic studies that to the uninitiate almost rivalled the mysteries of the ancient Hermetica." Nevertheless, Gibb ends on a generous note, remarking that

> for us, the lesson which by his example he impressed upon the Orientalists of his generation was that even classical Orientalism is no longer adequate without some degree of committedness to the vital forces that have given meaning and value to the diverse aspects of Eastern cultures.[75]

That, of course, was Massignon's greatest contribution, and it is true that in contemporary French Islamology (as it is sometimes called) there has grown up a tradition of identifying with "the vital forces" informing "Eastern culture"; one need only mention the extraordinary achievements of scholars like Jacques Berque, Maxime Rodinson, Yves Lacoste, Roger Arnaldez—all of them differing widely among themselves in approach and intention—to be struck with the seminal example of Massignon, whose intellectual impress upon them all is unmistakable.

Yet in choosing to focus his comments almost anecdotally upon Massignon's various strengths and weaknesses, Gibb misses the obvious things about Massignon, things that make him so different from Gibb and yet, when taken as a whole, make him the mature symbol of so crucial a development within French Orientalism. One is Massignon's personal background, which quite beautifully illustrates the simple truth of Lévi's description of French Orientalism. The very idea of "un esprit humain" was something more or less foreign to the intellectual and religious background out of which Gibb, like so many modern British Orientalists, developed: in Massignon's case the notion of "esprit," as an aesthetic as well as religious, moral, and historical reality, was something he seemed to have been nourished upon from childhood. His family was friendly with such people as Huysmans, and in nearly everything he wrote Massignon's early education in the intellectual ambience as well as the ideas of late Symbolisme is evident, even to the particular brand of Catholicism (and Sufi mysticism) in which he was interested. There is no austerity in Massignon's work, which is formulated in one of the great French styles of the century. His ideas about human experience draw plentifully upon thinkers and artists contemporary with him, and it is the very wide cultural range of his style itself that puts him in a different category altogether from Gibb's. His early ideas come out of the period of so-called aesthetic decadence, but they are also indebted to people like Bergson, Durkheim, and Mauss. His first contact with Orientalism came through Renan, whose lectures he heard as a young man; he was also a student of Sylvain Lévi, and came to include among his friends such figures as Paul Claudel, Gabriel Bounoure, Jacques and Raïssa Maritain, and Charles de Foucauld. Later he was able to absorb work done in such relatively recent fields as urban sociology, structural linguistics, psychoanalysis, contemporary anthropology, and the New History. His essays, to say nothing of the monumental study of al-Hallaj, draw effortlessly on the entire corpus of Islamic literature; his mystifying erudition and almost familiar personality sometimes make him appear to be a scholar invented by Jorge Luis Borges. He was very sensitive to "Oriental" themes in European literature;

this was one of Gibb's interests, too, but unlike Gibb, Massignon was attracted primarily neither to European writers who "understood" the Orient nor to European texts that were independent artistic corroborations of what later Orientalist scholars would reveal (e.g., Gibb's interest in Scott as a source for the study of Saladin). Massignon's "Orient" was completely consonant with the world of the Seven Sleepers or of the Abrahamanic prayers (which are the two themes singled out by Gibb as distinctive marks of Massignon's unorthodox view of Islam): offbeat, slightly peculiar, wholly responsive to the dazzling interpretative gifts which Massignon brought to it (and which in a sense made it up as a subject). If Gibb liked Scott's Saladin, then Massignon's symmetrical predilection was for Nerval, as suicide, *poète maudit*, psychological oddity. This is not to say that Massignon was essentially a student of the past; on the contrary, he was a major presence in Islamic–French relations, in politics as well as culture. He was obviously a passionate man who believed that the world of Islam could be penetrated, not by scholarship exclusively, but by devotion to all of its activities, not the least of which was the world of Eastern Christianity subsumed within Islam, one of whose subgroups, the Badaliya Sodality, was warmly encouraged by Massignon.

Massignon's considerable literary gifts sometimes give his scholarly work an appearance of capricious, overly cosmopolitan, and often private speculation. This appearance is misleading, and in fact is rarely adequate as a description of his writing. What he wished deliberately to avoid was what he called "l'analyse analytique et statique de l'orientalisme,"[76] a sort of inert piling up, on a supposed Islamic text or problem, of sources, origins, proofs, demonstrations, and the like. Everywhere his attempt is to include as much of the context of a text or problem as possible, to animate it, to surprise his reader, almost, with the glancing insights available to anyone who, like Massignon, is willing to cross disciplinary and traditional boundaries in order to penetrate to the human heart of any text. No modern Orientalist—and certainly not Gibb, his closest peer in achievement and influence—could refer so easily (and accurately) in an essay to a host of Islamic mystics and to Jung, Heisenberg, Mallarmé, and Kierkegaard; and certainly very few Orientalists had that range together with the concrete political experience of which he was able to speak in his 1952 essay "L'Occident devant l'Orient: Primauté d'une solution culturelle."[77] And yet his intellectual world was a clearly defined one. It had a definite structure, intact from the beginning to the end of his career, and it was laced up, despite its almost unparalleled richness of scope and reference, in a set of basically unchanging ideas. Let us briefly describe the structure and list the ideas in a summary fashion.

Massignon took as his starting point the existence of the three Abrahamanic religions, of which Islam is the religion of Ishmael, the monotheism of a people excluded from the divine promise made to Isaac. Islam is therefore a religion of resistance (to God the Father, to Christ the Incarnation), which yet keeps within it the sadness that began in Hagar's tears. Arabic as a result is the very language of tears, just as the whole notion of *jihad* in Islam (which Massignon explicitly says is the epic form in Islam that Renan could not see or understand) has an important intellectual dimension whose mission is war against Christianity and Judaism as exterior enemies, and against heresy as an interior enemy. Yet within Islam, Massignon believed he was able to discern a type of countercurrent, which it became his chief intellectual mission to study, embodied in mysticism, a road towards divine grace. The principal feature of mysticism was of course its subjective character, whose nonrational and even inexplicable tendencies were towards the singular, the individual, the momentary experience of participation in the Divine. All of Massignon's extraordinary work on mysticism was thus an attempt to describe the itinerary of souls out of the limiting consensus imposed on them by the orthodox Islamic community, or Sunna. An Iranian mystic was more intrepid than an Arab one, partly because he was Aryan (the old nineteenth-century labels "Aryan" and "Semitic" have a compelling urgency for Massignon, as does also the legitimacy of Schlegel's binary opposition between the two language families[78]) and partly because he was a man seeking the Perfect; the Arab mystic, in Massignon's view, inclined towards what Waardenburg calls a testimonial monism. The exemplary figure for Massignon was al-Hallaj, who sought liberation for himself outside the orthodox community by asking for, and finally getting, the very crucifixion refused by Islam as a whole; Mohammed, according to Massignon, had deliberately rejected the opportunity offered him to bridge the gap separating him from God. Al-Hallaj's achievement was therefore to have achieved a mystical union with God against the grain of Islam.

The rest of the orthodox community lives in a condition of what Massignon calls "soif ontologique"—ontological thirst. God presents himself to man as a kind of absence, a refusal to be present, yet the devout Muslim's consciousness of his submission to God's will (Islam) gives rise to a jealous sense of God's transcendence and an intolerance of idolatry of any sort. The seat of these ideas, according to Massignon, is the "circumcised heart," which while it is in the grip of its testimonial Muslim fervor can, as is the case with mystics like al-Hallaj, also be inflamed with a divine passion or love of God. In either case, God's transcendental unity (*tawhid*) is something to be achieved and understood over and over by the devout Muslim, either through testifying to it or through mystic love of God: and this, Massignon wrote in a complex essay, defines the "intention" of Islam.[79] Clearly Massignon's sympathies lay with the mystic vocation in Islam, as much for its closeness to his own temperament as a devout Catholic as for its disrupting influence within the orthodox body of beliefs. Massignon's image of Islam is of a religion ceaselessly implicated in its refusals, its latecoming (with reference to the other Abrahamanic creeds), its comparatively barren sense of worldly reality, its massive structures of defense against "psychic commotions" of the sort practiced by al-Hallaj and other Sufi mystics, its loneliness as the only remaining "Oriental" religion of the three great monotheisms.[80]

But so obviously stern a view of Islam, with its "invariants simples"[81] (especially for so luxuriant a thought as Massignon's), entailed no deep hostility towards it on his part. In reading Massignon one is struck by his repeated insistence on the need for complex reading—injunctions whose absolute sincerity it is impossible to doubt. He wrote in 1951 that his kind of Orientalism was "ni une manie d'exotisme, ni un reniement de l'Europe, mais une mise au niveau entre nos méthodes de recherches et les traditions vécues d'antiques civilisations."[82] Put into practice in the reading of an Arabic or Islamic text, this kind of Orientalism produced interpretations of an almost overwhelming intelligence; one would be foolish not to respect the sheer genius and novelty of Massignon's mind. Yet what must catch our attention in his definition of his Orientalism are two phrases: "nos méthodes de recherches" and "les traditions vécues d'antiques civilisations." Massignon saw what he did as the synthesis of two roughly opposed quantities, yet it is the peculiar asymmetry between them that troubles one, and not merely the fact of the opposition between Europe and Orient. Massignon's implication is that the essence of the difference between East and West is between modernity and ancient tradition. And indeed in his writings on political and contemporary problems, which is where one can see most immediately the limitations of Massignon's method, the East-West opposition turns up in a most peculiar way.

At its best, Massignon's vision of the East-West encounter assigned great responsibility to the West for its invasion of the East, its colonialism, its relentless attacks on Islam. Massignon was a tireless fighter on behalf of Muslim civilization and, as his numerous essays and letters after 1948 testify, in support of Palestinian refugees, in the defense of Arab Muslim and Christian rights in Palestine against Zionism, against what, with reference to something said by Abba Eban, he scathingly called Israeli "bourgeois colonialism."[83] Yet the framework in which Massignon's vision was held also assigned the Islamic Orient to an essentially ancient time and the West to modernity. Like Robertson Smith, Massignon considered the Oriental to be not a modern man but a Semite; this reductive category had a powerful grip on his thought. When, for example, in 1960 he and Jacques Berque, his colleague at the Collège de France, published their dialogue on "the Arabs" in *Esprit*, a good deal of the time was spent in arguing whether the best way to look at the problems of the contemporary Arabs was simply to say, in the main instance, that the Arab-Israeli conflict was really a *Semitic* problem. Berque tried to demur gently, and to nudge Massignon towards the possibility that like the rest of the world the Arabs had undergone what he called an "anthropological variation": Massignon refused the notion out of hand.[84] His repeated efforts to understand and report on the Palestine conflict, for all their profound humanism, never really got past the quarrel between Isaac and Ishmael or, so far as his quarrel with Israel was concerned, the tension between Judaism and Christianity. When Arab cities and villages were captured by the Zionists, it was Massignon's religious sensibilities that were offended.

Europe, and France in particular, were seen as *contemporary* realities. Partly because of his initial political encounter with the British during the First World War, Massignon retained a pronounced dislike of England and English policy; Lawrence and his type represented a too-complex policy which he, Massignon, opposed in his dealings with Faisal. "Je cherchais avec Faysal . . . à pénétrer dans le sens même de sa tradition à lui." The British seemed to represent "expansion" in the Orient, amoral economic policy, and an outdated philosophy of political influence.[85] The Frenchman was a more modern man, who was obliged to get from the Orient what he had lost in spirituality, traditional values, and the like. Massignon's investment in this view came, I think, by way of the entire nineteenth-century tradition of the Orient as thera-peutic for the West, a tradition whose earliest adumbration is to be found in Quinet. In Massignon, it was joined to a sense of Christian compassion:

> So far as Orientals are concerned, we ought to have recourse to this science of compassion, to this "participation" even in the construction of their language and of their mental structure, in which indeed we must participate: because ultimately this science bears witness either to verities that are ours too, or else to verities that we have lost and must regain. Finally, because in a profound sense everything that exists is good in some way, and those poor colonized people do not exist only for our purposes but in and for themselves [en soi].[86]

Nevertheless the Oriental, en soi, was incapable of appreciating or understanding himself. Partly because of what Europe had done to him, he had lost his religion and his philosophie; Muslims had "un vide immense" within them; they were close to anarchy and suicide. It became France's obligation, then, to associate itself with the Muslims' desire to defend their traditional culture, the rule of their dynastic life, and the patrimony of believers.[87]

No scholar, not even a Massignon, can resist the pressures on him of his nation or of the scholarly tradition in which he works. In a great deal of what he said of the Orient and its relationship with the Occident, Massignon seemed to refine and yet to repeat the ideas of other French Orientalists. We must allow, however, that the refinements, the personal style, the individual genius, may finally supersede the political restraints operating impersonally through tradition and through the national ambience. Even so, in Massignon's case we must also recognize that in one direction his ideas about the Orient remained thoroughly traditional and Orientalist, their personality and remarkable eccentricity notwith-standing. According to him, the Islamic Orient was spiritual, Semitic, tribalistic, radically monotheistic, un-Aryan: the adjectives resemble a catalogue of late-nineteenth-century anthropological descriptions. The relatively earthbound experiences of war, colonial-ism, imperialism, economic oppression, love, death, and cultural exchange seem always in Massignon's eyes to be filtered through metaphysical, ultimately dehumanized lenses: they are Semitic,

European, Oriental, Occidental, Aryan, and so on. The categories structured his world and gave what he said a kind of deep sense— to him, at least. In the other direction, among the individual and immensely detailed ideas of the scholarly world, Massignon maneuvered himself into a special position. He reconstructed and defended Islam against Europe on the one hand and against its own orthodoxy on the other. This intervention—for it was that—into the Orient as animator and champion symbolized his own accept- ance of the Orient's difference, as well as his efforts to change it into what he wanted. Both together, the will to knowledge over the Orient and on its behalf in Massignon are very strong. His al-Hallaj represents that will perfectly. The disproportionate importance accorded al-Hallaj by Massignon signifies first, the scholar's deci- sion to promote one figure above his sustaining culture, and second, the fact that al-Hallaj had come to represent a constant challenge, even an irritant, to the Western Christian for whom belief was not (and perhaps could not be) the extreme self-sacrifice it was for the Sufi. In either case, Massignon's al-Hallaj was intended literally to embody, to incarnate, values essentially outlawed by the main doctrinal system of Islam, a system that Massignon himself de- scribed mainly in order to circumvent it with al-Hallaj.

Nevertheless we need not say immediately of Massignon's work that it was perverse, or that its greatest weakness was that it mis- represented Islam as an "average" or "common" Muslim might adhere to the faith. A distinguished Muslim scholar has argued precisely for this last position, although his argument did not name Massignon as an offender.[88] Much as one may be inclined to agree with such theses—since, as this book has tried to demonstrate, Islam *has* been fundamentally misrepresented in the West—the real issue is whether indeed there can be a true representation of anything, or whether any and all representations, because they *are* representations, are embedded first in the language and then in the culture, institutions, and political ambience of the representer. If the latter alternative is the correct one (as I believe it is), then we must be prepared to accept the fact that a representation is *eo ipso* implicated, intertwined, embedded, interwoven with a great many other things besides the "truth," which is itself a representation. What this must lead us to methodologically is to view representa- tions (or misrepresentations—the distinction is at best a matter of degree) as inhabiting a common field of play defined for them, not by some inherent common subject matter alone, but by some common history, tradition, universe of discourse. Within this field, which no single scholar can create but which each scholar receives and in which he then finds a place for himself, the individual researcher makes his contribution. Such contributions, even for the exceptional genius, are strategies of redisposing material within the field; even the scholar who unearths a once-lost manuscript produces the "found" text in a context already prepared for it, for that is the real meaning of *finding* a new text. Thus each individual contribution first causes changes within the field and then promotes a new stability, in the way that on a surface covered with twenty compasses the introduction of a twenty-first will cause all the others to quiver, then to settle into a new accommodating configuration.

The representations of Orientalism in European culture amount to what we can call a discursive consistency, one that has not only history but material (and institutional) presence to show for itself. As I said in connection with Renan, such a consistency was a form of cultural praxis, a system of opportunities for making statements about the Orient. My whole point about this system is not that it is a misrepresentation of some Oriental essence—in which I do not for a moment believe—but that it operates as representations usually do, for a purpose, according to a tendency, in a specific historical, intellectual, and even economic setting. In other words, representations have purposes, they are effective much of the time, they accomplish one or many tasks. Representations are formations, or as Roland Barthes has said of all the operations of language, they are deformations. The Orient as a representation in Europe is formed—or deformed—out of a more and more specific sensitivity towards a geographical region called "the East." Specialists in this region do their work on it, so to speak, because in time their profession as Orientalists requires that they present their society with images of the Orient, knowledge about it, insight into it. And to a very large extent the Orientalist provides his own society with representations of the Orient (*a*) that bear his distinctive imprint, (*b*) that illustrate his conception of what the Orient can or ought to be, (*c*) that consciously contest someone else's view of the Orient, (*d*) that provide Orientalist discourse with what, at that moment, it seems most in need of, and (*e*) that respond to certain cultural, professional, national, political, and economic requirements of the epoch. It will be evident that even though it will never be absent, the role of positive knowledge is far from absolute. Rather, "knowledge"—never raw, unmediated, or simply objective—is what the five attributes of Orientalist representation listed above *distribute*, and redistribute.

Seen in such a way, Massignon is less a mythologized "genius" than he is a kind of system for producing certain kinds of statements, disseminated into the large mass of discursive formations that together make up the archive, or cultural material, of his time. I do not think that we dehumanize Massignon if we recognize this, nor do we reduce him to being subject to vulgar determinism. On the contrary, we will see in a sense how a very human being had, and was able to acquire more of, a cultural and productive capacity that had an institutional, or extrahuman, dimension to it: and this surely is what the finite human being must aspire to if he is not to be content with his merely mortal presence in time and space. When Massignon said "nous sommes tous des Sémites" he was indicating the range of his ideas over his society, showing the extent to which his ideas about the Orient could transcend the local anecdotal circumstances of a Frenchman and of French society. The category of Semite drew its nourishment out of Massignon's Orientalism, but its force derived from its tendency to extend out of the confines of the discipline, out into a broader history and anthropology, where it seemed to have a certain validity and power.[89]

On one level at least, Massignon's formulations and his representations of the Orient did have a direct influence, if not an unquestioned validity: among the guild of professional Orientalists. As I said above, Gibb's recognition of Massignon's achievement constitutes an awareness that as an alternative to Gibb's own work (by implication, that is), Massignon was to be dealt with. I am of course imputing things to Gibb's obituary that are there only as traces, not as actual statements, but they are obviously important if we look now at Gibb's own career as a foil for Massignon's. Albert Hourani's memorial essay on Gibb for the British Academy (to which I have referred several times) admirably summarizes the man's career, his leading ideas, and the importance of his work: with Hourani's assessment, in its broad lines, I have no disagreement. Yet something is missing from it, although this lack is partly made up for in a lesser piece on Gibb, William Polk's "Sir Hamilton Gibb Between Orientalism and History."[90] Hourani tends to view Gibb as the product of personal encounters, personal influences, and the like; whereas Polk, who is far less subtle in his general understanding of Gibb than Hourani, sees Gibb as the culmination of a specific academic tradition, what—to use an expression that does not occur in Polk's prose—we can call an academic-research consensus or paradigm.

Borrowed in this rather gross fashion from Thomas Kuhn, the idea has a worthwhile relevance to Gibb, who as Hourani reminds us was in many ways a profoundly institutional figure. Everything that Gibb said or did, from his early career at London to the middle years at Oxford to his influential years as director of Harvard's Center for Middle Eastern Studies, bears the unmistakable stamp of a mind operating with great ease inside established institutions. Massignon was irremediably the outsider, Gibb the insider. Both men, in any case, achieved the very pinnacle of prestige and influence in French and Anglo-American Orientalism, respectively. The Orient for Gibb was not a place one encountered directly; it was something one read about, studied, wrote about within the confines of learned societies, the university, the scholarly conference. Like Massignon, Gibb boasted of friendships with Muslims, but they seemed—like Lane's—to have been useful friendships, not determining ones. Consequently Gibb is a dynastic figure within the academic framework of British (and later of American) Orientalism, a scholar whose work quite consciously demonstrated the national tendencies of an academic tradition, set inside universities, governments, and research foundations.

One index of this is that in his mature years Gibb was often to be met with speaking and writing for policy-determining organizations. In 1951, for instance, he contributed an essay to a book significantly entitled *The Near East and the Great Powers*, in which he tried to explain the need for an expansion in Anglo-American programs of Oriental studies:

> . . . the whole situation of the Western countries in regard to the countries of Asia and Africa has changed. We can no longer rely on that factor of prestige which seemed to play a large part in prewar thinking, neither can we any longer expect the peoples of Asia and Africa or of Eastern Europe to come to us and learn from us, while we sit back. We have to learn about them so that we can learn to work with them in a relationship that is closer to terms of mutuality.[91]

The terms of this new relationship were spelled out later in "Area Studies Reconsidered." Oriental studies were to be thought of not so much as scholarly activities but as instruments of national policy towards the newly independent, and possibly intractable,

nations of the postcolonial world. Armed with a refocused awareness of his importance to the Atlantic commonwealth, the Orientalist was to be the guide of policymakers, of businessmen, of a fresh
generation of scholars.

What counted most in Gibb's later vision was not the Orientalist's positive work as a scholar (for example, the kind of scholar
Gibb had been in his youth when he studied the Muslim invasions
of Central Asia) but its adaptability for use in the public world.
Hourani puts this well:

> . . . it became clear to him [Gibb] that modern governments and
> elites were acting in ignorance or rejection of their own traditions
> of social life and morality, and that their failures sprang from this.
> Henceforth his main efforts were given to the elucidation, by
> careful study of the past, of the specific nature of Muslim society
> and the beliefs and culture which lay at the heart of it. Even this
> problem he tended to see at first mainly in political terms.[92]

Yet no such later vision could have been possible without a fairly
rigorous amount of preparation in Gibb's earlier work, and it is
there that we must first seek to understand his ideas. Among Gibb's
earliest influences was Duncan Macdonald, from whose work Gibb
clearly derived the concept that Islam was a coherent system of
life, a system made coherent not so much by the people who led
that life as by virtue of some body of doctrine, method of religious
practice, idea of order, in which all the Muslim people participated.
Between the people and "Islam" there was obviously a dynamic encounter of sorts, yet what mattered to the Western student was the
supervening power of Islam to make intelligible the experiences
of the Islamic people, not the other way around.

For Macdonald and subsequently for Gibb, the epistemological
and methodological difficulties of "Islam" as an object (about
which large, extremely general statements could be made) are never
tackled. Macdonald for his part believed that in Islam one could
perceive aspects of a still more portentous abstraction, the Oriental
mentality. The entire opening chapter of his most influential book
(whose importance for Gibb cannot be minimized), *The Religious
Attitude and Life in Islam*, is an anthology of unarguable declara-
tives about the Eastern or Oriental mind. He begins by saying that
"it is plain, I think,. and admitted that the conception of the Unseen
is much more immediate and real to the Oriental than to the
western peoples." The "large modifying elements which seem, from

time to time, almost to upset the general law" do not upset it, nor do
they upset the other equally sweeping and general laws governing
the Oriental mind. "The essential difference in the Oriental mind is
not credulity as to unseen things, but inability to construct a system
as to seen things." Another aspect of this difficulty—which Gibb
was later to blame for the absence of form in Arabic literature and
for the Muslim's essentially atomistic view of reality—is "that the
difference in the Oriental is not essentially religiosity, but the lack
of the sense of law. For him, there is no immovable order of nature."
If such a "fact" seems not to account for the extraordinary achievements of Islamic science, upon which a great deal in modern Western science is based, then Macdonald remains silent. He continues
his catalogue: "It is evident that anything is possible to the Oriental.
The supernatural is so near that it may touch him at any moment."
That an *occasion*—namely, the historical and geographical birth
of monotheism in the Orient—should in Macdonald's argument
become an entire theory of difference between East and West
signifies the degree of intensity to which "Orientalism" has committed Macdonald. Here is his summary:

> *Inability*, then, to see life steadily, and see it whole, to under-
> stand that a theory of life must cover all the facts, and *liability* to
> be stampeded by a single idea and blinded to everything else—
> therein, I believe, is the difference between the East and the
> West.[93]

None of this, of course, is particularly new. From Schlegel to
Renan, from Robertson Smith to T. E. Lawrence, these ideas get
repeated and re-repeated. They represent a decision about the
Orient, not by any means a fact of nature. Anyone who, like Macdonald and Gibb, consciously entered a profession called Orientalism did so on the basis of a decision made: that the Orient was the
Orient, that it was different, and so forth. The elaborations, refinements, consequent articulations of the field therefore sustain and
prolong the decision to confine the Orient. There is no perceivable
irony in Macdonald's (or Gibb's) views about Oriental liability
to be stampeded by a single idea; neither man seems able to recognize the extent of *Orientalism*'s liability to be stampeded by the
single idea of Oriental difference. And neither man is concerned
by such wholesale designations as "Islam" or "the Orient" being
used as proper nouns, with adjectives attached and verbs streaming
forth, as if they referred to persons and not to Platonic ideas.

It is no accident, therefore, that Gibb's master theme, in almost everything he wrote about Islam and the Arabs, was the tension between "Islam" as a transcendent, compelling Oriental fact and the realities of everyday human experience. His investment as a scholar and as a devout Christian was in "Islam," not so much in the (to him) relatively trivial complications introduced into Islam by nationalism, class struggle, the individualizing experiences of love, anger, or human work. Nowhere is the impoverishing character of this investment more evident than in *Whither Islam?*, a volume edited and contributed to, in the title essay, by Gibb in 1932. (It also includes an impressive article on North African Islam by Massignon.) Gibb's task as he saw it was to assess Islam, its present situation, its possible future course. In such a task the individual and manifestly different regions of the Islamic world were to be, not refutations of Islam's unity, but examples of it. Gibb himself proposed an introductory definition of Islam; then, in the concluding essay, he sought to pronounce on its actuality and its real future. Like Macdonald, Gibb seems entirely comfortable with the idea of a monolithic East, whose existential circumstances cannot easily be reduced to race or racial theory; in resolutely denying the value of racial generalization Gibb rises above what had been most reprehensible in preceding generations of Orientalists. Gibb has a correspondingly generous and sympathetic view of Islam's universalism and tolerance in letting diverse ethnic and religious communities coexist peacefully and democratically within its imperium. There is a note of grim prophecy in Gibb's singling out the Zionists and the Maronite Christians, alone amongst ethnic communities in the Islamic world, for their inability to accept coexistence.[94]

But the heart of Gibb's argument is that Islam, perhaps because it finally represents the Oriental's exclusive concern not with nature but with the Unseen, has an ultimate precedence and domination over all life in the Islamic Orient. For Gibb Islam *is* Islamic orthodoxy, *is* also the community of believers, *is* life, unity, intelligibility, values. It *is* law and order too, the unsavory disruptions of jihadists and communist agitators notwithstanding. In page after page of Gibb's prose in *Whither Islam?*, we learn that the new commercial banks in Egypt and Syria are facts of Islam or an Islamic initiative; schools and an increasing literacy rate are Islamic facts, too, as are journalism, Westernization, and intellectual societies. At no point does Gibb speak of European colonialism when he discusses the rise of nationalism and its "toxins." That the history of modern Islam might be more intelligible for its resistance, political and nonpolitical, to colonialism, never occurs to Gibb, just as it seems to him finally irrelevant to note whether the "Islamic" governments he discusses are republican, feudal, or monarchical.

"Islam" for Gibb is a sort of superstructure imperiled both by politics (nationalism, communist agitation, Westernization) and by dangerous Muslim attempts to tamper with its intellectual sovereignty. In the passage that follows, note how the word *religion* and its cognates are made to color the tone of Gibb's prose, so much so that we feel a decorous annoyance at the mundane pressures directed at "Islam":

> Islam, as a religion, has lost little of its force, but Islam as the arbiter of social life [in the modern world] is being dethroned; alongside it, or above it, new forces exert an authority which is sometimes in contradiction to its traditions and its social prescriptions, but nevertheless forces its way in their teeth. To put the position in its simplest terms, what has happened is this. Until recently, the ordinary Muslim citizen and cultivator had no political interests or functions, and no literature of easy access except religious literature, had no festivals and no communal life except in connection with religion, saw little or nothing of the outside world except through religious glasses. *To him, in consequence, religion meant everything.* Now, however, more in all the advanced countries, his interests have expanded and his activities are no longer bounded by religion. He has political questions thrust on his notice; he reads, or has read to him, a mass of articles on subjects of all kinds which have nothing to do with religion, and in which the religious point of view may not be discussed at all and the verdict held to lie with some quite different principles. . . . [Emphasis added][95]

Admittedly, the picture is a little difficult to see, since unlike any other religion *Islam is or means everything.* As a description of a human phenomenon the hyperbole is, I think, unique to Orientalism. Life itself—politics, literature, energy, activity, growth —is an intrusion upon this (to a Westerner) unimaginable Oriental totality. Yet as "a complement and counterbalance to European civilisation" Islam in its modern form is nevertheless a useful object: this is the core of Gibb's proposition about modern Islam. For "in the broadest aspect of history, what is now happening between

Europe and Islam is the reintegration of western civilization, artificially sundered at the Renaissance and now reasserting its unity
with overwhelming force."[96]

Unlike Massignon, who made no effort to conceal his metaphysical speculations, Gibb delivered such observations as this
as if they were objective knowledge (a category he found wanting
in Massignon). Yet by almost any standards most of Gibb's general
works on Islam *are* metaphysical, not only because he uses abstractions like "Islam" as if they have a clear and distinct meaning but
also because it is simply never clear where in concrete time and
space Gibb's "Islam" is taking place. If on the one hand, following
Macdonald, he puts Islam definitively outside the West, on the
other hand, in much of his work, he is to be found "reintegrating"
it with the West. In 1955 he made this inside-outside question a
bit clearer: the West took from Islam only those nonscientific
elements that it had originally derived from the West, whereas in
borrowing much from Islamic science, the West was merely following the law making "natural science and technology . . . indefinitely
transmissible."[97] The net result is to make Islam in "art, aesthetics,
philosophy and religious thought" a second-order phenomenon
(since those came from the West), and so far as science and technology are concerned, a mere conduit for elements that are not *sui
generis* Islamic.

Any clarity about what Islam is in Gibb's thought ought to be
found *within* these metaphysical constraints, and indeed his two
important works of the forties, *Modern Trends in Islam* and
Mohammedanism: An Historical Survey, flesh out matters considerably. In both books Gibb is at great pains to discuss the present
crisis in Islam, opposing its inherent, essential being to modern
attempts at modifying it. I have already mentioned Gibb's hostility
to modernizing currents in Islam and his stubborn commitment to
Islamic orthodoxy. Now it is time to mention Gibb's preference
for the word *Mohammedanism* over *Islam* (since he says that Islam
is really based upon an idea of apostolic succession culminating
in Mohammed) and his assertion that the Islamic master science
is law, which early on replaced theology. The curious thing about
these statements is that they are assertions made about Islam, not
on the basis of evidence internal to Islam, but rather on the basis
of a logic deliberately outside Islam. No Muslim would call himself
a Mohammedan, nor so far as is known would he necessarily feel
the importance of law over theology. But what Gibb does is to

situate himself as a scholar within contradictions he himself discerns, at that point in "Islam" where "there is a certain unexpressed dislocation between the formal outward process and the inner realities."[98]

The Orientalist, then, sees his task as expressing the dislocation and consequently speaking the truth about Islam, which by definition—since its contradictions inhibit its powers of self-discernment —it cannot express. Most of Gibb's general statements about Islam supply concepts to Islam that the religion or culture, again by *his* definition, is incapable of grasping: "Oriental philosophy had never appreciated the fundamental idea of justice in Greek philosophy." As for Oriental societies, "in contrast to most western societies, [they] have generally devoted [themselves] to building stable social organizations [more than] to constructing ideal systems of philosophical thought." The principal internal weakness of Islam is the "breaking of association between the religious orders and the Muslim upper and middle classes."[99] But Gibb is also aware that Islam has never remained isolated from the rest of the world and therefore must stand in a series of external dislocations, insufficiencies, and disjunctions between itself and the world. Thus he says that modern Islam is the result of a classical religion coming into disynchronous contact with Romantic Western ideas. In reaction to this assault, Islam developed a school of modernists whose ideas everywhere reveal hopelessness, ideas unsuited to the modern world: Mahdism, nationalism, a revived caliphate. Yet the conservative reaction to modernism is no less unsuited to modernity, for it has produced a kind of stubborn Luddism. Well then, we ask, what is Islam finally, if it cannot conquer its internal dislocations nor deal satisfactorily with its external surroundings? The answer can be sought in the following central passage from *Modern Trends*:

> Islam is a living and vital religion, appealing to the hearts, minds, and consciences of tens and hundreds of millions, setting them a standard by which to live honest, sober, and god-fearing lives. It is not Islam that is petrified, but its orthodox formulations, its systematic theology, its social apologetic. It is here that the dislocation lies, that the dissatisfaction is felt among a large proportion of its most educated and intelligent adherents, and that the danger for the future is most evident. No religion can ultimately resist disintegration if there is a perpetual gulf between its demands upon the will and its appeal to the intellect of its followers.

That for the vast majority of Muslims the problem of dislocation
has not yet arisen justifies the ulema in refusing to be rushed into
the hasty measures which the modernists prescribe; but the spread
of modernism is a warning that re-formulation cannot be indefinitely shelved.

In trying to determine the origins and causes of this petrifac-
tion of the formulas of Islam, we may possibly also find a clue to
the answer to the question which the modernists are asking, but
have so far failed to resolve—the question, that is, of the way in
which the fundamental principles of Islam may be re-formulated
without affecting their essential elements.[100]

The last part of this passage is familiar enough: it suggests the
now traditional Orientalist ability to reconstruct and reformulate
the Orient, given the Orient's inability to do so for itself. In part,
then, Gibb's Islam exists *ahead* of Islam as it is practiced, studied,
or preached in the Orient. Yet this prospective Islam is no mere
Orientalist fiction, spun out of his ideas: it is based on an "Islam"
that—since it cannot truly exist—*appeals* to a whole community
of believers. The reason that "Islam" can exist in some more or
less future Orientalist formulation of it is that in the Orient Islam
is usurped and traduced by the language of its clergy, whose claim
is upon the community's mind. So long as it is silent in its appeal,
Islam is safe; the moment the reforming clergy takes on its (legitimate) role of reformulating Islam in order for it to be able to
enter modernity, the trouble starts. And that trouble, of course, is
dislocation.

Dislocation in Gibb's work identifies something far more significant than a putative intellectual difficulty within Islam. It identifies,
I think, the very privilege, the very ground on which the Orientalist
places himself so as to write about, legislate for, and reformulate
Islam. Far from being a chance discernment of Gibb's, dislocation
is the epistemological passageway into his subject, and subsequently, the observation platform from which in all his writing, and
in every one of the influential positions he filled, he could survey
Islam. Between the silent appeal of Islam to a monolithic community of orthodox believers and a whole merely verbal articulation of Islam by misled corps of political activists, desperate clerks,
and opportunistic reformers: there Gibb stood, wrote, reformulated.
His writing said either what Islam could not say or what its clerics
would not say. What Gibb wrote was in one sense temporally
ahead of Islam, in that he allowed that at some point in the future

Islam would be able to say what it could not say now. In another important sense, however, Gibb's writings on Islam predated the religion as a coherent body of "living" beliefs, since his writing was able to get hold of "Islam" as a silent appeal made to Muslims *before* their faith became a matter for worldly argument, practice, or debate.

The contradiction in Gibb's work—for it is a contradiction to speak of "Islam" as neither what its clerical adherents in fact say it is nor what, if they could, its lay followers would say about it— is muted somewhat by the metaphysical attitude governing his work, and indeed governing the whole history of modern Oriental- ism which he inherited, through mentors like Macdonald. The Orient and Islam have a kind of extrareal, phenomenologically reduced status that puts them out of reach of everyone except the Western expert. From the beginning of Western speculation about the Orient, the one thing the Orient could not do was to represent itself. Evidence of the Orient was credible only after it had passed through and been made firm by the refining fire of the Orientalist's work. Gibb's *oeuvre* purports to be Islam (or Mohammedanism) both *as it is* and *as it might be*. Metaphysically—and only meta- physically—essence and potential are made one. Only a meta- physical attitude could produce such famous Gibb essays as "The Structure of Religious Thought in Islam" or "An Interpretation of Islamic History" without being troubled by the distinction made between objective and subjective knowledge in Gibb's criticism of Massignon.[101] The statements about "Islam" are made with a confidence and a serenity that are truly Olympian. There is no dis- location, no felt discontinuity between Gibb's page and the phenomenon it describes, for each, according to Gibb himself, is ultimately reducible to the other. As such, "Islam" and Gibb's description of it have a calm, discursive plainness whose common element is the English scholar's orderly page.

I attach a great deal of significance to the appearance of and to the intended model for the Orientalist's page as a printed object. I have spoken in this book about d'Herbelot's alphabetic encyclo- pedia, the gigantic leaves of the *Description de l'Égypte,* Renan's laboratory-museum notebook, the ellipses and short episodes of Lane's *Modern Egyptians,* Sacy's anthological excerpts, and so forth. These pages are signs of some Orient, and of some Oriental- ist, *presented* to the reader. There is an order to these pages by which the reader apprehends not only the "Orient" but also the

Orientalist, as interpreter, exhibitor, personality, mediator, representative (and representing) expert. In a remarkable way Gibb and Massignon produced pages that recapitulate the history of Orientalist writing in the West as that history has been embodied in a varied generic and topographical style, reduced finally to a scholarly, monographic uniformity. The Oriental specimen; the Oriental excess; the Oriental lexicographic unit; the Oriental series; the Oriental exemplum: all these have been subordinated in Gibb and Massignon to the linear prose authority of discursive analysis, presented in essay, short article, scholarly book. In their time, from the end of World War I till the early sixties, three principal forms of Orientalist writing were radically transformed: the encyclopedia, the anthology, the personal record. Their authority was redistributed or dispersed or dissipated: to a committee of experts (*The Encyclopedia of Islam*, *The Cambridge History of Islam*), to a lower order of service (elementary instruction in language, which would prepare one not for diplomacy, as was the case with Sacy's *Chrestomathie*, but for the study of sociology, economics, or history), to the realm of sensational revelation (having more to do with personalities or governments—Lawrence is the obvious example—than with knowledge). Gibb, with his quietly heedless but profoundly sequential prose; Massignon, with the flair of an artist for whom no reference is too extravagant so long as it is governed by an eccentric interpretative gift: the two scholars took the essentially *ecumenical* authority of European Orientalism as far as it could go. After them, the new reality—the new specialized style—was, broadly speaking, Anglo–American, and more narrowly speaking, it was American Social Scientese. In it, the old Orientalism was broken into many parts; yet all of them still served the traditional Orientalist dogmas.

IV

The Latest Phase

Since World War II, and more noticeably after each of the Arab-Israeli wars, the Arab Muslim has become a figure in American popular culture, even as in the academic world, in the policy

planner's world, and in the world of business very serious attention
is being paid the Arab. This symbolizes a major change in the international configuration of forces. France and Britain no longer
occupy center stage in world politics; the American imperium has
displaced them. A vast web of interests now links all parts of the
former colonial world to the United States, just as a proliferation
of academic subspecialties divides (and yet connects) all the former
philological and European-based disciplines like Orientalism. The
area specialist, as he is now called, lays claims to regional expertise,
which is put at the service of government or business or both. The
massive, quasi-material knowledge stored in the annals of modern
European Orientalism—as recorded, for example, in Jules Mohl's
nineteenth-century logbook of the field—has been dissolved and
released into new forms. A wide variety of hybrid representations
of the Orient now roam the culture. Japan, Indochina, China, India,
Pakistan: their representations have had, and continue to have,
wide repercussions, and they have been discussed in many places
for obvious reasons. Islam and the Arabs have their own representations, too, and we shall treat them here as they occur in that
fragmentary—yet powerfully and ideologically coherent—persistence, a far less frequently discussed one, into which, in the United
States, traditional European Orientalism disbursed itself.

1. *Popular images and social science representations*. Here are
a few examples of how the Arab is often represented today. Note
how readily "the Arab" seems to accommodate the transformations and reductions—all of a simply tendentious kind—into which
he is continually being forced. The costume for Princeton's tenth-
reunion class in 1967 had been planned before the June War. The
motif—for it would be wrong to describe the costume as more than
crudely suggestive—was to have been Arab: robes, headgear,
sandals. Immediately after the war, when it had become clear that
the Arab motif was an embarrassment, a change in the reunion
plans was decreed. Wearing the costume as had been originally
planned, the class was now to walk in procession, hands above
heads in a gesture of abject defeat. This was what the Arab had
become. From a faintly outlined stereotype as a camel-riding nomad
to an accepted caricature as the embodiment of incompetence and
easy defeat: that was all the scope given the Arab.

Yet after the 1973 war the Arab appeared everywhere as something more menacing. Cartoons depicting an Arab sheik standing
behind a gasoline pump turned up consistently. These Arabs, how-

ever, were clearly "Semitic": their sharply hooked noses, the evil mustachioed leer on their faces, were obvious reminders (to a largely non-Semitic population) that "Semites" were at the bottom of all "our" troubles, which in this case was principally a gasoline shortage. The transference of a popular anti-Semitic animus from a Jewish to an Arab target was made smoothly, since the figure was essentially the same.

Thus if the Arab occupies space enough for attention, it is as a negative value. He is seen as the disrupter of Israel's and the West's existence, or in another view of the same thing, as a surmountable obstacle to Israel's creation in 1948. Insofar as this Arab has any history, it is part of the history given him (or taken from him: the difference is slight) by the Orientalist tradition, and later, the Zionist tradition. Palestine was seen—by Lamartine and the early Zionists —as an empty desert waiting to burst into bloom; such inhabitants as it had were supposed to be inconsequential nomads possessing no real claim on the land and therefore no cultural or national reality. Thus the Arab is conceived of now as a shadow that dogs the Jew. In that shadow—because Arabs and Jews are Oriental Semites—can be placed whatever traditional, latent mistrust a Westerner feels towards the Oriental. For the Jew of pre-Nazi Europe has bifurcated: what we have now is a Jewish hero, constructed out of a reconstructed cult of the adventurer-pioneer-Orientalist (Burton, Lane, Renan), and his creeping, mysteriously fearsome shadow, the Arab Oriental. Isolated from everything except the past created for him by Orientalist polemic, the Arab is chained to a destiny that fixes him and dooms him to a series of reactions periodically chastised by what Barbara Tuchman gives the theological name "Israel's terrible swift sword."

Aside from his anti-Zionism, the Arab is an oil supplier. This is another negative characteristic, since most accounts of Arab oil equate the oil boycott of 1973–1974 (which principally benefitted Western oil companies and a small ruling Arab elite) with the absence of any Arab moral qualifications for owning such vast oil reserves. Without the usual euphemisms, the question most often being asked is why such people as the Arabs are entitled to keep the developed (free, democratic, moral) world threatened. From such questions comes the frequent suggestion that the Arab oil fields be invaded by the marines.

In the films and television the Arab is associated either with lechery or bloodthirsty dishonesty. He appears as an oversexed degenerate, capable, it is true, of cleverly devious intrigues, but essentially sadistic, treacherous, low. Slave trader, camel driver, moneychanger, colorful scoundrel: these are some traditional Arab roles in the cinema. The Arab leader (of marauders, pirates, "native" insurgents) can often be seen snarling at the captured Western hero and the blond girl (both of them steeped in wholesomeness), "My men are going to kill you, but—they like to amuse themselves before." He leers suggestively as he speaks: this is a current debasement of Valentino's Sheik. In newsreels or newsphotos, the Arab is always shown in large numbers. No individuality, no personal characteristics or experiences. Most of the pictures represent mass rage and misery, or irrational (hence hopelessly eccentric) gestures. Lurking behind all of these images is the menace of *jihad*. Consequence: a fear that the Muslims (or Arabs) will take over the world.

Books and articles are regularly published on Islam and the Arabs that represent absolutely no change over the virulent anti-Islamic polemics of the Middle Ages and the Renaissance. For no other ethnic or religious group is it true that virtually anything can be written or said about it, without challenge or demurral. The 1975 course guide put out by the Columbia College undergraduates said about the Arabic course that every other word in the language had to do with violence, and that the Arab mind as "reflected" in the language was unremittingly bombastic. A recent article by Emmett Tyrrell in *Harper's* magazine was even more slanderous and racist, arguing that Arabs are basically murderers and that violence and deceit are carried in the Arab genes.[102] A survey entitled *The Arabs in American Textbooks* reveals the most astonishing misinformation, or rather the most callous representations of an ethnic-religious group. One book asserts that "few people of this [Arab] area even know that there is a better way to live," and then goes on to ask disarmingly, "What links the people of the Middle East together?" The answer, given unhesitatingly, is, "The last link is the Arab's hostility—hatred—toward the Jews and the nation of Israel." Along with such material goes this about Islam, in another book: "The Moslem religion, called Islam, began in the seventh century. It was started by a wealthy businessman of Arabia, called Mohammed. He claimed that he was a prophet. He found followers among other Arabs. He told them that they were picked to rule the world." This bit of knowledge is followed by another, equally accurate: "Shortly after Mohammed's death, his teachings

were recorded in a book called the Koran. It became the holy book
of Islam."[103]

These crude ideas are supported, not contradicted, by the academic whose business is the study of the Arab Near East. (It is
worth noting incidentally that the Princeton event I referred to
above took place in a university that prides itself on its department
of Near Eastern Studies founded in 1927, the oldest such department in the country.) Take as an instance the report produced in
1967 by Morroe Berger, a professor of sociology and Near Eastern
studies at Princeton, at the behest of the Department of Health,
Education, and Welfare; he was then president of the Middle East
Studies Association (MESA), the professional association of
scholars concerned with all aspects of the Near East, "primarily
since the rise of Islam and from the viewpoint of the social science
and humanistic disciplines,"[104] and founded in 1967. He called his
paper "Middle Eastern and North African Studies: Developments
and Needs," and had it published in the second issue of the *MESA
Bulletin*. After surveying the strategic, economic, and political importance of the region to the United States, and after endorsing the
various United States government and private foundation projects
to support programs in universities—the National Defense Education Act of 1958 (a directly Sputnik-inspired initiative), the
establishing of links between the Social Science Research Council
and Middle Eastern studies, and so on—Berger came to the following conclusions:

> The modern Middle East and North Africa is not a center of great
> cultural achievement, nor is it likely to become one in the near
> future. The study of the region or its languages, therefore, does
> not constitute its own reward so far as modern culture is
> concerned.
>
>   . . . Our region is not a center of great political power nor does
> it have the potential to become one. . . . The Middle East (less
> so North Africa) has been receding in immediate political im-
> portance to the U.S. (and even in "headline" or "nuisance"
> value) relative to Africa, Latin America and the Far East.
>
>   . . . The contemporary Middle East, thus, has only in small
> degree the kinds of traits that seem to be important in attracting
> scholarly attention. This does not diminish the validity and in-
> tellectual value of studying the area or affect the quality of work
> scholars do on it. It does, however, put limits, of which we should
> be aware, on the field's capacity for growth in the numbers who
> study and teach.[105]

As a prophecy, of course, this is fairly lamentable; what makes it even more unfortunate is that Berger was commissioned not only because he was an expert on the modern Near East but also—as is clear from the report's conclusion—because he was expected to be in a good position to predict its future, and the future of policy. His failure to see that the Middle East was of great political significance, and potentially of great political power, was no chance aberration of judgment, I think. Both of Berger's main mistakes derive from the first and last paragraphs, whose genealogy is the history of Orientalism as we have been studying it. In what Berger has to say about the absence of great cultural achievement, and in what he concludes about future study—that the Middle East does not attract scholarly attention because of its intrinsic weaknesses—we have an almost exact duplication of the canonical Orientalist opinion that the Semites never produced a great culture and that, as Renan frequently said, the Semitic world was too impoverished ever to attract universal attention. Moreover, in making such time-honored judgments and in being totally blind to what is before his eyes—after all, Berger was not writing fifty years ago, but during a period when the United States was already importing about 10 percent of its oil from the Middle East and when its strategic and economic investments in the area were unimaginably huge—Berger was ensuring the centrality of his own position as Orientalist. For what he says, in effect, is that without people such as he the Middle East would be neglected; and that without his mediating, interpretative role the place would not be understood, partly because what little there is to understand is fairly peculiar, and partly because only the Orientalist can interpret the Orient, the Orient being radically incapable of interpreting itself.

The fact that Berger was not so much a classical Orientalist when he wrote (he wasn't and isn't) as he was a professional sociologist does not minimize the extent of his indebtedness to Orientalism and its ideas. Among those ideas is the specially legitimated antipathy towards and downgrading of the material forming the main basis of his study. So strong is this in Berger that it obscures the actualities before his eyes. And more impressively still, it makes it unnecessary for him to ask himself why, if the Middle East "is not a center of great cultural achievement," he should recommend that anyone devote his life, as he has, to the study of its culture. Scholars—more than, say, doctors—study what they like and what interests them; only an exaggerated sense of cultural duty drives a scholar to the study of what he does not think well of. Yet it is just such a sense of duty Orientalism has fostered, because for generations the culture at large put the Orientalist at the barricades, where in his professional work he confronted the East—its barbarities, its eccentricities, its unruliness—and held it at bay on behalf of the West.

I mention Berger as an instance of the academic attitude towards the Islamic Orient, as an instance of how a learned perspective can support the caricatures propagated in the popular culture. Yet Berger stands also for the most current transformation overtaking Orientalism: its conversion from a fundamentally philological discipline and a vaguely general apprehension of the Orient into a social science specialty. No longer does an Orientalist try first to master the esoteric languages of the Orient; he begins instead as a trained social scientist and "applies" his science to the Orient, or anywhere else. This is the specifically American contribution to the history of Orientalism, and it can be dated roughly from the period immediately following World War II, when the United States found itself in the position recently vacated by Britain and France. The American experience of the Orient prior to that exceptional moment was limited. Cultural isolatos like Melville were interested in it; cynics like Mark Twain visited and wrote about it; the American Transcendentalists saw affinities between Indian thought and their own; a few theologians and Biblical students studied the Biblical Oriental languages; there were occasional diplomatic and military encounters with Barbary pirates and the like, the odd naval expedition to the Far Orient, and of course the ubiquitous missionary to the Orient. But there was no deeply invested tradition of Orientalism, and consequently in the United States knowledge of the Orient never passed through the refining and reticulating and reconstructing processes, whose beginning was in philological study, that it went through in Europe. Furthermore, the imaginative investment was never made either, perhaps because the American frontier, the one that counted, was the westward one. Immediately after World War II, then, the Orient became, not a broad catholic issue as it had been for centuries in Europe, but an administrative one, a matter for policy. Enter the social scientist and the new expert, on whose somewhat narrower shoulders was to fall the mantle of Orientalism. In their turn, as we shall see, they made such changes in it that it became scarcely recognizable. In any event, the new Orientalist took over the attitudes of cultural hostility and kept them.

One of the striking aspects of the new American social-science attention to the Orient is its singular avoidance of literature. You can read through reams of expert writing on the modern Near East and never encounter a single reference to literature. What seem to matter far more to the regional expert are "facts," of which a literary text is perhaps a disturber. The net effect of this remarkable omission in modern American awareness of the Arab or Islamic Orient is to keep the region and its people conceptually emasculated, reduced to "attitudes," "trends," statistics: in short, dehumanized. Since an Arab poet or novelist—and there are many—writes of his experiences, of his values, of his humanity (however strange that may be), he effectively disrupts the various patterns (images, clichés, abstractions) by which the Orient is represented. A literary text speaks more or less directly of a living reality. Its force is not that it is Arab, or French, or English; its force is in the power and vitality of words that, to mix in Flaubert's metaphor from *La Tentation de Saint Antoine*, tip the idols out of the Orientalists' arms and make them drop those great paralytic children—which are their ideas of the Orient—that attempt to pass for the Orient.

The absence of literature and the relatively weak position of philology in contemporary American studies of the Near East are illustrations of a new eccentricity in Orientalism, where indeed my use of the word itself is anomalous. For there is very little in what academic experts on the Near East do now that resembles traditional Orientalism of the sort that ended with Gibb and Massignon; the main things that are reproduced are, as I said, a certain cultural hostility and a sense based not so much on philology as on "expertise." Genealogically speaking, modern American Orientalism derives from such things as the army language schools established during and after the war, sudden government and corporate interest in the non-Western world during the postwar period, Cold War competition with the Soviet Union, and a residual missionary attitude towards Orientals who are considered ripe for reform and re-education. The nonphilological study of esoteric Oriental languages is useful for obvious rudimentary strategic reasons; but it is also useful for giving a cachet of authority, almost a mystique, to the "expert" who appears able to deal with hopelessly obscure material with firsthand skill.

In the social-science order of things, language study is a mere tool for higher aims, certainly not for reading literary texts. In 1958, for example, the Middle East Institute—a quasi-governmental body founded to oversee and sponsor research interest in the Middle East—produced a *Report on Current Research*. The contribution "Present State of Arabic Studies in the United States" (done, interestingly enough, by a professor of Hebrew) is prefaced by an epigraph announcing that "no longer is knowledge of foreign languages, for instance, the sole province of the scholars in the humanities. It is a working tool of the engineer, the economist, the social scientist, and many other specialists." The whole report stresses the importance of Arabic to oil-company executives, technicians, and military personnel. But the report's main talking point is this trio of sentences: "Russian universities are now producing fluent Arabic speakers. Russia has realized the importance of appealing to men through their minds, by using their own language. The United States need wait no longer in developing its foreign language program."[106] Thus Oriental languages are part of some policy objective—as to a certain extent they have always been—or part of a sustained propaganda effort. In both these aims the study of Oriental languages becomes the instrument carrying out Harold Lasswell's theses about propaganda, in which what counts is not what people are or think but what they can be made to be and think.

The propagandist outlook in fact combines respect for individuality with indifference to formal democracy. The respect for individuality arises from the dependence of large scale operations upon the support of the mass and upon experience with the variability of human preferences. . . . This regard for men in the mass rests upon no democratic dogmatisms about men being the best judges of their own interests. The modern propagandist, like the modern psychologist, recognizes that men are often poor judges of their own interests, flitting from one alternative to the next without solid reason or clinging timorously to the fragments of some mossy rock of ages. Calculating the prospect of securing a permanent change in habits and values involves much more than the estimation of the preferences of men in general. It means taking account of the tissue of relations in which men are webbed, searching for signs of preference which may reflect no deliberation and directing a program towards a solution which fits in fact. . . . With respect to those adjustments which do require mass action the task of the propagandist is that of inventing goal symbols which serve the double function of facilitating adoption and adaptation. The symbols must induce acceptance spontaneously. . . . It follows that the management ideal is control of a situation not by imposition but by divination. . . . The propagandist takes it for granted that the world is completely caused but that it is only partly predictable. . . .[107]

The acquired foreign language is therefore made part of a subtle assault upon populations, just as the study of a foreign region like the Orient is turned into a program for control by divination.

Yet such programs must always have a liberal veneer, and usually this is left to scholars, men of good will, enthusiasts to attend to. The idea encouraged is that in studying Orientals, Muslims, or Arabs "we" can get to know another people, their way of life and thought, and so on. To this end it is always better to let them speak for themselves, to represent themselves (even though underlying this fiction stands Marx's phrase—with which Lasswell is in agreement—for Louis Napoleon: "They cannot represent themselves; they must be represented"). But only up to a point, and in a special way. In 1973, during the anxious days of the October Arab-Israeli War, the *New York Times Magazine* commissioned two articles, one representing the Israeli and one the Arab side of the conflict. The Israeli side was presented by an Israeli lawyer; the Arab side, by an American former ambassador to an Arab country who had no formal training in Oriental studies. Lest we jump immediately to the simple conclusion that the Arabs were believed incapable of representing themselves, we would do well to remember that both Arabs and Jews in this instance were Semites (in the broad cultural designation I have been discussing) and that both *were being made to be* represented for a Western audience. It is worthwhile here to remember this passage from Proust, in which the sudden appearance of a Jew into an aristocratic salon is described as follows:

> The Rumanians, the Egyptians, the Turks may hate the Jews. But in a French drawing-room the differences between those people are not so apparent, and an Israelite making his entry as though he were emerging from the heart of the desert, his body crouching like a hyaena's, his neck thrust obliquely forward, spreading himself in proud "salaams," completely satisfies a certain taste for the oriental [*un goût pour l'orientalisme*].[108]

2. *Cultural relations policy*. While it is true to say that the United States did not in fact become a world empire until the twentieth century, it is also true that during the nineteenth century the United States was concerned with the Orient in ways that prepared for its later, overtly imperial concern. Leaving aside the

campaigns against the Barbary pirates in 1801 and 1815, let us consider the founding of the American Oriental Society in 1842. At its first annual meeting in 1843 its president, John Pickering, made the very clear point that America proposed for itself the study of the Orient in order to follow the example of the imperial European powers. Pickering's message was that the framework of Oriental studies—then as now—was political, not simply scholarly. Note in the following summary how the lines of argument for Orientalism leave little room for doubt as to their intention:

> At the first annual meeting of the American Society in 1843, President Pickering began a remarkable sketch of the field it was proposed to cultivate by calling attention to the especially favorable circumstances of the time, the peace that reigned everywhere, the freer access to Oriental countries, and the greater facilities for communication. The earth seemed quiet in the days of Metternich and Louis Philippe. The treaty of Nanking had opened Chinese ports. The screw-propellor had been adopted in ocean-going vessels; Morse had completed his telegraph and he had already suggested the laying of a trans-Atlantic cable. The objects of the Society were to cultivate learning in Asiatic, African, and Polynesian language, and in everything concerning the Orient, to create a taste for Oriental Studies in this country, to publish texts, translations and communications, and to collect a library and cabinet. Most of the work has been done in the Asiatic field, and particularly in Sanskrit and the Semitic languages.[109]

Metternich, Louis-Philippe, the Treaty of Nanking, the screw propellor: all suggest the imperial constellation facilitating Euro-American penetration of the Orient. This has never stopped. Even the legendary American missionaries to the Near East during the nineteenth and twentieth centuries took their role as set not so much by God as by *their* God, *their* culture, and *their* destiny.[110] The early missionary institutions—printing presses, schools, universities, hospitals, and the like—contributed of course to the area's well-being, but in their specifically imperial character and their support by the United States government, these institutions were no different from their French and British counterparts in the Orient. During the First World War, what was to become a major United States policy interest in Zionism and the colonization of Palestine played an estimable role in getting the United States into the war; British discussions prior to and after the Balfour Declaration (November 1917) reflect the seriousness with which the declaration was taken by the United States.[111] During and after the Second World War, the escalation in United States interest in the Middle East was remarkable. Cairo, Teheran, and North Africa were important arenas of war, and in that setting, with the exploitation of its oil, strategic, and human resources pioneered by Britain and France, the United States prepared for its new postwar imperial role.

Not the least aspect of this role was "a cultural relations policy," as it was defined by Mortimer Graves in 1950. Part of this policy was, he said, the attempt to acquire "every significant publication in every important Near Eastern language published since 1900," an attempt "which our Congress ought to recognize as a measure of our national security." For what was clearly at stake, Graves argued (to very receptive ears, by the way), was the need for "much better American understanding of the forces which are contending with the American idea for acceptance by the Near East. The principal of these are, of course, communism and Islam."[112] Out of such a concern, and as a contemporary adjunct to the more backward-looking American Oriental Society, was born the entire vast apparatus for research on the Middle East. The model, both in its frankly strategic attitude and in its sensitivity to public security and policy (not, as is often postured, to pure scholarship), was the Middle East Institute, founded May 1946 in Washington under the aegis of, if not entirely within or by, the federal government.[113] Out of such organizations grew the Middle East Studies Association, the powerful support of the Ford and other foundations, the various federal programs of support to universities, the various federal research projects, research projects carried out by such entities as the Defense Department, the RAND Corporation, and the Hudson Institute, and the consultative and lobbying efforts of banks, oil companies, multinationals, and the like. It is no reduction to say of all this that it retains, in most of its general as well as its detailed functioning, the traditional Orientalist outlook which had been developed in Europe.

The parallel between European and American imperial designs on the Orient (Near and Far) is obvious. What is perhaps less obvious is (a) the extent to which the European tradition of Orientalist scholarship was, if not taken over, then accommodated, normalized, domesticated, and popularized and fed into the postwar efflorescence of Near Eastern studies in the United States; and (b) the extent to which the European tradition has given rise in the United States to a coherent attitude among most scholars, institutions, styles of discourse, and orientations, despite the contemporary appearance of refinement, as well as the use of (again) highly sophisticated-appearing social-science techniques. I have already discussed Gibb's ideas; it needs to be pointed out, however, that in the middle 1950s he became director of the Harvard Center for Middle East Studies, from which position his ideas and style exerted an important influence. Gibb's presence in the United States was different in what it did for the field from Philip Hitti's presence at Princeton since the late 1920s. The Princeton department produced a large group of important scholars, and its brand of Oriental studies stimulated great scholarly interest in the field. Gibb, on the other hand, was more truly in touch with the public-policy aspect of Orientalism, and far more than Hitti's at Princeton his position at Harvard focused Orientalism on a Cold War area-studies approach.

Gibb's own work, nevertheless, did not overtly employ the language of cultural discourse in the tradition of Renan, Becker, and Massignon. Yet this discourse, its intellectual apparatus, and its dogmas were impressively present, principally (although not exclusively) in the work and institutional authority, at Chicago and then at UCLA, of Gustave von Grunebaum. He came to the United States as part of the intellectual immigration of European scholars fleeing fascism.[114] Thereafter he produced a solid Orientalist *oeuvre* that concentrated on Islam as a holistic culture about which, from beginning to end of his career, he continued to make the same set of essentially reductive, negative generalizations. His style, which bore often chaotic evidence of his Austro-Germanic polymathy, of his absorption of the canonical pseudoscientific prejudices of French, British, and Italian Orientalism, as well as of an almost desperate effort to remain the impartial scholar-observer, was next to unreadable. A typical page of his on the Islamic self-image will jam together half-a-dozen references to Islamic texts drawn from as many periods as possible, references as well to Husserl and the pre-Socratics, references to Lévi-Strauss and various American social scientists. All this, nevertheless, does not obscure von Grunebaum's almost virulent dislike of Islam. He has no difficulty presuming that Islam is a unitary phenomenon, unlike any other religion or civilization, and thereafter he shows it to be antihuman, incapable of development, self-knowledge, or objectivity, as well as uncreative, unscientific, and authoritarian. Here are two typical excerpts—and we must remember that von Grunebaum wrote with the unique authority of a European scholar in the United States, teaching, administering, giving grants to a large network of scholars in the field.

> It is essential to realize that Muslim civilization is a cultural entity that does not share our primary aspirations. It is not vitally interested in the structured study of other cultures, either as an end in itself or as a means towards clearer understanding of its own character and history. If this observation were to be valid merely for contemporary Islam, one might be inclined to connect it with the profoundly disturbed state of Islam, which does not permit it to look beyond itself unless forced to do so. But as it is valid for the past as well, one may perhaps seek to connect it with the basic anti-humanism of this [Islamic] civilization, that is, the determined refusal to accept man to any extent whatever as the arbiter or the measure of things, and the tendency to be satisfied with the truth as the description of mental structures, or in other words, with psychological truth.

> [Arab or Islamic nationalism] lacks, in spite of its occasional use as a catchword, the concept of the divine right of a nation, it lacks a formative ethic, it also lacks, it would seem, the later nineteenth century belief in mechanistic progress; above all it lacks the intellectual vigor of a primary phenomenon. Both power and the will to power are ends in themselves. [This sentence seems to serve no purpose in the argument; yet it doubtless gives von Grunebaum the security of a philosophical-sounding nonsentence, as if to assure himself that he speaks wisely, not disparagingly, of Islam.] The resentment of political slights [felt by Islam] engenders impatience and impedes long-range analysis and planning in the intellectual sphere.[115]

In most other contexts such writing would politely be called polemical. For Orientalism, of course, it is relatively orthodox, and it passed for canonical wisdom in American study of the Middle East after World War II, mainly because of the cultural prestige associated with European scholars. The point is, however, that von Grunebaum's work is accepted uncritically by the field, even though the field itself today cannot reproduce people like him. Yet only one scholar has undertaken a serious critique of von Grunebaum's views: Abdullah Laroui, a Moroccan historian and political theorist.

Using the motif of reductive repetition in von Grunebaum's work as a practical tool of critical anti-Orientalist study, Laroui manages his case impressively on the whole. He asks himself what it is that

caused von Grunebaum's work, despite the enormous mass of its
detail and its apparent range, to remain reductive. As Laroui says,
"the adjectives that von Grunebaum affixes to the word Islam
(medieval, classical, modern) are neutral or even superfluous: there
is no difference between classical Islam and medieval Islam or
Islam plain and simple. . . . There is therefore [for von Grunebaum]
only *one* Islam that changes within itself."[116] Modern Islam, according to von Grunebaum, has turned away from the West because it
remains faithful to its original sense of itself; and yet Islam can
modernize itself only by a self-reinterpretation from a Western
point of view—which, of course, von Grunebaum shows is impossible. In describing von Grunebaum's conclusions, which add
up to a portrait of Islam as a culture incapable of innovation,
Laroui does not mention that the need for Islam to use Western
methods to improve itself has, as an idea, perhaps because of von
Grunebaum's wide influence, become almost a truism in Middle
Eastern studies. (For example, David Gordon, in *Self-Determination and History in the Third World*,[117] urges "maturity" on Arabs,
Africans, and Asians; he argues that this can be gained only by
learning from Western objectivity.)

Laroui's analysis shows also how von Grunebaum employed
A. L. Kroeber's culturalist theory to understand Islam, and how
this tool necessarily entailed a series of reductions and eliminations
by which Islam could be represented as a closed system of exclu-
sions. Thus, each of the many diverse aspects of Islamic culture
could be seen by von Grunebaum as a direct reflection of an unvary-
ing matrix, a particular theory of God, that compels them all into
meaning and order: development, history, tradition, reality in
Islam are therefore interchangeable. Laroui rightly maintains that
history as a complex order of events, temporalities, and meanings
cannot be reduced to such a notion of culture, in the same way
that culture cannot be reduced to ideology, nor ideology to theology.
Von Grunebaum has fallen prey both to the Orientalist dogmas he
inherited and to a particular feature of Islam which he has chosen
to interpret as a shortcoming: that there is to be found in Islam a
highly articulated theory of religion and yet very few accounts of
religious experience, highly articulate political theory and few
precise political documents, a theory of social structure and very
few individualized actions, a theory of history and very few dated
events, an articulated theory of economics and very few quantified
series, and so on.[118] The net result is a historical vision of Islam

entirely hobbled by the theory of a culture incapable of doing justice to, or even examining, its existential reality in the experience of its adherents. Von Grunebaum's Islam, after all, is the Islam of the earlier European Orientalists—monolithic, scornful of ordinary human experience, gross, reductive, unchanging.

At bottom such a view of Islam is political, not even euphemistically impartial. The strength of its hold on the new Orientalist (younger, that is, than von Grunebaum) is due in part to its traditional authority, and in part to its use-value as a handle for grasping a vast region of the world and proclaiming it an entirely coherent phenomenon. Since Islam has never easily been encompassed by the West politically—and certainly since World War II Arab nationalism has been a movement openly declaring its hostility to Western imperialism—the desire to assert intellectually satisfying things about Islam in retaliation increases. One authority has said of Islam (without specifying *which* Islam or aspect of Islam he means) that it is "one prototype of closed traditional societies." Note here the edifying use of the word *Islam* to signify all at once a society, a religion, a prototype, and an actuality. But all this will be subordinated by the same scholar to the notion that, unlike normal ("our") societies, Islam and Middle Eastern societies are totally "political," an adjective meant as a reproach to Islam for not being "liberal," for not being able to separate (as "we" do) politics from culture. The result is an invidiously ideological portrait of "us" and "them":

> To understand Middle Eastern society as a whole must remain our great aim. Only a society [like "ours"] that has already achieved a dynamic stability can afford to think of politics, economics, or culture as genuinely autonomous realms of existence and not merely convenient divisions for study. In a traditional society that does nct separate the things of Caesar from those of God, or that is entirely in flux, the connection between, say, politics and all other aspects of life is the heart of the issue. Today, for example, whether a man is to marry four wives or one, fast or eat, gain or lose land, rely on revelation or reason, have all become political issues in the Middle East. . . . No less than the Moslem himself, the new Orientalist must inquire anew what the significant structures and relationships of Islamic society may be.[119]

The triviality of most of the examples (marrying four wives, fasting or eating, etc.) is meant as evidence of Islam's all-inclusiveness, and its tyranny. As to *where* this is supposed to be happening, we are not told. But we are reminded of the doubtless nonpolitical fact that Orientalists "are largely responsible for having given Middle Easterners themselves an accurate appreciation of their past,"[120] just in case we might forget that Orientalists know things by definition that Orientals cannot know on their own.

If this sums up the "hard" school of the new American Orientalism, the "soft" school emphasizes the fact that traditional Orientalists have given us the basic outlines of Islamic history, religion, and society but have been "all too often content to sum up the meaning of a civilization on the basis of a few manuscripts."[121] Against the traditional Orientalist, therefore, the new area-studies specialist argues philosophically:

> Research methodology and disciplinary paradigms are not to determine what is selected for study, and they are not to limit observation. Area studies, from this perspective, hold that true knowledge is only possible of things that exist, while methods and theories are abstractions, which order observations and offer explanations according to non-empirical criteria.[122]

Good. But *how* does one know the "things that exist," and to what extent are the "things that exist" *constituted* by the knower? This is left moot, as the new value-free apprehension of the Orient as something that exists is institutionalized in area-studies programs. Without tendentious theorizing, Islam is *rarely* studied, *rarely* researched, *rarely* known: the naiveté of this conception scarcely conceals what ideologically it means, the absurd theses that man plays no part in setting up both the material and the processes of knowledge, that the Oriental reality is static and "exists," that only a messianic revolutionary (in Dr. Kissinger's vocabulary) will not admit the difference between reality out there and in his head.

Between the hard and soft schools, however, more or less diluted versions of the old Orientalism flourish—in the new academic jargons in some cases, in the old ones in others. But the principal dogmas of Orientalism exist in their purest form today in studies of the Arabs and Islam. Let us recapitulate them here: one is the absolute and systematic difference between the West, which is rational, developed, humane, superior, and the Orient, which is aberrant, undeveloped, inferior. Another dogma is that abstractions about the Orient, particularly those based on texts representing a "classical" Oriental civilization, are always preferable to direct evidence drawn from modern Oriental realities. A third dogma is that the Orient is eternal, uniform, and incapable of defining itself; therefore it is assumed that a highly generalized and systematic vocabulary for describing the Orient from a Western standpoint is inevitable and even scientifically "objective." A fourth dogma is that the Orient is at bottom something either to be feared (the Yellow Peril, the Mongol hordes, the brown dominions) or to be controlled (by pacification, research and development, outright occupation whenever possible).

The extraordinary thing is that these notions persist without significant challenge in the academic and governmental study of the modern Near Orient. Lamentably, there has been no demonstrable effect—if there has been a challenging gesture at all—made by Islamic or Arab scholars' work disputing the dogmas of Orientalism; an isolated article here or there, while important for its time and place, cannot possibly affect the course of an imposing research consensus maintained by all sorts of agencies, institutions, and traditions. The point of this is that Islamic Orientalism has led a contemporary life quite different from that of the other Orientalist subdisciplines. The Committee of Concerned Asia Scholars (who are primarily Americans) led a revolution during the 1960s in the ranks of East Asia specialists; the African studies specialists were similarly challenged by revisionists; so too were other Third World area specialists. Only the Arabists and Islamologists still function unrevised. For them there are still such things as *an* Islamic society, *an* Arab mind, *an* Oriental psyche. Even the ones whose specialty is the modern Islamic world anachronistically use texts like the Koran to read into every facet of contemporary Egyptian or Algerian society. Islam, or a seventh-century ideal of it constituted by the Orientalist, is assumed to possess the unity that eludes the more recent and important influences of colonialism, imperialism, and even ordinary politics. Clichés about how Muslims (or Mohammedans, as they are still sometimes called) behave are bandied about with a nonchalance no one would risk in talking about blacks or Jews. At best, the Muslim is a "native informant" for the Orientalist. Secretly, however, he remains a despised heretic who for his sins must additionally endure the entirely thankless position of being known—negatively, that is—as an anti-Zionist.

There is of course a Middle East studies establishment, a pool of interests, "old boy" or "expert" networks linking corporate business, the foundations, the oil companies, the missions, the military, the foreign service, the intelligence community together

with the academic world. There are grants and other rewards, there
are organizations, there are hierarchies, there are institutes, centers,
faculties, departments, all devoted to legitimizing and maintaining
the authority of a handful of basic, basically unchanging ideas about
Islam, the Orient, and the Arabs. A recent critical analysis of the
Middle East studies operation in the United States shows, not that
the field is "monolithic," but that it is complex, that it contains old-
style Orientalists, deliberately marginal specialists, counterinsurg-
ency specialists, policymakers, as well as "a small minority . . . of
academic power brokers."[123] In any event, the core of Orientalist
dogma persists.

As an instance of what, in its highest and most intellectually
prestigious form, the field now produces, let us consider briefly the
two-volume *Cambridge History of Islam*, which was first published
in England in 1970 and is a regular summa of Orientalist orthodoxy. To say of this work by numerous luminaries that it is an
intellectual failure by any standards other than those of Orientalism
is to say that it could have been a different and better history of
Islam. In fact, as several more thoughtful scholars have noted,[124]
this kind of history was already doomed when first planned and
could not have been different or better in execution: too many
ideas were uncritically accepted by its editors; there was too much
reliance on vague concepts; little emphasis was placed on methodological issues (which were left as they have been standing in
Orientalist discourse for almost two centuries); and no effort was
put forth to make even the idea of Islam seem interesting. Moreover, not only does *The Cambridge History of Islam* radically mis-
conceive and misrepresent Islam as a religion; it also has no
corporate idea of itself as a history. Of few such enormous enterprises can it be true, as it is of this one, that ideas and methodological intelligence are almost entirely absent from it.

Erfan Shahid's chapter on pre-Islamic Arabia, which opens the
history, intelligently sketches the fruitful consonance between
topography and human economy out of which Islam appeared in
the seventh century. But what can one fairly say of a history of
Islam, defined by P. M. Holt's introduction rather airily as a "cultural synthesis,"[125] that proceeds directly from pre-Islamic Arabia
to a chapter on Mohammed, then to a chapter on the Patriarchal
and Umayyad caliphates, and entirely bypasses any account of
Islam as a system of belief, faith, or doctrine? For hundreds of
pages in volume 1, Islam is understood to mean an unrelieved

chronology of battles, reigns, and deaths, rises and heydays, comings and passings, written for the most part in a ghastly monotone.

Take the Abbasid period from the eighth to the eleventh century as an instance. Anyone who has the slightest acquaintance with Arab or Islamic history will know that it was a high point of Islamic civilization, as brilliant a period of cultural history as the High Renaissance in Italy. Yet nowhere in the forty pages of description does one get an inkling of any richness; what is found instead is sentences like this: "Once master of the caliphate, [al-Ma'mun] seemed henceforth to shrink from contact with Baghdad society and remained settled at Merv, entrusting the government of Iraq to one of his trusted men, al-Hasan b. Sahl, the brother of al-Fadl, who was faced almost at once with a serious Shi'i revolt, that of Abu'l-Saraya, who in Jumada II 199/January 815 sent out a call to arms from Kufa in support of the Hasanid Ibn Tabataba."[126] A non-Islamicist will not know at this point what a Shi'i or a Hasanid is. He will have no idea what Jumada II is, except that it clearly designates a date of some sort. And of course he will believe that the Abbasids, including Harun al-Rashid, were an incorrigibly dull and murderous lot, as they sat sulking in Merv.

The Central Islamic lands are defined as excluding North Africa and Andalusia, and *their* history is an orderly march from the past till modern times. In volume 1, therefore, Islam is a geographical designation applied chronologically and selectively as it suits the experts. But nowhere in the chapters on classical Islam is there an adequate preparation for the disappointments in store for us when we come to "recent times," as they are called. The chapter on the modern Arab lands is written without the slightest understanding of the revolutionary developments in the area. The author takes a schoolmarmish, openly reactionary attitude towards the Arabs ("it must be said that during this period the educated and uneducated youth of the Arab countries, with their enthusiasm and idealism, became a fertile soil for political exploitation and, at times, perhaps without realizing it, the tools of unscrupulous extremists and agitators"[127]), tempered by occasional praise of Lebanese nationalism (although we are never told that the appeal of fascism to a small number of Arabs during the thirties also infected the Lebanese Maronites, who in 1936 founded the Falanges libanaises as a copy of Mussolini's Black Shirts). "Unrest and agitation" are ascribed to 1936 without a mention of Zionism, and the very notions of anti-colonialism and anti-imperialism are never allowed to violate the serenity of the narrative. As for the chapters on "the political impact of the West" and "economic and social change"—ideas left no more specific than that—they are tacked on as reluctant concessions to Islam as having something to do with "our" world in general. Change is unilaterally equated with modernization, even though it is nowhere made clear why other kinds of change need be so imperiously dismissed. Since it is assumed that Islam's only worthwhile relations have been with the West, the importance of Bandung or of Africa or of the Third World generally is ignored; this blithe indifference to a good three-quarters of reality somewhat explains the amazingly cheerful statement that "the historical ground has been cleared [by whom, for what, in what way?] for a new relationship between the West and Islam . . . based on equality and cooperation."[128]

If by the end of volume 1 we are mired in a number of contradictions and difficulties about what Islam really is, there is no help to be had in volume 2. Half the book is devoted to covering the tenth to the twentieth centuries in India, Pakistan, Indonesia, Spain, North Africa, and Sicily; there is more distinction in the chapters on North Africa, although the same combination of professional Orientalist jargon with unguided historical detail prevails pretty much everywhere. So far, after approximately twelve hundred pages of dense prose, "Islam" appears to be no more a cultural synthesis than any other roll call of kings, battles, and dynasties. But in the last half of volume 2, the great synthesis completes itself with articles on "The Geographical Setting," "Sources of Islamic Civilization," "Religion and Culture," and "Warfare."

Now one's legitimate questions and objections seem more justified. Why is a chapter commissioned on Islamic warfare when what is really discussed (interestingly, by the way) is the sociology of some Islamic armies? Is one to assume that there is an Islamic mode of war different, say, from Christian warfare? Communist war versus capitalist war proposes itself as a suitably analogous topic. Of what use for the understanding of Islam—except as a display of Gustave von Grunebaum's indiscriminate erudition—are the opaque quotations from Leopold von Ranke which, along with other equally ponderous and irrelevant material, dot his pages on Islamic civilization? Is it not mendacious thus to disguise the real Grunebaumian thesis, that Islamic civilization rests on an unprincipled borrowing by Muslims from the Judeo-Christian, Hellenistic, and Austro-Germanic civilizations? Compare with this idea—

that Islam is by definition a plagiaristic culture—the one put forward in volume 1 that "so-called Arabic literature" was written by Persians (no proof offered, no names cited). When Louis Gardet treats "Religion and Culture," we are told summarily that only the first five centuries of Islam are to be discussed; does this mean that religion and culture in "modern times" cannot be "synthesized," or does it mean that Islam achieved its final form in the twelfth century? Is there really such a thing as "Islamic geography," which seems to include the "planned anarchy" of Muslim cities, or is it mainly an invented subject to demonstrate a rigid theory of geographical-racial determinism? As a hint we are reminded of "the Ramadan fast with its active nights," from which we are expected to conclude that Islam is a religion "designed for town dwellers." This is explanation in need of explanation.

The sections on economic and social institutions, on law and justice, mysticism, art and architecture, science, and the various Islamic literatures are on an altogether higher level than most of the *History*. Yet nowhere is there evidence that their authors have much in common with modern humanists or social scientists in other disciplines: the techniques of the conventional history of ideas, of Marxist analysis, of the New History, are noticeably absent. Islam, in short, seems to its historians to be best suited to a rather Platonic and antiquarian bias. To some writers of the *History* Islam is a politics and a religion; to others it is a style of being; to others it is "distinguishable from Muslim society"; to still others it is a mysteriously known essence; to *all* the authors Islam is a remote, tensionless thing, without much to teach us about the complexities of today's Muslims. Hanging over the whole disjointed enterprise which is *The Cambridge History of Islam* is the old Orientalist truism that Islam is about texts, not about people.

The fundamental question raised by such contemporary Orientalist texts as *The Cambridge History* is whether ethnic origins and religion are the best, or at least the most useful, basic, and clear, definitions of human experience. Does it matter more in understanding contemporary politics to know that X and Y are disadvantaged in certain very concrete ways, or that they are Muslims or Jews? This is of course a debatable question, and we are very likely in rational terms to insist on both the religious-ethnic and the socio-economic descriptions; Orientalism, however, clearly posits the Islamic category as the dominant one, and this is the main consideration about its retrograde intellectual tactics.

3. *Merely Islam*. So deeply entrenched is the theory of Semitic simplicity as it is to be found in modern Orientalism that it operates with little differentiation in such well-known anti-Semitic European writings as *The Protocols of the Elders of Zion* and in remarks such as these by Chaim Weizmann to Arthur Balfour on May 30, 1918:

> The Arabs, who are superficially clever and quick witted, worship one thing, and one thing only—power and success. . . . The British authorities . . . knowing as they do the treacherous nature of the Arabs . . . have to watch carefully and constantly. . . . The fairer the English regime tries to be, the more arrogant the Arab becomes. . . . The present state of affairs would necessarily tend toward the creation of an Arab Palestine, if there were an Arab people in Palestine. It will not in fact produce that result because the fellah is at least four centuries behind the times, and the effendi . . . is dishonest, uneducated, greedy, and as unpatriotic as he is inefficient.[129]

The common denominator between Weizmann and the European anti-Semite is the Orientalist perspective, seeing Semites (or subdivisions thereof) as by nature lacking the desirable qualities of Occidentals. Yet the difference between Renan and Weizmann is that the latter had already gathered behind his rhetoric the solidity of institutions whereas the former had not. Is there not in twentieth-century Orientalism that same unaging "gracious childhood" — heedlessly allied now with scholarship, now with a state and all its institutions—that Renan saw as the Semites' unchanging mode of being?

Yet with what greater harm has the twentieth-century version of the myth been maintained. It has produced a picture of the Arab as seen by an "advanced" quasi-Occidental society. In his resistance to foreign colonialists the Palestinian was either a stupid savage, or a negligible quantity, morally and even existentially. According to Israeli law only a Jew has full civic rights and unqualified immigration privileges; even though they are the land's inhabitants, Arabs are given less, more simple rights: they cannot immigrate, and if they seem not to have the same rights, it is because they are "less developed." Orientalism governs Israeli policy towards the Arabs throughout, as the recently published Koenig Report amply proves. There are good Arabs (the ones who do as they are told) and bad Arabs (who do not, and are therefore terrorists). Most of all there are all those Arabs who, once defeated, can be expected to sit obediently behind an infallibly fortified line, manned by the smallest possible number of men, on the theory that Arabs have had to accept the myth of Israeli superiority and will never dare attack. One need only glance through the pages of General Yehoshafat Harkabi's *Arab Attitudes to Israel* to see how—as Robert Alter put it in admiring language in *Commentary*[130]—the Arab mind, depraved, anti-Semitic to the core, violent, unbalanced, could produce only rhetoric and little more. One myth supports and produces another. They answer each other, tending towards symmetries and patterns of the sort that as Orientals the Arabs themselves can be expected to produce, but that as a human being no Arab can truly sustain.

Of itself, in itself, as a set of beliefs, as a method of analysis, Orientalism cannot develop. Indeed, it is the doctrinal antithesis of development. Its central argument is the myth of the arrested development of the Semites. From this matrix other myths pour forth, each of them showing the Semite to be the opposite of the Westerner and irremediably the victim of his own weaknesses. By a concatenation of events and circumstances the Semitic myth bifurcated in the Zionist movement; one Semite went the way of Orientalism, the other, the Arab, was forced to go the way of the Oriental. Each time tent and tribe are solicited, the myth is being employed; each time the concept of Arab national character is evoked, the myth is being employed. The hold these instruments have on the mind is increased by the institutions built around them. For every Orientalist, quite literally, there is a support system of staggering power, considering the ephemerality of the myths that Orientalism propagates. This system now culminates in the very institutions of the state. To write about the Arab Oriental world, therefore, is to write with the authority of a nation, and not with the affirmation of a strident ideology but with the unquestioning certainty of absolute truth backed by absolute force.

In its February 1974 issue *Commentary* gave its readers an article by Professor Gil Carl Alroy entitled "Do the Arabs Want Peace?" Alroy is a professor of political science and is the author of two works, *Attitudes Towards Jewish Statehood in the Arab World* and *Images of Middle East Conflict*; he is a man who professes to "know" the Arabs, and is obviously an expert on image making. His argument is quite predictable: that the Arabs want to destroy Israel, that the Arabs really say what they mean (and Alroy makes ostentatious use of his ability to cite evidence from Egyptian newspapers, evidence he everywhere identifies with "Arabs" as if the two, Arabs and Egyptian newspapers, were one), and so on and on, with unflagging, one-eyed zeal. Quite the center of his article, as it is the center of previous work by other "Arabists" (synonymous with "Orientalists"), like General Harkabi, whose province is the "Arab mind," is a working hypothesis on what Arabs, if one peels off all the outer nonsense, are really like. In other words, Alroy must prove that because Arabs are, first of all, as one in their bent for bloody vengeance, second, psychologically incapable of peace, and third, congenitally tied to a concept of justice that means the opposite of that, they are not to be trusted and must be fought interminably as one fights any other fatal disease. For evidence Alroy's principal exhibit is a quotation taken from Harold W. Glidden's essay "The Arab World" (to which I referred in Chapter One). Alroy finds Glidden able to have "captured the cultural differences between the Western and the Arab view" of things "very well." Alroy's argument is clinched, therefore—the Arabs are unregenerate savages—and thus an authority on the Arab mind has told a wide audience of presumably concerned Jews that they must continue to watch out. And he has done it academically, dispassionately, fairly, using evidence taken from the Arabs themselves —who, he says with Olympian assurance, have "emphatically ruled out . . . real peace"—and from psychoanalysis.[131]

One can explain such statements by recognizing that a still more implicit and powerful difference posited by the Orientalist as against the Oriental is that the former *writes* about, whereas the latter *is written* about. For the latter, passivity is the presumed role; for the former, the power to observe, study, and so forth; as Roland Barthes has said, a myth (and its perpetuators) can invent itself (themselves) ceaselessly.[132] The Oriental is given as fixed, stable, in need of investigation, in need even of knowledge about himself. No dialectic is either desired or allowed. There is a source of information (the Oriental) and a source of knowledge (the Orientalist), in short, a writer and a subject matter otherwise inert. The relationship between the two is radically a matter of power, for which there are numerous images. Here is an instance taken from Raphael Patai's *Golden River to Golden Road*:

> In order properly to evaluate what Middle Eastern culture will
> *willingly accept* from the embarrassingly rich storehouses of
> Western civilization, a better and sounder understanding of Middle
> Eastern culture *must first be acquired*. The same prerequisite is
> necessary in order *to gauge* the probable effects *of newly intro-*

duced traits on the cultural context of tradition directed peoples. Also, the ways and means *in which new cultural offerings can be made palatable* must be studied much more thoroughly than was hitherto the case. In brief, the only way in which *the Gordian knot of resistance* to Westernization in the Middle East *can be unraveled* is that of studying the Middle East, *of obtaining a fuller picture* of its traditional culture, a better understanding of *the processes of change taking place* in it at present, and *a deeper insight* into the psychology of human groups brought up in Middle Eastern culture. *The task is taxing, but the prize, harmony between the West* and a neighboring world area of crucial importance, is well worth it.[133]

The metaphorical figures propping up this passage (I have indicated them by italics) come from a variety of human activities, some commercial, some horticultural, some religious, some veterinary, some historical. Yet in each case the relation between the Middle East and the West is really defined as sexual: as I said earlier in discussing Flaubert, the association between the Orient and sex is remarkably persistent. The Middle East is resistant, as any virgin would be, but the male scholar wins the prize by bursting open, penetrating through the Gordian knot despite "the taxing task." "Harmony" is the result of the conquest of maidenly coyness; it is not by any means the coexistence of equals. The underlying power relation between scholar and subject matter is never once altered: it is uniformly favorable to the Orientalist. Study, understanding, knowledge, evaluation, masked as blandishments to "harmony," are instruments of conquest.

The verbal operations in such writing as Patai's (who has outstripped even his previous work in his recent *The Arab Mind*[134]) aim at a very particular sort of compression and reduction. Much of his paraphernalia is anthropological—he describes the Middle East as a "culture area"—but the result is to eradicate the plurality of differences among the Arabs (whoever they may be in fact) in the interest of one difference, that one setting Arabs off from everyone else. As a subject matter for study and analysis, they can be controlled more readily. Moreover, thus reduced they can be made to permit, legitimate, and valorize general nonsense of the sort one finds in works such as Sania Hamady's *Temperament and Character of the Arabs*. Item:

> The Arabs so far have demonstrated an incapacity for disciplined and abiding unity. They experience collective outbursts

of enthusiasm but do not pursue patiently collective endeavors, which are usually embraced half-heartedly. They show lack of coordination and harmony in organization and function, nor have they revealed an ability for cooperation. Any collective action for common benefit or mutual profit is alien to them.[135]

The style of this prose tells more perhaps than Hamady intends. Verbs like "demonstrate," "reveal," "show," are used without an indirect object: to whom are the Arabs revealing, demonstrating, showing? To no one in particular, obviously, but to everyone in general. This is another way of saying that these truths are self-evident only to a privileged or initiated observer, since nowhere does Hamady cite generally available evidence for her observations. Besides, given the inanity of the observations, what sort of evidence could there be? As her prose moves along, her tone increases in confidence: "Any collective action . . . is alien to them." The categories harden, the assertions are more unyielding, and the Arabs have been totally transformed from people into no more than the putative subject of Hamady's style. The Arabs exist only as an occasion for the tyrannical observer: "The world is *my* idea."

And so it is throughout the work of the contemporary Orientalist: assertions of the most bizarre sort dot his or her pages, whether it is a Manfred Halpern arguing that even though all human thought processes can be reduced to eight, the Islamic mind is capable of only four,[136] or a Morroe Berger presuming that since the Arabic language is much given to rhetoric Arabs are consequently incapable of true thought.[137] One can call these assertions myths in their function and structure, and yet one must try to understand what other imperatives govern their use. Here one is speculating, of course. Orientalist generalizations about the Arabs are very detailed when it comes to itemizing Arab characteristics critically, far less so when it comes to analyzing Arab strengths. The Arab family, Arab rhetoric, the Arab character, despite copious descriptions by the Orientalist, appear de-natured, without human potency, even as these same descriptions possess a fullness and depth in their sweeping power over the subject matter. Hamady again:

Thus, the Arab lives in a hard and frustrating environment. He has little chance to develop his potentialities and define his position in society, holds little belief in progress and change, and finds salvation only in the hereafter.[138]

What the Arab cannot achieve himself is to be found in the writing about him. The Orientalist is supremely certain of *his* potential, is not a pessimist, is able to define his position, his own and the Arab's. The picture of the Arab Oriental that emerges is determinedly negative; yet, we ask, why this endless series of works on him? What grips the Orientalist, if it is not—as it certainly is not—love of Arab science, mind, society, achievement? In other words, what is the nature of Arab presence in mythic discourse about him?

Two things: number and generative power. Both qualities are reducible to each other ultimately, but we ought to separate them for the purposes of analysis. Almost without exception, every contemporary work of Orientalist scholarship (especially in the social sciences) has a great deal to say about the family, its male-dominated structure, its all-pervasive influence in the society. Patai's work is a typical example. A silent paradox immediately presents itself, for if the family is an institution for whose general failures the only remedy is the placebo of "modernization," we must acknowledge that the family continues to produce itself, is fertile, and is the source of Arab existence in the world, such as it is. What Berger refers to as "the great value men place upon their own sexual prowess"[139] suggests the lurking power behind Arab presence in the world. If Arab society is represented in almost completely negative and generally passive terms, to be ravished and won by the Orientalist hero, we can assume that such a representation is a way of dealing with the great variety and potency of Arab diversity, whose source is, if not intellectual and social, then sexual and biological. Yet the absolutely inviolable taboo in Orientalist discourse is that that very sexuality must never be taken seriously. It can never be explicitly blamed for the absence of achievement and "real" rational sophistication the Orientalist everywhere discovers among the Arabs. And yet this is, I think, the missing link in arguments whose main object is criticism of "traditional" Arab society, such as Hamady's, Berger's, and Lerner's. They recognize the power of the family, note the weaknesses of the Arab mind, remark the "importance" of the Oriental world to the West, but never say what their discourse implies, that what is really left to the Arab after all is said and done is an undifferentiated sexual drive. On rare occasions—as in the work of Leon Mugniery—we do find the implicit made clear: that there is a "powerful sexual appetite . . . characteristic of those hot-blooded southerners."[140] Most of the time, however, the belittlement of Arab society and its reduction of platitudes inconceivable for any except the racially inferior are carried on over an undercurrent of sexual exaggeration: the Arab produces himself, endlessly, sexually, and little else. The Orientalist says nothing about this, although his argument depends on it: "But co-operation in the Near East is still largely a family affair and little of it is found outside the blood group or village."[141] Which is to say that the only way in which Arabs count is as mere biological beings; institutionally, politically, culturally they are nil, or next to nil. Numerically and as the producers of families, Arabs are actual.

The difficulty with this view is that it complicates the passivity amongst Arabs assumed by Orientalists like Patai and even Hamady and the others. But it is in the logic of myths, like dreams, exactly to welcome radical antitheses. For a myth does not analyze or solve problems. It represents them as already analyzed and solved; that is, it presents them as already assembled images, in the way a scarecrow is assembled from bric-a-brac and then made to stand for a man. Since the image *uses* all material to its own end, and since by definition the myth displaces life, the antithesis between an over-fertile Arab and a passive doll is not functional. The discourse papers over the antithesis. An Arab Oriental is that impossible creature whose libidinal energy drives him to paroxysms of over-stimulation—and yet, he is as a puppet in the eyes of the world, staring vacantly out at a modern landscape he can neither understand nor cope with.

It is in recent discussions of Oriental political behavior that such an image of the Arab seems to be relevant, and it is often occasioned by scholarly discussion of those two recent favorites of Orientalist expertise, revolution and modernization. Under the auspices of the School of Oriental and African Studies there appeared in 1972 a volume entitled *Revolution in the Middle East and Other Case Studies*, edited by P. J. Vatikiotis. The title is overtly medical, for we are expected to think of Orientalists as finally being given the benefit of what "traditional" Orientalism usually avoided: psychoclinical attention. Vatikiotis sets the tone of the collection with a quasi-medical definition of revolution, but since Arab revolution is in his mind and in his readers', the hostility of the definition seems acceptable. There is a very clever irony here about which I shall speak later. Vatikiotis's theoretical support is Camus—whose colonial mentality was no friend of revolution or of the Arabs, as Conor Cruise O'Brien has recently shown—but the phrase "revolution destroys both men and principles" is accepted from Camus as having "fundamental sense." Vatikiotis continues:

> . . . all revolutionary ideology is in direct conflict with (actually, is a head-on attack upon) man's rational, biological and psychological make-up.
>
> Committed as it is to a methodical metastasis, revolutionary ideology demands fanaticism from its adherents. Politics for the revolutionary is not only a question of belief, or a substitute for religious belief. It must stop being what it has always been, namely, an adaptive activity in time for survival. Metastatic, soteriological politics abhors adaptiveness, for how else can it eschew the difficulties, ignore and bypass the obstacles of the complex biological-psychological dimension of man, or mesmerize his subtle though limited and vulnerable rationality? It fears and shuns the concrete and discrete nature of human problems and the preoccupations of political life: it thrives on the abstract and the Promethean. It subordinates all tangible values to the one supreme value: the harnessing of man and history in a grand design of human liberation. It is not satisfied with human politics, which has so many irritating limitations. It wishes instead to create a new world, not adaptively, precariously, delicately, that is, humanly, but by a terrifying act of Olympian pseudo-divine creation. Politics in the service of man is a formula that is unacceptable to the revolutionary ideologue. Rather man exists to serve a politically contrived and brutally decreed order.[142]

Whatever else this passage says—purple writing of the most extreme sort, counterrevolutionary zealotry—it is saying nothing less than that revolution is a bad kind of sexuality (pseudo-divine act of creation), and also a cancerous disease. Whatever is done by the "human," according to Vatikiotis, is rational, right, subtle, discrete, concrete; whatever the revolutionary proclaims is brutal, irrational, mesmeric, cancerous. Procreation, change, and continuity are identified not only with sexuality and with madness but, a little paradoxically, with abstraction.

Vatikiotis's terms are weighted and colored emotionally by appeals (from the right) to humanity and decency and by appeals (against the left) safeguarding humanity from sexuality, cancer, madness, irrational violence, revolution. Since it is Arab revolution that is in question, we are to read the passage as follows: This is what revolution is, and if the Arabs want it, then that is a fairly telling comment on them, on the kind of inferior race they are. They are *only* capable of sexual incitement and not of Olympian (Western, modern) reason. The irony of which I spoke earlier now comes into play, for a few pages later we find that the Arabs are so inept that they cannot even aspire to, let alone consummate, the ambitions of revolution. By implication, Arab sexuality need not be feared for itself but for its failure. In short, Vatikiotis asks his reader to believe that revolution in the Middle East is a threat precisely because revolution cannot be attained.

> The major source of political conflict and potential revolution in many countries of the Middle East, as well as Africa and Asia today, is the inability of so-called radical nationalist regimes and movements to manage, let alone resolve, the social, economic and political problems of independence. . . . Until the states in the Middle East can control their economic activity and create or produce their own technology, their access to revolutionary experience will remain limited. The very political categories essential to a revolution will be lacking.[148]

Damned if you do, and damned if you don't. In this series of dissolving definitions revolutions emerge as figments of sexually crazed minds which on closer analysis turn out not to be capable even of the craziness Vatikiotis truly respects—which is human, not Arab, concrete, not abstract, asexual, not sexual.

The scholarly centerpiece of Vatikiotis's collection is Bernard Lewis's essay "Islamic Concepts of Revolution." The strategy here appears refined. Many readers will know that for Arabic speakers today the word *thawra* and its immediate cognates mean revolution; they will know this also from Vatikiotis's introduction. Yet Lewis does not describe the meaning of *thawra* until the very end of his article, after he has discussed concepts such as *dawla*, *fitna*, and *bughat* in their historical and mostly religious context. The point there is mainly that "the Western doctrine of the right to resist bad government is alien to Islamic thought," which leads to "defeatism" and "quietism" as political attitudes. At no point in the essay is one sure where all these terms are supposed to be taking place except somewhere in the history of words. Then near the end of the essay we have this:

> In the Arabic-speaking countries a different word was used for [revolution] *thawra*. The root *th-w-r* in classical Arabic meant to rise up (e.g. of a camel), to be stirred or excited, and hence, especially in Maghribi usage, to rebel. It is often used in the context of establishing a petty, independent sovereignty; thus, for

example, the so-called party kings who ruled in eleventh century Spain after the break-up of the Caliphate of Cordova are called *thuwwar* (sing. *tha'ir*). The noun *thawra* at first means excitement, as in the phrase, cited in the Sihah, a standard medieval Arabic dictionary, *intazir hatta taskun hadhihi 'lthawra*, wait till this excitement dies down—a very apt recommendation. The verb is used by al-Iji, in the form of *thawaran* or *itharat fitna*, stirring up sedition, as one of the dangers which should discourage a man from practising the duty of resistance to bad government. *Thawra* is the term used by Arabic writers in the nineteenth century for the French Revolution, and by their successors for the approved revolutions, domestic and foreign, of our own time.[144]

The entire passage is full of condescension and bad faith. Why introduce the idea of a camel rising as an etymological root for modern Arab revolution except as a clever way of discrediting the modern? Lewis's reason is patently to bring down revolution from its contemporary valuation to nothing more noble (or beautiful) than a camel about to raise itself from the ground. Revolution is excitement, sedition, setting up a petty sovereignty—nothing more; the best counsel (which presumably only a Western scholar and gentleman can give) is "wait till the excitement dies down." One wouldn't know from this slighting account of *thawra* that innumerable people have an active commitment to it, in ways too complex for even Lewis's sarcastic scholarship to comprehend. But it is this kind of essentialized description that is natural for students and policymakers concerned with the Middle East: that revolutionary stirrings among "the Arabs" are about as consequential as a camel's getting up, as worthy of attention as the babblings of yokels. All the canonical Orientalist literature will for the same ideological reason be unable to explain or prepare one for the confirming revolutionary upheaval in the Arab world in the twentieth century.

Lewis's association of *thawra* with a camel rising and generally with excitement (and not with a struggle on behalf of values) hints much more broadly than is usual for him that the Arab is scarcely more than a neurotic sexual being. Each of the words or phrases he uses to describe revolution is tinged with sexuality: *stirred*, *excited*, *rising up*. But for the most part it is a "bad" sexuality he ascribes to the Arab. In the end, since Arabs are really not equipped for serious action, their sexual excitement is no more noble than a camel's rising up. Instead of revolution there is sedition, setting up a petty sovereignty, and more excitement, which is as much as saying that instead of copulation the Arab can only achieve foreplay, masturbation, coitus interruptus. These, I think, are Lewis's implications, no matter how innocent his air of learning, or parlorlike his language. For since he is so sensitive to the nuances of words, he must be aware that *his* words have nuances as well.

Lewis is an interesting case to examine further because his standing in the political world of the Anglo-American Middle Eastern Establishment is that of the learned Orientalist, and everything he writes is steeped in the "authority" of the field. Yet for at least a decade and a half his work in the main has been aggressively ideological, despite his various attempts at subtlety and irony. I mention his recent writing as a perfect exemplification of the academic whose work purports to be liberal objective scholarship but is in reality very close to being propaganda *against* his subject material. But this should come as no surprise to anyone familiar with the history of Orientalism; it is only the latest—and in the West, the most uncriticized—of the scandals of "scholarship."

So intent has Lewis become upon his project to debunk, to whittle down, and to discredit the Arabs and Islam that even his energies as a scholar and historian seem to have failed him. He will, for example, publish a chapter called "The Revolt of Islam" in a book in 1964, then republish much of the same material twelve years later, slightly altered to suit the new place of publication (in this case *Commentary*) and retitled "The Return of Islam." From "Revolt" to "Return" is of course a change for the worse, a change intended by Lewis to explain to his latest public why it is that the Muslims (or Arabs) still will not settle down and accept Israeli hegemony over the Near East.

Let us look more closely at how he does this. In both of his pieces he mentions an anti-imperialist riot in Cairo in 1945, which in both cases he describes as anti-Jewish. Yet in neither instance does he tell us how it was anti-Jewish; in fact, as his material evidence for anti-Jewishness, he produces the somewhat surprising intelligence that "several churches, Catholic, Armenian and Greek Orthodox, were attacked and damaged." Consider the first version, done in 1964:

> On November 2, 1945 political leaders in Egypt called for demonstrations on the anniversary of the Balfour Declaration. These rapidly developed into anti-Jewish riots, in the course of which a Catholic, an Armenian, and a Greek Orthodox church were

attacked and damaged. What, it may be asked, had Catholics, Armenians and Greeks to do with the Balfour Declaration?[145]

And now the *Commentary* version, done in 1976:

As the nationalist movement has become genuinely popular, so it has become less national and more religious—in other words less Arab and more Islamic. In moments of crisis—and these have been many in recent decades—it is the instinctive communal loyalty which outweighs all others. A few examples may suffice. On November 2, 1945, demonstrations were held in Egypt [note here how the phrase "demonstrations were held" is an attempt to show instinctive loyalties; in the previous version "political leaders" were responsible for the deed] on the anniversary of the issue by the British Government of the Balfour Declaration. Though this was certainly not the intention of the political leaders who sponsored it, the demonstration soon developed into an anti-Jewish riot and the anti-Jewish riot into a more general outbreak in the course of which several churches, Catholic, Armenian, and Greek Orthodox [another instructive change: the impression here is that many churches, of three kinds, were attacked; the earlier version is specific about three churches], were attacked and damaged.[146]

Lewis's polemical, not scholarly, purpose is to show, here and elsewhere, that Islam is an anti-Semitic ideology, not merely a religion. He has a little logical difficulty in trying to assert that Islam is a fearful mass phenomenon and at the same time "not genuinely popular," but this problem does not detain him long. As the second version of his tendentious anecdote shows, he goes on to proclaim that Islam is an irrational herd or mass phenomenon, ruling Muslims by passions, instincts, and unreflecting hatreds. The whole point of his exposition is to frighten his audience, to make it never yield an inch to Islam. According to Lewis, Islam does not develop, and neither do Muslims; they merely are, and they are to be watched, on account of that pure essence of theirs (according to Lewis), which happens to include a long-standing hatred of Christians and Jews. Lewis everywhere restrains himself from making such inflammatory statements flat out; he always takes care to say that of course the Muslims are not anti-Semitic the way the Nazis were, but their religion can too easily accommodate itself to anti-Semitism and has done so. Similarly with regard to Islam and racism, slavery, and other more or less "Western" evils. The core of Lewis's ideology about Islam is that it never changes, and his

whole mission is now to inform conservative segments of the Jewish
reading public, and anyone else who cares to listen, that any
political, historical, and scholarly account of Muslims must begin
and end with the fact that Muslims are Muslims.

> For to admit that an entire civilization can have religion as its
> primary loyalty is too much. Even to suggest such a thing is
> regarded as offensive by liberal opinion, always ready to take
> protective umbrage on behalf of those whom it regards as its
> wards. This is reflected in the present inability, political, journal-
> istic, and scholarly alike, to recognize the importance of the
> factor of religion in the current affairs of the Muslim world and
> in the consequent recourse to the language of left-wing and right-
> wing, progressive and conservative, and the rest of the Western
> terminology, the use of which in explaining Muslim political
> phenomena is about as accurate and as enlightening as an account
> of a cricket match by a baseball correspondent. [Lewis is so fond
> of this last simile that he quotes it verbatim from his 1964
> polemic.][147]

In a later work Lewis tells us what terminology is more accurate
and useful, although the terminology seems no less "Western"
(whatever "Western" means): Muslims, like most other former
colonial peoples, are incapable of telling the truth or even of seeing
it. According to Lewis, they are addicted to mythology, along with
"the so-called revisionist school in the United States, which look
back to a golden age of American virtue and ascribe virtually all
the sins and crimes of the world to the present establishment in their
country."[148] Aside from being a mischievous and totally inaccurate
account of revisionist history, this kind of remark is designed to
put Lewis as a great historian above the petty underdevelopment
of mere Muslims and revisionists.

Yet so far as being accurate is concerned, and so far as living
up to his own rule that "the scholar, however, will not give way to
his prejudices,"[149] Lewis is cavalier with himself and with his cause.
He will, for example, recite the Arab case against Zionism (using
the "in" language of the Arab nationalist) without at the same time
mentioning—anywhere, in any of his writings—that there was such
a thing as a Zionist invasion and colonization of Palestine despite
and in conflict with the native Arab inhabitants. No Israeli would
deny this, but Lewis the Orientalist historian simply leaves it out.
He will speak of the absence of democracy in the Middle East,

except for Israel, without ever mentioning the Emergency Defense Regulations used in Israel to rule the Arabs; nor has he anything to say about "preventive detention" of Arabs in Israel, nor about the dozens of illegal settlements on the militarily occupied West Bank of Gaza, nor about the absence of human rights for Arabs, principal among them the right of immigration, in former Palestine. Instead, Lewis allows himself the scholarly liberty to say that "imperialism and Zionism [so far as the Arabs are concerned were] long familiar under their older names as the Christians and Jews."[150] He quotes T. E. Lawrence on "the Semites" to bolster his case against Islam, he never discusses Zionism in parallel with Islam (as if Zionism were a French, not a religious, movement), and he tries everywhere to demonstrate that any revolution anywhere is at best a form of "secular millenarianism."

One would find this kind of procedure less objectionable as political propaganda—which is what it is, of course—were it not accompanied by sermons on the objectivity, the fairness, the impartiality of a real historian, the implication always being that Muslims and Arabs cannot be objective but that Orientalists like Lewis writing about Muslims and Arabs are, by definition, by training, by the mere fact of their Westernness. This is the culmination of Orientalism as a dogma that not only degrades its subject matter but also blinds its practitioners. But let us listen finally to Lewis telling us how the historian ought to conduct himself. We may well ask whether it is only the Orientals who are subject to the prejudices he chastises.

> [The historian's] loyalties may well influence his choice of subject of research; they should not influence his treatment of it. If, in the course of his researches, he finds that the group with which he identifies himself is always right, and those other groups with which it is in conflict are always wrong, then he would be well advised to question his conclusions, and to reexamine the hypothesis on the basis of which he selected and interpreted his evidence; for it is not in the nature of human communities [presumably, also, the community of Orientalists] always to be right.
>
> Finally the historian must be fair and honest in the way he presents his story. That is not to say that he must confine himself to a bare recital of definitely established facts. At many stages in his work the historian must formulate hypotheses and make judgments. The important thing is that he should do so consciously

and explicitly, reviewing the evidence for and against his conclusions, examining the various possible interpretations, and stating
explicitly what his decision is, and how and why he reached it.[151]

To look for a conscious, fair, and explicit judgment by Lewis of
the Islam he has treated as he has treated it is to look in vain. He
prefers to work, as we have seen, by suggestion and insinuation. One
suspects, however, that he is unaware of doing this (except perhaps
with regard to "political" matters like pro-Zionism, anti-Arab nationalism, and strident Cold Warriorism), since he would be
certain to say that the whole history of Orientalism, of whom he is
the beneficiary, has made these insinuations and hypotheses into
indisputable truths.

Perhaps the most indisputable of these rock-bottom "truths,"
and the most peculiar (since it is hard to believe it could be maintained for any other language), is that Arabic as a language is a
dangerous ideology. The contemporary *locus classicus* for this view
of Arabic is E. Shouby's essay "The Influence of the Arabic Language on the Psychology of the Arabs."[152] The author is described
as "a psychologist with training in both Clinical and Social Psychology," and one presumes that a main reason his views have such
wide currency is that he is an Arab himself (a self-incriminating
one, at that). The argument he proposes is lamentably simple-
minded, perhaps because he has no notion of what language is and
how it operates. Nevertheless the subheadings of his essay tell a
good deal of his story; Arabic is characterized by "General vagueness of Thought," "Overemphasis on Linguistic Signs," "Over-
assertion and Exaggeration." Shouby is frequently quoted as an
authority because he speaks like one and because what he hypos-
tasizes is a sort of mute Arab who at the same time is a great
word-master playing games without much seriousness or purpose.
Muteness is an important part of what Shouby is talking about,
since in his entire paper he never once quotes from the literature
of which the Arab is so inordinately proud. Where, then, does
Arabic influence the Arab mind? Exclusively within the mythological world created for the Arab by Orientalism. The Arab is a
sign for dumbness combined with hopeless overarticulateness,
poverty combined with excess. That such a result can be attained
by philological means testifies to the sad end of a formerly complex
philological tradition, exemplified today only in very rare individuals. The reliance of today's Orientalist on "philology" is the last

infirmity of a scholarly discipline completely transformed into social-science ideological expertise.

In everything I have been discussing, the language of Orientalism plays the dominant role. It brings opposites together as "natural," it presents human types in scholarly idioms and methodologies, it ascribes reality and reference to objects (other words) of its own making. Mythic language is discourse, that is, it cannot be anything but systematic; one does not really make discourse at will, or statements in it, without first belonging—in some cases unconsciously, but at any rate involuntarily—to the ideology and the institutions that guarantee its existence. These latter are always the institutions of an advanced society dealing with a less advanced society, a strong culture encountering a weak one. The principal feature of mythic discourse is that it conceals its own origins as well as those of what it describes. "Arabs" are presented in the imagery of static, almost ideal types, and neither as creatures with a potential in the process of being realized nor as history being made. The exaggerated value heaped upon Arabic as a language permits the Orientalist to make the language equivalent to mind, society, history, and nature. For the Orientalist the language *speaks* the Arab Oriental, not vice versa.

4. *Orientals Orientals Orientals*. The system of ideological fictions I have been calling Orientalism has serious implications not only because it is intellectually discreditable. For the United States today is heavily invested in the Middle East, more heavily than anywhere else on earth: the Middle East experts who advise policymakers are imbued with Orientalism almost to a person. Most of this investment, appropriately enough, is built on foundations of sand, since the experts instruct policy on the basis of such marketable abstractions as political elites, modernization, and stability, most of which are simply the old Orientalist stereotypes dressed up in policy jargon, and most of which have been completely inadequate to describe what took place recently in Lebanon or earlier in Palestinian popular resistance to Israel. The Orientalist now tries to see the Orient as an imitation West which, according to Bernard Lewis, can only improve itself when its nationalism "is prepared to come to terms with the West."[153] If in the meantime the Arabs, the Muslims, or the Third and Fourth Worlds go unexpected ways after all, we will not be surprised to have an Orientalist tell us that this testifies to the incorrigibility of Orientals and therefore proves that they are not to be trusted.

The methodological failures of Orientalism cannot be accounted
for either by saying that the *real* Orient is different from Orientalist
portraits of it, or by saying that since Orientalists are Westerners for
the most part, they cannot be expected to have an inner sense of
what the Orient is all about. Both of these propositions are false. It
is not the thesis of this book to suggest that there is such a thing as
a real or true Orient (Islam, Arab, or whatever); nor is it to make
an assertion about the necessary privilege of an "insider" perspective over an "outsider" one, to use Robert K. Merton's useful
distinction.[154] On the contrary, I have been arguing that "the
Orient" is itself a constituted entity, and that the notion that there
are geographical spaces with indigenous, radically "different" inhabitants who can be defined on the basis of some religion, culture,
or racial essence proper to that geographical space is equally a
highly debatable idea. I certainly do not believe the limited proposition that only a black can write about blacks, a Muslim about
Muslims, and so forth.

And yet despite its failures, its lamentable jargon, its scarcely
concealed racism, its paper-thin intellectual apparatus, Orientalism
flourishes today in the forms I have tried to describe. Indeed, there
is some reason for alarm in the fact that its influence has spread to
"the Orient" itself: the pages of books and journals in Arabic (and
doubtless in Japanese, various Indian dialects, and other Oriental
languages) are filled with second-order analyses by Arabs of "the
Arab mind," "Islam," and other myths. Orientalism has also spread
in the United States now that Arab money and resources have
added considerable glamour to the traditional "concern" felt for
the strategically important Orient. The fact is that Orientalism has
been successfully accommodated to the new imperialism, where its
ruling paradigms do not contest, and even confirm, the continuing
imperial design to dominate Asia.

In the one part of the Orient that I can speak about with some
direct knowledge, the accommodation between the intellectual class
and the new imperialism might very well be accounted one of the
special triumphs of Orientalism. The Arab world today is an intellectual, political, and cultural satellite of the United States. This is
not in itself something to be lamented; the specific form of the
satellite relationship, however, is. Consider first of all that universities in the Arab world are generally run according to some
pattern inherited from, or once directly imposed by, a former
colonial power. New circumstances make the curricular actualities

almost grotesque: classes populated with hundreds of students, badly trained, overworked, and underpaid faculty, political appointments, the almost total absence of advanced research and of research facilities, and most important, the lack of a single decent library in the entire region. Whereas Britain and France once dominated intellectual horizons in the East by virtue of their prominence and wealth, it is now the United States that occupies that place, with the result that the few promising students who manage to make it through the system are encouraged to come to the United States to continue their advanced work. And while it is certainly true that some students from the Arab world continue to go to Europe to study, the sheer numerical preponderance comes to the United States; this is as true of students from so-called radical states as it is of students from conservative states like Saudi Arabia and Kuwait. Besides, the patronage system in scholarship, business, and research makes the United States a virtual hegemonic commander of affairs; the source, however much it may not be a real source, is considered to be the United States.

Two factors make the situation even more obviously a triumph of Orientalism. Insofar as one can make a sweeping generalization, the felt tendencies of contemporary culture in the Near East are guided by European and American models. When Taha Hussein said of modern Arab culture in 1936 that it was European, not Eastern, he was registering the identity of the Egyptian cultural elite, of which he was so distinguished a member. The same is true of the Arab cultural elite today, although the powerful current of anti-imperialist Third World ideas that has gripped the region since the early 1950s has tempered the Western edge of the dominant culture. In addition, the Arab and Islamic world remains a second-order power in terms of the production of culture, knowledge, and scholarship. Here one must be completely realistic about using the terminology of power politics to describe the situation that obtains. No Arab or Islamic scholar can afford to ignore what goes on in scholarly journals, institutes, and universities in the United States and Europe; the converse is not true. For example, there is no major journal of Arab studies published in the Arab world today, just as there is no Arab educational institution capable of challenging places like Oxford, Harvard, or UCLA in the study of the Arab world, much less in any non-Oriental subject matter. The predictable result of all this is that Oriental students (and Oriental professors) still want to come and sit at the feet of

American Orientalists, and later to repeat to their local audiences the clichés I have been characterizing as Orientalist dogmas. Such a system of reproduction makes it inevitable that the Oriental scholar will use his American training to feel superior to his own people because he is able to "manage" the Orientalist system; in his relations with his superiors, the European or American Orientalists, he will remain only a "native informant." And indeed this is his role in the West, should he be fortunate enough to remain there after his advanced training. Most elementary courses in Oriental languages are taught by "native informants" in United States universities today; also, power in the system (in universities, foundations, and the like) is held almost exclusively by non-Orientals, although the numerical ratio of Oriental to non-Oriental resident professionals does not favor the latter so overwhelmingly.

There are all kinds of other indications of how the cultural domination is maintained, as much by Oriental consent as by direct and crude economic pressure from the United States. It is sobering to find, for instance, that while there are dozens of organizations in the United States for studying the Arab and Islamic Orient, there are none in the Orient itself for studying the United States, by far the greatest economic and political influence in the region. Worse, there are scarcely any institutes of even modest stature in the Orient devoted to study of the Orient. But all this, I think, is small in comparison with the second factor contributing to the triumph of Orientalism: the fact of consumerism in the Orient. The Arab and Islamic world as a whole is hooked into the Western market system. No one needs to be reminded that oil, the region's greatest resource, has been totally absorbed into the United States economy. By that I mean not only that the great oil companies are controlled by the American economic system; I mean also that Arab oil revenues, to say nothing of marketing, research, and industry management, are based in the United States. This has effectively made the oil-rich Arabs into huge customers of American exports: this is as true of states in the Persian Gulf as it is of Libya, Iraq, and Algeria—radical states all. My point is that the relationship is a one-sided one, with the United States a selective customer of a very few products (oil and cheap manpower, mainly), the Arabs highly diversified consumers of a vast range of United States products, material and ideological.

This has had many consequences. There is a vast standardization of taste in the region, symbolized not only by transistors, blue jeans, and Coca-Cola but also by cultural images of the Orient supplied by American mass media and consumed unthinkingly by the mass television audience. The paradox of an Arab regarding himself as an "Arab" of the sort put out by Hollywood is but the simplest result of what I am referring to. Another result is that the Western market economy and its consumer orientation have produced (and are producing at an accelerating rate) a class of educated people whose intellectual formation is directed to satisfying market needs. There is a heavy emphasis on engineering, business, and economics, obviously enough; but the intelligentsia itself is auxiliary to what it considers to be the main trends stamped out in the West. Its role has been prescribed and set for it as a "modernizing" one, which means that it gives legitimacy and authority to ideas about modernization, progress, and culture that it receives from the United States for the most part. Impressive evidence for this is found in the social sciences and, surprisingly enough, among radical intellectuals whose Marxism is taken wholesale from Marx's own homogenizing view of the Third World, as I discussed it earlier in this book. So if all told there is an intellectual acquiescence in the images and doctrines of Orientalism, there is also a very powerful reinforcement of this in economic, political, and social exchange: the modern Orient, in short, participates in its own Orientalizing.

But in conclusion, what of some alternative to Orientalism? Is this book an argument only *against* something, and not *for* something positive? Here and there in the course of this book I have spoken about "decolonializing" new departures in the so-called area studies—the work of Anwar Abdel Malek, the studies published by members of the Hull group on Middle Eastern studies, the innovative analyses and proposals of various scholars in Europe, the United States, and the Near East[155]—but I have not attempted to do more than mention them or allude to them quickly. My project has been to describe a particular system of ideas, not by any means to displace the system with a new one. In addition, I have attempted to raise a whole set of questions that are relevant in discussing the problems of human experience: How does one *represent* other cultures? What is *another* culture? Is the notion of a distinct culture (or race, or religion, or civilization) a useful one, or does it always get involved either in self-congratulation (when one discusses one's own) or hostility and aggression (when one discusses the "other")? Do cultural, religious, and racial differences matter more than socio-economic categories, or politicohistorical ones? How do ideas acquire authority, "normality," and even the status of "natural" truth? What is the role of the intellectual? Is he there to validate the culture and state of which he is a part? What importance must he give to an independent critical consciousness, an *oppositional* critical consciousness?

I hope that some of my answers to these questions have been implicit in the foregoing, but perhaps I can speak a little more explicitly about some of them here. As I have characterized it in this study, Orientalism calls in question not only the possibility of nonpolitical scholarship but also the advisability of too close a relationship between the scholar and the state. It is equally apparent, I think, that the circumstances making Orientalism a continuingly persuasive type of thought will persist: a rather depressing matter on the whole. Nevertheless there is some rational expectation in my own mind that Orientalism need not always be so unchallenged, intellectually, ideologically, and politically, as it has been.

I would not have undertaken a book of this sort if I did not also believe that there is scholarship that is not as corrupt, or at least as blind to human reality, as the kind I have been mainly depicting. Today there are many individual scholars working in such fields as Islamic history, religion, civilization, sociology, and anthropology whose production is deeply valuable as scholarship. The trouble sets in when the guild tradition of Orientalism takes over the scholar who is not vigilant, whose individual consciousness as a scholar is not on guard against *idées reçues* all too easily handed down in the profession. Thus interesting work is most likely to be produced by scholars whose allegiance is to a discipline defined intellectually and not to a "field" like Orientalism defined either canonically, imperially, or geographically. An excellent recent instance is the anthropology of Clifford Geertz, whose interest in Islam is discrete and concrete enough to be animated by the specific societies and problems he studies and not by the rituals, preconceptions, and doctrines of Orientalism.

On the other hand, scholars and critics who are trained in the traditional Orientalist disciplines are perfectly capable of freeing themselves from the old ideological straitjacket. Jacques Berque's and Maxime Rodinson's training ranks with the most rigorous available, but what invigorates their investigations even of traditional problems is their methodological self-consciousness. For if Orientalism has historically been too smug, too insulated, too positivistically confident in its ways and its premises, then one way of opening oneself to what one studies in or about the Orient is reflexively to submit one's method to critical scrutiny. This is what characterizes Berque and Rodinson, each in his own way. What one finds in their work is always, first of all, a direct sensitivity to the material before them, and then a continual self-examination of their methodology and practice, a constant attempt to keep their work responsive to the material and not to a doctrinal preconception. Certainly Berque and Rodinson, as well as Abdel Malek and Roger Owen, are aware too that the study of man and society—whether Oriental or not—is best conducted in the broad field of all the human sciences; therefore these scholars are critical readers, and students of what goes on in other fields. Berque's attention to recent discoveries in structural anthropology, Rodinson's to sociology and political theory, Owen's to economic history: all these are instructive correctives brought from the contemporary human sciences to the study of so-called Oriental problems.

But there is no avoiding the fact that even if we disregard the Orientalist distinctions between "them" and "us," a powerful series of political and ultimately ideological realities inform scholarship today. No one can escape dealing with, if not the East/West division, then the North/South one, the have/have-not one, the imperialist/anti-imperialist one, the white/colored one. We cannot get around them all by pretending they do not exist; on the contrary, contemporary Orientalism teaches us a great deal about the intellectual dishonesty of dissembling on that score, the result of which is to intensify the divisions and make them both vicious and permanent. Yet an openly polemical and right-minded "progressive" scholarship can very easily degenerate into dogmatic slumber, a prospect that is not edifying either.

My own sense of the problem is fairly shown by the kinds of questions I formulated above. Modern thought and experience have taught us to be sensitive to what is involved in representation, in studying the Other, in racial thinking, in unthinking and uncritical acceptance of authority and authoritative ideas, in the sociopolitical role of intellectuals, in the great value of a skeptical critical consciousness. Perhaps if we remember that the study of human experience usually has an ethical, to say nothing of a political, consequence in either the best or worst sense, we will not be indifferent to what we do as scholars. And what better norm for the scholar than human freedom and knowledge? Perhaps too we should remember that the study of man in society is based on concrete human history and experience, not on donnish abstractions, or on obscure laws or arbitrary systems. The problem then is to make the study fit and in some way be shaped by the experience, which would be illuminated and perhaps changed by the study. At all costs, the goal of Orientalizing the Orient again and again is to be avoided, with consequences that cannot help but refine knowledge and reduce the scholar's conceit. Without "the Orient" there would be scholars, critics, intellectuals, human beings, for whom the racial, ethnic, and national distinctions were less important than the common enterprise of promoting human community.

Positively, I do believe—and in my other work have tried to show —that enough is being done today in the human sciences to provide the contemporary scholar with insights, methods, and ideas that could dispense with racial, ideological, and imperialist stereotypes of the sort provided during its historical ascendancy by Orientalism. I consider Orientalism's failure to have been a human as much as an intellectual one; for in having to take up a position of irreducible opposition to a region of the world it considered alien to its own, Orientalism failed to identify with human experience, failed also to see it as human experience. The worldwide hegemony of Orientalism and all it stands for can now be challenged, if we can benefit properly from the general twentieth-century rise to political and historical awareness of so many of the earth's peoples. If this book has any future use, it will be as a modest contribution to that challenge, and as a warning: that systems of thought like Orientalism, discourses of power, ideological fictions—mind-forg'd manacles—are all too easily made, applied, and guarded. Above all, I hope to have shown my reader that the answer to Orientalism is not Occidentalism. No former "Oriental" will be comforted by the thought that having been an Oriental himself he is likely—too likely—to study new "Orientals"—or "Occidentals"—of his own making. If the knowledge of Orientalism has any meaning, it is in being a reminder of the seductive degradation of knowledge, of any knowledge, anywhere, at any time. Now perhaps more than before.

Afterword (1995)

I

Orientalism was completed in the last part of 1977, and was published a year later. It was (and still is) the only book that I wrote as one continuous gesture, from research, through several drafts, to final version, each following the other without interruption or serious distraction. With the exception of a wonderfully civilized and relatively burdenless year spent as a Fellow at the Stanford Center for Advanced Study in the Behavioral Sciences (1975–6), I had very little in the way of support or interest from the outside world. I received encouragement from one or two friends and my immediate family, but it was far from clear whether such a study of the ways in which the power, scholarship and imagination of a two-hundred-year-old tradition in Europe and America viewed the Middle East, the Arabs and Islam *might* interest a general audience. I recall, for instance, that it was very difficult at first to interest a serious publisher in the project. One academic press in particular very tentatively suggested a modest contract for a small monograph, so unpromising and slender did the whole enterprise seem at the outset. But luckily (as I describe my good fortune with my first publisher in *Orientalism*'s original page of Acknowledgments) things changed for the better very quickly after I finished writing the book.

In both America and England (where a separate UK edition appeared in 1979) the book attracted a great deal of attention, some of it (as was to be expected) very hostile, some of it uncomprehending, but most of it positive and enthusiastic. Beginning in 1980 with the French edition, a whole series of translations started to appear, increasing in number to this day, many of which have generated controversies and discussions in languages that I am incompetent to understand. There was a remarkable and still controversial Arabic translation by the gifted Syrian poet and critic Kamal Abu Deeb; I shall say more about that in a moment. Thereafter *Orientalism* has appeared in Japanese, German, Portuguese, Italian, Polish, Spanish, Catalan, Turkish, Serbo-Croat, and Swedish (in 1993 it became a bestseller in Sweden, which mystified the local publisher as much as it did me). There are several editions (Greek, Russian, Norwegian, and Chinese) either under way or about to appear. Other European translations are rumored, as is an Israeli version, according to one or two reports. There have been partial translations pirated in Iran and Pakistan. Many of the translations that I have known about directly (in particular, the Japanese) have gone through more than one edition; all are still in print and appear on occasion to give rise to local discussions that go very far beyond anything I was thinking about when I wrote the book.

The result of all this is that *Orientalism*, in almost a Borgesian way, has become several different books. And in so far as I have been able to follow and understand these subsequent versions, that strange, often disquieting and certainly unthought-of polymorphousness is what I should like to discuss here, reading back into the book that I wrote what others have said, in addition to what I myself wrote after *Orientalism* (eight or nine books plus many articles). Obviously I shall try to correct misreadings and, in a few instances, wilful misinterpretations.

Yet I shall also be rehearsing arguments and intellectual developments that acknowledge *Orientalism* to be a helpful book in ways that I foresaw only very partially at the time. The point of all this is neither to settle scores nor to heap congratulations on myself, but to chart and record a much-expanded sense of authorship that goes well beyond the egoism of the solitary beings we feel ourselves to be as we undertake a piece of work. For in all sorts of ways *Orientalism* now seems to me a collective book that I think supersedes me as its author more than I could have expected when I wrote it.

Let me begin with the one aspect of the book's reception that I most regret and find myself trying hardest now (in 1994) to overcome. That is the book's alleged anti-Westernism, as it has been misleadingly and rather too sonorously called by commentators both hostile and sympathetic. This notion has two parts to it, sometimes argued together, sometimes separately. The first is the claim imputed to me that the phenomenon of Orientalism is a synecdoche, or miniature symbol, of the entire West, and indeed ought to be taken to represent the West as a whole. Since this is so, the argument continues, therefore the entire West is an enemy of the Arab and Islamic or for that matter the Iranian, Chinese, Indian and many other non-European peoples who suffered Western colonialism and prejudice. The second part of the argument ascribed to me is no less far reaching. It is that a predatory West and Orientalism have violated Islam and the Arabs. (Note that the terms "Orientalism" and "West" have been collapsed into each other.) Since that is so, the very existence of Orientalism and Orientalists is seized upon as a pretext for arguing the exact opposite, namely, that Islam is perfect, that it is the only way (*al-hal al-wahid*), and so on and so on. To criticize Orientalism, as I did in my book, is in effect to be a supporter of Islamism or Muslim fundamentalism.

One scarcely knows what to make of these caricatural permutations of a book that to its author and in its arguments is explicitly anti-essentialist, radically skeptical about all categorical designations such as Orient and Occident, and painstakingly careful about *not* "defending" or even discussing the Orient and Islam. Yet *Orientalism* has in fact been read and written about in the Arab world as a systematic defense of Islam and the Arabs, even though I say explicitly that I have no interest in, much less capacity for, showing what the true Orient or Islam really are. Actually I go a great deal further when, very early in the book, I say that words such as "Orient" and "Occident" correspond to no stable reality that exists as a natural fact. Moreover, all such geographical designations are an odd combination of the empirical and imaginative. In the case of the Orient as a notion in currency in Britain, France and America, the idea derives to a great extent from the impulse not simply to describe, but also to dominate and somehow defend against it. As I try to show, this is powerfully true with reference to Islam as a particularly dangerous embodiment of the Orient.

The central point in all this is, however, as Vico taught us, that human history is made by human beings. Since the struggle for control over territory is part of that history, so too is the struggle over historical and social meaning. The task for the critical scholar is not to separate one struggle from another, but to connect them, despite the contrast between the overpowering materiality of the former and the apparent other-worldly refinements of the latter. My way of doing this has been to show that the development and maintenance of every culture require the existence of another different and competing *alter ego*. The construction of identity – for identity, whether of Orient or Occident, France or Britain, while obviously a repository of distinct collective experiences, *is* finally a construction – involves establishing opposites and "others" whose actuality is always subject to the continuous interpretation and re-interpretation of their differences from "us". Each age and society re-creates its "Others". Far from a static thing then, identity of self or of "other" is a much worked-over historical, social, intellectual, and political process that takes place as a contest involving individuals and institutions in all societies. Debates today about "Frenchness" and "Englishness" in France and Britain respectively, or about Islam in countries such as Egypt and Pakistan, are part of that same interpretive process which involves the identities of different "others," whether they be outsiders and refugees, or apostates and infidels. It should be obvious in all cases that these processes are not mental exercises but urgent social contests involving such concrete political issues as immigration laws, the legislation of personal conduct, the constitution of orthodoxy, the legitimization of violence and/or insurrection, the character and content of education, and the direction of foreign policy, which very often has to do with the designation of official enemies. In short, the construction of identity is bound up with the disposition of power and powerlessness in each society, and is therefore anything but mere academic wool-gathering.

What makes all these fluid and extraordinarily rich actualities difficult to accept is that most people resist the underlying notion: that human identity is not only not natural and stable, but constructed, and occasionally even invented outright. Part of the resistance and hostility to books like *Orientalism*, or after it *The Invention of Tradition*, and *Black Athena*,[1] stems from the fact that they seem to undermine the naïve belief in the certain positivity and unchanging historicity of a culture, a self, a national identity. *Orientalism* can only be read as a defense of Islam by suppressing half of my argument, in which I say (as I do in a subsequent book, *Covering Islam*) that even the primitive community we belong to natally is not immune from the interpretive contest, and that what appears in the West to be the emergence, return to, or resurgence of Islam is in fact a struggle in Islamic societies over the definition of Islam. No one person, authority, or institution has total control over that definition; hence, of course, the contest. Fundamentalism's epistemological mistake is to think that "fundamentals" are ahistorical categories, not subject to and therefore outside the critical scrutiny of true believers, who are supposed to accept them on faith. To the adherents of a restored or revived version of early Islam, Orientalists are considered (like Salman Rushdie) to be dangerous because they tamper with that version, cast doubt on it, show it to be fraudulent and non-divine. To them, therefore, the virtues of my book were that it pointed out the malicious dangers of the Orientalists and somehow prised Islam from their clutches.

Now this is hardly what I saw myself doing, but the view persists anyway. There are two reasons for this. In the first place, no one finds it easy to live uncomplainingly and fearlessly with the thesis that human reality is constantly being made and unmade, and that anything like a stable essence is constantly under threat. Patriotism, extreme xenophobic nationalism, and downright unpleasant chauvinism are common responses to this fear. We all need some foundation on which to stand; the question is how extreme and unchangeable is our formulation of what this foundation is. My position is that in the case of an essential Islam or Orient, these images are no more than images, and are upheld as such both by the community of the Muslim faithful and (the correspondence is significant) by the community of Orientalists. My objection to what I have called Orientalism is not that it is just the antiquarian study of Oriental languages, societies, and peoples, but that as a system of thought it approaches a heterogeneous, dynamic, and complex human reality from an uncritically essentialist standpoint; this suggests both an enduring Oriental reality and an opposing but no less enduring Western essence, which observes the Orient from afar and, so to speak, from above. This false position hides historical change. Even more important, from my standpoint, it hides the *interests* of the

Orientalist. Those, despite attempts to draw subtle distinctions between Orientalism as an innocent scholarly endeavor and Orientalism as an accomplice to empire, can never unilaterally be detached from the general imperial context that begins its modern global phase with Napoleon's invasion of Egypt in 1798.

I have in mind the striking contrast between the weaker and stronger party that is evident from the beginning of Europe's modern encounters with what it called the Orient. The studied solemnity and grandiose accents of Napoleon's *Déscription de l'Egypte* – its massive, serried volumes testifying to the sytematic labors of an entire corps of *savants* backed by a modern army of colonial conquest – dwarfs the individual testimony of people like Abd al-Rahman al-Jabarti, who in three separate volumes describes the French invasion from the point of view of the invaded. One might say that the *Déscription* is just a scientific, and therefore objective, account of Egypt in the early nineteenth century, but the presence of Jabarti (who is both unknown and ignored by Napoleon) suggests otherwise. Napoleon's is an "objective" account from the standpoint of someone powerful trying to hold Egypt within the French imperial orbit; Jabarti's is an account by someone who paid the price, was figuratively captured and vanquished.

In other words, rather than remaining as inert documents that testify to an eternally opposed Occident and Orient, the *Déscription* and Jabarti's chronicles together constitute a historical experience, out of which others evolved, and before which others existed. Studying the historical dynamics of this set of experiences is more demanding than sliding back into stereotypes like "the conflict of East and West." That is one reason why *Orientalism* is mistakenly read as a surreptitiously anti-Western work and, by an act of unwarranted and even wilful retrospective endowment, this reading (like all readings based on a supposedly stable binary opposition) elevates the image of an innocent and aggrieved Islam.

The second reason why the anti-essentialism of my arguments has proved hard to accept is political and urgently ideological. I had absolutely no way of knowing that, a year after the book was published, Iran would be the site of an extraordinarily far-reaching Islamic revolution, nor that the battle between Israel and the Palestinians would take such savage and protracted forms, from the 1982 invasion of Lebanon to the start of the *intifada* in late 1987. The end of the Cold War did not mute, much less terminate, the apparently unending conflict between East and West as represented by the Arabs and Islam on one side and the Christian West on the other. More recent, but no less acute contests developed as a result of the Soviet Union's invasion of Afghanistan; the challenge to the *status quo* made during the 1980s and 1990s by Islamic groups in countries as diverse as Algeria, Jordan, Lebanon, Egypt, and the Occupied Territories, and the various American and European responses; the creation of Islamic brigades to fight the Russians in Afghanistan from bases in Pakistan; the Gulf War; the continued support of Israel; and the emergence of "Islam" as a topic of alarmed, if not always precise and informed, journalism and scholarship. All this inflamed the sense of persecution felt by people forced, on almost a daily basis, to declare themselves to be either Westerners or Easterners. No one seemed to be free from the opposition between "us" and "them," resulting in a sense of reinforced, deepened, hardened identity that has not been particularly edifying.

In such a turbulent context, *Orientalism*'s fate was both fortunate and unfortunate. To those in the Arab and Islamic world who felt Western encroachment with anxiety and stress it appeared to be the first book that gave a serious answer back to a West that had never actually listened to or forgiven the Oriental for being an Oriental at all. I recall one early Arabic review of the book that described the author as a champion of Arabism, a defender of the downtrodden and abused, whose mission was to engage Western authorities in a kind of epic and romantic *mano-a-mano*. Despite the exaggeration, it did convey some real sense of the West's enduring hostility as felt by Arabs, and it also conveyed a response that many educated Arabs felt was appropriate.

I will not deny that I *was* aware, when writing the book, of the subjective truth insinuated by Marx in the little sentence I quoted as one of the book's epigraphs ("They cannot represent themselves; they must be represented"), which is that if you feel you have been denied the chance to speak your piece, you will try extremely hard to get that chance. For indeed, the subaltern *can* speak, as the history of liberation movements in the twentieth century eloquently attests. But I never felt that I was perpetuating the hostility between two rival political and cultural monolithic blocks, whose construction I was describing and whose terrible effects I was trying to reduce. On the contrary, as I said earlier, the Orient-versus-Occident opposition was both misleading and highly undesirable; the less it was given credit for actually describing anything more than a fascinating history of interpretations and contesting interests, the better. I am happy to record that many readers in Britain and America, as well as in English-speaking Africa, Asia, Australia, and the Caribbean, saw the book as stressing the actualities of what was later to be called multiculturalism, rather than xenophobia and aggressive, race-oriented nationalism.

Nevertheless, *Orientalism* has more often been thought of as a kind of testimonial to subaltern status – the wretched of the earth talking back – than as a multicultural critique of power using knowledge to advance itself. Thus as its author I have been seen as playing an assigned role: that of self-representing consciousness of what had formerly been suppressed and distorted in the learned texts of a discourse historically conditioned to be read not by Orientals but by other Westerners. This is an important point, and it adds to the sense of fixed identities battling across a permanent divide that my book quite specifically abjures, but which it paradoxically presupposes and depends on. None of the Orientalists I write about seems ever to have intended an Oriental as a reader. The discourse of Orientalism, its internal consistency and rigorous procedures, were all designed for readers and consumers in the metropolitan West. This goes as much for people I genuinely admire like Edward Lane and Gustave Flaubert, who were fascinated by Egypt, as it does for haughty colonial administrators like Lord Cromer, brilliant scholars like Ernest Renan, and baronial aristocrats like Arthur Balfour, all of whom condescended to and disliked the Orientals they either ruled or studied. I must confess to a certain pleasure in listening in, uninvited, to their various pronouncements and inter-Orientalist discussions, and an equal pleasure in making known my findings to both Europeans and non-Europeans. I have no doubt that this was made possible because I traversed the imperial East–West divide, entered into the life of the West, and yet retained some organic connection with the place I originally came from. I would repeat that this was very much a procedure of crossing, rather than maintaining, barriers; I believe *Orientalism* as a book shows it, especially when I speak of humanistic study as seeking ideally to go beyond coercive limitations on thought towards a non-dominative and non-essentialist type of learning.

These considerations did in fact add to the pressures on my book to represent a sort of testament of wounds and a record of sufferings, the recital of which was felt as a long overdue striking back at the West. I deplore so simple a characterization of a work that is – here I am not going to be falsely modest – quite nuanced and discriminating in what it says about different people, different periods, and different styles of Orientalism. Each of my analyses varies the picture, increases the difference and discriminations, separates authors and periods from each other, even though all pertain to Orientalism. To read my analyses of Chateaubriand and Flaubert, or of Burton and Lane, with exactly the same emphasis, deriving the same reductive message from the banal formula "an attack on Western civilization" is, I believe, to be both simplistic and wrong. But I also believe that it is entirely correct to read recent Orientalist authorities such as the almost comically persistent Bernard Lewis as the politically motivated and hostile witnesses that their suave accents and unconvincing displays of learning attempt to hide.

Once again, then, we return to the book's political and historical context, which I do not pretend is irrelevant to its contents. One of the most generously perspicacious and intelligently discriminating statements of that conjuncture was laid out in a review by Basim Musallam (MERIP, 1979). He begins by comparing my book with an earlier demystification of Orientalism by the Lebanese scholar Michael Rustum in 1895 (*Kitab al-Gharib fi al-Gharb*), but then says that the main difference between us is that my book is about loss, whereas Rustum's is not. Musallam says:

> Rustum writes as a free man and a member of a free society: a Syrian, Arab by speech, citizen of a still-independent Ottoman state ... unlike Michael Rustum, Edward Said has no generally accepted identity, his very *people* are in dispute. It is possible that Edward Said and his generation sometimes feel that they stand on nothing more solid than the remnants of the destroyed society of

Michael Rustum's Syria, and on memory. Others in Asia
and Africa have had their successes in this age of national
liberation; here, in painful contrast, there has been desperate resistance against overwhelming odds and, until
now, defeat. It is not just any "Arab" who wrote this
book, but one with a particular background and experience. (p. 22)

Musallam correctly notes that an Algerian would not have
written the same kind of generally pessimistic book, especially
one like mine that does very little with the history of French
relations with North Africa, Algeria most particularly. So while
I would accept the overall impression that *Orientalism* is
written out of an extremely concrete history of personal loss
and national disintegration – only a few years before I wrote
Orientalism Golda Meir made her notorious and deeply Orientalist comment about there being no Palestinian people –
I would also like to add that neither in this book nor in the
two that immediately followed it, *The Question of Palestine*
(1980) and *Covering Islam* (1981), did I want only to suggest
a political program of restored identity and resurgent nationalism. There was, of course, an attempt in both of the later
books to supply what was missing in *Orientalism*, namely a
sense of what an alternative picture of parts of the Orient –
Palestine and Islam respectively – might be, from a personal
point of view.

But in all my works I remained fundamentally critical of a
gloating and uncritical nationalism. The picture of Islam that I
represented was not one of assertive discourse and dogmatic
orthodoxy, but was based instead on the idea that communities
of interpretation exist within and outside the Islamic world,
communicating with each other in a dialogue of equals. My
view of Palestine, formulated originally in *The Question
of Palestine*, remains the same today: I expressed all sorts
of reservations about the insouciant nativism and militant
militarism of the nationalist consensus; I suggested instead a
critical look at the Arab environment, Palestinian history, and
Israeli realities, with the explicit conclusion that only a negot-
iated settlement between the two communities of suffering,
Arab and Jewish, would provide respite from the unending
war. (I should mention in passing that although my book on
Palestine was given a fine Hebrew translation in the early 1980s

by Mifras, a small Israeli publishing house, it remains untranslated in Arabic to this day. Every Arabic publisher who was interested in the book wanted me to change or delete those sections that are openly critical of one or another Arab regime (including the PLO), a request that I have always refused to comply with.)

I regret to say that the Arabic reception of *Orientalism*, despite Kamal Abu Deeb's remarkable translation, still managed to ignore that aspect of my book which diminished the nationalist fervor that some inferred from my critique of Orientalism, which I associated with those drives to domination and control also to be found in imperialism. The main achievement of Abu Deeb's painstaking translation was an almost total avoidance of Arabized Western expressions; technical words like *discourse*, *simulacrum*, *paradigm*, or *code* were rendered from within the classical rhetoric of the Arab tradition. His idea was to place my work inside one fully formed tradition, as if it were addressing another from a perspective of cultural adequacy and equality. In this way, he reasoned, it was possible to show that just as one could advance an epistemological critique from within the Western tradition, so too could one do it from within the Arabic tradition.

Yet the sense of confrontation between an often emotionally defined Arab world and an even more emotionally experienced Western world drowned out the fact that *Orientalism* was meant to be a study in critique, not an affirmation of warring and hopelessly antithetical identities. Moreover, the actuality I described in the book's last pages, of one powerful discursive system maintaining hegemony over another, was intended as the opening salvo in a debate that might stir Arab readers and critics to engage more determinedly with the sytem of Orientalism. I was either upbraided for not having paid closer attention to Marx (the passages in my own book that were most singled out by dogmatic critics in the Arab world and India, for instance, were those on Marx's own Orientalism), whose system of thought was claimed to have risen above his obvious prejudices, or I was criticized for not appreciating the great achievements of Orientalism, the West, etc. As with defenses of Islam, recourse to Marxism or "the West" as a coherent total system seems to me to have been a case of using one orthodoxy to shoot down another.

The difference between Arab and other responses to *Orientalism* is, I think, an accurate indication of how decades of loss, frustration and the absence of democracy have affected intellectual and cultural life in the Arab region. I intended my book as part of a pre-existing current of thought whose purpose was to liberate intellectuals from the shackles of systems such as Orientalism: I wanted readers to make use of my work so that they might then produce new studies of their own that would illuminate the historical experience of Arabs and others in a generous, enabling mode. That certainly happened in Europe, the United States, Australia, the Indian subcontinent, the Caribbean, Ireland, Latin America, and parts of Africa. The invigorated study of Africanist and Indological discourses, the analyses of subaltern history, the reconfiguration of post-colonial anthropology, political science, art history, literary criticism, musicology, in addition to the vast new developments in feminist and minority discourses – to all these, I am pleased and flattered that *Orientalism* often made a difference. That does not seem to have been the case (in so far as I can judge it) in the Arab world where, partly because my work is correctly perceived as Eurocentric in its texts, and partly because, as Musallam says, the battle for cultural survival is too engrossing, books like mine are interpreted less usefully, productively speaking, and more as defensive gestures either for or against the "West."

Yet among American and British academics of a decidedly rigorous and unyielding stripe, *Orientalism*, and indeed all of my other work, has come in for disapproving attacks because of its "residual" humanism, its theoretical inconsistencies, its insufficient, perhaps even sentimental, treatment of agency. I am glad that it has! *Orientalism* is a partisan book, not a theoretical machine. No one has convincingly shown that individual effort is not at some profoundly unteachable level both eccentric and, in Gerard Manley Hopkins's sense, *original*; this despite the existence of systems of thought, discourses and hegemonies (although none of them are in fact seamless, perfect, or inevitable). The interest I took in Orientalism as a cultural phenomenon (like the culture of imperialism I talked about in *Culture and Imperialism*, its 1993 sequel) derives from its variability and unpredictability, both qualities that give writers like Massignon and Burton their surprising force, and even attractiveness. What I tried to preserve in my analysis of Orientalism was its combination of consistency *and* inconsistency, its play, so to speak, which can only be rendered by preserving for oneself as writer and critic the right to some emotional force, the right to be moved, angered, surprised and even delighted. That is why, in the debate between Gayan Prakash on the one hand and Rosalind O'Hanlon and David Washbrook on the other, I think Prakash's more mobile post-structuralism has to be given its due.[2] By the same token the work of Homi Bhabha, Gayatri Spivak, Ashis Nandy, predicated on the sometimes dizzying subjective relationships engendered by colonialism, cannot be gainsaid for *its* contribution to our understanding of the humanistic traps laid by systems such as Orientalism.

Let me conclude this survey of *Orientalism*'s critical trans-mutations with a mention of the one group of people who were, not unexpectedly, the most vociferous in responding to my book, the Orientalists themselves. They were not my *principal* intended audience at all; I meant to cast some light on their practices so as to make other humanists aware of one field's particular procedures and genealogy. The word "Orientalism" itself has been confined for too long to a professional specialty; I tried to show its application and existence in general culture, literature, ideology, and social as well as political attitudes. To speak of someone as an Oriental, as the Orientalists did, was not just to designate that person as someone whose language, geography and history were the stuff of learned treatises: it was often meant as a derogatory expression signifying a lesser breed of human being. This is not to deny that for artists like Nerval and Segalen the word "Orient" was wonderfully, ingeniously connected to exoticism, glamour, mystery, and promise. But it was also a sweeping historical generalization. In addition to these uses of the words *Orient*, *Oriental*, and *Orientalism*, the term *Orientalist* also came to represent the erudite scholarly, mainly academic specialist in the languages and histories of the East. Yet, as the late Albert Hourani wrote me in March 1992 a few months before his untimely and much regretted death, due to the force of my argument (for which he said he could not reproach me), my book had the unfortunate effect of making it almost impossible to use the term "Orientalism" in a neutral sense, so much had it become a term of abuse. He concluded that he would have still liked to retain the word for use in describing "a limited, rather dull but valid discipline of scholarship."

In his generally balanced 1979 review of *Orientalism*, Hourani formulated one of his objections by suggesting that while I singled out the exaggerations, racism and hostility of much Orientalist writing, I neglected to mention its numerous scholarly and humanistic achievements. Names that he brought up included Marshall Hodgson, Claude Cahen, André Raymond, all of whom (along with the German authors who come up *de rigueur*) should be acknowledged as real contributors to human knowledge. This does not, however, conflict with what I say in *Orientalism*, with the difference that I do insist on the prevalence in the discourse itself of a structure of attitudes that cannot simply be waved away or discounted. Nowhere do I argue that Orientalism is evil, or sloppy, or uniformly the same in the work of each and every Orientalist. But I do say that the *guild* of Orientalists has a specific history of complicity with imperial power, which it would be Panglossian to call irrelevant.

So while I sympathize with Hourani's plea, I have serious doubts whether the notion of Orientalism properly understood can ever, in fact, be completely detached from its rather more complicated and not always flattering circumstances. I suppose that one can imagine at the limit that a specialist in Ottoman or Fatimid archives is an Orientalist in Hourani's sense, but we are still required to ask where, how and with what supporting institutions and agencies such studies take place *today*? Many who wrote after my book appeared asked exactly those questions of even the most recondite and other-worldly scholars, with sometimes devastating results.

Still, there has been one sustained attempt to mount an argument whose purport is that a critique of Orientalism (mine in particular) is both meaningless and somehow a violation of the very idea of disinterested scholarship. That attempt is made by Bernard Lewis, to whom I had devoted a few critical pages in my book. Fifteen years after *Orientalism* appeared, Lewis produced a series of essays, some of them collected in a book entitled *Islam and the West*. One of the main sections of this book consists of an attack on me, which he surrounds with chapters and other essays that mobilize a set of lax and characteristically Orientalist formulas – Muslims are enraged at modernity, Islam never made the separation between church and state, and so on, and so on – all of them pronounced with an extreme level of generalization and with scarcely a mention of the differences between individual Muslims, between Muslim societies, between Muslim traditions and eras. Since Lewis has in a sense appointed himself spokesman for the guild of Orientalists on which my critique was originally based, it may be worth spending a little more time on his procedures. His ideas are, alas, fairly current among his little acolytes and imitators, whose job seems to be to alert Western consumers to the threat of an enraged, congenitally undemocratic and violent Islamic world.

Lewis's verbosity scarcely conceals both the ideological underpinnings of his position and his extraordinary capacity for getting nearly everything wrong. Of course, these are familiar attributes of the Orientalists' breed, some of whom have at least had the courage to be honest in their active denigration of Islamic, as well as other non-European, peoples. Not Lewis. He proceeds by distorting the truth, making false analogies and, by innuendo, methods to which he adds that veneer of omniscient tranquil authority which he supposes is the way scholars talk. Take as a typical example the analogy he draws between my critique of Orientalism and a hypothetical attack on studies of classical antiquity, an attack which, he says, would be a foolish activity. It would be of course, but then Orientalism and Hellenism are radically incomparable. The former is an attempt to describe a whole region of the world as an accompaniment to that region's colonial conquest, the latter is not at all about the direct colonial conquest of Greece in the nineteenth and twentieth centuries; in addition Orientalism expresses antipathy to Islam, Hellenism sympathy for classical Greece.

Additionally, the present political moment, with its reams of racist anti-Arab and anti-Muslim stereotypes (and no attacks on classical Greece), allows Lewis to deliver ahistorical and wilful political assertions in the form of scholarly argument, a practice thoroughly in keeping with the least creditable aspects of old-fashioned colonialist Orientalism.[3] Lewis's work therefore is part of the present political, rather than purely intellectual, environment.

To imply, as he does, that the branch of Orientalism dealing with Islam and the Arabs is a learned discipline that can there-fore be fairly put in the same category as classical philology is preposterous, as appropriate as comparing one of the many Israeli Arabists and Orientalists who have worked for the occu-pation authorities of the West Bank and Gaza with scholars like Wilamowitz or Mommsen. On the one hand Lewis wishes to reduce Islamic Orientalism to the status of an innocent and enthusiastic department of scholarship; on the other hand he wishes to pretend that Orientalism is too complex, various and technical to exist in a form for any non-Orientalist (like myself and many others) to criticize. Lewis's tactic here is to suppress a significant amount of historical experience. As I suggest, European interest in Islam derived not from curiosity but from fear of a monotheistic, culturally and militarily formidable competitor to Christianity. The earliest European scholars of Islam, as numerous historians have shown, were medieval polemicists writing to ward off the threat of Muslim hordes and apostasy. In one way or another that combination of fear and hostility has persisted to the present day, both in scholarly and non-scholarly attention to an Islam which is viewed as belonging to a part of the world – the Orient – counterposed imaginatively, geographically, and historically *against* Europe and the West.

The most interesting problems about Islamic or Arabic Ori-entalism are, first, the forms taken by the medieval vestiges that persist so tenaciously, and, second, the history and sociology of connections between Orientalism and the societies that pro-duced it. There are strong *affiliations* between Orientalism and the literary imagination, for example, as well as the imperial consciousness. What is striking about many periods of Euro-pean history is the traffic between what scholars and specialists wrote and what poets, novelists, politicians, and journalists then said about Islam. In addition – and this is the crucial point that Lewis refuses to deal with – there is a remarkable (but none the less intelligible) parallel between the rise of modern Orientalist scholarship and the acquisition of vast Eastern em-pires by Britain and France.

Although the connection between a routine British classical education and the extension of the British empire is more com-plex than Lewis might suppose, no more glaring parallel exists

between power and knowledge in the modern history of philology than in the case of Orientalism. Much of the information and knowledge about Islam and the Orient that was used
by the colonial powers to justify their colonialism derived from
Orientalist scholarship: a recent study by many contributors,
Orientalism and the Postcolonial Predicament,[4] demonstrates
with copious documentation how Orientalist knowledge was
used in the colonial administration of South Asia. A fairly consistent interchange still continues between area scholars, such
as Orientalists, and government departments of foreign affairs.
In addition, many of the stereotypes of Islamic and Arabic
sensuality, sloth, fatalism, cruelty, degradation and splendor,
to be found in writers from John Buchan to V. S. Naipaul,
have also been presuppositions underlying the adjoining field
of academic Orientalism. In contrast, the trade in clichés between Indology and Sinology on the one hand, and general
culture on the other hand is not quite as flourishing, although
there are relationships and borrowings to be noted. Nor is
there much similarity between what obtains among Western
experts in Sinology and Indology and the fact that many professional scholars of Islam in Europe and the United States
spend their lives studying the subject, yet still find the religion
and culture impossible to like, much less admire.

To say, as Lewis and his imitators do, that all such observations are only a matter of espousing "fashionable causes" is
not quite to address the question of why, for example, so many
Islamic specialists were and still are routinely consulted by, and
actively work for, governments whose designs in the Islamic
world are economic exploitation, domination or outright aggression, or why so many scholars of Islam – like Lewis himself
– voluntarily feel that it is part of their duty to mount attacks
on modern Arab or Islamic peoples with the pretense that
"classical" Islamic culture can nevertheless be the object of disinterested scholarly concern. The spectacle of specialists in the
history of medieval Islamic guilds being sent on State Department missions to brief area embassies on US security interests
in the Gulf does not spontaneously suggest anything resembling the love of Hellas ascribed by Lewis to the supposedly
cognate field of classical philology.

It is therefore not surprising that the field of Islamic and
Arabic Orientalism, always ready to deny its complicity with

state power, had never until very recently produced an internal critique of the affiliations I have just been describing, and that Lewis can utter the amazing statement that a criticism of Orientalism would be "meaningless." It is also not surprising that, with a few exceptions, most of the negative criticism my work has elicited from "specialists" turns out to be, like Lewis's, no more than banal description of a barony violated by a crude trespasser. The only specialists (again with a few exceptions) who attempted to deal with what I discuss – which is not only the content of Orientalism, but its relationships, affiliations, political tendencies, world-view – were Sinologists, Indologists, and the younger generation of Middle-East scholars, susceptible to newer influences and also to the political arguments that the critique of Orientalism has entailed. One example is Benjamin Schwartz of Harvard, who used the occasion of his 1982 presidential address to the Asian Studies Association not only to disagree with some of my criticism, but also to welcome my arguments intellectually.

Many of the senior Arabists and Islamicists have responded with the aggrieved outrage that is for them a substitute for self-reflection; most use words such as "malign," "dishonor," "libel," as if criticism itself were an impermissible violation of their sacrosanct academic preserve. In Lewis's case the defense offered is an act of conspicuous bad faith, since he more than most Orientalists has been a passionate political partisan against Arab (and other) causes in such places as the US Congress, *Commentary* and elsewhere. The proper response to him must therefore include an account of what politically and sociologically he is all about when he pretends to be defending the "honour" of his field, a defense which, it will be evident enough, is an elaborate confection of ideological half-truths designed to mislead non-specialist readers.

In short, the relationship between Islamic or Arab Orientalism and modern European culture can be studied without at the same time cataloguing every Orientalist who ever lived, every Orientalist tradition, or everything written by Orientalists, then lumping them together as rotten and worthless imperialism. I never did that anyway. It is benighted to say that Orientalism is a conspiracy or to suggest that "the West" is evil: both are among the fatuities that Lewis and one of his epigones, the Iraqi publicist Kanan Makiya, have had the tem-

erity to ascribe to me. On the other hand it is hypocritical to
suppress the cultural, political, ideological, and institutional
contexts in which people write, think and talk about the Orient,
whether they are scholars or not. And as I said earlier, it is
extremely important to understand that the reason why Orientalism is opposed by so many thoughtful non-Westerners is that
its modern discourse is correctly perceived as a discourse of
power originating in an era of colonialism, the subject of an
excellent recent symposium, *Colonialism and Culture*.[5] In this
kind of discourse, based mainly upon the assumption that
Islam is monolithic and unchanging and therefore marketable
by "experts" for powerful domestic political interests, neither
Muslims nor Arabs nor any of the other dehumanized lesser
peoples recognize themselves as human beings or their observers as simple scholars. Most of all they see in the discourse of
modern Orientalism, and its counterparts in similar knowledges constructed for native Americans and Africans, a
chronic tendency to deny, suppress or distort the cultural context of such systems of thought in order to maintain the fiction
of its scholarly disinterest.

II

Yet I would not want to suggest that, current though such
views as Lewis's may be, they are the only ones that have either
emerged or been reinforced during the past decade and a half.
Yes, it is true that ever since the demise of the Soviet Union
there has been a rush by some scholars and journalists in the
United States to find in an Orientalized Islam a new empire
of evil. Consequently, both the electronic and print media have
been awash with demeaning stereotypes that lump together
Islam and terrorism, or Arabs and violence, or the Orient and
tyranny. And there has also been a return in various parts of the
Middle and Far East to nativist religion and primitive nationalism, one particularly disgraceful aspect of which is the continuing Iranian *fatwa* against Salman Rushdie. But this is not the
whole picture, and what I want to do in the remaining part of
this essay is to talk about new trends in scholarship, criticism,

and interpretation that, although accepting the basic premises of my book, go well beyond it in ways, I think, that enrich our sense of the complexity of historical experience.

None of those trends has emerged out of the blue, of course; nor have they gained the status of fully established knowledges and practices. The worldly context remains both perplexingly stirred-up and ideologically fraught, volatile, tense, changeable and even murderous. Even though the Soviet Union has been dismembered and the East European countries have attained political independence, patterns of power and dominance remain unsettlingly in evidence. The global South – once referred to romantically and even emotionally as the Third World – is enmeshed in a debt trap, broken into dozens of fractured or incoherent entities, beset with problems of poverty, disease and underdevelopment that have increased in the past ten or fifteen years. Gone are the Non-Aligned movement and the charismatic leaders who undertook decolonization and independence. An alarming pattern of ethnic conflict and local wars, not confined to the global South as the tragic case of the Bosnians attests, has sprung up all over again. And in places like Central America, the Middle East and Asia, the United States still remains the dominant power, with an anxious and still un-unified Europe straggling behind.

Explanations for the current world scene and attempts to comprehend it culturally and politically have emerged in some strikingly dramatic ways. I have already mentioned fundamentalism. The secular equivalents are a return to nationalism and theories that stress the radical distinction – a falsely all-inclusive one, I believe – between different cultures and civilizations. Recently, for example, Professor Samuel Huntington of Harvard University advanced the far-from-convincing proposition that Cold War bi-polarism has been superseded by what he called the "clash of civilizations", a thesis based on the premise that Western, Confucian and Islamic civilizations, among several others, were rather like water-tight compartments whose adherents were at bottom mainly interested in fending off all the others.[6]

This is preposterous, since one of the great advances in modern cultural theory is the realization, almost universally acknowledged, that cultures are hybrid and heterogeneous and, as I argued in *Culture and Imperialism*, that cultures and civiliz-

ations are so interrelated and interdependent as to beggar any
unitary or simply delineated description of their individuality.
How can one today speak of "Western civilization" except as
in large measure an ideological fiction, implying a sort of detached superiority for a handful of values and ideas, none of
which has much meaning outside the history of conquest, immigration, travel and the mingling of peoples that gave the
Western nations their present mixed identities? This is especially true of the United States, which today can only be
described as an enormous palimpsest of different races and
cultures sharing a problematic history of conquests, extermin-
ations, and of course major cultural and political achievements.
And this was one of the implied messages of *Orientalism*, that
any attempt to force cultures and peoples into separate and
distinct breeds or essences exposes not only the misrepresentations and falsifications that ensue, but also the way in which
understanding is complicit with the power to produce such
things as the "Orient" or the "West."

Not that Huntington, and behind him all the theorists and
apologists of an exultant Western tradition, like Francis Fuku-
yama, haven't retained a good deal of their hold on the public
consciousness. They have, as is evident in the symptomatic case
of Paul Johnson, once a Left intellectual, now a retrograde
social and political polemicist. In the 18 April 1993 issue of the
New York Times Magazine, by no means a marginal publication, Johnson published an essay entitled "Colonialism's back
– and not a moment too soon," whose main idea was that "the
civilized nations" ought to take it upon themselves to re-
colonize Third World countries "where the most basic conditions of civilized life had broken down," and to do this by
means of a system of imposed trusteeships. His model is explicitly a nineteenth-century colonial one: he says that in order
for the Europeans to trade profitably they had to impose political order.

Johnson's argument has numerous subterranean echoes in
the works of US policy-makers, the media, and of course US
foreign policy itself, which remains interventionist in the
Middle East, Latin America, and Eastern Europe, and frankly
missionary everywhere else, especially in its policies towards
Russia and the former Soviet republics. The important point,
however, is that a largely unexamined but serious rift has

opened in the public consciousness between the old ideas of Western hegemony (of which the sytem of Orientalism was a part) on the one hand, and, on the other hand, newer ideas that have taken hold among subaltern and disadvantaged communities and among a wide sector of intellectuals, academics, and artists. It is now very strikingly no longer the case that the lesser peoples – formerly colonized, enslaved, suppressed – are silent or unaccounted for except by senior European or American males. There has been a revolution in the consciousness of women, minorities and marginals so powerful as to affect mainstream thinking world-wide. Although I had some sense of it when I was working on *Orientalism* in the 1970s, it is now so dramatically apparent as to demand the attention of everyone seriously concerned with the scholarly and theoretical study of culture.

Two broad currents can be distinguished: post-colonialism and post-modernism; their use of the prefix "post" suggests not so much the sense of going beyond but rather, as Ella Shohat puts it in a seminal article on the post-colonial, "continuities and discontinuities; but its emphasis is on the new modes and forms of the old colonialist practices, not on a 'beyond'."[7] Both post-colonialism and post-modernism emerged as related topics of engagement and investigation during the 1980s and, in many instances, seemed to take account of such works as *Orientalism* as antecedents. It would be impossible here to go into the immense terminological debates that surround both words, some of them dwelling at length on whether the phrases should or should not be hyphenated. The point here is therefore not to talk about isolated instances of excess or risible jargon, but to locate those currents and efforts which, from the perspective of a book published in 1978, seem to some extent now to involve it in 1994.

Much of the most compelling work on the new political and economic order has concerned what, in a recent article, Harry Magdoff has described as "globalisation," a system by which a small, financial élite expanded its power over the whole globe, inflating commodity and service prices, redistributing wealth from lower-income sectors (usually in the non-Western world) to the higher-income ones.[8] Along with this, as discussed in astringent terms by Masao Miyoshi and Arif Dirlik, there has emerged a new transnational order in which states no longer have borders, labor and income are subject only to global managers, and colonialism has reappeared in the subservience of the South to the North.[9] Both Miyoshi and Dirlik go on to show how the interest of Western academics in subjects such as multiculturalism and "post-coloniality" can in fact be a cultural and intellectual retreat from the new realities of global power: "What we need," Miyoshi says, "is a rigorous political and economic scrutiny rather than a gesture of pedagogic expediency," exemplified by the "liberal self-deception" contained in such new fields as cultural studies and multiculturalism (751).

But even if we take such injunctions seriously (as we must), there is a solid basis in historical experience for the appearance today of interest in both post-modernism and its quite different counterpart, post-colonialsim. First of all, there is a much greater Eurocentric bias in the former, as well as a preponderance of theoretical and aesthetic emphasis stressing the local and the contingent, as well as the almost decorative weightlessness of history, pastiche, and above all consumerism. The earliest studies of the post-colonial were by such distinguished thinkers as Anwar Abdel Malek, Samir Amin, C. L. R. James; almost all were based on studies of domination and control made from the standpoint of either a completed political independence or an incomplete liberationist project. Yet whereas post-modernism in one of its most famous programmatic statements (by Jean-François Lyotard) stresses the disappearance of the grand narratives of emancipation and enlightenment, the emphasis behind much of the work done by the first generation of post-colonial artists and scholars is exactly the opposite: the grand narratives remain, even though their implementation and realization are at present in abeyance, deferred, or circumvented. This crucial difference between the urgent historical and political imperatives of post-colonialism and post-modernism's relative detachment makes for altogether different approaches and results, although there is some overlap between them (in the technique of "magical realism," for example).

I think it would be wrong to suggest that in much of the best post-colonial work that has proliferated so dramatically since the early 1980s there hasn't been a great emphasis on the local, regional and contingent: there has, but it seems to me to be most interestingly connected in its general approach to a universal set of concerns, all of them relating to emancipation, revisionist attitudes towards history and culture, a widespread use of recurring theoretical models and styles. A leading motif has been the consistent critique of Eurocentrism and patriarchy. Across US and European campuses in the 1980s students and faculties alike worked assiduously to expand the academic focus of so-called core curricula to include writing by women, non-European artists and thinkers, subalterns. This was accompanied by important changes in approach to area studies, long in the hands of classical Orientalists and their equivalents in other fields. Anthropology, political science, literature, sociology, and above all history felt the effects of a wide-ranging critique of sources, the introduction of theory, and the dislodgement of the Eurocentric perspective. Perhaps the most brilliant revisionist work was done not in Middle East studies, but in the field of Indology with the advent of Subaltern Studies, a group of remarkable scholars and researchers led by Ranajit Guha. Their aim was nothing less than a revolution in historiography, the immediate goal being to rescue the writing of Indian history from the domination of the nationalist élite and restore to it the important role of the urban poor and the rural masses. I think it would be wrong to say of such mostly academic work that it was easily cooptable and complicit with "transnational" neo-colonialism. We need to record and acknowledge the achievement while warning of the later pitfalls.

What has been of special interest for me is the extension of post-colonial concerns to the problems of geography. After all, Orientalism is a study based on the re-thinking of what had for centuries been believed to be an unbridgeable chasm separating East from West. My aim, as I said earlier, was not so much to dissipate difference itself – for who can deny the constitutive role of national as well as cultural differences in the relations between human beings – but to challenge the notion that difference implies hostility, a frozen reified set of opposed essences, and a whole adversarial knowledge built out of those things. What I called for in Orientalism was a new way of conceiving the separations and conflicts that had stimulated generations of hostility, war, and imperial control. And indeed, one of the most interesting developments in post-colonial studies was a re-reading of the canonical cultural works, not to demote or somehow dish dirt on them, but to re-investigate some of their assumptions, going beyond the stifling hold on them of some version of the master-slave binary dialectic. This has certainly been the comparable effect of astoundingly resourceful novels such as Rushdie's *Midnight's Children*, the narratives of C. L. R. James, the poetry of Aimé Césaire and of Derek Walcott, works whose daring new formal achievements are in effect a re-appropriation of the historical experience of colonialism, revitalized and transformed into a new aesthetic of sharing and often transcendent re-formulation.

One sees a similar development in the work of the group of distinguished Irish writers who in 1980 established themselves as a collective called Field Day. The preface to a collection of their works says about them:

> (these writers) believed that Field Day could and should contribute to the solution of the present crisis by producing analyses of the established opinion, myths and stereotypes which had become both a symptom and cause of the current situation (between Ireland and the North). The collapse of constitutional and political arrangements and the recrudescence of the violence which they had been designed to repress or contain, made this a more urgent requirement in the North than in the Republic ... The company, therefore, decided to embark upon a succession of publications, starting with a series of pamphlets (in addition to an impressive series of poems by Seamus Heaney, essays by Seamus Deane, plays by Brian Friel and Tom Paulin) in which the nature of the Irish problem could be explored and, as a result, more successfully confronted than it had been hitherto.[10]

The idea of rethinking and re-formulating historical experiences which had once been based on the geographical separation of peoples and cultures is at the heart of a whole spate of scholarly and critical works. It is to be found, to mention only three, in Amiel Alcalay's *Beyond Arabs and Jews: Remaking Levantine Culture*, Paul Gilroy's *The Black Atlantic: Modernity and Double Consciousness*, and Moira Ferguson's *Subject to Others: British Women Writers and Colonial Slavery, 1670–1834*.[11] In these works, domains once believed to have been exclusive to one people, gender, race or class are re-examined and shown to have involved others. Long represented as a battleground for Arabs and Jews, the Levant emerges in Alcalay's book as a Mediterranean culture common to both peoples; according to Gilroy a similar process alters, indeed doubles, our perception of the Atlantic Ocean, previously thought of as principally a European passage. And in re-examining the adversarial relationship between English slave-owners and African slaves, Ferguson allows a more complex pattern dividing white female from white male to stand out, with new demotions and dislocations appearing as a result in Africa.

I could go on giving more and more examples. I shall conclude briefly by saying that although the animosities and inequities still exist from which my interest in Orientalism as a cultural and political phenomenon began, there is now at least a general acceptance that these represent not an eternal order but a historical experience whose end, or at least partial abatement, may be at hand. Looking back at it from the distance afforded by fifteen eventful years and the availability of a massive new interpretive and scholarly enterprise to reduce the effects of imperialist shackles on thought and human relations, *Orientalism* at least had the merit of enlisting itself openly in the struggle, which continues of course in "West" and "East" together.

E. W. S.

New York
March 1994

Notes

Introduction

1. Thierry Desjardins, *Le Martyre du Liban* (Paris: Plon, 1976), p. 14.

2. K. M. Panikkar, *Asia and Western Dominance* (London: George Allen & Unwin, 1959).

3. Denys Hay, *Europe: The Emergence of an Idea*, 2nd ed. (Edinburgh: Edinburgh University Press, 1968).

4. Steven Marcus, *The Other Victorians: A Study of Sexuality and Pornography in Mid-Nineteenth Century England* (1966; reprint ed., New York: Bantam Books, 1967), pp. 200–19.

5. See my *Criticism Between Culture and System* (Cambridge, Mass.: Harvard University Press, forthcoming).

6. Principally in his *American Power and the New Mandarins: Historical and Political Essays* (New York: Pantheon Books, 1969) and *For Reasons of State* (New York: Pantheon Books, 1973).

7. Walter Benjamin, *Charles Baudelaire: A Lyric Poet in the Era of High Capitalism*, trans. Harry Zohn (London: New Left Books, 1973), p. 71.

8. Harry Bracken, "Essence, Accident and Race," *Hermathena* 116 (Winter 1973): 81–96.

9. In an interview published in *Diacritics* 6, no. 3 (Fall 1976): 38.

10. Raymond Williams, *The Long Revolution* (London: Chatto & Windus, 1961), pp. 66–7.

11. In my *Beginnings: Intention and Method* (New York: Basic Books, 1975).

12. Louis Althusser, *For Marx*, trans. Ben Brewster (New York: Pantheon Books, 1969), pp. 65–7.

13. Raymond Schwab, *La Renaissance orientale* (Paris: Payot, 1950); Johann W. Fück, *Die Arabischen Studien in Europa bis in den Anfang des 20. Jahrhunderts* (Leipzig: Otto Harrassowitz, 1955); Dorothee Metlitzki, *The Matter of Araby in Medieval England* (New Haven, Conn.: Yale University Press, 1977).

14. E. S. Shaffer, *"Kubla Khan" and The Fall of Jerusalem: The Mythological School in Biblical Criticism and Secular Literature, 1770–1880* (Cambridge: Cambridge University Press, 1975).

15. George Eliot, *Middlemarch: A Study of Provincial Life* (1872; reprint ed., Boston: Houghton Mifflin Co., 1956), p. 164.

16. Antonio Gramsci, *The Prison Notebooks: Selections*, trans. and ed. Quintin Hoare and Geoffrey Nowell Smith (New York: International Publishers, 1971), p. 324. The full passage, unavailable in the Hoare and Smith translation, is to be found in Gramsci, *Quaderni del Carcere*, ed. Valentino Gerratana (Turin: Einaudi Editore, 1975), 2: 1363.

17. Raymond Williams, *Culture and Society, 1780–1950* (London: Chatto & Windus, 1958), p. 376.

Chapter 1.　The Scope of Orientalism

1. This and the preceding quotations from Arthur James Balfour's speech to the House of Commons are from Great Britain, *Parliamentary Debates* (Commons), 5th ser., 17 (1910): 1140–46. See also A. P. Thornton, *The Imperial Idea and Its Enemies: A Study in British Power* (London: Mac-Millan & Co., 1959), pp. 357–60. Balfour's speech was a defense of Eldon Gorst's policy in Egypt; for a discussion of that see Peter John Dreyfus Mellini, "Sir Eldon Gorst and British Imperial Policy in Egypt," unpublished Ph.D. dissertation, Stanford University, 1971.

2. Denis Judd, *Balfour and the British Empire: A Study in Imperial Evolution, 1874–1932* (London: MacMillan & Co., 1968), p. 286. See also p. 292: as late as 1926 Balfour spoke—without irony—of Egypt as an "independent nation."

3. Evelyn Baring, Lord Cromer, *Political and Literary Essays, 1908–1913* (1913; reprint ed., Freeport, N. Y.: Books for Libraries Press, 1969), pp. 40, 53, 12–14.

4. Ibid., p. 171.

5. Roger Owen, "The Influence of Lord Cromer's Indian Experience on British Policy in Egypt 1883–1907," in *Middle Eastern Affairs, Number Four: St. Antony's Papers Number 17*, ed. Albert Hourani (London: Oxford University Press, 1965), pp. 109–39.

6. Evelyn Baring, Lord Cromer, *Modern Egypt* (New York: Macmillan Co., 1908), 2: 146–67. For a British view of British policy in Egypt that runs totally counter to Cromer's, see Wilfrid Scawen Blunt, *Secret History of the English Occupation of Egypt: Being a Personal Narrative of Events* (New York: Alfred A. Knopf, 1922). There is a valuable discussion of Egyptian opposition to British rule in Mounah A. Khouri, *Poetry and the Making of Modern Egypt, 1882–1922* (Leiden: E. J. Brill, 1971).

7. Cromer, *Modern Egypt*, 2: 164.

8. Cited in John Marlowe, *Cromer in Egypt* (London: Elek Books, 1970), p. 271.

9. Harry Magdoff, "Colonialism (1763–c. 1970)," *Encyclopaedia Britannica*, 15th ed. (1974), pp. 893–4. See also D. K. Fieldhouse, *The Colonial Empires: A Comparative Survey from the Eighteenth Century* (New York: Delacorte Press, 1967), p. 178.

10. Quoted in Afaf Lutfi al-Sayyid, *Egypt and Cromer: A Study in Anglo-Egyptian Relations* (New York: Frederick A. Praeger, 1969), p. 3.

11. The phrase is to be found in Ian Hacking, *The Emergence of Probability: A Philosophical Study of Early Ideas About Probability, Induction and Statistical Inference* (London: Cambridge University Press, 1975), p. 17.

12. V. G. Kiernan, *The Lords of Human Kind: Black Man, Yellow Man, and White Man in an Age of Empire* (Boston: Little, Brown & Co., 1969), p. 55.

13. Edgar Quinet, *Le Génie des religions*, in *Oeuvres complètes* (Paris: Paguerre, 1857), pp. 55–74.

14. Cromer, *Political and Literary Essays*, p. 35.

15. See Jonah Raskin, *The Mythology of Imperialism* (New York: Random House, 1971), p. 40.

16. Henry A. Kissinger, *American Foreign Policy* (New York: W. W. Norton & Co., 1974), pp. 48–9.

17. Harold W. Glidden, "The Arab World," *American Journal of Psychiatry* 128, no. 8 (February 1972): 984–8.

18. R. W. Southern, *Western Views of Islam in the Middle Ages* (Cambridge, Mass.: Harvard University Press, 1962), p. 72. See also Francis Dvornik, *The Ecumenical Councils* (New York: Hawthorn Books, 1961), pp. 65–6: "Of special interest is the eleventh canon directing that chairs for teaching Hebrew, Greek, Arabic and Chaldean should be created at the main universities. The suggestion was Raymond Lull's, who advocated learning Arabic as the best means for the conversion of the Arabs. Although the canon remained almost without effect as there were few teachers of Oriental languages, its acceptance indicates the growth of the missionary idea in the West. Gregory X had already hoped for the conversion of the Mongols, and Franciscan friars had penetrated into the depths of Asia in their missionary zeal. Although these hopes were not fulfilled, the missionary spirit continued to develop." See also Johann W. Fück, *Die Arabischen Studien in Europa bis in den Anfang des 20. Jahrhunderts* (Leipzig: Otto Harrassowitz, 1955).

19. Raymond Schwab, *La Renaissance orientale* (Paris: Payot, 1950). See also V.-V. Barthold, *La Découverte de l'Asie: Histoire de l'orientalisme en Europe et en Russie*, trans. B. Nikitine (Paris: Payot, 1947), and the relevant pages in Theodor Benfey, *Geschichte der Sprachwissenschaft und Orientalischen Philologie in Deutschland* (Munich: Gottafschen, 1869). For an instructive contrast see James T. Monroe, *Islam and the Arabs in Spanish Scholarship* (Leiden: E. J. Brill, 1970).

20. Victor Hugo, *Oeuvres poétiques*, ed. Pierre Albouy (Paris: Gallimard, 1964), 1: 580.

21. Jules Mohl, *Vingt-sept Ans d'histoire des études orientales: Rapports faits à la Société asiatique de Paris de 1840 à 1867*, 2 vols. (Paris: Reinwald, 1879–80).

22. Gustave Dugat, *Histoire des orientalistes de l'Europe du XIIᵉ au XIXᵉ siècle*, 2 vols. (Paris: Adrien Maisonneuve, 1868–70).

23. See René Gérard, *L'Orient et la pensée romantique allemande* (Paris: Didier, 1963), p. 112.

24. Kiernan, *Lords of Human Kind*, p. 131.

25. University Grants Committee, *Report of the Sub-Committee on Oriental, Slavonic, East European and African Studies* (London: Her Majesty's Stationery Office, 1961).

26. H. A. R. Gibb, *Area Studies Reconsidered* (London: School of Oriental and African Studies, 1964).

27. See Claude Lévi-Strauss, *The Savage Mind* (Chicago: University of Chicago Press, 1967), chaps. 1–7.

28. Gaston Bachelard, *The Poetics of Space*, trans. Maria Jolas (New York: Orion Press, 1964).

29. Southern, *Western Views of Islam*, p. 14.

30. Aeschylus, *The Persians*, trans. Anthony J. Podleck (Englewood Cliffs, N. J.: Prentice-Hall, 1970), pp. 73–4.

31. Euripides, *The Bacchae*, trans. Geoffrey S. Kirk (Englewood Cliffs, N. J.: Prentice-Hall, 1970), p. 3. For further discussion of the Europe-Orient distinction see Santo Mazzarino, *Fra oriente e occidente: Ricerche di storia greca arcaica* (Florence: La Nuova Italia, 1947), and Denys Hay, *Europe: The Emergence of an Idea* (Edinburgh: Edinburgh University Press, 1968).

32. Euripides, *Bacchae*, p. 52.

33. René Grousset, *L'Empire du Levant: Histoire de la question d'Orient* (Paris: Payot, 1946).

34. Edward Gibbon, *The History of the Decline and Fall of the Roman Empire* (Boston: Little, Brown & Co., 1855), 6: 399.

35. Norman Daniel, *The Arabs and Medieval Europe* (London: Longmans, Green & Co., 1975), p. 56.

36. Samuel C. Chew, *The Crescent and the Rose: Islam and England During the Renaissance* (New York: Oxford University Press, 1937), p. 103.

37. Norman Daniel, *Islam and the West: The Making of an Image* (Edinburgh: University Press, 1960), p. 33. See also James Kritzeck, *Peter the Venerable and Islam* (Princeton, N. J.: Princeton University Press, 1964).

38. Daniel, *Islam and the West*, p. 252.

39. Ibid., pp. 259–60.

40. See for example William Wistar Comfort, "The Literary Rôle of the Saracens in the French Epic," *PMLA* 55 (1940): 628–59.

41. Southern, *Western Views of Islam*, pp. 91–2, 108–9.

42. Daniel, *Islam and the West*, pp. 246, 96, and passim.

43. Ibid., p. 84.

44. Duncan Black Macdonald, "Whither Islam?" *Muslim World* 23 (January 1933): 2.

45. P. M. Holt, Introduction to *The Cambridge History of Islam*, ed. P. M. Holt, Anne K. S. Lambton, and Bernard Lewis (Cambridge: Cambridge University Press, 1970), p. xvi.

46. Antoine Galland, prefatory "Discours" to Barthélemy d'Herbelot, *Bibliothèque orientale, ou Dictionnaire universel contenant tout ce qui fait connaître les peuples de l'Orient* (The Hague: Neaulme & van Daalen, 1777), 1: vii. Galland's point is that d'Herbelot presented real knowledge, not legend or myth of the sort associated with the "marvels of the East." See R. Wittkower, "Marvels of the East: A Study in the History of Monsters," *Journal of the Warburg and Courtauld Institutes* 5 (1942): 159–97.

47. Galland, prefatory "Discours" to d'Herbelot, *Bibliothèque orientale*, pp. xvi, xxxiii. For the state of Orientalist knowledge immediately before d'Herbelot, see V. J. Parry, "Renaissance Historical Literature in Relation to the New and Middle East (with Special Reference to Paolo Giovio)," in *Historians of the Middle East*, ed. Bernard Lewis and P. M. Holt (London: Oxford University Press, 1962), pp. 277–89.

48. Barthold, *La Découverte de l'Asie*, pp. 137–8.

49. D'Herbelot, *Bibliothèque orientale*, 2: 648.

50. See also Montgomery Watt, "Muhammad in the Eyes of the West," *Boston University Journal* 22, no. 3 (Fall 1974): 61–9.

51. Isaiah Berlin, *Historical Inevitability* (London: Oxford University Press, 1955), pp. 13–14.

52. Henri Pirenne, *Mohammed and Charlemagne*, trans. Bernard Miall (New York: W. W. Norton & Co., 1939), pp. 234, 283.

53. Quoted by Henri Baudet in *Paradise on Earth: Some Thoughts on European Images of Non-European Man*, trans. Elizabeth Wentholt (New Haven, Conn.: Yale University Press, 1965), p. xiii.

54. Gibbon, *Decline and Fall of the Roman Empire*, 6: 289.

55. Baudet, *Paradise on Earth*, p. 4.

56. See Fieldhouse, *Colonial Empires*, pp. 138–61.

57. Schwab, *La Renaissance orientale*, p. 30.

58. A. J. Arberry, *Oriental Essays: Portraits of Seven Scholars* (New York: Macmillan Co., 1960), pp. 30, 31.

59. Raymond Schwab, *Vie d'Anquetil-Duperron suivie des Usages civils et religieux des Perses par Anquetil-Duperron* (Paris: Ernest Leroux, 1934), pp. 10, 96, 4, 6.

60. Arberry, *Oriental Essays*, pp. 62–6.

61. Frederick Eden Pargiter, ed., *Centenary Volume of the Royal Asiatic Society of Great Britain and Ireland 1823–1923* (London: Royal Asiatic Society, 1923), p. viii.

62. Quinet, *Le Génie des religions*, p. 47.

63. Jean Thiry, *Bonaparte en Égypte décembre 1797–24 août 1799* (Paris: Berger-Levrault, 1973), p. 9.

64. Constantin-François Volney, *Voyage en Égypte et en Syrie* (Paris: Bossange, 1821), 2: 241 and passim.

65. Napoleon, *Campagnes d'Égypte et de Syrie, 1798–1799: Mémoires pour servir à l'histoire de Napoléon* (Paris: Comou, 1843), 1: 211.

66. Thiry, *Bonaparte en Égypte*, p. 126. See also Ibrahim Abu-Lughod, *Arab Rediscovery of Europe: A Study in Cultural Encounters* (Princeton, N. J.: Princeton University Press, 1963), pp. 12–20.

67. Abu-Lughod, *Arab Rediscovery of Europe*, p. 22.

68. Quoted from Arthur Helps, *The Spanish Conquest of America* (London, 1900), p. 196, by Stephen J. Greenblatt, "Learning to Curse: Aspects of Linguistic Colonialism in the Sixteenth Century," in *First Images of America: The Impact of the New World on the Old*, ed. Fredi Chiapelli (Berkeley: University of California Press, 1976), p. 573.

69. Thiry, *Bonaparte en Égypte*, p. 200. Napoleon was not just being cynical. It is reported of him that he discussed Voltaire's *Mahomet* with Goethe, and defended Islam. See Christian Cherfils, *Bonaparte et l'Islam d'après les documents français arabes* (Paris: A. Pedone, 1914), p. 249 and passim.

70. Thiry, *Bonaparte en Égypte*, p. 434.

71. Hugo, *Les Orientales*, in *Oeuvres poétiques*, 1: 684.

72. Henri Dehérain, *Silvestre de Sacy, ses contemporains et ses disciples* (Paris: Paul Geuthner, 1938), p. v.

73. *Description de l'Égypte, ou Recueil des observations et des recherches* *qui ont été faites in Égypte pendant l'expédition de l'armée française, publié par les ordres de sa majesté l'empereur Napoléon le grand,* 23 vols. (Paris: Imprimerie impériale, 1809–28).

74. Fourier, *Préface historique,* vol. 1 of *Description de l'Égypte,* p. 1.

75. Ibid., p. iii.

76. Ibid., p. xcii.

77. Étienne Geoffroy Saint-Hilaire, *Histoire naturelle des poissons du Nil,* vol. 17 of *Description de l'Égypte,* p. 2.

78. M. de Chabrol, *Essai sur les moeurs des habitants modernes de l'Égypte,* vol. 14 of *Description de l'Égypte,* p. 376.

79. This is evident in Baron Larrey, *Notice sur la conformation physique des égyptiens et des différentes races qui habitent en Égypte, suivie de quelques réflexions sur l'embaumement des momies,* vol. 13 of *Description de l'Égypte.*

80. Cited by John Marlowe, *The Making of the Suez Canal* (London: Cresset Press, 1964), p. 31.

81. Quoted in John Pudney, *Suez: De Lesseps' Canal* (New York: Frederick A. Praeger, 1969), pp. 141–2.

82. Marlowe, *Making of the Suez Canal,* p. 62.

83. Ferdinand de Lesseps, *Lettres, journal et documents pour servir à l'histoire du Canal de Suez* (Paris: Didier, 1881), 5: 310. For an apt characterization of de Lesseps and Cecil Rhodes as mystics, see Baudet, *Paradise on Earth,* p. 68.

84. Cited in Charles Beatty, *De Lesseps of Suez: The Man and His Times* (New York: Harper & Brothers, 1956), p. 220.

85. De Lesseps, *Lettres, journal et documents,* 5: 17.

86. Ibid., pp. 324–33.

87. Hayden White, *Metahistory: The Historical Imagination in Nineteenth-Century Europe* (Baltimore: Johns Hopkins University Press, 1973), p. 12.

88. Anwar Abdel Malek, "Orientalism in Crisis," *Diogenes* 44 (Winter 1963): 107–8.

89. Friedrich Schlegel, *Über die Sprache und Weisheit der Indier: Ein Beitrag zur Begrundung der Altertumstunde* (Heidelberg: Mohr & Zimmer, 1808), pp. 44–59; Schlegel, *Philosophie der Geschichte: In achtzehn Vorlesungen gehalten zu Wien im Jahre 1828,* ed. Jean-Jacques Anstett, vol. 9 of *Kritische Friedrich-Schlegel-Ausgabe,* ed. Ernest Behler (Munich: Ferdinand Schöningh, 1971), p. 275.

90. Léon Poliakov, *The Aryan Myth: A History of Racist and Nationalist Ideas in Europe,* trans. Edmund Howard (New York: Basic Books, 1974).

91. See Derek Hopwood, *The Russian Presence in Syria and Palestine, 1843–1943: Church and Politics in the Near East* (Oxford: Clarendon Press, 1969).

92. A. L. Tibawi, *British Interests in Palestine, 1800–1901* (London: Oxford University Press, 1961), p. 5.

93. Gérard de Nerval, *Oeuvres,* ed. Albert Béguin and Jean Richet (Paris: Gallimard, 1960), 1: 933.

94. Hugo, *Oeuvres poétiques,* 1: 580.

95. Sir Walter Scott, *The Talisman* (1825; reprint ed., London: J. M. Dent, 1914), pp. 38–9.

96. See Albert Hourani, "Sir Hamilton Gibb, 1895–1971," *Proceedings of the British Academy* 58 (1972): 495.

97. Quoted by B. R. Jerman, *The Young Disraeli* (Princeton, N. J.: Princeton University Press, 1960), p. 126. See also Robert Blake, *Disraeli* (London: Eyre & Spottiswoode, 1966), pp. 59–70.

98. *Flaubert in Egypt: A Sensibility on Tour*, trans. and ed. Francis Steegmuller (Boston: Little, Brown & Co., 1973), pp. 44–5. See Gustave Flaubert, *Correspondance*, ed. Jean Bruneau (Paris: Gallimard, 1973), 1: 542.

99. This is the argument presented in Carl H. Becker, *Das Erbe der Antike im Orient und Okzident* (Leipzig: Quelle & Meyer, 1931).

100. See Louis Massignon, *La Passion d'al-Hosayn-ibn-Mansour al-Hallaj* (Paris: Paul Geuthner, 1922).

101. Abdel Malek, "Orientalism in Crisis," p. 112.

102. H. A. R. Gibb, *Modern Trends in Islam* (Chicago: University of Chicago Press, 1947), p. 7.

103. Gibb, *Area Studies Reconsidered*, pp. 12, 13.

104. Bernard Lewis, "The Return of Islam," *Commentary*, January 1976, pp. 39–49.

105. See Daniel Lerner and Harold Lasswell, eds., *The Policy Sciences: Recent Developments in Scope and Method* (Stanford, Calif.: Stanford University Press, 1951).

106. Morroe Berger, *The Arab World Today* (Garden City, N. Y.: Doubleday & Co., 1962), p. 158.

107. There is a compendium of such attitudes listed and criticized in Maxime Rodinson, *Islam and Capitalism*, trans. Brian Pearce (New York: Pantheon Books, 1973).

108. Ibrahim Abu-Lughod, "Retreat from the Secular Path? Islamic Dilemmas of Arab Politics," *Review of Politics* 28, no. 4 (October 1966): 475.

Chapter 2.   Orientalist Structures and Restructures

1. Gustave Flaubert, *Bouvard et Pécuchet*, vol. 2 of *Oeuvres*, ed. A. Thibaudet and R. Dumesnil (Paris: Gallimard, 1952), p. 985.

2. There is an illuminating account of these visions and utopias in Donald G. Charlton, *Secular Religions in France, 1815–1870* (London: Oxford University Press, 1963).

3. M. H. Abrams, *Natural Supernaturalism: Tradition and Revolution in Romantic Literature* (New York: W. W. Norton & Co., 1971), p. 66.

4. For some illuminating material see John P. Nash, "The Connection of Oriental Studies with Commerce, Art, and Literature During the 18th–19th Centuries," *Manchester Egyptian and Oriental Society Journal* 15 (1930): 33–9; also John F. Laffey, "Roots of French Imperialism in the Nineteenth Century: The Case of Lyon," *French Historical Studies* 6, no. 1 (Spring 1969): 78–92, and R. Leportier, *L'Orient Porte des Indes* (Paris: Éditions France-Empire, 1970). There is a great deal of information in Henri Omont, *Missions archéologiques françaises en Orient aux XVIIe et XVIIIe siècles*, 2 vols. (Paris: Imprimerie nationale, 1902), and in Margaret T. Hodgen, *Early Anthropology in the Sixteenth and Seventeenth Centuries* (Philadelphia: University of Pennsylvania Press, 1964), as well as in Norman

Daniel, *Islam, Europe and Empire* (Edinburgh: University Press, 1966). Two indispensable short studies are Albert Hourani, "Islam and the Philosophers of History," *Middle Eastern Studies* 3, no. 3 (April 1967): 206–68, and Maxime Rodinson, "The Western Image and Western Studies of Islam," in *The Legacy of Islam*, ed. Joseph Schacht and C. E. Bosworth (Oxford: Clarendon Press, 1974), pp. 9–62.

5. P. M. Holt, "The Treatment of Arab History by Prideaux, Ockley, and Sale," in *Historians of the Middle East*, ed. Bernard Lewis and P. M. Holt (London: Oxford University Press, 1962), p. 302. See also Holt's *The Study of Modern Arab History* (London: School of Oriental and African Studies, 1965).

6. The view of Herder as populist and pluralist is advocated by Isaiah Berlin, *Vico and Herder: Two Studies in the History of Ideas* (New York: Viking Press, 1976).

7. For a discussion of such motifs and representations, see Jean Starobinski, *The Invention of Liberty, 1700–1789*, trans. Bernard C. Smith (Geneva: Skira, 1964).

8. There are a small number of studies on this too-little-investigated subject. Some well-known ones are: Martha P. Conant, *The Oriental Tale in England in the Eighteenth Century* (1908; reprint ed., New York: Octagon Books, 1967); Marie E. de Meester, *Oriental Influences in the English Literature of the Nineteenth Century, Anglistische Forschungen*, no. 46 (Heidelberg, 1915); Byron Porter Smith, *Islam in English Literature* (Beirut: American Press, 1939). See also Jean-Luc Doutrelant, "L'Orient tragique au XVIIIe siècle," *Revue des Sciences Humaines* 146 (April–June 1972): 255–82.

9. Michel Foucault, *The Order of Things: An Archaeology of the Human Sciences* (New York: Pantheon Books, 1970), pp. 138, 144. See also François Jacob, *The Logic of Life: A History of Heredity*, trans. Betty E. Spillmann (New York: Pantheon Books, 1973), p. 50 and passim, and Georges Canguilhem, *La Connaissance de la vie* (Paris: Gustave-Joseph Vrin, 1969), pp. 44–63.

10. See John G. Burke, "The Wild Man's Pedigree: Scientific Method and Racial Anthropology," in *The Wild Man Within: An Image in Western Thought from the Renaissance to Romanticism*, ed. Edward Dudley and Maximillian E. Novak (Pittsburgh, Pa.: University of Pittsburgh Press, 1972), pp. 262–8. See also Jean Biou, "Lumières et anthropophagie," *Revue des Sciences Humaines* 146 (April–June 1972): 223–34.

11. Henri Dehérain, *Silvestre de Sacy: Ses Contemporains et ses disciples* (Paris: Paul Geuthner, 1938), p. 111.

12. For these and other details see ibid., pp. i–xxxiii.

13. Duc de Broglie, "Éloge de Silvestre de Sacy," in Sacy, *Mélanges de littérature orientale* (Paris: E. Ducrocq, 1833), p. xii.

14. Bon Joseph Dacier, *Tableau historique de l'érudition française, ou Rapport sur les progrès de l'histoire et de la littérature ancienne depuis 1789* (Paris: Imprimerie impériale, 1810), pp. 23, 35, 31.

15. Michel Foucault, *Discipline and Punish: The Birth of the Prison*, trans. Alan Sheridan (New York: Pantheon Books, 1977), pp. 193–4.

16. Broglie, "Éloge de Silvestre de Sacy," p. 107.

17. Sacy, *Mélanges de littérature orientale*, pp. 107, 110, 111–12.

18. Silvestre de Sacy, *Chrestomathie arabe, ou Extraits de divers écrivains arabes, tant en prose qu'en vers, avec une traduction française et des notes, à l'usage des élèves de l'École royale et spéciale des langues orientales vivantes* (vol. 1, 1826; reprint ed., Osnabrück: Biblio Verlag, 1973), p. viii.

19. For the notions of "supplementarity," "supply," and "supplication," see Jacques Derrida, *De la grammatologie* (Paris: Éditions de Minuit, 1967), p. 203 and passim.

20. For a partial list of Sacy's students and influence see Johann W. Fück, *Die Arabischen Studien in Europa bis in den Anfang des 20. Jahrhunderts* (Leipzig: Otto Harrassowitz, 1955), pp. 156–7.

21. Foucault's characterization of an archive can be found in *The Archaeology of Knowledge and the Discourse on Language*, trans. A. M. Sheridan Smith and Rupert Sawyer (New York: Pantheon Books, 1972), pp. 79–131. Gabriel Monod, one of Renan's younger and very perspicacious contemporaries, remarks that Renan was by no means a revolutionary in linguistics, archaeology, or exegesis, yet because he had the widest and the most precise learning of anyone in his period, he was its most eminent representative (*Renan, Taine, Michelet* [Paris: Calmann-Lévy, 1894], pp. 40–1). See also Jean-Louis Dumas, "La Philosophie de l'histoire de Renan," *Revue de Métaphysique et de Morale* 77, no. 1 (January–March 1972): 100–28.

22. Honoré de Balzac, *Louis Lambert* (Paris: Calmann-Lévy, n.d.), p. 4.

23. Nietzsche's remarks on philology are everywhere throughout his works. See principally his notes for "Wir Philologen" taken from his notebooks for the period January–July 1875, translated by William Arrowsmith as "Notes for 'We Philologists,'" *Arion*, N. S. ½ (1974): 279–380; also the passages on language and perspectivism in *The Will to Power*, trans. Walter Kaufmann and R. J. Hollingdale (New York: Vintage Books, 1968).

24. Ernest Renan, *L'Avenir de la science: Pensées de 1848*, 4th ed. (Paris: Calmann-Lévy, 1890), pp. 141, 142–5, 146, 148, 149.

25. Ibid., p. xiv and passim.

26. The entire opening chapter—bk. 1, chap. 1—of the *Histoire générale et système comparé des langues sémitiques*, in *Oeuvres complètes*, ed. Henriette Psichari (Paris: Calmann-Lévy, 1947–61), 8: 143–63, is a virtual encyclopedia of race prejudice directed against Semites (i.e., Moslems and Jews). The rest of the treatise is sprinkled generously with the same notions, as are many of Renan's other works, including *L'Avenir de la science*, especially Renan's notes.

27. Ernest Renan, *Correspondance; 1846–1871* (Paris: Calmann-Lévy, 1926), 1: 7–12.

28. Ernest Renan, *Souvenirs d'enfance et de jeunesse*, in *Oeuvres complètes*, 2: 892. Two works by Jean Pommier treat Renan's mediation between religion and philology in valuable detail: *Renan, d'après des documents inédits* (Paris: Perrin, 1923), pp. 48–68, and *La Jeunesse cléricale d'Ernest Renan* (Paris: Les Belles Lettres, 1933). There is a more recent account in J. Chaix-Ruy, *Ernest Renan* (Paris: Emmanuel Vitte, 1956), pp. 89–111. The standard description—done more in terms of Renan's religious vocation—is still valuable also: Pierre Lasserre, *La Jeunesse d'Ernest Renan: Histoire de la crise religieuse au XIXᵉ siècle*, 3 vols. (Paris: Garnier Frères, 1925). In vol. 2, pp. 50–166 and 265–98 are useful on the relations between philology, philosophy, and science.

29. Ernest Renan, "Des services rendus aux sciences historiques par la philologie," in *Oeuvres complètes* 8: 1228.

30. Renan, *Souvenirs*, p. 892.

31. Foucault, *The Order of Things*, pp. 290–300. Along with the discrediting of the Edenic origins of language, a number of other events—the Deluge, the building of the Tower Babel—also were discredited as explanations. The most comprehensive history of theories of linguistic origin is Arno Borst, *Der Turmbau von Babel: Geschichte der Meinungen über Ursprung und Vielfalt der Sprachen und Volker*, 6 vols. (Stuttgart: Anton Hiersemann, 1957–63).

32. Quoted by Raymond Schwab, *La Renaissance orientale* (Paris: Payot, 1950), p. 69. On the dangers of too quickly succumbing to generalities about Oriental discoveries, see the reflections of the distinguished contemporary Sinologist Abel Rémusat, *Mélanges postumes d'histoire et littérature orientales* (Paris: Imprimerie royale, 1843), p. 226 and passim.

33. Samuel Taylor Coleridge, *Biographia Literaria*, chap. 16, in *Selected Poetry and Prose of Coleridge*, ed. Donald A. Stauffer (New York: Random House, 1951), pp. 276–7.

34. Benjamin Constant, *Oeuvres*, ed. Alfred Roulin (Paris: Gallimard, 1957), p. 78.

35. Abrams, *Natural Supernaturalism*, p. 29.

36. Renan, *De l'origine du langage*, in *Oeuvres complètes*, 8: 122.

37. Renan, "De la part des peuples sémitiques dans l'histoire de la civilisation," in *Oeuvres complètes*, 2: 320.

38. Ibid., p. 333.

39. Renan, "Trois Professeurs au Collège de France: Étienne Quatremère," in *Oeuvres complètes*, 1: 129. Renan was not wrong about Quatremère, who had a talent for picking interesting subjects to study and then making them quite uninteresting. See his essays "Le Goût des livres chez les orientaux" and "Des sciences chez les arabes," in his *Mélanges d'histoire et de philologie orientales* (Paris: E. Ducrocq, 1861), pp. 1–57.

40. Honoré de Balzac, *La Peau de chagrin*, vol. 9 (*Études philosophiques* 1) of *La Comédie humaine*, ed. Marcel Bouteron (Paris: Gallimard, 1950), p. 39; Renan, *Histoire générale des langues sémitiques*, p. 134.

41. See, for instance, *De l'origine du langage*, p. 102, and *Histoire générale*, p. 180.

42. Renan, *L'Avenir de la science*, p. 23. The whole passage reads as follows: "Pour moi, je ne connais qu'un seul résultat à la science, c'est de résoudre l'énigme, c'est de dire définitivement à l'homme le mot des choses, c'est de l'expliquer à lui-même, c'est de lui donner, au nom de la seule autorité légitime qui est la nature humaine toute entière, le symbole que les religions lui donnaient tout fait et qu'ils ne peut plus accepter."

43. See Madeleine V.-David, *Le Débat sur les écritures et l'hiéroglyphe aux XVIIᵉ et XVIIIᵉ siècles et l'application de la notion de déchiffrement aux écritures mortes* (Paris: S.E.V.P.E.N., 1965), p. 130.

44. Renan is mentioned only in passing in Schwab's *La Renaissance orientale*, not at all in Foucault's *The Order of Things*, and only somewhat disparagingly in Holger Pederson's *The Discovery of Language: Linguistic Science in the Nineteenth Century*, trans. John Webster Spargo (1931; reprint ed., Bloomington: Indiana University Press, 1972). Max Müller in his *Lectures on the Science of Language* (1861–64; reprint ed., New York: Scribner, Armstrong, & Co., 1875) and Gustave Dugat in his *Histoire des orientalistes de l'Europe du XIIe au XIXe siècle*, 2 vols. (Paris: Adrien Maisonneuve, 1868–70) do not mention Renan at all. James Darmesteter's *Essais Orientaux* (Paris: A. Lévy, 1883)—whose first item is a history, "L'Orientalisme en France"—is dedicated to Renan but does not mention his contribution. There are half-a-dozen short notices of Renan's production in Jules Mohl's encyclopedic (and extremely valuable) quasi-logbook, *Vingt-sept ans d'histoire des études orientales: Rapports faits à la Société asiatique de Paris de 1840 à 1867*, 2 vols. (Paris: Reinwald, 1879–80).

45. In works dealing with race and racism Renan occupies a position of some importance. He is treated in the following: Ernest Seillière, *La Philosophie de l'impérialisme*, 4 vols. (Paris: Plon, 1903–8); Théophile Simar, *Étude critique sur la formation de la doctrine des races au XVIIIe siècle et son expansion au XIXe siècle* (Brussels: Hayez, 1922); Erich Voegelin, *Rasse und Staat* (Tübingen: J. C. B. Mohr, 1933), and here one must also mention his *Die Rassenidee in der Geistesgeschichte von Ray bis Carus* (Berlin: Junker und Dunnhaupt, 1933), which, although it does not deal with Renan's period, is an important complement to *Rasse und Staat*; Jacques Barzun, *Race: A Study in Modern Superstition* (New York: Harcourt, Brace & Co., 1937).

46. In *La Renaissance orientale* Schwab has some brilliant pages on the museum, on the parallelism between biology and linguistics, and on Cuvier, Balzac, and others; see p. 323 and passim. On the library and its importance for mid-nineteenth-century culture, see Foucault, "La Bibliothèque fantastique," which is his preface to Flaubert's *La Tentation de Saint Antoine* (Paris: Gallimard, 1971), pp. 7–33. I am indebted to Professor Eugenio Donato for drawing my attention to these matters; see his "A Mere Labyrinth of Letters: Flaubert and the Quest for Fiction," *Modern Language Notes* 89, no. 6 (December 1974): 885–910.

47. Renan, *Histoire générale*, pp. 145–6.

48. See *L'Avenir de la science*, p. 508 and passim.

49. Renan, *Histoire générale*, p. 214.

50. Ibid., p. 527. This idea goes back to Friedrich Schlegel's distinction between organic and agglutinative languages, of which latter type Semitic is an instance. Humboldt makes the same distinction, as have most Orientalists since Renan.

51. Ibid., pp. 531–2.

52. Ibid., p. 515 and passim.

53. See Jean Seznec, *Nouvelles Études sur "La Tentation de Saint Antoine"* (London: Warburg Institute, 1949), p. 80.

54. See Étienne Geoffroy Saint-Hilaire, *Philosophie anatomique: Des monstruosités humaines* (Paris: published by the author, 1822). The complete title of Isidore Geoffroy Saint-Hilaire's work is: *Histoire générale et particulière des anomalies de l'organisation chez l'homme et les animaux, ouvrage comprenante des recherches sur les caractères, la classification, l'influence physiologique et pathologique, les rapports généraux, les lois et les causes des monstruosités, des variétés et vices de conformation, ou traité de tératologie*, 3 vols. (Paris: J.-B. Baillière, 1832–36). There are some valuable pages on Goethe's biological ideas in Erich Heller, *The Disinherited Mind* (New York: Meridian Books, 1959), pp. 3–34. See also Jacob, *The Logic of Life*, and Canguilhem, *La Connaissance de la vie*, pp. 174–84, for

very interesting accounts of the Saint-Hilaires' place in the development of the life sciences.

55. E. Saint-Hilaire, *Philosophie anatomique*, pp. xxii–xxiii.

56. Renan, *Histoire générale*, p. 156.

57. Renan, *Oeuvres complètes*, 1: 621–2 and passim. See H. W. Wardman, *Ernest Renan: A Critical Biography* (London: Athlone Press, 1964), p. 66 and passim, for a subtle description of Renan's domestic life; although one would not wish to force a parallel between Renan's biography and what I have called his "masculine" world, Wardman's descriptions here are suggestive indeed—at least to me.

58. Renan, "Des services rendus au sciences historiques par la philologie," in *Oeuvres complètes*, 8: 1228, 1232.

59. Ernst Cassirer, *The Problem of Knowledge: Philosophy, Science, and History since Hegel*, trans. William H. Woglom and Charles W. Hendel (New Haven, Conn.: Yale University Press, 1950), p. 307.

60. Renan, "Réponse au discours de réception de M. de Lesseps (23 avril 1885)," in *Oeuvres complètes*, 1: 817. Yet the value of being truly contemporary was best shown with reference to Renan by Sainte-Beuve in his articles of June 1862. See also Donald G. Charlton, *Positivist Thought in France During the Second Empire* (Oxford: Clarendon Press, 1959), and his *Secular Religions in France*. Also Richard M. Chadbourne, "Renan and Sainte-Beuve," *Romanic Review* 44, no. 2 (April 1953): 126–35.

61. Renan, *Oeuvres complètes*, 8: 156.

62. In his letter of June 26, 1856, to Gobineau, *Oeuvres complètes*, 10: 203–4. Gobineau's ideas were expressed in his *Essai sur l'inégalité des races humaines* (1853–55).

63. Cited by Albert Hourani in his excellent article "Islam and the Philosophers of History," p. 222.

64. Caussin de Perceval, *Essai sur l'histoire des Arabes avant l'Islamisme, pendant l'époque de Mahomet et jusqu'à la réduction de toutes les tribus sous la loi musulmane* (1847–48; reprint ed., Graz, Austria: Akademische Druck- und Verlagsanstalt, 1967), 3: 332–9.

65. Thomas Carlyle, *On Heroes, Hero-Worship, and the Heroic in History* (1841; reprint ed., New York: Longmans, Green & Co., 1906), p. 63.

66. Macaulay's Indian experiences are described by G. Otto Trevelyan, *The Life and Letters of Lord Macaulay* (New York: Harper & Brothers, 1875), 1: 344–71. The complete text of Macaulay's "Minute" is conveniently to be found in Philip D. Curtin, ed., *Imperialism: The Documentary History of Western Civilization* (New York: Walker & Co., 1971), pp. 178–91. Some consequences of Macaulay's views for British Orientalism are discussed in A. J. Arberry, *British Orientalists* (London: William Collins, 1943).

67. John Henry Newman, *The Turks in Their Relation to Europe*, vol. 1 of his *Historical Sketches* (1853; reprint ed., London: Longmans, Green & Co., 1920).

68. See Marguerite-Louise Ancelot, *Salons de Paris, foyers éteints* (Paris: Jules Tardieu, 1858).

69. Karl Marx, *Surveys from Exile*, ed. David Fernbach (London: Pelican Books, 1973), pp. 306–7.

70. Ibid., p. 320.

71. Edward William Lane, Author's Preface to *An Account of the Manners and Customs of the Modern Egyptians* (1836; reprint ed., London: J. M. Dent, 1936), pp. xx, xxi.

72. Ibid., p. 1.

73. Ibid., pp. 160–1. The standard biography of Lane, published in 1877, was by his great-nephew, Stanley Lane-Poole. There is a sympathetic account of Lane by A. J. Arberry in his *Oriental Essays: Portraits of Seven Scholars* (New York: Macmillan Co., 1960), pp. 87–121.

74. Frederick Eden Pargiter, ed., *Centenary Volume of the Royal Asiatic Society of Great Britain and Ireland, 1823–1923* (London: Royal Asiatic Society, 1923), p. x.

75. *Société asiatique: Livre du centenaire, 1822–1922* (Paris: Paul Geuthner, 1922), pp. 5–6.

76. Johann Wolfgang von Goethe, *Westöstlicher Diwan* (1819; reprint ed., Munich: Wilhelm Golmann, 1958), pp. 8–9, 12. Sacy's name is invoked with veneration in Goethe's apparatus for the *Diwan*.

77. Victor Hugo, *Les Orientales*, in *Oeuvres poétiques*, ed. Pierre Albouy (Paris: Gallimard, 1964), 1: 616–18.

78. François-René de Chateaubriand, *Oeuvres romanesques et voyages*, ed. Maurice Regard (Paris: Gallimard, 1969), 2: 702.

79. See Henri Bordeaux, *Voyageurs d'Orient: Des pélerins aux méharistes de Palmyre* (Paris: Plon, 1926). I have found useful the theoretical ideas about pilgrims and pilgrimages contained in Victor Turner, *Dramas, Fields, and Metaphors: Symbolic Action in Human Society* (Ithaca, N.Y.: Cornell University Press, 1974), pp. 166–230.

80. Hassan al-Nouty, *Le Proche-Orient dans la littérature française de Nerval à Barrès* (Paris: Nizet, 1958), pp. 47–8, 277, 272.

81. Chateaubriand, *Oeuvres*, 2: 702 and note, 1684, 769–70, 769, 701, 808, 908.

82. Ibid., pp. 1011, 979, 990, 1052.

83. Ibid., p. 1069.

84. Ibid., p. 1031.

85. Ibid., p. 999.

86. Ibid., pp. 1126–27, 1049.

87. Ibid., p. 1137.

88. Ibid., pp. 1148, 1214.

89. Alphonse de Lamartine, *Voyage en Orient* (1835; reprint ed., Paris: Hachette, 1887), 1: 10, 48–9, 179, 178, 148, 189, 118, 245–6, 251.

90. Ibid., 1: 363; 2: 74–5; 1: 475.

91. Ibid., 2: 92–3.

92. Ibid., 2: 526–7, 533. Two important works on French writers in the Orient are Jean-Marie Carré, *Voyageurs et écrivains français en Égypte*, 2 vols. (Cairo: Institut français d'archéologie orientale, 1932), and Moënis Taha-Hussein, *Le Romantisme français et l'Islam* (Beirut: Dar-el-Maeref, 1962).

93. Gérard de Nerval, *Les Filles du feu*, in *Oeuvres*, ed. Albert Béguin and Jean Richet (Paris: Gallimard, 1960), 1: 297–8.

94. Mario Praz, *The Romantic Agony*, trans. Angus Davison (Cleveland, Ohio: World Publishing Co., 1967).

95. Jean Bruneau, *Le "Conte Orientale" de Flaubert* (Paris: Denoel, 1973), p. 79.

96. These are all considered by Bruneau in *ibid.*

97. Nerval, *Voyage en Orient*, in *Oeuvres*, 2: 68, 194, 96, 342.

98. Ibid., p. 181.

99. Michel Butor, "Travel and Writing," trans. John Powers and K. Lisker, *Mosaic* 8, no. 1 (Fall 1974): 13.

100. Nerval, *Voyage en Orient*, p. 628.

101. Ibid., pp. 706, 718.

102. *Flaubert in Egypt: A Sensibility on Tour*, trans. and ed. Francis Steegmuller (Boston: Little, Brown & Co., 1973), p. 200. I have also consulted the following texts, in which all Flaubert's "Oriental" material is to be found: *Oeuvres complètes de Gustave Flaubert* (Paris: Club de l'Honnête homme, 1973), vols. 10, 11; *Les Lettres d'Égypte, de Gustave Flaubert*, ed. A. Youssef Naaman (Paris: Nizet, 1965); Flaubert, *Correspondance*, ed. Jean Bruneau (Paris, Gallimard, 1973), 1: 518 ff.

103. Harry Levin, *The Gates of Horn: A Study of Five French Realists* (New York: Oxford University Press, 1963), p. 285.

104. *Flaubert in Egypt*, pp. 173, 75.

105. Levin, *Gates of Horn*, p. 271.

106. Flaubert, *Catalogue des opinions chic*, in *Oeuvres*, 2: 1019.

107. *Flaubert in Egypt*, p. 65.

108. Ibid., pp. 220, 130.

109. Flaubert, *La Tentation de Saint Antoine*, in *Oeuvres*, 1: 85.

110. See Flaubert, *Salammbô*, in *Oeuvres*, 1: 809 ff. See also Maurice Z. Shroder, "On Reading *Salammbô*," *L'Esprit créateur* 10, no. 1 (Spring 1970): 24–35.

111. *Flaubert in Egypt*, pp. 198–9.

112. Foucault, "La Bibliothèque fantastique," in Flaubert, *La Tentation de Saint Antoine*, pp. 7–33.

113. *Flaubert in Egypt*, p. 79.

114. Ibid., pp. 211–2.

115. For a discussion of this process see Foucault, *Archaeology of Knowledge*; also Joseph Ben-David, *The Scientist's Role in Society* (Englewood Cliffs, N.J.: Prentice-Hall, 1971). See also Edward W. Said, "An Ethics of Language," *Diacritics* 4, no. 2 (Summer 1974): 28–37.

116. See the invaluable listings in Richard Bevis, *Bibliotheca Cisorientalia: An Annotated Checklist of Early English Travel Books on the Near and Middle East* (Boston: G. K. Hall & Co., 1973).

117. For discussions of the American travelers see Dorothee Metlitski Finkelstein, *Melville's Orienda* (New Haven, Conn.: Yale University Press, 1961), and Franklin Walker, *Irreverent Pilgrims: Melville, Browne, and Mark Twain in the Holy Land* (Seattle; University of Washington Press, 1974).

118. Alexander William Kinglake, *Eothen, or Traces of Travel Brought Home from the East*, ed. D. G. Hogarth (1844; reprint ed., London: Henry Frowde, 1906), pp. 25, 68, 241, 220.

119. *Flaubert in Egypt*, p. 81.

120. Thomas J. Assad, *Three Victorian Travellers: Burton, Blunt and Doughty* (London: Routledge & Kegan Paul, 1964), p. 5.

121. Richard Burton, *Personal Narrative of a Pilgrimage to al-Madinah and Meccah*, ed. Isabel Burton (London: Tylston & Edwards, 1893), 1: 9, 108–10.

122. Richard Burton, "Terminal Essay," in *The Book of the Thousand and One Nights* (London: Burton Club, 1886), 10: 63–302.

123. Burton, *Pilgrimage*, 1: 112, 114.

Chapter 3. Orientalism Now

1. Friedrich Nietzsche, "On Truth and Lie in an Extra-Moral Sense," in *The Portable Nietzsche*, ed. and trans. Walter Kaufmann (New York: Viking Press, 1954), pp. 46–7.

2. The number of Arab travelers to the West is estimated and considered by Ibrahim Abu-Lughod in *Arab Rediscovery of Europe: A Study in Cultural Encounters* (Princeton, N.J.: Princeton University Press, 1963), pp. 75–6 and passim.

3. See Philip D. Curtin, ed., *Imperialism: The Documentary History of Western Civilization* (New York: Walker & Co., 1972), pp. 73–105.

4. See Johann W. Fück, "Islam as an Historical Problem in European Historiography since 1800," in *Historians of the Middle East*, ed. Bernard Lewis and P. M. Holt (London: Oxford University Press, 1962), p. 307.

5. Ibid., p. 309.

6. See Jacques Waardenburg, *L'Islam dans le miroir de l'Occident* (The Hague: Mouton & Co., 1963).

7. Ibid., p. 311.

8. P. Masson-Oursel, "La Connaissance scientifique de l'Asie en France depuis 1900 et les variétés de l'Orientalisme," *Revue Philosophique* 143, nos. 7–9 (July–September 1953): 345.

9. Evelyn Baring, Lord Cromer, *Modern Egypt* (New York: Macmillan Co., 1908), 2: 237–8.

10. Evelyn Baring, Lord Cromer, *Ancient and Modern Imperialism* (London: John Murray, 1910), pp. 118, 120.

11. George Nathaniel Curzon, *Subjects of the Day: Being a Selection of Speeches and Writings* (London: George Allen & Unwin, 1915), pp. 4–5, 10, 28.

12. Ibid., pp. 184, 191–2. For the history of the school, see C. H. Phillips, *The School of Oriental and African Studies, University of London, 1917–1967: An Introduction* (London: Design for Print, 1967).

13. Eric Stokes, *The English Utilitarians and India* (Oxford: Clarendon Press, 1959).

14. Cited in Michael Edwardes, *High Noon of Empire: India Under Curzon* (London: Eyre & Spottiswoode, 1965), pp. 38–9.

15. Curzon, *Subjects of the Day*, pp. 155–6.

16. Joseph Conrad, *Heart of Darkness*, in *Youth and Two Other Stories* (Garden City, N.Y.: Doubleday, Page, 1925), p. 52.

17. For an illustrative extract from de Vattel's work see Curtin, ed., *Imperialism*, pp. 42–5.

18. Cited by M. de Caix, *La Syrie* in Gabriel Hanotaux, *Histoire des colonies françaises*, 6 vols. (Paris: Société de l'histoire nationale, 1929–33), 3: 481.

19. These details are to be found in Vernon McKay, "Colonialism in the French Geographical Movement," *Geographical Review* 33, no. 2 (April 1943): 214–32.

20. Agnes Murphy, *The Ideology of French Imperialism, 1817–1881* (Washington: Catholic University of America Press, 1948), pp. 46, 54, 36, 45.

21. Ibid., pp. 189, 110, 136.

22. Jukka Nevakivi, *Britain, France, and the Arab Middle East, 1914–1920* (London: Athlone Press, 1969), p. 13.

23. Ibid., p. 24.

24. D. G. Hogarth, *The Penetration of Arabia: A Record of the Development of Western Knowledge Concerning The Arabian Peninsula* (New York: Frederick A. Stokes, 1904). There is a good recent book on the same subject: Robin Bidwell, *Travellers in Arabia* (London: Paul Hamlyn, 1976).

25. Edmond Bremond, *Le Hedjaz dans la guerre mondiale* (Paris: Payot, 1931), pp. 242 ff.

26. Le Comte de Cressaty, *Les Intérêts de la France en Syrie* (Paris: Floury, 1913).

27. Rudyard Kipling, *Verse* (Garden City, N.Y.: Doubleday & Co., 1954), p. 280.

28. The themes of exclusion and confinement in nineteenth-century culture have played an important role in Michel Foucault's work, most recently in his *Discipline and Punish: The Birth of the Prison* (New York: Pantheon Books, 1977), and *The History of Sexuality, Volume I: An Introduction* (New York: Pantheon Books, 1978).

29. *The Letters of T. E. Lawrence of Arabia*, ed. David Garnett (1938; reprint ed., London: Spring Books, 1964), p. 244.

30. Gertrude Bell, *The Desert and the Sown* (London: William Heinemann, 1907), p. 244.

31. Gertrude Bell, *From Her Personal Papers, 1889–1914*, ed. Elizabeth Burgoyne (London: Ernest Benn, 1958), p. 204.

32. William Butler Yeats, "Byzantium," *The Collected Poems* (New York: Macmillan Co., 1959), p. 244.

33. Stanley Diamond, *In Search of the Primitive: A Critique of Civilization* (New Brunswick, N.J.: Transaction Books, 1974), p. 119.

34. See Harry Bracken, "Essence, Accident and Race," *Hermathena* 116 (Winter 1973): pp. 81–96.

35. George Eliot, *Middlemarch: A Study of Provincial Life* (1872; reprint ed., Boston: Houghton Mifflin Co., 1956), p. 13.

36. Lionel Trilling, *Matthew Arnold* (1939; reprint ed., New York: Meridian Books, 1955), p. 214.

37. See Hannah Arendt, *The Origins of Totalitarianism* (New York: Harcourt Brace Jovanovich, 1973), p. 180, note 55.

38. W. Robertson Smith, *Kinship and Marriage in Early Arabia*, ed.

Stanley Cook (1907; reprint ed., Oesterhout, N.B.: Anthropological Publications, 1966), pp. xiii, 241.

39. W. Robertson Smith, *Lectures and Essays*, ed. John Sutherland Black and George Chrystal (London: Adam & Charles Black, 1912), pp. 492–3.

40. Ibid., pp. 492, 493, 511, 500, 498–9.

41. Charles M. Doughty, *Travels in Arabia Deserta*, 2nd ed., 2 vols. (New York: Random House, n.d.), 1: 95. See also the excellent article by Richard Bevis, "Spiritual Geology: C. M. Doughty and the Land of the Arabs," *Victorian Studies* 16 (December 1972), 163–81.

42. T. E. Lawrence, *The Seven Pillars of Wisdom: A Triumph* (1926; reprint ed., Garden City, N.Y.: Doubleday, Doran & Co., 1935), p. 28.

43. For a discussion of this see Talal Asad, "Two European Images of Non-European Rule," in *Anthropology and the Colonial Encounter*, ed. Talal Asad (London: Ithaca Press, 1975), pp. 103–18.

44. Arendt, *Origins of Totalitarianism*, p. 218.

45. T. E. Lawrence, *Oriental Assembly*, ed. A. W. Lawrence (New York: E. P. Dutton & Co., 1940), p. 95.

46. Cited in Stephen Ely Tabachnick, "The Two Veils of T. E. Lawrence," *Studies in the Twentieth Century* 16 (Fall 1975): 96–7.

47. Lawrence, *Seven Pillars of Wisdom*, pp. 42–3, 661.

48. Ibid., pp. 549, 550–2.

49. E. M. Forster, *A Passage to India* (1924; reprint ed., New York: Harcourt, Brace & Co., 1952), p. 322.

50. Maurice Barrès, *Une Enquête aux pays du Levant* (Paris: Plon, 1923), 1: 20; 2: 181, 192, 193, 197.

51. D. G. Hogarth, *The Wandering Scholar* (London: Oxford University Press, 1924). Hogarth describes his style as that of "the explorer first and the scholar second" (p. 4).

52. Cited by H. A. R. Gibb, "Structure of Religious Thought in Islam," in his *Studies on the Civilization of Islam*, ed. Stanford J. Shaw and William R. Polk (Boston: Beacon Press, 1962), p. 180.

53. Frédéric Lefèvre, "Une Heure avec Sylvain Lévi," in *Mémorial Sylvain Lévi*, ed. Jacques Bacot (Paris: Paul Hartmann, 1937), pp. 123–4.

54. Paul Valéry, *Oeuvres*, ed. Jean Hytier (Paris: Gallimard, 1960), 2: 1556–7.

55. Cited in Christopher Sykes, *Crossroads to Israel* (1965; reprint ed., Bloomington: Indiana University Press, 1973), p. 5.

56. Cited in Alan Sandison, *The Wheel of Empire: A Study of the Imperial Idea in Some Late Nineteenth and Early Twentieth Century Fiction* (New York: St. Martin's Press, 1967), p. 158. An excellent study of the French equivalent is Martine Astier Loutfi, *Littérature et colonialisme: L'Expansion coloniale vue dans la littérature romanesque française, 1871–1914* (The Hague: Mouton & Co., 1971).

57. Paul Valéry, *Variété* (Paris: Gallimard, 1924), p. 43.

58. George Orwell, "Marrakech," in *A Collection of Essays* (New York: Doubleday Anchor Books, 1954), p. 187.

59. Valentine Chirol, *The Occident and the Orient* (Chicago: University of Chicago Press, 1924), p. 6.

60. Élie Faure, "Orient et Occident," *Mercure de France* 229 (July 1–August 1, 1931): 263, 264, 269, 270, 272.

61. Fernand Baldensperger, "Où s'affrontent l'Orient et l'Occident intellectuels," in *Études d'histoire littéraire*, 3rd ser. (Paris: Droz, 1939), p. 230.

62. I. A. Richards, *Mencius on the Mind: Experiments in Multiple Definitions* (London: Routledge & Kegan Paul, 1932), p. xiv.

63. *Selected Works of C. Snouck Hurgronje*, ed. G. H. Bousquet and J. Schacht (Leiden: E. J. Brill, 1957), p. 267.

64. H. A. R. Gibb, "Literature," in *The Legacy of Islam*, ed. Thomas Arnold and Alfred Guillaume (Oxford: Clarendon Press, 1931), p. 209.

65. The best general account of this period in political, social, economic, and cultural terms is to be found in Jacques Berque, *Egypt: Imperialism and Revolution*, trans. Jean Stewart (New York: Praeger Publishers, 1972).

66. There is a useful account of the intellectual project informing their work in Arthur R. Evans, Jr., ed., *On Four Modern Humanists: Hofmannsthal, Gundolf, Curtius, Kantorowicz* (Princeton, N.J.: Princeton University Press, 1970).

67. Erich Auerbach, *Mimesis: The Representation of Reality in Western Literature*, trans. Willard R. Trask (1946; reprint ed., Princeton, N.J.: Princeton University Press, 1968), and his *Literary Language and Its Public in Late Latin Antiquity and in the Middle Ages*, trans. Ralph Manheim (New York: Bollingen Books, 1965).

68. Erich Auerbach, "Philology and *Weltliteratur*," trans. M. and E. W. Said, *Centennial Review* 13, no. 1 (Winter 1969): 11.

69. Ibid., p. 17.

70. For example, in H. Stuart Hughes, *Consciousness and Society: The Reconstruction of European Social Thought, 1890–1930* (1958; reprint ed., New York: Vintage Books, 1961).

71. See Anwar Abdel Malek, "Orientalism in Crisis," *Diogenes* 44 (Winter 1963): 103–40.

72. R. N. Cust, "The International Congresses of Orientalists," *Hellas* 6, no. 4 (1897): 349.

73. See W. F. Wertheim, "Counter-insurgency Research at the Turn of the Century—Snouck Hurgronje and the Acheh War," *Sociologische Gids* 19 (September–December 1972).

74. Sylvain Lévi, "Les Parts respectives des nations occidentales dans les progrès de l'indianisme," in *Mémorial Sylvain Lévi*, p. 116.

75. H. A. R. Gibb, "Louis Massignon (1882–1962)," *Journal of the Royal Asiatic Society* (1962), pp. 120, 121.

76. Louis Massignon, *Opera Minora*, ed. Y. Moubarac (Beirut: Dar-el-Maaref, 1963), 3: 114. I have used the complete bibliography of Massignon's work by Moubarac: *L'Oeuvre de Louis Massignon* (Beirut: Éditions du Cénacle libanais, 1972–73).

77. Massignon, "L'Occident devant l'Orient: Primauté d'une solution culturelle," in *Opera Minora*, 1: 208–23.

78. Ibid., p. 169.

79. See Waardenburg, *L'Islam dans le miroir de l'Occident*, pp. 147, 183, 186, 192, 211, 213.

80. Massignon, *Opera Minora*, 1: 227.

81. Ibid., p. 355.

82. Quoted from Massignon's essay on Biruni in Waardenburg, *L'Islam dans le miroir de l'Occident*, p. 225.

83. Massignon, *Opera Minora*, 3: 526.

84. Ibid., pp. 610–11.

85. Ibid., p. 212. Also p. 211 for another attack on the British, and pp. 423–7 for his assessment of Lawrence.

86. Quoted in Waardenburg, *L'Islam dans le miroir de l'Occident*, p. 219.

87. Ibid., pp. 218–19.

88. See A. L. Tibawi, "English-Speaking Orientalists: A Critique of Their Approach to Islam and Arab Nationalism, Part I," *Islamic Quarterly* 8, nos. 1, 2 (January–June 1964): 25–44; "Part II," *Islamic Quarterly* 8, nos. 3, 4 (July–December 1964): 73–88.

89. "Une figure domine tous les genres [of Orientalist work], celle de Louis Massignon": Claude Cahen and Charles Pellat, "Les Études arabes et islamiques," *Journal asiatique* 261, nos. 1, 4 (1973): 104. There is a very detailed survey of the Islamic-Orientalist field to be found in Jean Sauvaget, *Introduction à l'histoire de l'Orient musulman: Éléments de bibliographie*, ed. Claude Cahen (Paris: Adrien Maisonneuve, 1961).

90. William Polk, "Sir Hamilton Gibb Between Orientalism and History," *International Journal of Middle East Studies* 6, no. 2 (April 1975): 131–9. I have used the bibliography of Gibb's work in *Arabic and Islamic Studies in Honor of Hamilton A. R. Gibb*, ed. George Makdisi (Cambridge, Mass.: Harvard University Press, 1965), pp. 1–20.

91. H. A. R. Gibb, "Oriental Studies in the United Kingdom," in *The Near East and the Great Powers*, ed. Richard N. Frye (Cambridge, Mass.: Harvard University Press, 1951), pp. 86–7.

92. Albert Hourani, "Sir Hamilton Gibb, 1895–1971," *Proceedings of the British Academy* 58 (1972): p. 504.

93. Duncan Black Macdonald, *The Religious Attitude and Life in Islam* (1909; reprint ed., Beirut: Khayats Publishers, 1965), pp. 2–11.

94. H. A. R. Gibb, "Whither Islam?" in *Whither Islam? A Survey of Modern Movements in the Moslem World*, ed. H. A. R. Gibb (London: Victor Gollancz, 1932), pp. 328, 387.

95. Ibid., p. 335.

96. Ibid., p. 377.

97. H. A. R. Gibb, "The Influence of Islamic Culture on Medieval Europe," *John Rylands Library Bulletin* 38, no. 1 (September 1955): 98.

98. H. A. R. Gibb, *Mohammedanism: An Historical Survey* (London: Oxford University Press, 1949), pp. 2, 9, 84.

99. Ibid., pp. 111, 88, 189.

100. H. A. R. Gibb, *Modern Trends in Islam* (Chicago: University of Chicago Press, 1947), pp. 108, 113, 123.

101. Both essays are to be found in Gibb's *Studies on the Civilization of Islam*, pp. 176–208 and 3–33.

102. R. Emmett Tyrell, Jr., "Chimera in the Middle East," *Harper's*, November 1976, pp. 35–8.

103. Cited in Ayad al-Qazzaz, Ruth Afiyo, et al., *The Arabs in American Textbooks*, California State Board of Education, June 1975, pp. 10, 15.

104. "Statement of Purpose," *MESA Bulletin* 1, no. 1 (May 1967): 33.

105. Morroe Berger, "Middle Eastern and North African Studies: Developments and Needs," *MESA Bulletin* 1, no. 2 (November 1967): 16.

106. Menachem Mansoor, "Present State of Arabic Studies in the United States," in *Report on Current Research 1958*, ed. Kathleen H. Brown (Washington: Middle East Institute, 1958), pp. 55–6.

107. Harold Lasswell, "Propaganda," *Encyclopedia of the Social Sciences* (1934), 12: 527. I owe this reference to Professor Noam Chomsky.

108. Marcel Proust, *The Guermantes Way*, trans. C. K. Scott Moncrieff (1925; reprint ed., New York: Vintage Books, 1970), p. 135.

109. Nathaniel Schmidt, "Early Oriental Studies in Europe and the Work of the American Oriental Society, 1842–1922," *Journal of the American Oriental Society* 43 (1923): 11. See also E. A. Speiser, "Near Eastern Studies in America, 1939–45," *Archiv Orientalni* 16 (1948): 76–88.

110. As an instance there is Henry Jessup, *Fifty-Three Years in Syria*, 2 vols. (New York: Fleming H. Revell, 1910).

111. For the connection between the issuing of the Balfour Declaration and United States war policy, see Doreen Ingrams, *Palestine Papers 1917–1922: Seeds of Conflict* (London: Cox & Syman, 1972), pp. 10 ff.

112. Mortimer Graves, "A Cultural Relations Policy in the Near East," in *The Near East and the Great Powers*, ed. Frye, pp. 76, 78.

113. George Camp Keiser, "The Middle East Institute: Its Inception and Its Place in American International Studies," in *The Near East and the Great Powers*, ed. Frye, pp. 80, 84.

114. For an account of this migration, see *The Intellectual Migration: Europe and America, 1930–1960*, ed. Donald Fleming and Bernard Bailyn (Cambridge, Mass.: Harvard University Press, 1969).

115. Gustave von Grunebaum, *Modern Islam: The Search for Cultural Identity* (New York: Vintage Books, 1964), pp. 55, 261.

116. Abdullah Laroui, "Pour une méthodologie des études islamiques: L'Islam au miroir de Gustave von Grunebaum," *Diogène* 38 (July–September 1973): 30. This essay has been collected in Laroui's *The Crisis of the Arab Intellectuals: Traditionalism or Historicism?* trans. Diarmid Cammell (Berkeley: University of California Press, 1976).

117. David Gordon, *Self-Determination and History in the Third World* (Princeton, N.J.: Princeton University Press, 1971).

118. Laroui, "Pour une méthodologie des études islamiques," p. 41.

119. Manfred Halpern, "Middle East Studies: A Review of the State of the Field with a Few Examples," *World Politics* 15 (October 1962): 121–2.

120. Ibid., p. 117.

121. Leonard Binder, "1974 Presidential Address," *MESA Bulletin* 9, no. 1 (February 1975): 2.

122. Ibid., p. 5.

123. "Middle East Studies Network in the United States," *MERIP Reports* 38 (June 1975): 5.

124. The two best critical reviews of the *Cambridge History* are by Albert Hourani, *The English Historical Review* 87, no. 343 (April 1972): 348–57, and Roger Owen, *Journal of Interdisciplinary History* 4, no. 2 (Autumn 1973): 287–98.

125. P. M. Holt, Introduction, *The Cambridge History of Islam*, ed. P. M. Holt, Anne K. S. Lambton, and Bernard Lewis, 2 vols. (Cambridge: Cambridge University Press, 1970), 1: xi.

126. D. Sourdel, "The Abbasid Caliphate," *Cambridge History of Islam*, ed. Holt et al., 1: 121.

127. Z. N. Zeine, "The Arab Lands," *Cambridge History of Islam*, ed. Holt et al., 1: 575.

128. Dankwart A. Rustow, "The Political Impact of the West," *Cambridge History of Islam*, ed. Holt et al., 1: 697.

129. Cited in Ingrams, *Palestine Papers, 1917–1922*, pp. 31–2.

130. Robert Alter, "Rhetoric and the Arab Mind," *Commentary*, October 1968, pp. 61–85. Alter's article was an adulatory review of General Yehoshafat Harkabi's *Arab Attitudes to Israel* (Jerusalem: Keter Press, 1972).

131. Gil Carl Alroy, "Do The Arabs Want Peace?" *Commentary*, February 1974, pp. 56–61.

132. Roland Barthes, *Mythologies*, trans. Annette Lavers (New York: Hill & Wang, 1972), pp. 109–59.

133. Raphael Patai, *Golden River to Golden Road: Society, Culture, and Change in the Middle East* (Philadelphia: University of Pennsylvania Press, 1962; 3rd rev. ed., 1969), p. 406.

134. Raphael Patai, *The Arab Mind* (New York: Charles Scribner's Sons, 1973). For an even more racist work see John Laffin, *The Arab Mind Considered: A Need for Understanding* (New York: Taplinger Publishing Co., 1976).

135. Sania Hamady, *Temperament and Character of the Arabs* (New York: Twayne Publishers, 1960), p. 100. Hamady's book is a favorite amongst Israelis and Israeli apologists; Alroy cites her approvingly, and so does Amos Elon in *The Israelis: Founders and Sons* (New York: Holt, Rinehart & Winston, 1971). Morroe Berger (see note 137 below) also cites her frequently. Her model is Lane's *Manners and Customs of the Modern Egyptians*, but she has none of Lane's literacy or general learning.

136. Manfred Halpern's thesis is presented in "Four Contrasting Repertories of Human Relations in Islam: Two Pre-Modern and Two Modern Ways of Dealing with Continuity and Change, Collaboration and Conflict and the Achieving of Justice," a paper presented to the 22nd Near East Conference at Princeton University on Psychology and Near Eastern Studies, May 8, 1973. This treatise was prepared for by Halpern's "A Redefinition of the Revolutionary Situation," *Journal of International Affairs* 23, no. 1 (1969): 54–75.

137. Morroe Berger, *The Arab World Today* (New York: Doubleday Anchor Books, 1964), p. 140. Much the same sort of implication underlies the clumsy work of quasi-Arabists like Joel Carmichael and Daniel Lerner; it is there more subtly in political and historical scholars such as Theodore Draper, Walter Laqueur, and Élie Kedourie. It is strongly in evidence in such highly regarded works as Gabriel Baer's *Population and Society in the Arab East*, trans. Hanna Szoke (New York: Frederick A. Praeger, 1964), and Alfred Bonné's *State and Economics in the Middle East: A Society in Transition* (London: Routledge & Kegan Paul, 1955). The consensus seems to be that if they think at all, Arabs think differently—i.e., not necessarily with reason, and often without it. See also Adel Daher's RAND study, *Current Trends in Arab Intellectual Thought* (RM-5979-FF, December

1969) and its typical conclusion that "the concrete problem-solving approach is conspicuously absent from Arab thought" (p. 29). In a review-essay for the *Journal of Interdisciplinary History* (see note 124 above), Roger Owen attacks the very notion of "Islam" as a concept for the study of history. His focus is *The Cambridge History of Islam*, which, he finds, in certain ways perpetuates an idea of Islam (to be found in such writers as Carl Becker and Max Weber) "defined essentially as a religious, feudal, and antirational system, [that] lacked the necessary characteristics which had made European progress possible." For a sustained proof of Weber's total inaccuracy, see Maxime Rodinson's *Islam and Capitalism*, trans. Brian Pearce (New York: Pantheon Books, 1974), pp. 76–117.

138. Hamady, *Character and Temperament*, p. 197.

139. Berger, *Arab World*, p. 102.

140. Quoted by Irene Gendzier in *Frantz Fanon: A Critical Study* (New York: Pantheon Books, 1973), p. 94.

141. Berger, *Arab World*, p. 151.

142. P. J. Vatikiotis, ed., *Revolution in the Middle East, and Other Case Studies; proceedings of a seminar* (London: George Allen & Unwin, 1972), pp. 8–9.

143. Ibid., pp. 12, 13.

144. Bernard Lewis, "Islamic Concepts of Revolution," in ibid., pp. 33, 38–9. Lewis's study *Race and Color in Islam* (New York: Harper & Row, 1971) expresses similar disaffection with an air of great learning; more explicitly political—but no less acid—is his *Islam in History: Ideas, Men and Events in the Middle East* (London: Alcove Press, 1973).

145. Bernard Lewis, "The Revolt of Islam," in *The Middle East and The West* (Bloomington: Indiana University Press, 1964), p. 95.

146. Bernard Lewis, "The Return of Islam," *Commentary*, January 1976, p. 44.

147. Ibid., p. 40.

148. Bernard Lewis, *History—Remembered, Recovered, Invented* (Princeton, N.J.: Princeton University Press, 1975), p. 68.

149. Lewis, *Islam in History*, p. 65.

150. Lewis, *The Middle East and the West*, pp. 60, 87.

151. Lewis, *Islam in History*, pp. 65–6.

152. Originally published in *Middle East Journal* 5 (1951). Collected in *Readings in Arab Middle Eastern Societies and Cultures*, ed. Abdulla Lutfiyye and Charles W. Churchill (The Hague: Mouton & Co., 1970), pp. 688–703.

153. Lewis, *The Middle East and the West*, p. 140.

154. Robert K. Merton, "The Perspectives of Insiders and Outsiders," in his *The Sociology of Science: Theoretical and Empirical Investigations*, ed. Norman W. Storer (Chicago: University of Chicago Press, 1973), pp. 99–136.

155. See, for example, the recent work of Anwar Abdel Malek, Yves Lacoste, and the authors of essays published in *Review of Middle East Studies 1 and 2* (London: Ithaca Press, 1975, 1976), the various analyses of Middle Eastern politics by Noam Chomsky, and the work done by the Middle East Research and Information Project (MERIP). A good prospectus is provided in Gabriel Ardant, Kostas Axelos, Jacques Berque, et al., *De l'impérialisme à la décolonisation* (Paris: Éditions de Minuit, 1965).

Afterword

1. Martin Bernal, *Black Athena* (New Brunswick: Rutgers University Press, Volume I, 1987; Volume II, 1991); Eric J. Hobsbawm and Terence Rangers, eds., *The Invention of Tradition* (Cambridge: Cambridge University Press, 1984).

2. O'Hanlon and Washbrook, "After Orientalism: Culture, Criticism, and Politics in the Third World"; Prakash, "Can the Subaltern Ride? A Reply to O'Hanlon and Washbrook," both in *Comparative Studies in Society and History*, IV, 9 (January 1992), 141–84.

3. In one particularly telling instance, Lewis's habits of tendentious generalization do seem to have gotten him in legal trouble. According to *Libération* (1 March 1994) and the *Guardian* (8 March 1994), Lewis now faces both criminal and civil suits brought against him in France by Armenian and human rights organizations. He is being charged under the same statute that makes it a crime in France to deny that the Nazi Holocuast took place; the charge against him is denying (in French newspapers) that a genocide of Armenians occurred under the Ottoman empire.

4. Carol Breckenridge and Peter van der Veer, eds., *Orientalism and the Postcolonial Predicament* (Philadelphia: University of Pennsylvania Press, 1993).

5. Nicholas B. Dirks, ed., *Colonialism and Culture* (Ann Arbor: The University of Michigan Press, 1992).

6. "The Clash of Civilizations," *Foreign Affairs* 71, 3 (Summer 1993), 22–49.

7. "Notes on the 'Post-Colonial'," *Social Text*, 31/32 (1992), 106.

8. Magdoff, "Globalisation – To What End?," *Socialist Register 1992: New World Order?*, ed. Ralph Milliband and Leo Panitch (New York: Monthly Review Press, 1992), 1–32.

9. Miyoshi, "A Borderless World? From Colonialism to Transnationalism and the Decline of the Nation-State," *Critical Inquiry*, 19, 4 (Summer 1993), 726–51; Dirlik, "The Postcolonial Aura: Third World Criticism in the Age of Global Capitalism," *Critical Inquiry*, 20, 2 (Winter 1994), 328–56.

10. *Ireland's Field Day* (London: Hutchinson, 1985), pp. vii–viii.

11. Alcalay (Minneapolis: University of Minnesota Press, 1993); Gilroy (Cambridge: Harvard University Press, 1993); Ferguson (London: Routledge, 1992).

Index

Index

Index

Index

authority with Hashimites, 246; contrasted with Burton, 195; definition and vision in narrative of, 228–9, 239, 240, 247; imperial agent, 196, 224, 225, 238, 240–1, 246; Orientalism as sensational revelation in, 284; personal vision of, 241, 242–3, 248; and primitive clarity of the Arab, 229–31; reverse pilgrimage of, 170–1; struggle to arouse Orient, 241–2

Layard, Austen, 195
Le Bon, Gustave, 207
Le Mascrier, Abbé, 84
La Strange, Guy, 224
Lebanon, 1, 109, 177, 182, 191, 192, 321
Leconte, Casimir, 90
Legacy of Islam, The (1931, ed. Arnold and Guillaume), 256, 372
Legrain, Georges, 170
Leibnitz, Baron Gottfried Wilhelm von, 124, 125
Leopardi, Conte Giacomo, 131
Lepanto, battle of, 74
Lepic, Ludovic, 170
Lerner, Daniel, 311, 361, 375
Leroy-Beaulieu, Paul, 219
Lesseps, Ferdinand-Marie de, 88–92, 94–5, 148, 218, 219, 220, 360
Lesseps, Mathieu de, 89
Lettres d'Égypte, de Gustave Flaubert, Les (ed. Naaman), 368
Lévi, Sylvain, 248–9, 250, 264, 266, 372
Lévi-Strauss, Claude, 53, 296, 357
Levin, Harry, 184, 368
Lewis, Bernard, 105, 107, 315–21, 358, 361, 362, 370, 375, 376
Libya, 324
Life of Mahomet (Muir), 151
Linnaeus, Carolus, 119
"Literature" (Gibb), 256
literature, imaginative: contrasted with professional Orientalism, 157–8, 168–9, 170–1, 181, 183, 189, 192; English Orientalist contrasted with French, 192–3; and Oriental residence, 157–8; Orientalist genre of, 2–3, 8, 18, 21, 22, 26, 40, 43, 52–3, 60, 88, 99, 100–102, 157–8, 167–9, 170–6, 177–190, 192–4, 224, 256, 267, 284; and pilgrimage to Orient, 168–9, 170, 171–5, 177–90, 192–3; political bearing on, 9–11, 14–15, 24, 169; social-cultural constraints upon, 43, 169, 201–2. *See also* individual writers

Locke, John, 13
Lois psychologiques de l'évolution des peuples, Les (Le Bon), 207
London University School of Oriental and African Studies, 214
Long Revolution, The (Williams), 14, 355
Lorrain, Claude, 178
Loti, Pierre, 99, 252
Louis Lambert (Balzac), 131, 363
Louis-Philippe, 294
Louÿs, Pierre, 208
Lowth, Robert, 17
Lugard, Frederick Dealtry, 1st Baron Lugard, 213
"Lui" (Hugo), 82–3
Lukacs, Georg, 259
"Lustful Turk, The," 8
Luther, Martin, 61, 71
Lyall, Sir Alfred Comyn, 38, 47, 151
Lyall, Sir Charles James, 224
Lycurgus, 85

Macaulay, Thomas Babington, 14, 152, 196, 366
Macdonald, Duncan Black, 105, 106, 209, 210, 247, 248, 276–8, 280, 283, 358, 373
Maeterlinck, Maurice, 250
Magic Flute, The (Mozart), 118
Mahdism, 281
Mahomet (Voltaire), 359
"Mahometgesang" (Goethe), 100
Mallarmé, Stéphane, 267
Malraui, André, 248
Mamelukes, 82
Mandeville, Sir John, 31, 58
manifest Orientalism, 206, 209; converges with latent Orientalism, 222–4
Manifesto (Napoleon), 124
Mannheim, Karl, 259
Mans, Raphael du, 65
Manu, 78, 120
Maqamat (al-Hariri), 126
Marcus, Steven, 8, 355
Marcus Aurelius, 147
Margoliouth, David Samuel, 224
Mariette, August-Edouard, 170
Marigny, François Augier de, 80
Maritain, Jacques and Raïssa, 266
Marlowe, Christopher, 63
Marlowe, John, 89, 356, 360
Maronites, 191, 220, 278, 303
Marrakech, 251
Marx, Karl, 3, 14, 16, 21, 32, 97, 102, 153–6, 157, 206, 231, 293, 325, 366
Marxism, 13, 43, 305, 325

Index

aesthetic in Orientalist writing, 158, 168, 169, 170, 179, 180–1; and female types, 180, 182, 184; imagination of Orient disappointed, 100, 101, 181, 184, 243; importance to Orientalism, 181, 183; internal dream world, 183–4; journey contrasted with Chateaubriand's, 183; Massignon's predilection for, 267; meaning of Orient to, 180–4, 190, 206; negative vision of Orient, 184; Orientalist constraints upon, 43

Nestorians, 220

Newman, John Henry, Cardinal, 14, 153, 228, 366

Nicholas of Cusa, 61

Nietzsche, Friedrich Wilhelm, 131, 132, 203, 204, 363, 369

Nicholson, Reynold Alleyne, 224

Nile, 162, 174, 187

Nöldeke, Theodor, 18, 209

North Africa, 19, 52, 74, 99, 191, 210, 218, 223, 225, 278, 288, 295, 303, 304

Notes of a Journey from Cornhill to Grand Cairo (Thackeray), 195

Nouty, Hassan al-, 170, 367

Novalis, 115

"Objects of Enquiry During My Residence in Asia" (Jones), 78

O'Brien, Conor Cruise, 312

"Occident and the Orient, The" (Chirol), 252–3, 371

"Occident devant l'Orient, L'" (Massignon), 267, 372

Ockley, Simon, 63, 64, 75–6

Omar I, 74, 172

On Liberty (Mill), 14

Order of Things, The (Foucault), 22, 362, 364

Oriental literature, 78, 96, 105, 305; anthologies of extracts from, 20, 64, 125, 128–9, 130, 142, 147, 151, 165, 176, 283, 284; avoided in social-scientist Orientalism, 291; Gibb on, 256–7, 277; "infinity" of, 77; Kinglake on, 193; and manifest Orientalism, 206; Massignon and, 209, 264, 266; Nerval emulates, 182, 183; poetry, 96, 128, 168, 178, 209, 256; religious, 279: tale in, 32, 52; value to West of, 128, 256–7; Western tribute to, 168

Orientales, Les (Hugo), 51, 101, 167, 359, 367

Orientalism: creates Orient, 5, 40, 87, 94, 121, 129–30, 140, 143,

145–6, 148, 221; crisis in, 104–9, 205, 249–50; current dogmas of, 300–2, 319; definitions of, 1–6, 12, 41, 42, 51, 73, 92, 95, 121, 202–3; demarcation of East and West in, 39–40, 42, 43, 45–9, 56, 57, 73, 96, 201, 206, 216, 227–30, 248, 250, 253, 256, 257, 259, 269–270, 277, 299, 300–1, 306–7, 308–309, 327; essentialist vision of, 97, 102–8, 148, 154–5, 156, 203, 205, 209–10, 221, 223, 229–34, 236–40, 246, 248, 251, 255, 256, 262, 278–80, 283, 296–9, 300–1, 305, 306–10, 315, 317–18, 321, 322, 375, 376; exteriority of, 20–1, 86–87, 97, 104, 105–8, 118, 127, 162, 229–30, 238, 247–8; general and particular perspectives on, 8, 11–12, 13–15, 50; in interwar years, 248–54, 255–72; as mode of Western dominance, 3, 5–6, 7, 11, 13, 15, 25, 28, 31–41, 46, 48, 53, 60, 73, 80–1, 86–7, 92, 94–6, 104, 108–9, 122–3, 141, 146, 152–3, 160, 166, 179, 192–4, 195, 197, 204, 222–4, 225, 231–4, 246, 253–254, 301, 306, 309–11, 321–5; modernization of, 43, 51,73, 76–79, 86–7, 92, 95, 116, 120–3, 124, 127, 129–30, 156, 197, 210, 255–284; retrogressive position of Islamic, 260–3, 269–70, 278–80, 296–8, 300–5, 307–21; schematization of Orient, 68–72, 80, 83, 85–7, 95, 98–9, 100–8, 146–8, 149–50, 154–5, 156, 189, 209, 229–30, 239, 300–1; on Semitic cultural decadence, 141, 145–6, 208, 231–4, 236–7, 260, 289, 300–301, 306–7; supplies agents and expertise to Empire, 196–7, 222–225, 228–31, 234, 237–46, 284, 321, 322; three senses of, 2–6. *See also* scholarship, Orientalist

"Orientalism in Crisis" (Abdel Malek), 360, 361, 372

Orientalizing, of Orient, 5–6, 65–7, 96, 104, 109, 155, 168, 181, 202, 328: by modern Orient of itself, 325

Orwell, George, 251–2, 371

Othello (Shakespeare), 71

Ottoman Empire, 59–60, 74, 75, 76, 100, 191, 207, 220, 225, 248, 253

"Où s'affrontent l'Orient et l' Occident intellectuels" (Baldensperger), 253, 372

Owen, Roger, 327, 356, 374, 376

396 Index

United States: Arab world satellite
of, 322–4; ascendancy in East, 3–
4, 11, 17, 25, 104, 107, 290, 293;
awareness of Orient, 1, 2, 11–12,
26, 107–8, 252–3; cultural relations with East, 293–302; geopolitical identity vis-à-vis Orient,
11, 12; ideal of pure scholarship
in, 10, 13; imperialist quality of
knowledge in, 11, 293–5, 321,
322; inherits Orientalist tradition,
6, 47–9, 107–8, 264, 275, 284,
285–93, 295–302, 307–21, 322–4,
374; interest in Zionist colonization of Palestine, 294, 374; limited
experience with Orient before
W.W. II, 290; Oriental pilgrims
from, 192, 368; and Orientalism,
6, 11, 12, 15, 16–17, 25, 43;
Orientalist confidence of, 46–9,
107–8; popular image of Arab in,
26–7, 285–8; role in Near Orient,
2, 26–7, 294–5, 321, 322–4; and
Third World, 46–7, 104, 107–8,
321
universities, Arab, 322–3
Untergang des Abendlandes, Der
(Spengler), 208
Upanishads, 77, 98
utilitarianism, and imperialism, 214–
215

Valéry, Paul, 250–1, 252, 371
Valle, Pietro della, 58
Varro, Marcus Terentius, 144
Varthema Lodovico di, 58
Vatikiotis, P. J., 312–14, 376
Vattel, Emer de, 216, 370
Vergleichende Grammatik (Bopp),
135
Verne, Jules, 218
Vico, Giovanni Battista, 4, 25, 53,
117, 118, 119, 120, 132, 133, 137,
138, 147, 148
Vico and Herder (Berlin), 362
Victoria, Queen, 31
Victory (Conrad), 186
Vie de Jésus (Renan), 146
Vietnam War, 11
Vigny, Alfred-Victor de, 99, 169
*Vingt–sept Ans d'histoire des études
orientales* (Mohl), 51
*Visit to the Monasteries of the
Levant* (Curzon), 195
Vogüe, Marquis de, 170
Voiney, Constantin-François de
Chasseboeuf, 39, 81, 168, 169,
170, 359

Voltaire, 76–7, 92, 359
Vossler, Karl, 258
Voyage en Égypte et en Syrie
(Volney), 81, 359
Voyage en Orient (Lamartine), 88,
111, 177–9, 367
Voyage en Orient (Nerval), 100,
158, 180–4, 368

Waardenburg, Jacques, 209–10, 268,
369, 372, 373
Wafd party, 257
Wagner, Richard, 131
Waley, Arthur, 252
Wandering Scholar, The (Hogarth).
245, 371
Warburton, Eliot, 169, 195
Weber, Max, 259, 376
Weil, Gustav, 99
Weizmann, Chaim, 306
Wellhausen, Julius, 209
Weltgeschichte (Ranke), 208
West: *see* Europe, United States
Westernization, in Islamic world,
278, 279, 308–9, 321–5
Westlake, John, 206–7
Westöstlicher Diwan (Goethe), 19,
51, 154, 155, 167, 367
Whiston, William, 76
White Man, 226–31, 235–43, 245–6
Whither Islam? (ed. Gibb), 278, 373
Wilde, Oscar, 145
Wilkins, Charles, 78
William of Tripoli, 71
Williams, Raymond, 14, 28, 355, 356
Wilson, Woodrow, 221, 251
Wolf, Friedrich August, 131, 132,
133
Wordsworth, William, 115
World War I, 104, 105, 123, 220,
223, 224, 240, 246, 255–6, 270,
284, 294
World War II, 4, 17, 18, 53, 107,
255, 258, 284, 290, 295, 297, 299

Xerxes 1, 56, 57

Yeats, William Butler, 110, 230, 252,
370
Yemen, 109
Yemen, Southern, 109

Zaghlul Pasha, Saad, 257
Zend-Avesta, 17, 42, 76–7, 98
Zionism, 27, 221, 270, 278, 286, 294,
301,303, 306–7, 318, 319, 320,
374
Zoroastrianism, 120, 232. *See also*
Zend-Avetsa